Terrorism, War, or Disease?

Terrorism, War, or Disease?

Unraveling the Use of Biological Weapons

Edited by

ANNE L. CLUNAN

PETER R. LAVOY

SUSAN B. MARTIN

STANFORD SECURITY STUDIES

An Imprint of Stanford University Press

Stanford, California 2008

Stanford University Press
Stanford, California
©2008 by the Board of Trustees of the
Leland Stanford Junior University

Chapter 4 ©2008 by Matthew S. Meselson and Julian Perry Robinson;
Chapter 8 ©2008 by Jeanne Guillemin

Library of Congress Cataloging-in-Publication Data

Terrorism, war, or disease? : unraveling the use of biological weapons /
edited by Anne L. Clunan, Peter R. Lavoy, Susan B. Martin.
    p. cm.
  Includes bibliographical references and index.
  ISBN 978-0-8047-5976-2 (cloth : alk. paper) —
  ISBN 978-0-8047-5977-9 (pbk. : alk. paper)
    1. Biological weapons—Case studies. 2. Biological weapons—
Government policy. 3. Biological arms control. 4. National security.
I. Clunan, Anne L. II. Lavoy, Peter R. (Peter René). III. Martin,
Susan B.
UG447.8.T47   2008
358'.3882—dc22

                                                      2008005321

Printed in the United States of America on acid-free, archival-
quality paper

Typeset at Stanford University Press in 10/14.5 Minion

Special discounts for bulk quantities of Stanford Security Series
are available to corporations, professional associations, and
other organizations. For details and discount information,
contact the special sales department of Stanford University Press.
Tel: (650) 736-1783, Fax: (650) 736-1784

For our families and children,
LOUISA, NATHANIEL, *and* ZOE

May they never experience this threat

Contents

Part II: Policy and Scholarly Implications

Tables and Figures

Tables

Figures

Preface

The international community's efforts to combat the spread of nuclear, biological, and chemical weapons have not kept up with the pace of proliferation, and urgently require improvement. This was a major finding of the 2005 WMD Commission report and it was a key conclusion I reached while serving as the counterproliferation policy director for the U.S. Secretary of Defense from 1998 through 2000.[1] Probably the hardest challenge we faced in the Pentagon was (and probably still is) to understand, monitor, and combat the global diffusion of expertise and materials used to develop and deliver biological warfare (BW) agents. This is because biological weapons are cheaper and easier to make than nuclear weapons—and they could be more deadly. Only a handful of scientists are needed to isolate and disseminate harmful pathogens. Not much money is required, nor are specialized facilities and equipment. Almost everything needed to make and employ BW agents—from skilled people and source materials to production and dissemination technologies—is available in commercial and academic settings. Further, the manipulation of bacteria, viruses, or toxins to cause harm emits few observable signs, making it almost impossible to give policymakers timely warning that a BW development program of a given country or non-state actor is nearing a critical threshold or, more ominously, that BW agents are being readied for use against unprotected populations.

Critics argue that heightened fears about the acute vulnerability of the public and armed forces to the malicious use of pathogens have led the U.S. government to take an alarmist view of the BW proliferation threat.[2] The exaggerated assessment of Iraq's capacity to conduct biological warfare in the early 2000s is cited as a case in point. But just because many governments got Iraq wrong does not mean that BW proliferation is waning, that the risk of biological warfare is any smaller, or that the steps required to counter this threat have become more manageable. The crucial lesson to be drawn from the Iraq WMD experience—one that the WMD Commission highlighted—is that the enormous dangers and complexities of the BW problem need to be approached with a new sense of urgency and with new strategies for information collection and analysis—not all of which require access to governmental sources or data.

BW agents have a number of attractive qualities from the perspective of their use, one of which is the wide spectrum of effects they can produce on humans—such as debilitating a large number of people or causing mass deaths—animals, and destroying agriculture without the likelihood of detection. Unlike nuclear or possibly chemical attacks, which can be traced back to a particular source, the conspirators behind a biological release have reason to believe they would not be attributed as perpetrators of the attack due to lack of identifying signatures. Moreover, because the effects of BW attacks often take days to manifest, and are potentially similar to the effects of naturally occurring diseases, it might not be clear if a BW agent has deliberately been released.

Because of these conditions, the history of biological warfare is replete with uncertainty, controversy, and innuendo. For example, only in 2002 did a district court in Japan formally acknowledge that Chinese prisoners and citizens had deliberately been infected with bubonic plague by Imperial Japan's notorious Unit 731. Controversy still exists on many other alleged BW outbreaks, including "Yellow Rain" in Southeast Asia and Afghanistan and the spread of Foot and Mouth Disease in Taiwan. In other known incidents of biological warfare or terrorism, the perpetrators remain unknown, including the "Amerithrax" case involving anthrax-filled letters in the United States. Biodefense planners thus face significant challenges in determining whether a deliberate BW attack has occurred, characterizing the agents involved, and identifying the perpetrators. This book is intended to help them.

The Naval Postgraduate School's Center for Contemporary Conflict and King's College London brought together academic and policy experts in a collaborative research project to highlight the difficulties involved in knowing when states or non-state actors have intentionally released pathogens in the past and to assess how governments fared in identifying and countering the agents used, managing the information campaign of attribution, and responding to allegations of attacks. The result of that effort—this book—features a broad collection of balanced, factual studies of confirmed, suspected, and fabricated BW agent releases, as well as an assessment of lessons that can be drawn and implemented by current-day policymakers to manage the problems of BW identification, characterization, and attribution.

This book could not have been produced without the valuable contribution of numerous organizations and individuals. David Hamon and Kerry Kartchner were instrumental in providing intellectual guidance and arranging financial support for the research effort from the Advanced Systems and Concepts Office of the U.S. Defense Threat Reduction Agency. Theo Farrell of King's College London organized a highly productive research conference in London. Randy Murch, Jim George, Kay Mereish, Paula DeSutter, David Omand, and Michael Goodman offered many valuable insights. And Elizabeth Stone of the Center for Contemporary Conflict provided all of the research support required for the project's success. The authors, of course, did the heavy lifting: any value this book might provide the communities seized with this problem is a result of their thoughtful, professional, and collegial contributions. Finally, my co-editors, Anne Clunan and Susan Martin, assumed the responsibility for editing the chapters of this volume in a highly attentive and efficient manner. Our aim was to make this book read as a coherent whole to a wide variety of audiences. If it does, it is entirely because of them.

Peter R. Lavoy

MacLean, VA, October 18, 2007

Notes

1. The Commission on the Intelligence Capabilities of the United States Regarding Weapons of Mass Destruction, *Report to the President of the United States*, March 31, 2005, http://www.wmd.gov/about.html.

2. Milton Leitenberg, *Assessing the Biological Weapons and Terrorism Threat*, Strategic Studies Institute monograph, U.S. Army War College, December 2005.

The Authors

Editors

ANNE L. CLUNAN is Assistant Professor of National Security Affairs at the Naval Postgraduate School. She specializes in the state responses to non-traditional security threats in the information age. Her most recent work has appeared in *Terrorism Financing and State Responses, Global Politics of Defense Reform,* and the journal *Political Science Quarterly.*

PETER R. LAVOY is National Intelligence Officer for South Asia at the National Intelligence Council. He previously directed the Center for Contemporary Conflict and taught in the National Security Affairs Department at the Naval Postgraduate School. He served as director for Counterproliferation Policy in the Office of the U.S. Secretary of Defense from 1998 through 2000.

SUSAN B. MARTIN is Lecturer at the Department of War Studies, King's College London. She is a founding member of CAMOS, the Committee for the Analysis of Military Operations and Strategy. Her current research focuses on chemical, biological, and nuclear weapons and her work has appeared in the *Journal of Strategic Studies* and *International Security.*

Contributors

GARY ACKERMAN is Research Director of the National Consortium for the Study of Terrorism and the Responses to Terrorism (NC-START), a Department of Homeland Security National Center of Excellence, based at the University of Maryland. He is also Director of the Center for Terrorism Intelligence Studies, a division of the Akribis Group.

VICTOR ASAL is Assistant Professor of Political Science at the University at Albany—SUNY. His research focuses on the interaction of international relations and domestic politics, notably how this interaction influences ethnic conflict and ethnic terrorism.

RON BARRETT is Assistant Professor of Medical Anthropological and Nursing at Emory University. His research interests concern the social dynamics of infectious diseases and medical decision making in India and the United States.

LEONARD A. COLE is an adjunct professor of political science at Rutgers University, Newark, New Jersey, where he teaches science and public policy. He is the author of seven books including *The Anthrax Letters: A Medical Detective Story* (2003) and *Terror: How Israel Has Coped and What America Can Learn* (2007).

JEANNE GUILLEMIN is a Senior Advisor at the MIT Security Studies Program and also a Senior Fellow at the Carr Center for Human Rights Policy at Harvard's Kennedy School of Government. She is the author of *Biological Weapons: From the Invention of State Programs to Contemporary Bioterrorism* (Columbia University Press, 2005).

ELISA D. HARRIS is a Senior Research Scholar at the Center for International and Security Studies at the University of Maryland (CISSM). From 1993 to 2001, she was Director for Nonproliferation and Export Controls on the National Security Council staff, where she had primary responsibility for coordinating U.S. policy on chemical, biological, and missile proliferation issues.

REBECCA KATZ is an Assistant Research Professor at the George Washington University School of Public Health and Health Services. She is also an expert consultant to the Office of Biological Weapons Affairs in the Bureau of Verification, Compliance, and Implementation, U.S. Department of State. Her current research focuses on global governance in public health.

MILTON LEITENBERG is Senior Research Scholar at the Center for International and Security Studies (CISSM) at the University of Maryland. He has written extensively on biological weapons and arms control, and has authored or edited a half dozen books, an equal number of commissioned book-length studies, and has written some 170 papers, monographs, and book chapters.

MATTHEW S. MESELSON is the Thomas Dudley Cabot Professor of the Natural Sciences in the Department of Molecular and Cellular Biology at Harvard University. His current research is in the field of molecular genetics and evolution. Dr. Meselson presently serves on the Committee on International Security and Arms Control of the National Academy of Sciences.

GRAHAM S. PEARSON is Visiting Professor in International Security in the Department of Peace Studies at the University of Bradford, Bradford, West Yorkshire, UK, where he is active particularly in the area of biological and chemical weapons arms control. He is author of *The UNSCOM Saga* and *The Search for Iraq's Weapons of Mass Destruction*. He was Director General and Chief Executive of the Chemical and Biological Defence Establishment at Porton Down, Salisbury, UK, from 1984 to 1995.

JULIAN PERRY ROBINSON, a chemist and lawyer by training, is a professorial fellow of SPRU—Science & Technology Policy Research, University of Sussex, UK, where he conducts research in the fields of arms control and technology policy with a focus on problems associated with chemical and biological warfare. This is a subject on which he has published or presented some 450 papers and monographs since 1967.

JONATHAN B. TUCKER is a Senior Fellow in the Washington, DC, office of the James Martin Center for Nonproliferation Studies (CNS) of the Monterey Institute of International Studies, where he specializes in the nonproliferation and control of biological and chemical weapons. Dr. Tucker was an arms control specialist with the U.S. government, including positions at the Department of State, the Congressional Office of Technology Assessment, and the Arms Control and Disarmament Agency.

RAYMOND A. ZILINSKAS is Director of the Chemical and Biological Weapons Nonproliferation Program at the James Martin Center for Nonproliferation Studies at the Monterey Institute for International Studies. He is the editor of *Biological Warfare: Modern Offense and Defense*, and co-editor of the *Encyclopedia of Bioterrorism Defense*.

CHAPTER ONE

Introduction

Identifying Biological Agents, Characterizing Events, and Attributing Blame

ANNE L. CLUNAN

The use of biological warfare (BW) agents by states or terrorists is one of the world's most frightening security threats. Killers such as anthrax, smallpox, botulism, tularemia, viral hemorrhagic fevers, and plague, and incapacitating diseases such as brucella, salmonella, typhoid, and shigellosis—the diseases commonly listed as BW agents—are invisible. Their effects may take days to manifest. BW agents can vary widely in the effects they can produce on humans—from incapacitating a population to causing mass deaths—and on animals and agriculture. Those who use BW may have impact without detection, and this possibility makes it more difficult for states to deter other states and terrorists from using biological weapons.

The risk that BW attacks might never be traced back to a particular source is greater than for nuclear or even chemical attacks, in part because BW attacks may look like those of naturally occurring disease. Historically, attributing blame for BW use has been fraught with controversy and may take a very long time. Only in 2002, for example, did a court in Japan formally acknowledge the Imperial Japanese Army's deliberate infection of Chinese prisoners and citizens with bubonic plague in 1940–42. Controversy still exists about aspects of many other alleged cases of BW, including the "Yellow Rain" episode in Southeast Asia. Even for other incidents known to be biological warfare or terrorism, such as the 2001 anthrax letters in the United States, the perpetrator remains unknown (see Table 9.1 for a summary of twentieth-century BW incidents, claims, and attempts).

The difficulties involved in determining whether terrorism, warfare, or disease is the source of a biological event may give the initiators of a BW release confidence that they might get away with a BW attack without being blamed or even suspected. Improved capabilities for accurate and rapid attribution of BW use are therefore central to the two key strategies available to policymakers: deterring an attack through the threat of retaliatory punishment, and deterring through denial of impact, by mitigating the consequences of an attack on the state and society.

Deterrence may require government capabilities to determine, first, what the agent of disease might be; second, whether a biological outbreak is terrorism or warfare, or is instead a naturally occurring disease; and third, if so, who is to blame. These are the three elements of the process of attribution, which are spelled out later in this chapter. First, however, I spell out how BW deterrence works, before explaining how the process of attribution works and how it may contribute to deterrence. The chapter then concludes with an overview of the rest of the book.

BW Mitigation and Deterrence

Enhanced mitigation of the effects of BW should have a deterrent effect on potential BW attackers: societies that are clearly capable of substantially limiting the consequences of a biological attack are much less likely to be targeted, since the desired outcome of the attack is less likely to be achieved. To succeed at such deterrence by denial, governments must be capable of determining, quickly and accurately, which biological agent has been used (this is step one of the three-step attribution process). Identification of the agent can increase the effectiveness of medical intervention, minimizing the public disruption and damage that are the aims of would-be attackers. Knowing whether the attack was deliberate and understanding the motives behind it (the second element of the attribution process) may also help emergency responders and public-health officials allocate appropriate resources and capabilities during the outbreak, and to prepare for further outbreaks. Capability of making such a determination may thus contribute to deterrence by denial, and is essential to deterrence by punishment.

Deterrence by punishment hinges on knowing whom to blame, the third element of the attribution process. Although nuclear weapons bear the unmistakable "signature" of the countries that manufactured their nuclear material, biological agents are unlikely to carry such signatures. Biological warfare agents could be found "in the wild," and rapid advances in biotechnology mean that new biological agents are being created in the commercial and scientific spheres that could also be used as weapons.[1]

Knowledge Makes for Better Policy

In the face of such challenges, the literature on biological warfare attribution is underdeveloped. Further, most of it predates the 2001 anthrax attacks in the United States and the Bush Administration's decision to withdraw from negotiations on a verification protocol for the Biological and Toxin Weapons Convention (BWC). Some studies have examined the nature of the BW threat, offered histories of state and non-state actors' BW programs, and explored the potential and the pitfalls of biological defensive efforts.[2] Some have focused on assessing the threat posed by biological weapons.[3] Notable is *Biological Weapons: Limiting the Threat* which, however, focuses on BW challenges primarily from a public-health perspective.[4] Other works examine how biological warfare might be carried out, and inter-state efforts at arms control and nonproliferation.[5] *Toxic Terror* concentrates on the types and nature of sub-state actors, such as terrorist groups, that have used biological or chemical weapons.[6] One recent work, *Scientific and Technical Means of Distinguishing Between Natural and Other Outbreaks of Disease*, focuses only on part of the BW attribution problem—distinguishing between natural and deliberate attacks—but does not examine the many sociopolitical factors that affect the attribution process.[7]

Much of this literature points out that the difficulty in identifying a biological warfare attack and accurately attributing its use hinders public-health responses, and also impedes deterrence of BW attacks, since deterrence requires knowing whom to blame. Little attention, however, has been devoted to understanding how to improve attribution of BW events, and much of that has focused on the scientific and technical difficulties and on biological, technical, legal, and criminological issues.[8] Yet, as this book shows, BW attribution is as much a political problem as it is a scientific one.[9]

This book seeks to fill the gap, addressing political, military, legal, and scientific challenges involved in determining when biological weapons have been used and who has used them. Internationally recognized experts offer detailed analyses of the most significant allegations of BW use from the Second World War to the present, assess past attempts at attribution of unusual biological events, and draw lessons from these cases for current attribution policy. They identify political, social, and economic as well as scientific factors that affect when, how, and with what success states may undertake attribution. A major contribution of this book, and the substance of this chapter, is to offer a defini-tion of the multifaceted problem of tracking down the perpetrators of biologi-cal warfare, and analysis of the forces that shape each phase of the attribution process. This chapter next outlines the three steps that make up the process of attribution.

The Three Steps of the Biological Weapons Attribution Process

The problem of identifying an intentional use of biological weapons and knowing whom to blame has three interrelated parts, each with its own par-ticular requirements: identification of the biological agent(s) responsible for an event; characterization of the event as intentional or unintentional; and attri-bution of use to a specific perpetrator. These three parts—identification, char-acterization, and attribution—make up what is referred to in this volume as the BW attribution process.[10] For example, in the U.S. anthrax cases (see Chapter 2 by Leonard Cole), identification of the agent as anthrax was the first step, and the most important in terms of public-health response. It was relatively simple to identify the agent used in the attacks and to characterize the event as deliberate, since the envelopes containing the anthrax also contained letters announcing its presence. As in most cases, however, attribution to a specific perpetrator is more difficult. Questions still remain about the strain of anthrax used and the method by which it was processed. Answering those questions would significantly narrow the field of possible perpetrators, but the case re-mains unresolved as of this writing.

In the event of an overt attack with military-grade weapons, the three-part process of attribution might be relatively uncomplicated.[11] However, a covert attack or one using non-military-grade strains of a BW agent would make the attribution process much more difficult.[12] The nature of biological agents, as well as the politics that surround characterization and attribution of a biological event, contribute significantly to the attribution problem. The cases described in this volume suggest that any effort to attribute BW use must attempt to accomplish the three elements of the attribution process within some agreed range of how much of the inevitable uncertainty is acceptable, aiming to avoid bias and preserve public trust.

The question of the degree of acceptable uncertainty highlights the crucial issue of what standards of evidence are necessary for BW attribution. In all three parts of the attribution problem, both legal-scientific and political standards for information are important. Throughout the BW attribution process, actors must attempt to meet legal and scientific standards for the collection of evidence if any attribution of use is to be credible internationally or in a court of law. In the United States, for example, public-health agencies may conduct searches without judicial warrants, but resulting evidence might be excluded from criminal cases if deemed the fruit of warrantless or unconstitutional searches. Legal evidentiary standards may govern search and seizure, wiretapping, or other forms of information collection. Close cooperation between law-enforcement and public-health officials is therefore required in order to meet appropriate standards for the collection of evidence and the custody of evidence.[13] Scientific standards require, among other things, the replicability of tests by independent researchers and establishing a degree of confidence in the results of analysis linking agent with disease and disease with intentional attack.

Both legal and scientific standards require that the evidence is demonstrably not tampered with. However, ensuring a properly documented chain of custody of evidence can be extraordinarily difficult in BW cases. Samples, control samples, and physical evidence must be collected, preserved, and transferred in such a manner as to protect them from contamination, to document where they came from, and to make it clear that they have not been tampered with. Yet in many cases, the first responders to a biological event may not know that it may become the subject of a BW investigation. The first people to collect what may become evidence may be the victims, or humanitarian relief workers operating in refugee camps, or emergency room doctors and primary-care physicians. As Chapters 4 and 5 on Yellow Rain in this volume make clear, there is considerable potential for controversy regarding the scientific validity of data, for both scientific and political reasons.

Charges of BW use must also be politically persuasive. The standard of proof must be sufficiently high that it allows a decision maker to make a well-informed decision on whether or not to take steps to apprehend or retaliate against the perpetrator. As deterrence rests on credible threats to retaliate, attribution must achieve a degree of certainty that allows policymakers to respond, but such responses must be widely viewed as legitimate, not misplaced or politically motivated. Given the domestic and international need for any retaliation to be seen as legitimate, meeting very demanding legal-scientific standards should be the goal in all cases, even though it may not be reached. Particularly in cases where a state alleges that a foreign actor used BW, the state must, at a minimum, act on the basis of a scientifically valid preliminary attribution process and show its willingness to have its investigation and methods reviewed by outside experts, and even better, to accept a multilateral investigation of the alleged attack under international auspices such as those of the United Nations. Only under these conditions are allegations of a biological weapons attack likely to be credible. If the accusing state has conducted its own investigation according to rigorous scientific standards, then it will have little reason not to invite outside scrutiny of its charges. Such standards would also serve to discourage states from making false allegations, such as those highlighted in Chapters 6 and 7, in the hopes of politically shaming an opponent, as any allegation that is not accompanied by openness to independent and multilateral investigation would be suspect.

Identification of the Disease Agent

The key biological agents most associated with warfare and terrorism, according to the World Health Organization (WHO), are *Bacillus anthracis* (anthrax), *Clostridium botulinum* (botulism toxin), *Yersinia pestis* (bubonic, septicemic, and pneumonic plague), *Francisella tularensis* (tularemia), and *Variola major* virus (smallpox). The U.S. Centers for Disease Control and Prevention (CDC) lists these and viral hemorrhagic fevers (filoviruses such as Ebola and Marburg, and arenaviruses such as Lassa and Machupol) as the disease agents of most concern because of their ease of human-to-human transmission (contagiousness), high mortality rates, potential for public panic and social disruption, and specialized public-health requirements. Less dangerous agents that are also listed by the CDC as potential BW agents include *Brucella* (brucellosis or undulant fever), *Clostridium perfringens* (epsilon toxin), *Salmonella typhimurium* and *Salmonella entriditis* (salmonella), *Escherichia coli* O157:H7, *Shigella sonnei, flexneri,* and *dysenteriae* (shigellosis), *Salmonella typhi* (typhoid fever), *Vibrio cholerae* (cholera), and emerging infectious diseases such as Nipah virus and hantavirus.[14]

The central issue in identifying a BW agent is distinguishing signals—pertinent information—from background noise, such as poor public-health and poor environmental conditions, the presence of diseases with symptoms similar to potential BW outbreaks, and the normal disease patterns of the locale.[15] As Leonard Cole notes in Chapter 2, in the U.S. anthrax case, the flu-like symptoms associated with inhalation anthrax led to many misdiagnoses of infected postal workers, despite widely broadcast signals that anthrax had been found in letters. In this case, first responders did not separate signals from noise, the disease was misidentified, and deaths resulted. Many of the diseases listed as BW agents have symptoms that may be confused with other common or endemic diseases, making it difficult to identify the disease agent correctly, especially as diagnosticians are trained to focus on the most likely hypotheses for the appearance of symptoms, rather than on rare or exotic causes.

Identification of the agent causing a disease is largely a medical and scientific issue. The primary actors are likely to be emergency room doctors, poison control centers, primary care physicians, veterinarians, humanitarian aid workers, epidemiologists, disease specialists, and biologists. Scientific knowledge, and especially technological advances in DNA sequencing, now allow pathogen identification at the strain level, which should generally meet law-enforcement standards of evidence. However, developments in genetic engineering mean that new agents, or agents that do not conform to known epidemiological patterns, may be created that would make characterization and attribution much more difficult. In such cases, information from public-health officials, academic experts, and the biotechnology community may be necessary to identify where a particular strain originated. However, as Chapters 4 and 5 on Yellow Rain suggest, it may be neither easy nor simple to reach agreement on what biological or toxic agent may be involved, even within the medical and scientific community let alone the political community.

A biological agent, once introduced, generally first manifests as a health problem, and is only detected if victims seek medical care. Healthcare professionals are therefore the frontline forces in biological terrorism and thus in BW attribution, particularly at the identification stage.[16] These would include

veterinarians or, in the case of plant pathogens, plant biologists. Such first responders will probably be the ones to notice that an unhealthy patient, animal,
or crop presents particular symptoms, and to identify and report disease outbreaks.[17] Domestic detection of a disease outbreak requires pooling information gathered by healthcare providers or other first responders, infection control
practitioners, and health departments. Internationally, this list includes disease
surveillance systems, national health ministries, international agencies such as
the WHO and the Animal Health Organization (OIE, Office des Epizooties),
and non-governmental organizations (NGOs), particularly humanitarian aid
organizations, as well as environmental monitors (who may be the first to note
the appearance of endemic, novel, or genetically modified organisms).[18]

The effectiveness of national or international surveillance systems rests
primarily on the type and nature of pathogen involved. Agents that are not
transmitted directly from human to human (non-contagious agents), such as
anthrax, are often detected only after everyone has already been exposed. For
contagious agents such as smallpox, early detection could limit the spread of
infection. However, speed of detection also varies with whether the infectious
pathogen spreads fast (like cholera, whose incubation period is under 1–5 days),
or slowly (symptoms of inhalation anthrax, for example, may appear 8 days to
2 months later, while smallpox has an incubation period of 10 days, and symptoms of HIV/AIDs may take years to manifest).[19]

From the perspective of attribution, deterrence, and international law or
treaty enforcement, early detection of BW is vital for both infectious and non-
infectious pathogens, as it increases the likelihood of collecting evidence from
living victims and identifying how the pathogen was introduced or delivered.
Identification is much more difficult when the investigation occurs in environments where access is limited or impossible. The Yellow Rain case illustrates the
difficulty of collecting and analyzing uncontaminated samples from a conflict
zone or other non-permissive environments. Lack of early access to the site of
alleged attacks hampered the interviewing of eyewitnesses and victims as well
as the collection of physical evidence.

Characterization of Outbreak as Intentionally Caused or Not

The second analytic step in the process of BW attribution is characterization
of the outbreak of a disease as deliberate, accidental, or naturally occurring.

Epidemiologists, public-health officials, and law-enforcement officials must determine whether reported patterns of disease outbreak are suspicious. Yet the majority of such reports are likely to represent unintentional biological events, or "noise," from a BW attribution perspective, especially if the biological pathogen occurs naturally or is endemic to an area. Over an eleven-year period in the United States, the CDC suspected only six of 1,099 reported outbreaks affecting human health to be potentially intentional.[20] Even in some cases involving a listed biological agent, healthcare professionals might not even report the event if the disease occurs naturally in their locale.[21] Characterizing outbreaks as intentional attacks or endemic diseases requires baseline data on the population in question. Domestic and international disease surveillance systems provide vital information for such a determination.

Characterization is primarily a medical, scientific, and investigative process, but it can be affected, usually adversely, by politics. As shown by the 1994 outbreak of plague in India (described by Barrett in Chapter 3), rumors about the source of an outbreak and lack of public trust in political officials can hamper efforts to characterize the outbreak. Cases involving charges against or by the United States (discussed in Chapters 4 by Meselson and Robinson, 5 by Katz, 6 by Leitenberg, 7 by Zilinskas, and 10 by Harris) illustrate how geopolitics frequently cloud characterization.

Even when politics and rumor are not involved, and even under permissive conditions, the characterization element of the attribution process can be quite lengthy. The CDC has found that it took as long as 26 days for suspicious events to be reported to the CDC, even in cases where the agents involved—brucella and shigellosis—were listed by the CDC as potential biological warfare agents.[22] Only in the case of suspected anthrax use was reporting time less than one day. If a disease occurs naturally in a region, reporting may be delayed as long as a year, or not reported at all, even for a disease listed as a potential BW agent.[23] This suggests that disease outbreaks that are not associated with specifically identified biological warfare agents are even less likely to be reported rapidly.[24] Because BW attacks are rare, the possibility that a BW agent is involved may not even occur to first responders and so they might not report it until much later, if at all.

However, if a large number of people suddenly contract a disease for which there is no obvious natural source, then alarm bells may ring. For example,

when at least 750 people were afflicted with salmonella poisoning in 1984 in
The Dalles, Oregon, the agent was traced to as many as ten restaurant salad
bars. However, even though foul play was immediately suspected, no one could
imagine a motive for such an attack. The case was not amenable to available
technical solutions, as the disease strain found was also used in many commercial clinical laboratories. No common supplier, food item, water supply,
or distribution could be identified. The investigation therefore stalled.[25] Only
a year later, when the leader of the cult publicly accused one of its members of
poisoning the local population, did blame focus on the Rajneeshee cult, resulting in further investigation and the conviction of three cult members.[26]

Epidemiology alone, therefore, is insufficient to determine whether an outbreak of disease is intentional or not; traditional forensic analysis must also
be incorporated.[27] This requires that analysts have sufficient knowledge of the
conditions on the ground to assess factors beyond clinical science, such as local political conditions, migration patterns, social contacts, and other factors
such as those described by Barrett in Chapter 3. The problem of characterizing
and attributing use of biological agents has spurred interest in forensic microbial epidemiology, which "combines principles of public-health epidemiology and law enforcement to identify patterns in a disease outbreak, determine
the pathogen involved, control its spread, and trace the microorganism to its
source—the perpetrator."[28] In the United States, this new discipline (variously
referred to as forensic microbial epidemiology and microbial forensics, or more
broadly as forensic epidemiology) has led to a rapidly evolving and deepening
relationship between public-health experts and law-enforcement officials, fos-
tered through training programs sponsored by the CDC.[29]

Characterizing a biological event as intentional or unintentional may require matching public-health data with information collected through local,
national, and international law-enforcement and intelligence communities,
such as surveillance of criminal and terrorist organizations and state-sponsored biological programs.[30]

However, even forensic investigation may be unable to characterize a biological event accurately. Socioeconomic, demographic, and political trends may
affect the process of determining whether an event was intentional or unintentional. As Ronald Barrett's analysis of the human ecology of plague in India
indicates, knowledge of local conditions may have to be very broad, detailed,

and diverse. Correctly characterizing the plague outbreak in that case required knowledge of the socioeconomic conditions that gave rise to a migrant labor force by which the disease spread. Detailed analysis of historical and current social, economic, and political data was essential to determining that the plague was an unintentional outbreak resulting from labor migration and demographic trends, rather than, as widely believed for a time, a terrorist attack by one ethnic community against another.

Attribution to a Perpetrator: Knowing Whom to Blame

The third part of the problem of BW attribution is fingering the person, organization, or government that perpetrated an attack. This involves the law-enforcement, intelligence, and policy communities. The process may be conducted by domestic law-enforcement officials, foreign intelligence and foreign-policy agencies, or by all three.

With heightened concerns over the possible use of biological weapons by terrorists and "rogue states," deterring the use of biological weapons use has increased the importance policymakers attach to the attribution process.[31] Policymakers recognize that attribution, if done accurately and quickly, significantly increases the chances of holding states and non-state actors accountable for the use or supply of BW. This supports the classic aims of deterrence by punishment, which require that states fear retaliation for the use or supply of BW and that non-state actors, too, face credible threats of detection and punishment.

In practice, the three parts of the attribution process outlined here may not be distinctly separate: as the case studies in this volume show, outbreaks are rarely investigated in the analytic sequence of identification, characterization, and attribution. Rumors, panic, and politics often delay and complicate the process, and as a result, critical samples and other evidence may be mishandled, altered, or otherwise compromised.

How This Book Is Organized

Part I of this book features empirical case studies from the Second World War to the present, while Part II draws lessons and generates policy recommendations.

Case Studies: Part I

The case studies include actual uses of BW agents, alleged uses, fabricated reports of BW use connected with real disease outbreaks and staged "evidence," and natural, non-deliberate occurrences of disease that implicate agents that could have been used intentionally.[32] Two chapters address confirmed cases of BW use: the 2001 dissemination of anthrax through the U.S. postal system, and the use of BW agents by the Japanese Imperial Army in China in the 1930s and 1940s. The contentious "Yellow Rain" case of the late 1970s and early 1980s—in which the U.S. government alleged that Vietnamese forces and the Soviet military used trichothecene mycotoxin as a weapon—is the subject of two chapters. Another chapter addresses an unintentional outbreak of plague in India that was initially suspected to be a bioterrorist attack. Two chapters discuss false allegations accusing the United States of BW use; one case covers events during the Korean War, and the other Cuban allegations starting in the 1960s.

In Chapter 2, Leonard Cole discusses a confirmed case of BW agent use, the U.S. anthrax letters of 2001. This case overturned many assumptions about the use of a biological agent for hostile purposes, surprising U.S. authorities on a number of fronts, from the method of delivery and breadth of contamination to the health effects on infected survivors. Who committed these attacks, and why, remain unknown; where the spores originated and how they were processed are still a matter of controversy. Given that the attacks were openly carried out in a permissive environment and in a country with significant scientific and technological capacity, the surprises and failures experienced in the U.S. anthrax case bear careful study, as it represents perhaps the best case scenario for BW attribution.

Chapter 3 by Ronald Barrett examines the 1994 plague outbreak in Surat, India, in which 1,000 people or more may have had pneumonic plague, and more than three dozen died of it. Evidence strongly indicates that the plague occurred through natural and non-deliberate factors. Initially, however, rumors of chemical and biological terrorism impeded early detection and treatment programs. They also delayed follow-up efforts to prevent future outbreaks. The 1994 plague and its aftermath hold important lessons for the attribution and control of infectious diseases, whether or not they are deliberately initiated.

Chapter 4, by Matthew Meselson and Julian Perry Robinson, and Chapter 5, by Rebecca Katz, both examine reports of the late 1970s and early 1980s of "Yellow Rain," alleged to be trichothecene mycotoxin weapons attacks, in Southeast Asia and Afghanistan. These allegations sparked the first large-scale investigation conducted by the United States into allegations of chemical or biological weapons use. Although the United States officially found that toxin weapons had been used in Southeast Asia and Afghanistan, a number of scientists and experts, including Meselson and Robinson and some British government experts, concluded that trichothecene mycotoxin was not present. Katz argues on the basis of newly declassified documents, however, that while trichothecene mycotoxin may not have been the weapon used, some form of toxin weapon was likely used. Both chapters discuss the lessons of the Yellow Rain case for improving capabilities for accurate and timely BW attribution, with attention to difficulties that can arise during an investigation, especially in a conflict zone. These include problems in obtaining good data, the challenges in confirming use and in reaching an attribution determination in the absence of good data, and the consequences that flow from these difficulties.

The most prominent accusation of biological weapons use in the twentieth century was made during the Korean War against the United States, as Milton Leitenberg recounts in Chapter 6. China, North Korea, and the USSR charged that the United States had used a wide range of biological warfare agents in China and North Korea. Based on documents from the former Soviet archives and other evidence earlier unavailable, Leitenberg concludes that the charges were contrived and fraudulent. The chapter shows how false allegations and attributions of BW use can be manufactured, and draws lessons for the means by which false allegations might be refuted.

Since the 1960s, Cuban politicians, led by Castro, have repeatedly alleged that the United States or its proxies deliberately carried out biological warfare attacks against Cuba's human, animal, and plant populations. However, as Raymond Zilinskas shows in Chapter 7, the Cuban government has never backed up its charges with any scientific evidence. Zilinskas analyzes the Cuban allegations, and suggests that they were lodged largely for domestic and international political reasons. The chapter discusses the implications of the Cuban actions for international biological arms control and emphasizes the role of the UN Secretary-General in future BW investigations.

In Chapter 8, Jeanne Guillemin examines China's 1942 allegations of Japanese biological warfare. The accusation that the Japanese army had attacked Chinese civilians with germ weapons represents the first modern historical dispute that turned on the question of natural versus deliberate epidemics. Instead of investigating China's claim that thousands of civilians had been infected and many killed by Japan's deliberate use of plague-infected fleas, the United States chose to offer immunity to Japan's BW scientists in exchange for information on its biological warfare program. The suppression of this information from war-crimes proceedings represents a missed opportunity to establish criminal liability under international law for individuals who commit war crimes involving BW; the gap remains unfilled to this day.

Gary Ackerman and Victor Asal provide a quantitative and comparative overview of confirmed or suspected cases of BW agent use. Chapter 9 discusses the available data sources, their comprehensiveness, and the credibility of the information they provide. It provides a compilation of data on all 31 confirmed and alleged BW uses of the twentieth century. They find that the number of confirmed BW cases produced far fewer casualties than naturally occurring disease outbreaks, though they warn that advances in biotechnology may make biological warfare more effective in the future. Their chapter concludes that, in the absence of consistent and reliable data on BW use, efforts to understand and improve BW attribution must rely on qualitative analyses, such as those carried out in the case studies elsewhere in this volume.

All of the case studies in the first part of the book describe what mechanisms were available and what steps were taken by government officials, quasi-governmental bodies, and non-governmental experts to identify the actors responsible for the events. They also suggest steps that might have facilitated more rapid and definitive identification and attribution of BW use. They highlight how political context and overarching strategic goals often hinder BW attribution efforts.

Lessons and Recommendations: Part II

Part II of the volume draws lessons from the cases and generates policy recommendations. It also looks to the future in its assessment of how states in the post–9/11 world are organizing to meet this challenge. Two chapters assess U.S. and British policies regarding BW attribution. Another evaluates the available multilateral tools for BW attribution and the reforms required to make them more effective. The penultimate chapter outlines methodologies and requirements for information-sharing and alerts within and across national agencies, the private sector, foreign governments, and international organizations such as the WHO, OIE, and the UN Food and Agriculture Organization (FAO).

Chapter 10 by Elisa Harris examines U.S. efforts to investigate the use of biological weapons in the Yellow Rain and the more recent anthrax letters cases, as well as the U.S. approach to attribution in cases where the United States has been accused of BW use, during the Korean War and by Cuba. She draws lessons from these and other cases to offer recommendations for future U.S. policy toward investigating and attributing the use of biological weapons, in particular the need for independent and multilateral investigations that would give attributions of BW use political legitimacy.

Graham Pearson assesses United Kingdom policies regarding biological weapons in Chapter 11. He notes that the UK has long focused on dissuading would-be state possessors of biological weapons, rather than on evaluating or determining whether an outbreak of disease has been intentional or natural, both because there have been few attempted uses, and because responses after use would not be as effective. Since the attacks of September 11, 2001, however, the UK has increased its attention to non-state possession and use, increasing the importance of evaluation and determination of an outbreak. Pearson concludes that more effort should focus on deterring states and non-state actors from acquiring BW.

In Chapter 12, Jonathan Tucker examines multilateral approaches to the investigation and attribution of biological weapons use, including a mechanism under the United Nations secretary-general. At the request of a member state, he or she may dispatch a group of experts to investigate an alleged chemical or biological attack. This procedure was established in 1980 in response to charges that the Soviet Union and its allies were using a toxic agent ("Yellow Rain") in Southeast Asia and Afghanistan; subsequent UN investigations of alleged chemical warfare took place during the Iran-Iraq War of the 1980s and in Mozambique and Azerbaijan in 1992. Tucker examines the successes and failures of these investigations, as well as other procedures under the BWC and the Chemical Weapons Convention, and suggests how they might be strengthened.

In Chapter 13, Anne Clunan explores how national, subnational, and transnational information networks may offer a crucial capacity for timely and accurate attribution of BW use. She assesses policy and trust issues involved in moving from a "need-to-know" limitation to a "need-to-share" presumption to facilitate quick and accurate determination of whether BW has been used and by whom. It surveys the perspectives of critical stakeholders in the attribution process, including policymakers, the intelligence community, business sectors, non-governmental organizations, and first responders and other public-health agents—who usually have first-hand knowledge of the event and the victims—as well as intergovernmental organizations.

Chapter 14 by Susan Martin and Anne Clunan concludes the book by drawing lessons from the preceding chapters regarding the identification, characterization, and attribution of biological weapons use. It finds that, for attributions of BW use to be politically credible, they must be based on investigations that are scientifically sound and which establish with a high degree of confidence that a particular culprit perpetrated a biological weapons attack. The development of capabilities for conducting all three phases of a BW investigation enhance both a state's ability to deter by the threat of punishment and its capacity to deter by denial (reducing the consequences of attack). Enhanced identification, characterization, and attribution capabilities increase the likelihood that a perpetrator will be identified and can therefore be punished, while improvements in the public-health system that facilitate accurate and timely BW attribution, such as epidemiological surveillance, sanitation, vaccination, and information-sharing programs, serve to reduce the loss of life and societal disruption that BW attackers seek.

Notes

The views expressed in this chapter do not represent the official position of the Department of Defense or the U.S. government, but are the sole responsibility of the author.

1. Rocco Casagrande, "Biological Terrorism Targeted at Agriculture: The Threat to U.S. National Security," *Nonproliferation Review* 7, 73 (Fall–Winter 2000): 92–105; René Gottschalk and Wolfgang Preiser, "Bioterrorism: Is It a Real Threat?" *Medical Microbiology and Immunology* 194, 3 (May 2005): 109–14; James B. Petro, Theodore R. Plasse, and Jack A. McNulty, "Biotechnology: Impact on Biological Warfare and Biodefense," *Biosecurity and Bioterrorism: Biodefense Strategy, Practice, and Science* 1, 3 (September 2003): 161–68.

2. Recent histories of biological warfare are Jeanne Guillemin, *Biological Weapons: From the Invention of State-sponsored Programs to Contemporary Bioterrorism* (New

York: Columbia University Press, 2006); and Mark Wheelis, Lajos Rozsa, and Malcolm Dando, eds., *Deadly Cultures: Biological Weapons since 1945* (Cambridge, MA: Harvard University Press, 2006).

3. Richard A. Falkenrath, Robert D. Newman, and Bradley A. Thayer, *America's Achilles' Heel: Nuclear, Biological, and Chemical Terrorism and Covert Attack* (Cambridge, MA: BCSIA/MIT Press, 1998); Milton Leitenberg, *Assessing the Biological Weapons and Bioterrorism Threat* (Carlisle, PA: Strategic Studies Institute, U.S. Army War College, 2005); Anthony Cordesman, *The Challenge of Biological Terrorism* (Washington, DC: Center for Strategic and International Studies, 2005); and Sidney D. Drell, Abraham D. Sofaer, and George D. Wilson, eds., *The New Terror: Facing the Threat of Biological and Chemical Weapons* (Palo Alto, CA: Hoover Institution Press, 1999).

4. Joshua Lederberg, ed., *Biological Weapons: Limiting the Threat* (Cambridge, MA: BCSIA/MIT Press, 1999).

5. Raymond Zilinskas, ed., *Biological Warfare: Modern Offense and Defense* (Boulder, CO: Lynne Rienner, 1999).

6. Jonathan Tucker, ed., *Toxic Terror: Assessing Terrorist Use of Chemical and Biological Weapons* (Cambridge, MA: BCSIA/MIT Press, 2000).

7. Malcolm Dando, Graham S. Pearson, and Bohumir Kriz, eds., *Scientific and Technical Means of Distinguishing Between Natural and Other Outbreaks of Disease* (Norwell, MA: Kluwer Academic Publishers, 2001).

8. Alexander Kelle, Malcolm R. Dando, and Kathryn Nixdorff, eds., *The Role of Biotechnology in Countering BTW Agents* (Norwell, MA: Kluwer Academic Publishers, 2001); and Luther E. Lindler, Frank J. Lebeda, and George Korch, eds., *Biological Weapons Defense: Infectious Disease and Counterbioterrorism* (Totowa, NJ: Humana Press, 2005).

9. For an introduction to the many epidemiological and political issues hindering BW attribution inspired by the project that produced this volume, but which focuses on anthrax, see Elizabeth Stone Bahr, "Biological Weapons Attribution: A Primer," Master's Thesis, Naval Postgraduate School, June 2007.

10. This understanding of "attribution" as identification of a perpetrator and "attribution process" as encompassing the three elements of identification of a BW agent, characterization as intentional or unintentional, and attribution to a perpetrator is distinct from, and broader than, the forensic-science definition of attribution, which limits attribution to mean that a piece of evidence did in fact originate from a source of known origin to a high degree of scientific certainty to the exclusion of all other sources. I thank Randall S. Murch for bringing this distinction to my attention.

11. Even investigations of suspected overt use are not simple. Concerns over the possible use of biological weapons against U.S. and coalition forces during the 1990 Gulf War led to detailed investigations that ultimately found no evidence that any biological weapon was used, but sampling problems, particularly issues about the chain of cus-

tody of the samples, plagued the operation. See U.S. Department of Defense, "Close-Out Report: Biological Warfare Investigation," February 13, 2001, 20001011-0000001 Ver. 1.1, <http://www.gulflink.osd.mil/bw_ii/>; and U.S. Department of Defense, "Information Paper: Medical Surveillance During Operations Desert Shield/Desert Storm," November 6, 1997, 1997197-0000-052, <http://www.gulflink.osd.mil/nfl/>, both accessed June 21, 2006.

12. On the covert aspect, see Falkenrath, Newman and Thayer, *America's Achilles' Heel.*

13. Goodman et al., "Forensic Epidemiology," 684–700.

14. Centers for Disease Control and Prevention, "Bioterrorism Agents/Diseases," *Bioterrorism*, <http://www.bt.cdc.gov/agent/agentlist-category.asp>, accessed March 22, 2007.

15. World Health Organization, "Specific Diseases Associated with Biological Weapons," *Epidemic and Pandemic Alert and Response (EPR)*, <http://www.who.int/csr/delibepidemics/disease/en/>, accessed March 22, 2007.

16. David A. Ashford, Robyn Kaiser, Michael E. Bales et al., "Planning against Biological Terrorism: Lessons from Outbreak Investigations," *Emerging Infectious Diseases* 9, no. 5 (May 2003), <http://www.cdc.gov/ncidod/EID/vol9no5/02-0388.htm>, accessed June 21, 2006.

17. Ashford et al., "Planning."

18. Barry Kellman, "The International Matrix for Biosecurity," paper presented at the Los Angeles Terrorism Early Warning Group Conference on Terrorism, Global Security, and the Law, Santa Monica, CA, June 1–2, 2005.

19. Michael A. Stoto, "Syndromic Surveillance," *Issues in Science and Technology* Spring 2005, <http://www.issues.org/21.3/stoto.html>, accessed June 21, 2006.

20. Ashford et al., "Planning."

21. Anne Clunan, personal communication with State Department official responsible for biological weapons verification and attribution, September 6, 2006.

22. Ashford et al., "Planning." For the particulars of this case, see J. Greenblatt, "Suspected Brucellosis Case Prompts Investigation of Possible Bioterrorism-Related Activity—New Hampshire and Massachusetts, 1999," *Morbidity and Mortality Weekly Report* (MMWR) 49, no. 23 (June 16 2000): 509–12, <http://www.cdc.gov/mmwr/preview/mmwrhtml/mm4923a1.htm>, accessed June 21, 2006.

23. Anne Clunan, personal communication with State Department official responsible for biological weapons verification and attribution, September 6, 2006.

24. Ashford et al., "Planning."

25. Seth W. Carus, "The Rajneeshees (1984)," in Jonathan B. Tucker, ed., *Toxic Terror: Assessing Terrorist Use of Chemical and Biological Weapons* (Cambridge, MA: MIT Press, 2000), 115–37; and T. J. Torok et al., "A Large Community Outbreak of Salmonellosis

caused by Intentional Contamination of Restaurant Salad Bars," *Journal of the American Medical Association* 278 (1997): 389–95.

26. Carus, "The Rajneeshees (1984)," 136; and Judith Miller, Stephen Engelberg, and William Broad, *Germs: Biological Weapons and America's Secret War* (New York: Simon and Schuster, 2001): 32. For an excellent analysis of the Rajneeshee case from the perspective of BW attribution, see Brian C. Bernett, "U.S. Biodefense and Homeland Security: Toward Detection and Attribution," Master's Thesis, Naval Postgraduate School (December 2006), 13–35.

27. Randall S. Murch, "Microbial Forensics: Building a National Capacity to Investigate Bioterrorism," *Biosecurity and Bioterrorism: Biodefense Strategy, Practice, and Science* 1, 2 (2003): 117–22.

28. American Academy of Microbiology, quoted in Richard A. Goodman, Judith W. Munson, Kim Danners, Zita Lazzarini, and John P. Barkely, "Forensic Epidemiology: Law at the Intersection of Public Health and Criminal Investigations," *Journal of Law, Medicine and Ethics*, 31 (2003): 685.

29. For the development of microbial forensics and its standards, see Bruce Budowle, Randall Murch, and Ranajit Chakraborty, "Microbial Forensics: The Next Forensic Challenge," *International Journal of Legal Medicine* 119, 6 (November 2005): 317–30, available at <http://www.springerlink.com/content/1437-1596/>; Bruce Budowle, Steven E. Schutzer, Michael S. Ascher, Ronald M. Atlas, James P. Burans, Ranajit Chakraborty, John J. Dunn, Claire M. Fraser, David R. Franz, Terrance J. Leighton, Stephen A. Morse, Randall S. Murch, Jacques Ravel, Daniel L. Rock, Thomas R. Slezak, Stephan P. Velsko, Anne C. Walsh, and Ronald A. Walters, "Toward a System of Microbial Forensics: From Sample Collection to Interpretation of Evidence," *Applied and Environmental Microbiology*, May 2005: 2209–13; Bruce Budowle, Martin D. Johnson, Claire M. Fraser, Terrance J. Leighton, Randall S. Murch, and Ranajit Chakraborty, "Genetic Analysis and Attribution of Microbial Forensics Evidence," *Critical Reviews in Microbiology* 31: 233–54; and J. Fletcher, C. Bender, B. Budowle, W. T. Cobb, S. E. Gold, C. A. Ishimaru, D. Luster, U. Melcher, R. Murch, H. Scherm, R. C. Seem, J. L. Sherwood, B. W. Sobral, and S. A. Tolin, "Plant Pathogen Forensics: Capabilities, Needs and Recommendations," *Microbiology and Molecular Biology Reviews*, June 2006: 450–71.

30. Such surveillance systems may be insufficient to provide the necessary baseline data. Massive data-mining programs could gather global public-health data and also data on ongoing research and development in the biotech industry and academia, and could even monitor biodiversity. Developing such a system would require use of existing international organizations and databases in the area of public health, the environment, and microorganisms and bio-science to create a complete picture of the background data of biological agents in order to better pick out an anomalous event. Kellman, "International Matrix." Yet many of the organizations collecting such information may be

quite reluctant to share data with law-enforcement, military, intelligence, or other government agencies.

31. See, for example, President of the United States, *National Strategy for Combating Terrorism*, September 2006, 14–15, http://www.whitehouse.gov/nsc/nsct/2006/nsct2006. pdf, accessed September 7, 2006; and Assistant Secretary of State Paula DeSutter, "Identification, Characterization, and Attribution of Biological Weapons Use," remarks at a Conference on Identification, Characterization, and Attribution of Biological Weapons Use, organized by the Naval Postgraduate School's Center for Contemporary Conflict and the Kings College London Centre for Science and Security Studies, London, United Kingdom, July 12, 2006. Available at http://www.state.gov/t/vci/rls/rm/69313.htm, accessed August 22, 2006.

32. Another category is accidental biological outbreaks, such as the unintentional release of aerosolized anthrax in Sverdlovsk in 1979 and the 1971 smallpox epidemic in Aralsk, Kazakhstan. In order to limit the size of this study, however, there is no specific discussion of accidental outbreaks. The attribution requirements for accidental outbreaks are no different from those needed to distinguish between unintentional events and intentional release of BW. For the purposes of this volume, an accidental release of a biological warfare agent would fall into the category of intentional release, as the agent was not introduced as a result of natural patterns of interactions with the environment by humans, animals, plants or insects, as was the case in the 1994 Indian plague outbreak. At the characterization phase, the only distinction would be to determine whether the release was accidental or deliberate, which is merely a question of expanding hypotheses for why the agent appeared.

Case Studies

CHAPTER TWO

The U.S. Anthrax Letters

A Confirmed Case of BW Agent Use

LEONARD A. COLE

A half-dozen letters, perhaps more, containing powdered anthrax spores were sent through the U.S. mail to journalists and politicians starting about a week after the attacks of September 11, 2001.[1] As a result, 22 people became infected, half with cutaneous anthrax, half with inhalation anthrax; five of the latter died. In several instances, initial diagnoses failed to recognize *Bacillus anthracis* as the cause of infection; the first case was not confirmed until October 4. The outbreak was characterized as intentional soon after, as spores were found at improbable locations, but the extent of illness and contamination of buildings, offices, and postal facilities was not grasped for several more weeks. Attribution as to the perpetrator proved elusive and remained uncertain more than six years later.

The anthrax bioattack of 2001 confounded many earlier assumptions about use of a biological agent for hostile purposes, from the manner of delivery to the health effects on infected survivors. This chapter reviews the unfolding events, from the first case to be confirmed in early October through the last one on November 21, and subsequent efforts to clarify uncertainties about the attack.

Although much about the anthrax letters is now understood, important questions remain unanswered: still unknown are the motivation as well as the identity of the perpetrator; the manner of exposure by which two women were fatally infected; the source of the anthrax spores; and the method by which they were processed before they were placed in the envelopes. Also unexpected is that, years after exposure, five of the six survivors of inhalation anthrax still had symptoms associated with the disease, including muscle and joint aches, shortness of breath, and malaise. The chapter examines these open questions and concludes with a discussion of lessons learned.

Discovering the Threat

On October 4, 2001, the U.S. Centers for Disease Control and Prevention (CDC) confirmed a Florida state laboratory finding that a 63-year-old man had tested positive for anthrax. The patient, Robert Stevens, was a photo-editor for the *Sun*, a supermarket tabloid published by American Media, Inc. (AMI) in Boca Raton, Florida. He had been hospitalized on October 2, two days earlier, and he died on October 5 of inhalation anthrax, an infection caused by breathing in anthrax bacteria. Inhalation anthrax is so rare that only eighteen cases in the United States had been recorded in the twentieth century. The most recent instance before 2001 was in 1976 when a California weaver was fatally infected by spores from wool that had been imported from Pakistan.[2]

Coming so soon after the attacks of September 11, and with associated publicity about anthrax as a potential biological weapon, some people immediately suspected that Stevens's anthrax infection might be associated with bioterrorism. But many officials initially discounted the possibility that the cause was intentional: state public-health authorities in Florida, and in North Carolina where Stevens had just vacationed, insisted that his infection in no way implied terrorism, while Tommy Thompson, the U.S. Secretary of Health and Human Services, at first declared that, "There is no terrorism."[3]

Meanwhile, CDC officials investigated dozens of places that Stevens had frequented in the months before his diagnosis. They swabbed surfaces and collected samples for analysis in restaurants, shops, parks, his home in Lantana, Florida, and his workplace in the AMI building. On October 7, two days after his death, tests indicated the presence of anthrax spores on Stevens's computer keyboard and in the AMI mailroom. These findings suddenly made clear that the dismissal of bioterrorism as a possible cause of his death had been premature.

During the following weeks, *Bacillus anthrax* was found to have infected

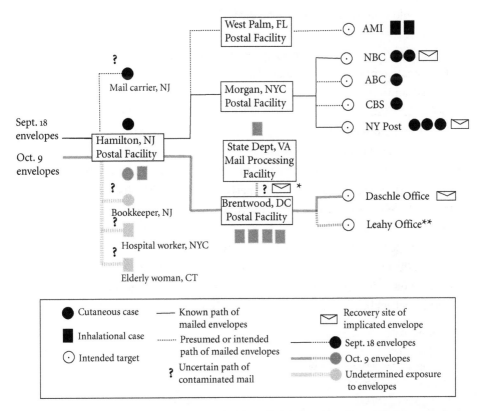

FIG. 2.1. Cases of Anthrax Associated with Mailed Paths of Implicated Envelopes and Intended Target Sites. Source: Redrawn from Daniel B. Jernigan et al., "Investigation of Bioterrorism-Related Anthrax, United States, 2001: Epidemiologic Findings," *Emerging Infectious Diseases* 8, no. 10 (October 2002): figure 2, <http://www.cdc.gov/ncidod/eid/vol8no10/02-0353-G2.htm>.

Abbreviations: NY, New York; NBC, National Broadcasting Company; AMI, American Media Inc.; USPS, United States Postal Service; CBS, Columbia Broadcasting System.

*Envelope addressed to Senator Leahy, found unopened on November 16, 2001, in a barrel of unopened mail sent to Capitol Hill.

**Dotted line indicates intended path of envelope addressed to Senator Leahy.

twenty-two residents of Washington, DC, and seven east coast states: Florida, Virginia, Maryland, Pennsylvania, New Jersey, New York, and Connecticut. (See Figure 2.1.) Eleven people, including Stevens, were stricken with inhalation anthrax, of whom five died. Another eleven contracted the less dangerous cutaneous form of the disease; all of them survived.[4] The last case to be reported was a

94-year-old Connecticut woman who died of inhalation anthrax on November 21, 2001.

During October and November, it became clear that the bacterium had been disseminated through the U.S. mail. Threat letters containing anthrax were recovered, and several postal sorting centers were found to be contaminated with spores, including the Hamilton, N.J., facility near Trenton, and the Brentwood Road facility in Washington, DC. Most anthrax victims were postal workers or otherwise known to have been in contact with contaminated mail.

Four letters, each containing 1–2 grams of dry anthrax spores, were found during this period. All four were postmarked "Trenton NJ," which meant that they had been processed at the Postal Sorting and Distribution Center (PSDC) in nearby Hamilton. Two of the envelopes were postmarked September 18, 2001; one was addressed to newscaster Tom Brokaw at NBC-TV (found on October 12), and the other to the editor of the *New York Post* (found on October 19). The message on a sheet inside of each was a photocopy of an original, which may have been kept by the mailer. In handwritten block letters, the text read:

09-11-01
THIS IS NEXT
TAKE PENACILIN [sic] NOW
DEATH TO AMERICA
DEATH TO ISRAEL
ALLAH IS GREAT[5]

The other two recovered envelopes, postmarked October 9, 2001, were addressed to Senator Tom Daschle (found October 15) and Senator Patrick Leahy (found at the State Department on November 16). The text in these two letters was identical, although somewhat different from the wording in the other pair:

09-11-01
YOU CAN NOT STOP US.
WE HAVE THIS ANTHRAX.
YOU DIE NOW.
ARE YOU AFRAID?
DEATH TO AMERICA.
DEATH TO ISRAEL.
ALLAH IS GREAT.[6]

Based on the trails of spores found, and the fact that infected individuals had been in their proximity, anthrax letters are also believed to have been sent to the ABC and CBS television studios in New York, as well as the offices of AMI, publisher of the *Sun* and another tabloid, the *National Inquirer*, in Boca Raton, Florida. The envelope flaps were sealed with tape, so it appears that the anthrax spores—each around one micron in diameter—leaked through the envelope paper's pores, which exceeded twenty microns in size. Although the bacteria could have been transported by cross-contamination from other mail containing anthrax spores, the fact that they were found in large concentrations at those locations suggested that the likely source was a letter containing anthrax spores.

In several instances, initial diagnoses of the victims failed to identify anthrax as a possible cause of their illness, nor was the extent of contamination in scores of buildings, offices, and postal facilities recognized at first. Retrospective assessments and testing eventually identified additional locations that had been exposed to the bacterium, as well as previously infected individuals who had recovered by the time the ailment was identified as anthrax. The presence of spores, along with several false alarms, prompted much of official Washington to shut down starting soon after the letter sent to Senator Daschle's office was opened, on October 15. At various times during this period, many buildings and offices were closed, including the Capitol and offices of members of the Senate and House of Representatives, as well as portions of the Pentagon, the State Department, the Federal Reserve Building, and the Supreme Court. Meanwhile, spores were found in postal facilities and other offices along the eastern seaboard and as far west as Kansas City, Missouri.[7] As succeeding days and weeks brought information about more victims and contaminated locations, the public became increasingly anxious, and people throughout the United States were afraid to open mail.

The anthrax attacks resulted in relatively few casualties, although they generated massive disruption and demonstrated the potential for devastating consequences. More than 30,000 people who were considered at risk of exposure to the bacterium were treated with prophylactic antibiotics.[8] Without this intervention, many of them could have become infected and some might have died. If the strain of bacterium had been drug-resistant, or if more anthrax let-

TABLE 2.1

Timeline of Anthrax Attack, 2001

9/11/01: Attacks on the Pentagon and World Trade Center.

9/18: The postmark date on the two letters recovered in New York, found 10/12 and 10/19 at NBC and the *NY Post* respectively.

9/21: The first symptomatic case (cutaneous), though not identified as anthrax until October 19 through belated testing (a *New York Post* journalist).

9/21–10/1: During this period, nine people in the states of Florida, New York, and New Jersey showed symptoms of anthrax (seven cutaneous and two inhalation), unrecognized as anthrax at first. Confirmation came during later weeks after retrospective assessments and testing.

10/4: The first confirmed case of anthrax (Robert Stevens in Boca Raton, Florida, who died the next day of inhalation anthrax).

10/7: The first environmental identification of anthrax spores (in the AMI building in Boca Raton, Florida).

10/9: The postmark date on the two letters recovered in Washington, DC (one found October 15 in the office of Senator Daschle, one found November 16 in impounded mail at the State Department, addressed to Senator Leahy).

10/12: The first recovered anthrax letter was found at NBC in New York City (postmarked 9/18).

10/15: The second recovered anthrax letter was found in Washington, DC, in the office of Senator Daschle (postmarked 10/9).

10/16: Congressional office buildings were closed—the day after the letter to Daschle was opened in the Hart Senate Office Building.

10/18: Environmental sampling was begun at selected sites inside the Hamilton and Brentwood postal facilities.

10/18: The Hamilton, NJ, Postal Sorting and Distribution Center (PSDC) was closed after a postal worker there was diagnosed with cutaneous anthrax.

10/19: The third recovered anthrax letter was found in a mail pile in the office of the *New York Post* (postmarked 9/18).

10/20: Presence of anthrax was confirmed at Hamilton postal facility.

10/21: The Brentwood PSDC was closed after tests confirmed the facility was contaminated with anthrax spores.

11/16: The fourth recovered letter, addressed to Senator Leahy, was found with other impounded mail in a storage bag at the State Department, where it had mistakenly been routed.

December 2003: The Brentwood postal facility was able to reopen following decontamination.

March 2005: The Hamilton postal facility was able to reopen following decontamination.

ters had been mailed, the numbers of deaths and illnesses might have been far greater. It is clear that responses to the unfolding outbreak were in many ways inadequate. A review of the events can illuminate weaknesses and the means to correct them. (See the timeline in Table 2.1.)

Grasping the Nature and Extent of the Attack

When Robert Stevens arrived, delirious, at the emergency room of JFK Hospital in Atlantis, Florida, at 2:00 a.m. on October 2, he was initially diagnosed as suffering from meningitis. No one on duty thought of anthrax as a cause of his illness. But later that day, when infectious disease specialist Dr. Larry Bush was called in to consult, he began to entertain a possibility that struck some at the hospital as preposterous. While examining Stevens's spinal fluid under a microscope, Bush thought that the unusual rod-shaped bacteria in view might be *Bacillus anthracis*. After preliminary testing at a local laboratory, Bush had the specimens sent to a state laboratory in Jacksonville, and then to the CDC, for advanced testing. While the tests were underway, colleagues and health officials continued to dismiss Bush's conjecture, though Dr. Jean Malecki, the Palm Beach County health director, was an exception who shared Bush's suspicion.[9] Even after the diagnosis of anthrax was confirmed by the CDC on October 4, several public officials rejected the possibility that the cause had been deliberate. The pattern of skepticism and rejection was also experienced with other early anthrax cases, most of which were only belatedly recognized.

Although Stevens was the first identified anthrax case, later analyses found that he was not the first to have become infected. Between September 21 and October 1, a total of nine individuals had displayed symptoms of anthrax; seven had contracted the cutaneous form of the disease, and two the inhalational (Stevens and another AMI employee in Florida). The two earliest cases are described here, because they were typical of the tardiness of identification as anthrax. The first person now known to show symptoms of anthrax was Joanna Huden, a 31-year-old journalist at the *New York Post*. On September 21, she noticed a blister on her right middle finger. In subsequent days the lesion oozed, itched, turned black, and became painful. Her physician believed the cause was an infected spider bite. Huden was initially treated with the antibiotic amoxicillin, but the sore continued to fester. On October 1, feeling feverish, Huden went to a New York hospital emergency room. The black lesion, she recalled, "caught the interest of several doctors—emergency specialists, internists and plastic surgeons."[10] After the doctors agreed that the lesion should be excised, a surgeon removed the affected tissue.[11] The lesion area began to heal, though Huden remained concerned about its cause.

Meanwhile, on October 12, a week after Robert Stevens's death, news reports indicated that an assistant to NBC journalist Tom Brokaw was found to have cutaneous anthrax. Erin O'Connor, 38, had noticed a sore on her chest on September 25. Her physician, an internist, believed the lesion had been caused by a spider bite, but considered anthrax a remote possibility. He sent a sample of the affected tissue to the New York City Health Department, where preliminary tests were, incorrectly as it turned out, negative for anthrax. The department forwarded some tissue to the CDC where, on October 12, advanced testing found the sample to be positive for anthrax.[12]

When the news broke about O'Connor's skin anthrax, Johanna Huden did a computer search for "anthrax." The images of cutaneous lesions struck her as similar to the one that had been on her finger. She reported her suspicion to another doctor, who sent tissue and blood specimens to the city health department, which forwarded samples to the CDC; there, testing eventually gave rise to a diagnosis of suspected anthrax. The finding, based on a positive serum immunoglobulin reactive test, was announced publicly on October 19.[13]

Huden and O'Connor, both in New York, turned out to be the first two anthrax cases. Their cases suggest three key observations. First, if their diagnoses had been accurate at the outset, the nation could have been made aware that anthrax had appeared at improbable locations more than a week before the Stevens case was confirmed. Second, as with most of the other infected individuals, few of their examining doctors initially considered anthrax as a likely cause of their patients' illnesses. Third, analytic capabilities to confirm the presence of anthrax were less dependable at state and local laboratories than at national laboratories, particularly those of the CDC and at the U.S. Army Medical Research Institute for Infectious Diseases (USAMRIID) at Fort Detrick, Maryland. USAMRIID is the nation's principal biodefense research institute; like the CDC, it fell behind in responding to demands for rapid testing of the thousands of suspected samples it received during the crisis.

Alternative Identification and Characterization Scenarios

An alternative scenario asks what might have happened if Huden, O'Connor, or any of the other early cases had been diagnosed with anthrax at the outset.[14] Huden first sought medical care at a walk-in clinic on September 28, a week after the onset of her symptoms. The doctor, though unsure of the cause of infection, prescribed amoxicillin. Her condition worsened and she later visited another doctor. She continued taking the amoxicillin which, as it happens, can be effective to some degree against *Bacillus anthracis*. On October 1, a surgeon removed the lesion, though its cause remained uncertain. She began to feel better, but was still eager for a diagnosis. By October 19, when the CDC concluded that her lesion had been caused by *Bacillus anthracis*, she had seen seven physicians.[15]

Huden's first doctors never considered anthrax in their diagnoses. Days after O'Connor's case was made public, Huden visited a physician at another hospital where additional tissue and blood specimens were taken and sent to the New York City Health Laboratory. Tests there were negative for anthrax, though the lab's testing techniques were limited, as was true at many community and state laboratories throughout the country. But the New York laboratory forwarded Huden's specimens to the CDC, where her blood sample tested positive for anthrax. The identification of this first case of anthrax, on October 19, nearly one month after the onset of symptoms, had also been delayed by the backlog of other specimens awaiting tests at both the local and national labs.[16] In the absence of a sense of urgency, a week elapsed before the finding on Huden's sample was established.

If the system had worked ideally, her first doctor would have suspected anthrax and sent a sample to the city laboratory. If a proper array of tests had been available and performed rapidly, the suspicion of anthrax would presumably have been quickly reinforced. The sample would then have been forwarded to CDC laboratories for rapid confirmation or disconfirmation. Although the CDC also had a backlog of items waiting to be tested for a variety of possible diseases, suspicion of anthrax, notwithstanding the negative findings of the city lab, should have caused Huden's specimen to receive priority handling; a conclusion could have been reached in 24 hours. With timely action and appropriate laboratory capabilities, Huden's lesion could have been identified as cutaneous anthrax before September 30. Had she sought medical care three days after her symptoms appeared rather than six, and if anthrax had been part of the differential diagnosis, confirmation of the disease could have come as early as September 25. The appearance of an anthrax case in New York City would have been broadly publicized. It would have alerted doctors and patients who were seeing similar lesions that were not being accurately diagnosed. Anthrax would have been considered a possibility in subsequent cases; for those whose inhalation anthrax was initially unrecognized by examining doctors, earlier prophylactic measures might have saved lives.

Another theoretical scenario focuses on the postal facilities. If the nation had been alerted even earlier to a finding of anthrax spores at odd locations, this might have led to earlier identification of the agent and characterization of the event as intentional. Prompted by the diagnosis of anthrax for a local postal worker, the postal facility in Hamilton, New Jersey, was closed on October 18, 2001, to test for the presence of anthrax bacteria. Spores were discovered throughout the facility, and the building remained shut for three years until decontamination could be completed.[17] Around the same time, after workers at the larger postal center on Brentwood Road in Washington, DC, became ill, testing there also indicated widespread contamination, prompting the closing of that center on October 21, 2001, for more than two years.[18] Soon after the discovery of spores at the two large postal centers, investigations found anthrax spores in various amounts in numerous postal facilities and other offices and buildings.[19]

If equipment to detect bioagents had been in place, anthrax spores might have been found in the New Jersey facility as early as September 18, the date the early letters were processed there. But the bacterial cargo in those letters went unrecognized, and spores continued to leak along the mail trail from New Jersey to the Morgan distribution center in downtown Manhattan, to local post offices, and to the ultimate recipients. The contamination might have been discovered at the smaller post offices as well, if detection machines had been near the sorting apparatus. However, the anthrax contamination of any postal facility was not confirmed until October 20. Had effective detectors been in place, the presence of spores could have been recognized more than a month earlier, and the public-health and law-enforcement communities could have understood the threat even sooner than in the first scenario.

Since the anthrax incidents, the U.S. Postal Service has sought a system of early identification of anthrax spores. By the end of 2005, 1,373 Biohazard Detection Systems had been installed in the 282 Postal Sorting and Distribution Centers across the country, at a cost of $375 million. Each system collects air samples from mail items. The samples then undergo polymerase chain reaction testing for the presence of anthrax DNA.[20] In 2006, plans were underway to expand the capability of the system to identify other threat agents as well, although postal authorities were unable to say when that would happen.[21]

The Danger Posed by Cross-Contamination

During the month between the earliest postmarked anthrax letters and the dates when the Hamilton and Brentwood postal centers were closed, 85 million pieces of mail were processed at the two facilities. Thousands or millions of letters may have been cross-contaminated during that period. The residue of spores on most pieces of mail was probably minimal, but the risk from exposure even to small amounts could not be entirely disregarded. Indeed, the deaths of two anthrax patients were likely due to such exposure.

All but two of the twenty-two anthrax victims were known to have been in locations where spores were found: contaminated postal facilities, offices, or buildings. The two exceptions were Kathy Nguyen and Ottilie Lundgren, both of whom died of inhalation anthrax. Nguyen, a 61-year-old stockroom employee at Manhattan's Eye, Ear and Throat Hospital, commuted to work by subway from her Bronx apartment. On October 28, critically ill, she was admitted to another Manhattan hospital where she died three days later. Extensive searches of her apartment, personal effects, workplace, shops she frequented, and even the subway she rode found no trace of anthrax bacteria.[22]

The case of Ottilie Lundgren, at 94 the oldest anthrax victim, was even more perplexing. Lundgren lived alone in a private home in the semi-rural town of Oxford, Connecticut. She was in good health for her age, although she remained home most of the time. Friends would drive her to a weekly appointment with her hairdresser, to church, occasionally to the library, or lunch at a local restaurant. Every place that Lundgren had visited in her last weeks was identified and, along with her home and personal effects, was examined carefully for anthrax. No spores were found. When she died on November 21, she was the last known victim of the anthrax letters. One clue may be the manner in which she disposed of her mail, as described by her niece Shirley Davis: after a friend brought the mail to her from the curbside mailbox, Lundgren would open the items and sort them, and she would tear in half each letter she did not plan to save and discard it into a wastebasket. Then she would empty the wastebasket into a garbage bin outside the back door.[23] Tearing might have released some powdered spores on a cross-contaminated letter and caused them to float up to her face.

Subsequent testing identified *Bacillus anthracis* spores in local post offices through which mail passed en route to Kathy Nguyen's and Ottilie Lundgren's mailboxes. Even though spores were not found in their mailboxes or homes, it may be supposed that the women became ill after inhaling bacteria from cross-contaminated mail. Extrapolations from animal studies show that a dose of 2,500 to 55,000 anthrax spores would be expected to kill 50 percent of the people exposed.[24] But for some individuals, inhaling even a single spore might cause infection and death.[25] Moreover, that no spores were detected does not show that no spores were ever present: a small residue of spores could have been swept away in the course of routine cleaning.[26]

Challenges for Early Identification and Diagnosis

The first challenge to early diagnosis of the anthrax victims arose because health professionals had only limited experience with the disease, as well as because some in the medical community may have been reluctant to allow for unusual possibilities. A tenet of diagnostic training is that a physician should give primacy to probable, rather than obscure, causes: symptoms such as fever and chills in Manhattan should first suggest the flu, not malaria. Despite heightened publicity about the threat of bioterrorism, most of the doctors who initially saw the anthrax victims failed to consider the disease in their possible diagnoses. Those few who did tended to meet with skepticism from colleagues, especially in small communities—Lantana and Boca Raton in Florida, Oxford, Connecticut, and Mount Holly, New Jersey—which were deemed unlikely targets for a terror attack. Skepticism greeted tentative diagnoses of anthrax in some larger communities as well, including New York City and Washington, DC.

The second challenge arose because of numerous bioterrorism hoaxes. The hoax phenomenon had grown dramatically in the late 1990s. In 1997, the Federal Bureau of Investigation (FBI) reported twenty-two instances in which threats involved anthrax or, less often, another biological material. By 2000, the number of anthrax threats exceeded 300 per year, and all had proven to be false alarms.[27] Thus, even after September 11, 2001, the thousand-odd previous hoaxes created expectations that more such biothreats would also be hoaxes.

A third challenge lay with obtaining timely and accurate tests of suspected specimens. In 1999, the CDC had established a bioterrorism preparedness and response program to help state laboratories adopt uniform testing methods for suspected bioagents. By 2001, eighty laboratories around the country were participating in the new "laboratory response network."[28] Proficiency varied among the laboratories—technicians at some locations were better prepared than others—but most labs lacked the supplies needed to perform a range of tests for several threat agents. Fortunately, the state laboratory in Jacksonville, Florida, was well equipped in this regard. Philip Lee, the lead technician there, had just completed a CDC course on testing for bioagents, which enabled him to conduct the tests on the Stevens specimens that first revealed the presence of anthrax.[29]

The sheer number of potential threats created a bottleneck at many state laboratories. During October and November 2001, laboratories in the response network tested more than 125,000 clinical specimens and around one million environmental specimens.[30] The huge volume meant that some samples were not tested until weeks after they arrived at a laboratory. By 2006, however, the number of laboratories in the network had grown to more than 140 and the level of proficiency was vastly improved.[31] Faced again with the need to test more than one million samples quickly, however, the system would still be hard pressed.

A final challenge was that of case definition, which crystallized with the illness of the other AMI victim in Florida. As Stevens lay ill in a hospital in Atlantis, Florida, Ernesto Blanco, a 73-year-old AMI mailroom clerk, was in a Miami hospital with similar symptoms. The cause of his illness had been a puzzle to his doctors; only after Stevens's diagnosis became known was Blanco viewed as a possible case of inhalation anthrax. One of Blanco's physicians then began treating him with massive volumes of intravenous ciprofloxacin, the antibiotic considered most effective against anthrax, and Blanco eventually recovered.[32] However, Blanco's condition was not confirmed as anthrax until weeks after he was deemed a suspect case.

Determining the criteria for particular diseases lies with the CDC. Prior to Blanco's case, the CDC's case definition for anthrax required isolation of *Bacillus anthracis* from a patient's specimen. If living bacteria could not be cultured, anthrax was not considered the cause of illness. But Blanco's blood samples failed to grow bacteria because he had begun taking antibiotics before his blood was tested for anthrax. Initial doses of the antibiotics had suppressed the bacteria. Blanco remained ill for some time because the toxin had already been released by the microorganisms and continued to wreak havoc in his body. When scientists at the CDC realized all this, they changed the criteria for the case definition. Now, according to the CDC's revised criteria, in the absence of viable bacteria, certain other laboratory tests may be used to define a case as confirmed or suspect. These tests include PCR (polymerase chain reaction), immunohistochemical staining, and ELISA (enzyme-linked immunosorbent assay). The tests may demonstrate the presence of an antigen, antibodies, or segments of anthrax DNA. If a patient's symptoms are clinically compatible with those of anthrax, and two of these tests are positive, the case is considered confirmed. If only one test is positive, the case is deemed suspect.[33]

Attribution: Identifying the Perpetrator

The most notorious unresolved question about the anthrax letters concerns the identity of the perpetrator. Notions about who prepared and mailed the letters have tended to fall into either of two camps. One holds that the mailer was probably a lone domestic scientist roughly matching a profile developed by the FBI.[34] The other contends that the perpetrator was foreign, perhaps associated with Al-Qaeda, and may have had advance knowledge of the September 11 attacks. (Speculation by some that the bacteria might have come from Iraq's former biological weapons program seems unlikely in view of its apparent cessation after the 1991 Gulf War.)[35] Publicly available information suggests that either a domestic or foreign source is possible; the evidence for each is suggestive, but far from definitive. The arguments that favor the domestic-loner hypothesis are based on the purported nature and preparation of the spores, doubts about Al-Qaeda's scientific capabilities, and the FBI's profile of the likely perpetrator. Support for the notion of an overseas connection arises from the close proximity in timing between 9/11 and the release of the bacterium, Al-Qaeda's known interest in using anthrax as a weapon, and activities of some of the 9/11 hijackers. Given the information that is publicly available, describing the perpetrator either as a domestic loner or as connected to an overseas source remains conjectural.

Domestic-Loner Hypothesis

All the letters contained the "Ames" strain of *Bacillus anthracis*. The Ames strain was identified in 1981 after it killed several cows in a Texas pasture, and was then acquired for study by the U.S. Army Medical Research Institute for Infectious Diseases (USAMRIID) in Fort Detrick, Maryland. The strain proved to be highly virulent; samples were sent for further study to other laboratories, mainly in the United States.

The spores in the letters were considered by many experts to be highly refined, especially those in the two letters postmarked October 9 (the spores in the September 18 letters reportedly were mixed with debris and could not be as readily aerosolized). The two batches may have been prepared differently, although that also is uncertain. The CDC suggests that the difference in potential for aerosolization might have come about because "the two mailings were made under or exposed to different environmental conditions (e.g., amount of moisture)."[36] A proponent of this notion was Douglas Beecher, an FBI microbiologist who worked on the anthrax investigation:

> Particle size distributions [of dried anthrax spores] are dynamic, changing as a powder experiences different conditions upon handling, such as compaction, friction, and humidity, among other factors. The size distribution of a recovered powder represents its state after an unknown period of aging and an unknowable set of conditions experienced during handling. It may not resemble the initial product.[37]

In any case, the spores in both batches were deadly. The disease apparently can occur any time from a few days to a few months after exposure.[38] The two inhalation victims at AMI became symptomatic toward the end of September. Although no anthrax letters to the AMI offices were recovered, the trails of spores indicated that two anthrax letters were sent to AMI tabloids—one to the *Sun* and the other to the *National Inquirer*.[39] Such letters may well have been sent at the same time as those sent to New York, around September 18.

The method used to process the spores remains in question. Normally, an electrostatic effect induces spores to cling to each other. Thus a preparation of dry spore powder ordinarily contains particles—dozens of spores clumped together—that are "large" though still microscopic. Such a powder would not float as freely as one composed of separate individual spores. Laboratory techniques can coat spores with silica or other materials to negate their electrostatic attraction so that they are more effectively aerosolized and can float as single particles. It is such a concentration of free-floating spores that is believed by some to have been in the October 9 letters sent to the U.S. Capitol, in contrast to the more clumpy mix in the September 18 letters.

Some analysts maintain that free-floating anthrax spores would not be technically difficult for a lone operator to produce, although others disagree. The difference of opinion extends even to experts who have experience with "weaponizing" anthrax and other bioagents. William Patrick and Richard Spertzel both worked in the U.S. offensive biological warfare program before it ended in 1969. Patrick maintains that the small amounts of anthrax found in the October 9 letters to Senators Daschle and Leahy could have been produced in a crude domestic laboratory.[40] In contrast, Spertzel thinks that the anthrax spores in those letters would have been difficult to process and that the material likely came from an overseas state program.[41] He believes he knows personally each of the handful of American scientists who could produce such a sophisticated product and that none of them could conceivably be the mailer.[42]

FBI microbiologist Douglas Beecher added yet another dimension to the issue. He wrote in 2006 that "a widely circulated misconception is that the spores were produced using additives and sophisticated engineering supposedly akin to military weapons production. The persistent credence given to this impression fosters erroneous preconceptions, which may . . . detract from the magnitude of hazards posed by simple spore preparations."[43] In other words, he is warning that a potent sample of dry anthrax spores might not be difficult to produce.

There is no solid evidence that Al-Qaeda ever weaponized anthrax. Its capability to do so remains a subject of debate. A comprehensive 2005 report to President George W. Bush on intelligence regarding weapons of mass destruction reflects this uncertainty.[44] After the war in Afghanistan began, intelligence officials found that Al-Qaeda's research and development on anthrax apparently were more advanced than previously believed. The organization had "'probably' acquired at least a small quantity of [a] virulent strain," according to some assessments. But the reliability of these suppositions is questionable, according to the report. Clarifying uncertainties about the source of the mailed anthrax, and Al-Qaeda's ability to produce it, could have important implications.[45] If the perpetrator were an amateur who was able to develop the material without advanced training, the matter would be especially ominous, expanding greatly the field of possible perpetrators, whether local or overseas.

On November 9, 2001, two weeks before the last anthrax victim was diagnosed, the FBI posted on its website a detailed portrayal of supposed characteristics of the perpetrator. The Bureau did so in hopes that someone might recognize an "acquaintance [who] might fit the profile."[46] According to the FBI site, the anthrax mailer was likely an adult male with scientific background who had access to a source of anthrax, probably from a U.S. laboratory. He is described as a non-confrontational person, someone who holds grudges and who prefers to be by himself. FBI officials acknowledged that the domestic-loner profile was patterned on Theodore Kaczynski, the Unabomber.[47] In the 18 years prior to his arrest in 1996, Kaczynski mailed several letter bombs that injured 29 people and killed three. It is unclear why Kaczynski's personal and professional attributes should have been considered a model for the anthrax mailer, but six years following the anthrax mailings, the FBI's profile remained on its website. Several individuals have been investigated, though none was charged with a crime.

Overseas Perpetrator

The proposition that the perpetrator might somehow have been associated with Al-Qaeda is no less intriguing and frustrating than the supposition that the perpetrator was a domestic loner. The letters postmarked September 18 meant they were mailed just six or seven days after 9/11. If the mailer had no foreknowledge of the 9/11 attacks, either he already possessed powdered bacteria (for reasons unknown) and suddenly decided to use it, or he worked with extraordinary speed to refine the bacteria, identify targets, and do the mailings. Neither possibility strengthens the case for a lone disaffected scientist as perpetrator, nor explains what his motivation might have been.

On the other hand, some reported connections between Al-Qaeda operatives and the anthrax letters, while also suggestive, fall short of proof. For example, in the summer of 2001, Gloria Irish, a south Florida realtor, had found rental apartments for Marwan Al-Shehhi and Hamza Alghamdi; they were among six hijackers who lived in the Boca Raton area through August. When her two clients told Gloria Irish they would be taking flying lessons nearby, she told them that her husband Mike flew a private plane from the same airport. Mike Irish was the editor of the *Sun* in Boca Raton where Robert Stevens worked, and which would apparently become a target of the anthrax mailer.[48] This may be a clue or it may be mere coincidence.

Another one of the six hijackers who had lived in the Boca Raton area, Ahmed Alhaznawi, had visited a Fort Lauderdale hospital in June 2001 for treatment of a black lesion on his leg. The emergency room doctor noted that Alhaznawi said he scraped his leg two months earlier. The doctor found the lesion puzzling, but cleaned it and prescribed an antibiotic. After the September 11 attacks and publicity about the anthrax cases, the doctor came to believe that the lesion may have been cutaneous anthrax. Physicians at the Johns Hopkins Center for Civilian Biodefense Strategies interviewed the doctor, reviewed his notes, and concluded that the diagnosis of anthrax was "the most probable and coherent interpretation of the data available."[49]

Another connection, or coincidence, was noted in a *Miami Herald* news article: "Investigators confirmed that two hijackers who died in the Sept. 11 terrorist attacks had subscriptions to tabloid newspapers published in the Boca Raton headquarters of American Media, Inc., where photo editor Robert Stevens is believed to have contracted the fatal disease."[50] The article did not name the tabloids, though elsewhere Hamza Alghamdi (one of Gloria Irish's rental clients) was reported to have purchased a subscription to *Mira!*, a Spanish-language tabloid published by American Media.[51]

All of the other anthrax letters targeted nationally prominent media and political offices; AMI was an exception, and of the seven tabloids published by AMI, the *Sun* was among the least prominent, having a relatively low circulation. If accomplices of the hijackers were involved in the anthrax letters, selecting American Media tabloids among the targets would seem more understandable. However, even if the hijackers and their accomplices were familiar with the *Sun* and other AMI tabloids, this does not constitute proof that they were connected to the anthrax letters. Anthrax spores were never found at any locations that the hijackers were known to have frequented, nor at the locations of the many domestic "persons of interest" who were investigated by the FBI.

Characterizing the Source of the Anthrax

In seeking to characterize the source of the anthrax, the FBI sought the services of several scientists. Among them was microbiologist Paul Keim of Northern Arizona University, who had amassed a collection 1,350 anthrax strains from around the world. Soon after discovery of the anthrax letters, samples were sent to Keim, who compared the genetic sequencing of the bacteria with that of known strains. On October 25, 2001, Tom Ridge, head of the homeland security office, announced the results of those analyses. Keim had identified bacteria as the highly virulent Ames strain.[52] Ultimately, bacterial samples from the recovered letters, the infected victims, and contaminated environments all proved to be of the Ames strain.

Anthrax spores commonly lie in the soil, where they remain inactive for long periods during which their DNA remains unchanged. Only when the spores are induced by a favorable environment into vegetative form do they reproduce, and only then does mutation become possible. Such a situation might occur, for example, if grazing livestock became infected after inhaling or ingesting some spores. However, anthrax outbreaks are infrequent, and therefore the genetic structures of long-dormant bacteria remain almost identical to each other.

Through painstaking work, Keim and his colleague Paul Jackson at the Los Alamos National Laboratory had developed a technique to detect the rare genetic inconsistencies within a single strain.[53] After he identified the spores as the Ames strain, Keim was asked by the FBI to analyze anthrax stocks at the various laboratories known to have the Ames strain. The hope was to identify the laboratory from which the spores were taken. At a conference on microbial genomes in 2002, Keim announced that he had found distinguishing features among the stocks, but because of an agreement with the FBI not to discuss the case, he was unable to say anything further.[54] It is therefore unclear whether his findings have helped to identify a particular laboratory as a possible source.[55]

If Keim had been able to narrow the search based on distinctions of the DNA features in various stocks of the Ames strain, this could be helpful but not necessarily definitive. The quality of record-keeping varies among laboratories, and inventories of bacterial samples at some locations are not always accurate. Moreover, not until 1997 were laboratories required to register with the CDC when transferring certain agents, including anthrax, from one laboratory to another.[56] As a result, no one can be certain which domestic or overseas laboratories may have received samples of Ames strain before that time.

Lessons

Lessons of the anthrax attacks in 2001 may be summarized as follows:

First, identification of a particular bioagent as the cause of illness can be challenging. As the disease outbreak in 2001 showed, healthcare workers often initially failed to consider anthrax in their diagnoses, and local laboratory tests were sometimes erroneous or ambiguous, while more advanced or reliable tests were often not available.

Second, characterization of an outbreak as intentional, and understanding the consequences if it is, can present challenges. Although the discovery of bacteria in an improbable location may suggest intentionality, even that finding does not necessarily signal the scope of the dispersion. Dissemination of the mailed anthrax spores was widespread, but this fact was not initially apparent. An experiment in early 2001 (conducted in a confined chamber with simulated anthrax powder) had demonstrated that spores in letters could readily disperse after an envelope was slit open.[57] But this study did not foretell the extensive leakage that could occur even from unopened letters, nor the large-scale contamination of buildings and cross-contamination of other mail that would result.

Third, long after anthrax was understood to be the cause, and even after the incident had been characterized as intentional because spores were discovered in improbable places, attribution as to the source remained elusive. Theories still vary about the motivation and identity of the perpetrator. More than six years after the attacks, no one had been charged and all suppositions remained speculative.

Fourth, the initial responder to a biological event may well be a healthcare worker rather than a police, fire, or military official. The first professional to see the anthrax victims during the 2001 attacks was, in most instances, a physician. The level of training and awareness of the healthcare provider therefore may be critical to recognition of a bioattack.

Fifth, anthrax victims resided or worked in remote communities as well as urban areas, a reminder that preparedness for bioterrorism is as necessary in rural and suburban areas as in large metropolitan centers.

Sixth, launching a bioattack could be simple: as simple as dropping a letter into a mailbox, which is how the anthrax assault began. Although acquiring and processing this bioagent could pose challenges, releasing it as an instrument of terror was easy.

Seventh, a small amount of bioagent can cause havoc. The total volume of powder in all the anthrax letters was very small (an estimated 7–14 grams). This small amount of powder became broadly dispersed, prompted widespread anxiety, and caused twenty-two casualties, including five deaths.

Eighth, ridding contaminated facilities of anthrax spores can be difficult and expensive. Many initial attempts at decontamination were unsuccessful, needed several repetitions, and took in some cases several years (Brentwood until the end of 2003 and Hamilton not until early 2005).

Ninth, doubts about the efficacy of delayed antibiotic therapy for inhalation anthrax proved overly pessimistic. Before the 2001 experience, it was commonly believed that following the onset of symptoms, mortality was "essentially 100 percent despite appropriate treatment."[58] In fact, all eleven inhalation cases in 2001 were symptomatic before receiving antibiotic therapy, and six of them survived. Also worth noting is the CDC's conclusion that prophylactic administration of antibiotics to more than 30,000 people who were at risk for exposure likely prevented "substantial illness and death."[59]

Tenth, the mode of recovery from inhalation anthrax is not fully understood. Six years after they became ill, five of the six inhalation survivors still had symptoms consistent with the disease (muscle ache, shortness of breath, neurological manifestations, malaise), though most reported continuing health improvement. Whether the cause of those lingering symptoms was physical or psychological remains unclear. A study of the possible long-term effects of anthrax disease, both inhalation and cutaneous, was begun in 2002 by the National Institute of Allergy and Infectious Diseases.[60]

Eleventh, launching a bioattack can be inexpensive, and if cost is not an obstacle, the pool of possible perpetrators is large; this complicates attribution efforts. In the 2001 event, samples of *Bacillus anthracis* may have been acquired for minimal costs. The equipment necessary to process the samples—an incubator, centrifuge, freeze dryer, spray dryer, protective clothing and apparatus, various chemicals, and possibly an electron microscope—probably cost less than $50,000 and perhaps as little as $5,000.

Twelfth, the consequences of a bioattack can be expensive. Expenses related to the 2001 event included costs for laboratory tests, drugs and other medical treatment, salaries of engaged personnel (FBI, CDC, state and local authorities), decontamination of infected locations, reduced postal revenue, and lawsuits by victims and families. The total likely exceeded $6 billion.[61]

Finally, procedures employed in a criminal investigation may conflict with those in an epidemiological investigation. According to the CDC, public-health investigators may have been denied access to information during the anthrax outbreak because it was protected for use in criminal prosecution.[62]

Conclusion

The attacks with anthrax in the mail moved the threat of bioterrorism from theory to reality in the United States. Perhaps the biggest surprise was the effectiveness of the mail as a means of delivering an agent of disease. This would be true especially for durable agents such as spore-forming organisms like anthrax and toxins (the potency of some other agents would be short-lived under typical mail conditions). Not only did the anthrax letters transport their poisons to the target addresses, they left a trail of spores along the way. Before the attacks took place, evidently no one considered the possibility that spores of 1 to 3 microns in size could leak through unopened envelopes; this delayed both identification of the causative agent and characterization of the intentionality behind the outbreak.

Even with all that is known about the events of September–November 2001, much remains uncertain about the anthrax letters. Some questions may yet be answered by ongoing studies, such as the long-term health effects on survivors and matching of bacterial isolates with stocks in various laboratories. But questions related to attribution, including the motivation behind the letters, the source of the mailed bacteria, and the manner in which they were processed, might remain unanswered unless the perpetrator, or perpetrators, can be apprehended.

Notes

1. Anthrax bacteria commonly exist as inactive hardy spores, but in favorable environments they may transform into vegetative, reproducing organisms.

2. "Anthrax in the United States: 1997–2002," Federation of American Scientists, <www.fas.org/ahead/disease/anx/outbreak/2001usa-sso.htm>, accessed August 4, 2006.

3. Gina Kolata, "Florida Man Is Hospitalized with Pulmonary Attack," *The New York Times*, October 5, 2001, A-6; Sanjay Bhatt, "Anthrax Source Said to Be Natural," *The Palm Beach Post*, October 7, 2001, 1-A.

4. Daniel B. Jernigan et al., "Investigation of Bioterrorism-Related Anthrax, United States, 2001: Epidemiologic Findings," *Emerging Infectious Diseases* 8, no. 10 (October 2002): 1019–28, available at <http://www.cdc.gov/ncidod/eid/vol8no10/02-0353-G2.htm>.

5. School of Public Health, UCLA, "Compilation of Mailed Anthrax Evidence," <www.ph.ucla.edu/EPI/bioter/detect/antdetect_letters_a.htm>, accessed July 31, 2006. See also Federal Bureau of Investigation, photos of anthrax letters to NBC, Senator Daschle, and *New York Post* <http://www.fbi.gov/pressrel/pressrel01/102301.htm>.

6. Ibid.

7. BBC News Online, November 23, 2001, <http://news.bbc.co.uk/1/low/world/americas/1617049.stm#cont>, accessed August 23, 2006.

8. H. Clifford Lane and Anthony S. Fauci, "Bioterrorism on the Home Front: A New Challenge for American Medicine," *Journal of the American Medical Association* 286, no. 20 (November 28, 2001): 2595–97.

9. Interviews described in Leonard A. Cole, *The Anthrax Letters: A Medical Detective Story* (Washington, DC: Joseph Henry Press, 2003), 10–13.

10. Johanna Huden, "Giving the Finger to Bioterrorists," *New York Post*, October 20, 2001, 1.

11. Author's interview with Joanna Huden, April 18, 2003; New York City Department of Health, Press Release, "Health Department Confirms Fourth Case of Cutaneous (Skin) Anthrax," October 19, 2001.

12. New York City Department of Health, Press Release, "Health Department Announces an Anthrax Case in New York City," October 12, 2001.

13. Michael B. Heller et al., "Laboratory Response to Anthrax Bioterrorism, New York City, 2001," *Emerging Infectious Diseases* 8, no. 10 (Oct. 2002): 1096–1102.

14. The first nine anthrax cases included seven cases of cutaneous anthrax (five people associated with or visiting media companies in New York City, plus two postal employees in New Jersey), in addition to two cases of inhalation anthrax, one fatal, both AMI employees in Florida.

15. Author's interview with Johanna Huden, April 18, 2003.

16. Mark S. Dworkin et al., "Fear of Bioterrorism and Implications for Public Health Preparedness," *Emerging Infectious Diseases* 9, no. 4 (April 2003): 504–5.

17. "Hamilton, NJ, Post Office Reopens After Anthrax Attacks," *USA Today.com*, March 14, 2005, <http://www.usatoday.com/news/nation/2005-03-14-anthrax-cleanup_x.htm>, accessed August 30, 2006.

18. Arthur Santana, "Ravaged by Anthrax, Postal Facility Reopens," *The Washington Post*, December 22, 2003, B-1.

19. David Ho, "Anthrax Roundup: Tiny Amounts found in D.C. Buildings," *Houston Chronicle* (on line), November 10, 2001, <www.chron.com/disp/story.mpl/special/terror/front/1127628.html>, accessed August 14, 2006.

20. David Francis, "Installation of Anthrax Detectors at Postal Facilities Nears End," *Global Security Newswire*, November 3, 2005, <http://38.118.42.202/story_page.cfm?articleid=32725&sid=28>, accessed August 12, 2006.

21. Leonard A. Cole, "Still a Mystery Five Years Later," *The Record* (Hackensack, NJ), October 15, 2006, O-1.

22. Guy Gugliotta and Ben White, "Kathy Nguyen's Mystery Link: Bronx Woman's Death from Spores Baffles Medical Experts," *The Washington Post*, November 11, 2001, A-10.

23. Author's interview with Shirley Davis, January 4, 2002; Bryn Mandel, "Life Back to Normal in Oxford Despite Continuing Probe into Woman's Death," *Republican-American* (Waterbury CT), November 21, 2004.

24. Thomas V. Inglesby et al., "Anthrax as a Biological Weapon, 2002: Updated Recommendations for Management," *Journal of the American Medical Association* 287, no. 11 (May 1, 2002): 2239.

25. Charles J. Peters and David M. Hartley, "Anthrax Inhalation and Lethal Human Infection," *Lancet* 359, no. 9307 (February 23, 2002): 710–11.

26. Leonard A. Cole, "Persistence of a Mock Bio-Agent in Cross-Contaminated Mail and Mailboxes," *Journal of Public Health Management and Practice* 9, no. 5 (September–October 2003): 357–60.

27. Robert M. Burnham, Federal Bureau of Investigation, Statement to the U.S. House of Representatives Subcommittee on Oversight and Investigations, May 20, 1999; Leonard A. Cole, "Anthrax Hoaxes: Hot New Hobby," *Bulletin of the Atomic Scientists*, July/August 1999: 7–9.

28. U.S. Department of Health and Human Services, "Fact Sheet: Biodefense Preparedness," News Release, April 28, 2004.

29. Author's interview with Philip Lee, May 14, 2002.

30. James M. Hughes and Julie Louise Gerberding, "Anthrax Bioterrorism: Lessons Learned and Future Directions," *Emerging Infectious Diseases* 8, no. 10 (October 2002): 1013.

31. Centers for Disease Control and Prevention, "Frequently Asked Questions About the Laboratory Response Network (LRN)," <www.bt.cdc.gov/lrn/faq.asp,> accessed August 7, 2006.

32. Cole, *The Anthrax Letters*: 22–32.

33. Jernigan et al., "Investigation of Bioterrorism-Related Anthrax," 1020.

34. Federal Bureau of Investigation, Amerithrax Press Briefing, "Linguistic/Behavioral Analysis of Anthrax Letters," Washington, DC, <www.fbi.gov/anthrax/amerithrax.htm>, posted November 9, 2001, accessed August 1, 2006.

35. "Report: No WMD Stockpiles in Iraq—CIA: Saddam Intended to Make Arms If Sanctions Ended," CNN, <http://www.cnn.com/2004/WORLD/meast/10/06/iraq.wmd. report/> posted October 7, 2004, accessed March 25, 2007.

36. Bradley A. Perkins, Tanja Popovic, and Kevin Yeskey, "Public Health in the Time of Bioterrorism," *Emerging Infectious Diseases* 8, no. 10 (October 2002): 1017.

37. Douglas J. Beecher, "Forensic Application of Microbiological Culture Analysis to Identify Mail Intentionally Contaminated with *Bacillus anthracis* Spores," *Applied and Environmental Microbiology* 72, no. 8 (August 2006): 5309.

38. Thomas V. Inglesby et al., "Anthrax as a Biological Weapon: Medical and Public Health Management," *Journal of the American Medical Association* 281, no. 18 (May 12, 1999): 1735–45.

39. Author's interview with Jean Malecki, April 13, 2002.

40. Paul Recer, "Inventor of Anthrax Process Says Spores Will Not Be 'Smoking Gun' to Identify Who Mailed Killer Letters," Associated Press, December 19, 2001, <http://www.anthraxinvestigation.com/ap.html> accessed August 4, 2006.

41. Guy Gugliotta and Gary Matsumoto, "FBI's Theory on Anthrax Is Doubted: Attacks Not Likely Work of One Person, Experts Say," *Washington Post*, October 28, 2002: A-1.

42. Spertzel interview on ABC News, cited in Don Foster, "The Message in the Anthrax," *Vanity Fair*, October 2003, 180–200.

43. Beecher, "Forensic Application," 5305.

44. The Commission on the Intelligence Capabilities of the United States Regarding Weapons of Mass Destruction, Report to the President of the United States, March 31, 2005, Washington, DC: 269–70.

45. The implications are noted in Milton Leitenberg, *Assessing the Biological Weapons and Bioterrorism Threat* (Carlisle, PA: Strategic Studies Institute, 2006), 40–41.

46. FBI, Amerithrax Press Briefing.

47. Eric Lichtblau and Megan Garvey, "Profile of Anthrax Mailer Portrays Loner, Opportunist," *Los Angeles Times*, November 10, 2001, A-8.

48. Author's interview with Gloria Irish, April 23, 2002.

49. William J. Broad and David Johnston, "Report Linking Anthrax and Hijackers Is Investigated," *The New York Times*, March 23, 2002, A-9. One of the Johns Hopkins physicians, Thomas Inglesby, was the lead author of the two *Journal of the Medical Association* articles that were considered authoritative on anthrax as a bioweapon: Inglesby et al., "Anthrax as a Biological Weapon," 1997; and Inglesby et al., "Anthrax As a Biological Weapon, 2002," 2002.

50. David Kidwell, Manny Garcia, and Larry Lebowitz, "Authorities Trace Anthrax That Killed Florida Man to Iowa Lab," *The Miami Herald*, October 10, 2001, 1-A.

51. Jeff Bercovici, "Media on Guard as Anthrax Threat Spreads," *Media Life*, October 15, 2001.

52. Paul J. Boyer, "The Ames Strain," *The New Yorker,* November 12, 2001.

53. Paul Keim et al., "Multiple-Locus Variable-Number Tandem Repeat Analysis Reveals Genetic Relationships Within Bacillus anthracis," *Journal of Bacteriology* 182, no. 10 (May 2000): 2928–36.

54. Nicholas Wade, "Scientist's Findings Could Aid Anthrax Inquiry," *The New York Times,* February 13, 2002.

55. Ibid.

56. Antiterrorism and Effective Death Penalty Act of 1996, Pub. L. No. 104-132, § 511, 110 Stat. 1214, 1284–85 (1996).

57. Bill Kournikakis et al., "Risk Assessment of Anthrax Threat Letters," Defence Research Establishment, Suffield, Canada, Technical Report, DRES TR-2001-048, September 2001.

58. Arthur M. Friedlander, "Anthrax," in Russ Zajtchuk, Editor-in-Chief, *Textbook of Military Medicine,* Part I: *Medical Aspects of Chemical and Biological Warfare* (Washington, DC: Office of the Surgeon General, 1997), 472.

59. Jernigan et al., "Investigation of Bioterrorism-Related Anthrax," 1025.

60. U.S. National Institutes of Health, "Natural History of Anthrax: A Study of Primary Infected, Recovered, and Exposed Individuals (SPoRE); and Evaluation of AVA-Vaccinated Recipients," <www.clinicaltrials.gov/ct/show/NCT00050310>, posted February 2006, accessed August 17, 2006.

61. Leonard A. Cole, "WMD and Lessons from the Anthrax Attacks," in David G. Kamien, ed., *The McGraw-Hill Homeland Security Handbook* (New York: McGraw-Hill, 2006), 170.

62. Jernigan et al., "Investigation of Bioterrorism-Related Anthrax," 1027.

CHAPTER THREE

The 1994 Plague in Western India

Human Ecology and the Risks
of Misattribution

RON BARRETT

In recent years, a number of studies have considered the possibility that plague bacillus (*Yersinia pestis*) might be used as a biological weapon. Several bio-security exercises have simulated governmental responses to deliberate plague epidemics.[1] The U.S. Centers for Disease Control and Prevention (CDC) have listed *Y. pestis* among those pathogens posing the greatest risks to national security.[2] Although historical instances of intentionally caused plague outbreaks have demonstrated that they are of questionable military efficacy at best, this disease nevertheless poses several issues for concern.[3] *Y. pestis* is relatively stable in diverse environments; it can be found in natural reservoirs (wild rodent populations) around the world; and it can develop much higher virulence in its pneumonic (respiratory) form.[4] Even in its attenuated (milder) and more readily treatable bubonic (vector-borne) form, plague could still be an effective weapon for the generation of public fear. This fear is partly due to the history of pandemics such as the Black Death and the association of plague with dirt, rats, and poverty.[5]

All of these issues arose at various stages of the 1994 plague epidemic in Western India. With more than 5,000 suspected cases (238 "confirmed") and 56 plague-related deaths, the epidemic comprised India's first reported human plague infections in 28 years and its largest number of plague-specific casualties in more than six decades.[6] Pneumonic plague cases were in unusually high proportion in Surat, an industrial city of some one and a half million people where the epidemic was centered. These events occurred in a region of great tension between Hindu and Muslim communities, fueling suspicions of terrorism. Although evidence would eventually point to a "natural" (that is, unintentional) outbreak, these suspicions contributed to mass panic and breakdown in public-health response as several hundred thousand people fled Surat.

Focusing on the 1994 plague epidemic, with a special focus on the city of Surat, this chapter explains how a combination of human and natural events created the conditions for the re-emergence of *Yersinia pestis* in India. It also examines how initial misattributions of symptoms to chemical or biological terrorism impeded early detection and treatment programs, and delayed efforts to prevent future outbreaks. Finally, this chapter explores how the municipal and public-health reforms that eventually resulted in Surat may have contributed to the subsequent absence of plague, as well as to declines in other vector-borne and water-borne diseases in Surat. The 1994 epidemic and its aftermath underscore the importance of public trust and a pre-existing public-health infrastructure for the attribution and control of infectious diseases, whether or not they are deliberately initiated.

The Human Ecology of Plague in Western India

With respect to questions of attribution, disease investigations are comparable to fire investigations: both require a deep understanding of behavioral and environmental factors, and both must trace these factors back in time to their ultimate sources. Amidst a combination of natural and anthropogenic factors, one can neither determine nor exclude human intentions as a cause or contributing factor without first understanding the broader circumstances preceding and surrounding the Indian plague of 1994. These circumstances can be analyzed in terms of human ecology, approaching the socioeconomic histories of human communities as part of a larger system of species interactions that, in turn, create selective conditions for and against infectious diseases.[7]

With this in mind, we begin with the question that originally raised suspicions of biowarfare in Surat: why did plague suddenly re-emerge in one of India's wealthiest cities after an absence of almost thirty years? To answer this question, we must consider some of the changes that occurred in this part of

India during the years leading up to the epidemic. With its high proportion of merchant-caste communities, the western Indian state of Gujarat has played an active role in international trade since the early days of the British Raj. This has been especially the case for the Gujarati city of Surat, where the east-west Tapi River empties into the Gulf of Khambhat (Cambay), providing a major port for ships passing through the Arabian Sea. In addition to its natural advantages, Surat had been known for its relative absence of organized labor, and the willingness of local authorities to turn a blind eye to property and excise taxes. These factors contributed to an economic boom in the 1970s as regional landowners invested in small-scale industries through rural-urban caste connections. By the early 1990s there were over a quarter-million power looms and embroidery shops scattered throughout the city, and Surat had become one of the world's largest centers for diamond processing.

As Surat's economic boom occurred, outlying rural areas were in decline. Despite the industrial growth of its cities, western India remains predominantly agrarian, relying upon the production of cereal grains, oil seeds, and cotton. This semi-arid region is subject to frequent droughts, partly due to fluctuating monsoon rains mediated by a weather system that stretches to the Horn of Africa.[8] Drought has been increasingly exacerbated by reliance on water-intensive cash crops, the over-extraction of groundwater resources, and the diversion of surface water to industrial power production. These practices have left farming communities with little margin to withstand the three droughts per decade that occur, on average, in this part of India.[9] To mitigate these risks, many rural families have migrated to cities like Surat in search of factory and service work. Meanwhile, more successful landowners diversified their holdings with more power looms and diamond polishing equipment. As a result, the population of Surat increased four-fold, from 318,000 to 1.5 million, over the thirty years leading up to the 1994 plague outbreak. The average population density is 13,483 people per square kilometer, and is as high as 52,000 in the city center.[10]

These rural-urban dynamics were reflected in the 1994 plague. It began as a vector-borne (bubonic) infection in a nearby village and quickly spread to the city as a respiratory (pneumonic) infection among its migrant labor communities. The first suspected plague cases were detected in August 1994 in Mamla, a farming village of 350 people located in the Beed District just across the border in the neighboring state of Maharasthra. There, thirteen cases presented themselves to a local primary health clinic (PMC) with signs indicative of bubonic plague—fever, headache, lethargy, and very swollen and painful lymph nodes (buboes)—following recent exposure to fleas and the sudden appearance of many dead rodents ("ratfall") in the village.

Y. pestis would later be identified in seven domestic rats (*Rattus rattus*) from Mamla. Numerous burrows of field rodents (*Bandicotta bengalensis*) were found in uncultivated areas along the western edge of the village. It was hypothesized that these wild rodents, their domestic counterparts (including the peridomestic *Tatera indica*), and associated fleas (*Xenopsylla cheopis*) had long maintained their populations in equilibrium at levels below those at which the occasional *Y. pestis* infection could be reasonably expected to transmit into human populations.[11]

This disease-vector equilibrium probably destabilized following an earthquake in September 1993. The earthquake, 6.5 on the Richter scale, was centered in the neighboring districts of Latur and Osmanabad, but significant tremors were also felt in Beed. Earthquakes have long been associated with increases in rat populations, possibly due to the simultaneous disruption of rodent burrows and human granaries.[12] In the particular case of Mamla, residents were so concerned about future earthquakes that they moved into their lighter-roofed storage shelters and granaries, storing grain in their houses for the rest of the year. With less protection against pests, these makeshift granaries were overrun with rats, followed by flea infestations in the weeks preceding the epidemic.[13] Even at this micro-level, events indicate that the plague was triggered by a combination of natural and human events.

The first suspected plague cases appeared in Surat in early September of 1994. By the time the epidemic was contained in late October, there were 1,061 suspected cases (71 confirmed seropositive)[14] and 54 related deaths. This represented more cases in Surat than in the rest of Gujarat and five other reporting states combined, and nearly all of the 56 related deaths from the entire epidemic (see Table 3.1).[15]

All plague-related deaths in Surat occurred among patients diagnosed with pneumonic plague, a respiratory disease capable of spreading from human to human via air droplets at short distances (2–5 feet). Bubonic plague, by contrast, is a lymphatic infection that is typically transmitted by fleas and other biting insects. Left untreated, bubonic plague has a case mortality rate of about

TABLE 3.1

*Number of Suspected Plague Cases and Seropositive Samples
by Indian State: August 26–October 5, 1994*

	Suspected	Confirmed
Maharasthra	2,793	79
Gujarat (including Surat)	1,391	106 (71 in Surat)
Delhi (national capital territory)	749	44
Andhra Pradesh, Haryana, Rajasthan, Uttar Pradesh, and West Bengal	169	9

SOURCE: World Health Organization (1994).

60 percent, but the disease can usually be cured with a ten-day course of antibiotics commonly available in India: tetracycline and aminoglycosides such as streptomycin and gentamicin. Pneumonic plague, however, is nearly 100 percent fatal if antibiotics are not initiated within 18 hours of symptom onset. This is largely due to certain temperature-activated genes that are associated with higher virulence but are not switched on when the bacterium grows in cold-blooded insect vectors.[16]

It is puzzling that most of the hospitalized Surat cases were diagnosed with pneumonic plague. Primary pneumonic plague is rare compared to bubonic plague, and secondary pneumonic infections occur in only about 5 percent of bubonic cases.[17] Given limited laboratory resources and the chaos that ensued during the epidemic, it is certainly possible that physicians might have erred on the side of sensitivity when diagnosing their patients, assuming pneumonic plague in the absence of buboes (lymphatic swellings) and treating patients empirically with antibiotics. Yet among serum samples taken from 27 presumptive pneumonic patients in Surat, 23 had sufficient antibody titers against F1 plague antigens to confirm diagnosis of pneumonic plague.[18] All available clinical and laboratory evidence, although limited, pointed to pneumonic plague. It should be noted, however, that the hospitalized cases were not necessarily representative of all cases. With medical resources stretched far beyond capacity, it is likely that only the sickest patients were triaged into beds during the epidemic. Better identification within this time frame would have required reasonably equipped hospital laboratory facilities that did not exist in Surat.

Living conditions in Surat city could have supported either bubonic or pneumonic plague outbreaks. Although one of the wealthiest cities in India, Surat also had a reputation for being among its filthiest. At the time of the epidemic, the city's solid waste collection was less than 40 percent of the waste generated, piped water was available to only 66 percent of the population, and only 27 percent of the municipal area had adequate drainage during the monsoon season.[19] Not surprisingly, Surat was known for having a very large population of domestic rats, which were increasingly visible following monsoon rains.

Conditions were even worse among Surat's 299 largely immigrant slum communities, comprising 29 percent of the city's 1.8 million population and more than 80 percent of its reported plague cases.[20] Only 40 percent of slum areas had any drainage system at all, and only 22 percent of slum residents had access to public or private toilets; the remainder had to defecate in open spaces.[21] Crowding was also a particularly difficult problem in the slums: among households with plague patients, 78 percent lived in dwellings of less than 600 square feet, and 52 percent lived in single-room dwellings with an estimated average of 100 square feet per person.[22]

Given these circumstances, and the size and the severity of the epidemic within the city, it could be hypothesized that bubonic plague originated in Surat, spread out into other areas, and eventually developed into pneumonic plague. This hypothesis has important implications for determining the pathogen's point of entry as well as its means of entry into the human population, key steps in the attribution of this epidemic. As evidence supporting this urban origin hypothesis, the city had just experienced a particularly heavy monsoon: a seasonal total of 1.9 meters representing 84 percent excess rainfall. This led to the overflow of the Tapi River with significant flooding throughout the city, especially in the slums, where standing water remained for five days just prior to the outbreak. It also left 5,000 metric tons of garbage on the city streets, ten times the municipal daily removal capacity.[23] Rat infestation was reported to be particularly high during this time and an unusually large number of rat carcasses were found on the streets after the floodwaters receded. Conditions were strongly selective for bubonic plague.

Conditions notwithstanding, however, an urban-origin hypothesis does not explain the sudden appearance of plague after an absence of almost three decades. Even the preceding rains were not that remarkable in a region prone to frequent floods and droughts. The rats observed in 1994 may have drowned in the floodwater, or may have been killed by the large amounts of malathion distributed as part of the post-flood clean-up campaign.[24] A study of Surat's urban ecology found insufficient habitat diversity to support non-urban rodent populations, except in a few small feral patches.[25] The domestic *R. rattus* would have been the next most likely host. Given the abundance of *rattus*, and its continued proximity to humans, one would expect at least some reports of bubonic plague during the years leading up to the epidemic, but this was not the case. Finally, the epidemic bypassed squatter communities adjacent to the aforementioned feral patches, where people lived under the very poorest conditions in makeshift shelters along the riverbanks.

An importation hypothesis explains these data much better than one of urban origin. The absence of plague in Surat's poorest squatter communities points to factors beyond those of infrastructure and economic scarcity alone. Certainly, most of the city's plague patients lived in poor conditions, but most were not so poor as to live with mud floors and plastic tarps, like the squatter communities. Instead, most had permanent structures with cement floors and some access to at least some sanitation facilities. In addition, plague was differently distributed within and between the slums from which 80 percent of plague victims came. Within these communities, 67 percent of the plague patients were male, 52 percent were between 16 and 35 years of age, and 78 percent were first-generation immigrants from other districts or states.[26] These demographics reflect the social dynamics of labor migration that largely contributed to Surat's population growth and density: the influx of working-age males into the city to seek new opportunities and generate income for extended rural families. They also evoke further questions about whether the social and geographic mobility of these males resulted in greater opportunities for disease transmission, or whether the stresses of working conditions, family pressures, and unhealthy behaviors might have increased their susceptibility to infection.

Plague was not equally distributed in slum communities that were otherwise of similar type and geography. Although slums were scattered throughout the city, most of the plague-related deaths and seropositive cases were clustered in slums along the Ved Road corridor from the city's north to northern-central zones; a smaller concentration was in the south zone. Just east of the Ved Road cluster, slums along Varaccha Road having similar amenities, and even closer to the river, were unaffected. Adjacent to the inland southern cluster, similar slums of Limbhayat and Dumbhal experienced neither deaths nor seropositive cases.[27]

The medical geography of Surat's plague epidemic reflects the sociocultural heterogeneity of its working-class communities. A comprehensive survey of Surati slums in 1993 found a high degree of segregation by natal origin, caste and, to some extent, primary language or dialect. [28] For example, some slums along Ved Road were composed almost entirely of Marathi farmer-weavers. Others were occupied by artisans from Saurastra who worked in diamond processing and construction. There were Saurastrans along Varaccha Road as well, but many worked the power looms, as did Oriyans in the same neighborhoods. These Saurastrans were relatively isolated from other Saurastrans in the city, and the Oriyans were isolated from everyone else. Each spoke a different primary language, and some spoke a different secondary language as well. Surat's immigrant laborers were segregated across a mosaic of ghettos.

Ghettos are a common feature of Indian cities. They are the products of urban migration based upon access to employment and housing through existing social networks of family and friends with ongoing connections between natal localities and destination cities.[29] Members of Surat's working-class communities are known to maintain close relationships with extended kin in their natal villages through regular visitation, such as the observance of weddings and other life events; and mutual remittances between city and village households.[30]

These social dynamics provide a persuasive explanation of the structure of pneumonic plague transmission in Surat during the 1994 epidemic. *Yersinia pestis* did not simply emerge and spread indiscriminately throughout the city's slums. It was propagated through particular social networks that had a greater likelihood of transmission between affiliated contacts than any other combination of infected and susceptible people. These dynamics also explain the origin of the plague, for the city's first cases were from a community with close connections to the Beed district of Maharasthra, where the very first cases of bubonic plague were detected. These connections present a likely conduit for the importation of plague into Surat city.

The re-emergence of plague in western India after nearly three decades was a natural but unintended consequence of deliberate human actions taken in particular biosocial circumstances. As in many parts of the world, plague had persisted as a low-level zoonotic (animal) infection, ecologically balanced among its nonhuman hosts for many years. This balance was disrupted by a combination of two unusual events: an earthquake, and the alteration of a village's living arrangements in response to that earthquake. This village was linked to the city by socioeconomic forces: industrial development created incentives for urban immigration (economic opportunities) as well as disincentives for remaining in rural areas (depleted resources). Subsequent migrations and resource flows became a conduit for the importation of plague into an urban environment. They also led to rapid population growth that, in the context of poverty and underdevelopment, created selective conditions for the amplification of *Yersinia pestis,* and its transformation from a vector-borne to a respiratory epidemic. A mosaic of different communities and their respective networks formed a pattern of disease transmission in which social proximity had more effect than physical geography. Such was the human ecology of plague in western India.

Misattribution, Mass Panic, and Economic Consequences

Misattributions of the plague in Surat created significant obstacles for disease control and the primary prevention of future epidemics. The first misattribution was a rumor that circulated in the early days of the urban epidemic, claiming that the city's water supplies had been deliberately poisoned. This rumor followed four sudden and at that point still unexplained deaths in three northern Ved Road area slums on September 19, 1994.[31] Word quickly spread of these simultaneous deaths, and with it, exaggerated numbers of casualties. Poisoned wells were added somewhere in the retelling. Rumors were reinforced as additional cases were admitted to local area hospitals.

The rumor claimed that Muslim terrorists had poisoned the wells in revenge for violence received during a major riot in 1992. Less than two years before the epidemic, Hindu nationalists had destroyed the Babri Masjid Mosque in the northern Indian city of Ayodhya. This sparked religious-based communal violence throughout India. Rioting was particularly intense in Surat. It sustained the second-highest casualty rate of any Indian city: 190 killed, with thousands more injured or raped, and many homes and businesses looted and burned. Both Hindus and Muslims had committed violent acts during the riot, but the Muslim minority were by far its hardest-hit victims.[32]

Events surrounding the 1992 violence may have influenced public response to the 1994 plague. Tensions between Hindu and Muslim communities were high in the state of Gujarat, which had become a political base for several Hindu nationalist organizations. Nevertheless, Surat had avoided major episodes

of communal violence from 1927 to 1992, despite a half-dozen nationwide incidents during those years.[33] For that matter, Surat did not experience any major
violence in the 14 years following the 1992 riots, not even during the widespread
Godhra train riots of 2002, when more than a thousand people were killed
thoughout the state of Gujarat.[34] One hypothesis is that the exceptional violence in Surat during 1992 was linked to the city's rapid economic expansion
in at least two ways. First, a black-market economy developed in parallel with
small-scale industries, increasing opportunities for criminal activity. Second,
Surat's new entrepreneurs (both legitimate and otherwise) had reshaped the
municipal government such that it was neither capable of, nor interested in, addressing the civic needs of India's fastest-growing city. Criminal activity combined with civic unrest contributed to the high levels of violence in 1992.[35]

This economic hypothesis sheds light on the issues of underdevelopment
leading up to the plague. It also stands as a warning about Surat's potential for
further violence in the event of increases in tension between Hindu and Muslim communities. The poisoned water rumor was certainly widespread: there
were reports that people from neighborhoods throughout Surat were dumping
their water caches, and that shops had quickly sold out of bottled water.[36] The
poisoning rumor persisted for a time even after newspapers first reported that
the illnesses were due to plague, for the public had little trust in statements
made by the media or government. Yet people did not have to believe in the
poisoned-well rumor in order to be affected by it; they had only to believe that
the rumor might cause violence. Some people from the Muslim community,
for example, declared that the plague was one of God's classic punishments and
asserted that the first neighborhoods affected were those that had produced
much of the 1992 violence.[37] Such pronouncements were likely to anger Hindus, instigating counteraccusations, and so on.

The 1992 riots had resulted in a major exodus from the city. Based on railway receipts and the net flow of outgoing pedestrian traffic, it is estimated that
200,000 people fled the city after violence erupted.[38] The exodus of 1992 did not
bode well for the epidemic of 1994, especially considering the additional stigma
of the plague itself. Plague could evoke memories of India's worst epidemics,
particularly the Third Pandemic with 12 million deaths in India between 1896
and 1930.[39] Such memories were rekindled when the media first reported the
plague on September 21; some described "instant" deaths at 100 times the actual

initial mortality.[40] Amidst these exaggerated reports, a rumor circulated that the government might place the city under quarantine.[41] Thus, whether one feared poison, plague, or the threat of violence, it appeared that bad things were happening in Surat from which there might soon be no escape.

A spot survey conducted by the Surat Municipal Corporation (SMC) on September 29, 1994, estimated that a half million people, roughly a third of the population, had already fled Surat.[42] People with vehicles were among the first to leave; these included many medical providers. Another SMC survey found that 78 percent of medical clinics were closed in the Ved Road area.[43] Many physicians were absent from public hospitals as well. Pharmacies quickly sold out of tetracycline and other antibiotics once it was announced that the plague could be treated with these medications. The remaining health workers did the best they could under the circumstances; mobile medical teams screened the most affected communities, distributed antibiotics when available, and referred suspect cases to the New Civil Hospital, although it was short-staffed and over-burdened with hundreds of additional patients.

Under these conditions, it was hard to distinguish plague (especially pneu-monic plague) from many other diseases that were endemic to the city such as malaria, typhoid, tuberculosis, and other pneumonias. Most suspected plague cases were diagnosed on the basis of clinical signs and bipolar staining of sam-ple smears. However, the criteria for suspected cases left significant room for alternative diagnoses. "Confirmed" cases were those where passive hemaggluti-nation assays (PHA) found elevated levels of antibodies to plague-specific (F1) antigens. But despite elevated antibodies, PHA testing in the early stages of the epidemic did not fully meet the World Health Organization (WHO) criteria for identification of plague, which requires a four-fold increase in antibodies between two samples taken a minimum of ten days apart, with the first taken before the administration of antibiotics. Later testing of these samples was problematic because of sample contamination (overgrowth) resulting from in-adequate hospital laboratory facilities.[44] A visiting team from the WHO pointed out these shortcomings but still accepted that many of the cases were plague.[45] This was a reasonable presumption for an outbreak in a community having poor health resources, where a rapid identification must be made with limited data, and the public health risks of a falsely positive determination (type I er-ror) are less than a falsely negative determination (type II error).

However, as the epidemic was beginning to receive international attention and support, questions arose whether there were any plague cases at all. An alternative hypothesis was that the "plague" was actually melioidosis, a bacterial infection caused by *Burkholderia pseudomallei*. Melioidosis was endemic to neighboring countries and it presented many of the same signs and symptoms as plague. The hypothesis was based upon an outbreak in the Pune area of Maharasthra in October of 1994. Here, 32 of 40 patients tested were found to have *B. pseudomallei*; and one of these patients originated from Beed district.[46] However, subsequent analyses confirmed plague among the hospitalized patients. Plague-specific antibodies were found in 23 of 27 convalescing pneumonic patients in December 1994.[47] Moreover, *Y. pestis* genes (f1 and pla) were found in each of 18 samples previously characterized as having plague (11 samples from pneumonic Surati patients; 7 rodent samples from Beed), and at least one of these two genes were found in each of 7 autopsy tissue samples from Surat.[48] These results confirmed that plague was present in at least some of the patients in Surat.

Additional molecular tests were performed on the aforementioned samples to determine how this particular *Y. pestis* was related to the 16 other genetically sequenced strains around in the world. Although the Surat strain shared some profiles with certain other strains (it was more than 99 percent related to the species as a whole), initial results showed the 1994 pathogen to be a new type, which was named "S" for Surat by the WHO *Yersinia* Reference Centre.[49]

Preliminary information of these results reached the Indian public indirectly in July of 1995. Around this time, the genetic sequence data was rumored to support another allegation: that the 1994 plague bacterium had been deliberately engineered for biological warfare. This rumor persisted from Bangalore to Delhi. In Surat, it coincided with debates about blame for shortcomings and difficult decisions about the future of governance and public services in Surat. This rumor would certainly have provided a convenient excuse: an enemy upon which to deflect the political blame. However, although the WHO declared the epidemic contained before the end of October 1994, Surat continued to suffer from the public stigma of plague, dirt, and rats well into the following year. The claim of bioterrorism, even if correct, could not have deflected this stigma; it could only have added to the blame.

It has been argued that, although the stigma of plague in Surat had negative consequences for immediate disease control, it also provided significant motivation for eventual civic reforms.[50] As Suratis escaped from the city, other people refused service and lodging to vehicles with Surati license plates. Railroad passengers refused to allow Suratis to board when trains stopped at the city station, and other stations flagged off trains originating from Surat. At an international level, the stigma of plague spread to the country as a whole. Over 400 international plane flights to India were cancelled. Milan and Rome fumigated incoming planes from India. Moscow instituted a six-day quarantine for people arriving from India. Twenty-five percent of international tourist itineraries for India were cancelled in the fall quarter of 1994.

Declining tourism was only part of the economic damage. After the BBC and CNN reported the plague, global depository receipts for India declined sharply in London, marking a major loss of investor confidence. The United Arab Emirates (UAE) banned all Indian imports, resulting in an estimated trade loss of 420 million dollars.[51] These events, in turn, led to a major decline in the Bombay Stock Exchange (BSE) and the SENSEX, the latter considered by many investors to be an important indicator of the state of the Indian economy. The SENSEX had been largely bullish following India's economic liberalization in 1992 and the opening of the BSE to international trade. This changed in October of 1994. The economic diagnosis was even worse at the local level: industrial production had come to a standstill for more than a month while Surat was being portrayed to the country and the world as India's filthiest city.

Reforms, Outcomes, and Lessons Learned

The economic forces responsible for the rapid growth of Surat could ill afford any further negligence in its infrastructural development. Just after the WHO declared an end to the plague epidemic in October 1994, an army of bulldozers entered the city and cleared away thousands of tons of garbage along with squatter settlements, market stands, and other "illegal structures."[52] This was followed by sporadic public-health campaigns that included intensive fumigation and rodent surveillance activities. Such efforts were not sustained, however, and the city fell back into its old patterns over the next six months.[53]

Lasting reforms did not commence until after May 1995, when voters elected a new city government. Charged with a strong public mandate, and with the

support of private business interests, the new municipal government decentral-
ized its civic management into six new zones, which in turn delegated responsibility to 52 sanitary districts. The new Surat Municipal Corporation (SMC)
sent a clear message that new policies would be enforced when it took disciplin-
ary actions against 1,200 negligent sanitation workers and managers. The SMC
created public-private partnerships for street sweeping and garbage removal,
resulting in a 2.5-fold increase in daily solid waste collection. It made major
investments in roads and drainage throughout the city. Many slums were paved
and given covered drains and public toilets. The SMC also made investments in
plague surveillance, rodent control, and malaria control units. A major public
relations campaign then touted Surat as the second cleanest city in India.[54]

For all these investments and changes, civic improvements are difficult to
quantify. Formal comparisons of conditions before and after the plague are
hindered by insufficient or unreliable baseline data, products of the earlier government. Telling outcomes would certainly include declining rates of infectious
diseases, with plague among the foremost. Yet even the disappearance of plague
in Surat—the evidence of its absence—lacks weight unless it can be tied to
changes in disease ecology. Unfortunately, vector data are not much help in this
regard. Government figures on trapped rats are not based upon standardized
sampling procedures. The flea indices of these rats have varied up and down
over the last decade, but these numbers are not that meaningful either: rats had
fleas before the plague outbreak, and rats continue to have fleas after it.[55]

Declines in other vector-borne diseases indicate that there has been improvement. Malaria, like plague, is closely tied to waste and water management
issues, but, unlike plague, measurable outcomes are based on decline rather
than absence of disease. Malaria admissions to the New Civil Hospital (NCH)
declined, from 1,130 cases in 1994 to 262 cases in 2004. Although the decline
had begun before 1994, over the next decade it generally showed significantly
greater proportions of chronic (*P. vivax*) malaria cases.[56] These proportions
reflect a higher share of chronic malaria cases compared to new malaria cases,
an expected outcome for a disease in decline.

The NCH also saw declines after 1994 in waterborne infections, despite an
ever-increasing population in need of public services (see Table 3.2). Yet it also
saw an increase in acute respiratory infections, perhaps because post-plague
reforms had been geared toward control of vectors associated with the bubonic

TABLE 3.2

Admissions to Surat's New Civil Hospital for Selected
Infectious Disease Categories: 1993–1997

	1993	1994	1995	1996	1997
Acute diarrheal	4,335	4,224	3,090	3,608	2,282
Enteric fever	629	564	309	135	102
Viral hepatitis	1,639	1,635	579	653	674
Acute respiratory	26,915	38,467	31,610	45,123	51,126

SOURCE: Surat Municipal Corporation (1998).

plague, and did not address the issues of crowding, co-morbidity, and overall poverty associated with the city's pneumonic plague cases. That these conditions of susceptibility persist is of particular concern in light of the recent detection of avian influenza in nearby rural districts having connections with Surati slums.[57] Should it ever evolve human-to-human transmissibility, avian influenza could present the same pattern of replication as the 1994 plague.

Respiratory infections notwithstanding, Surat has made demonstrable gains toward improving the conditions that would raise the risk of plague and other diseases in its population. It stands as a positive example for other cities throughout India and the rest of the world. If Surat holds lessons of what could happen in the event of a deliberate plague attack, then those lessons should include the successes as well as the shortcomings of its primary biodefenses: sanitation, drainage, and a public-health infrastructure.

Surat also holds lessons on the consequences of falsely attributing an epidemic to terrorism. Poisoned wells are the historical archetype of bioterrorism.[58] In 1994, rumors of poisoned water supplies instilled terror throughout Surat, compounded by very real fears that the rumor itself could initiate widespread communal violence. The resulting exodus created chaos and severely curtailed medical and other resources at a time when they were most needed to manage the early stages of the epidemic. If rumors of bioterrorism had persisted following the end of the epidemic, they might have deflected public attention and resources away from much needed primary prevention efforts. As it turned out, the rumors gave way before the economic interests of the city, reflecting another important lesson learned: bad health is bad for business.

Finally, there is the issue of the pathogen itself. Although the actual extent of the plague in Surat will never be known, it is clear that many people were infected with *Yersinia pestis*. Some argue that the determination of plague was premature, and that its public announcement created unnecessary panic and suffering.[59] However, it will often be the case that clinical decisions must be made rapidly and under less than optimal conditions. Had the government withheld its decision until all the WHO criteria were met, it could not have acted for weeks into the epidemic. Instead, the government erred in its diagnosis on the side of sensitivity and rapid response, an "error" that ultimately proved correct. It would not have been realistic to withhold this information anyway, for the existing political conditions were such that even the suspicion of plague could not remain secret for long. The plague epidemic was a crisis of confidence as much as a crisis of public health. Far better to be forthcoming about the pathogen, just as it was better to be forthcoming about the negligence from which it emerged. Such lessons apply to defense against future diseases, regardless of whether they are deliberately initiated.

Implications for Identification, Characterization, and Attribution

The lessons of the Indian plague of 1994 have important implications for the identification, characterization, and attribution of biological weapons in developing countries around the world. First, identification must be linked to a broader concept of risk assessment. For instance, it is important to identify in advance those communities that are at greater risk for infectious diseases, in order to determine differential vulnerability to specific biological weapons because, once released, they are likely to spread like any other pathogen of the same species. In the case of the 1994 plague, the disease emerged as a vector-borne infection in a small rural village, but quickly spread to a large urban area, where it amplified and developed into a respiratory infection among its slum-dwelling population. The major center for the transmission of plague was geographically distant but socially proximate to its point of origin. This spread could have been predicted, based on the strong networks of rural-urban exchange in Surat as well as the vulnerability of its migrant labor population. One could also predict a similar pattern for an epidemic resulting from a bioterrorist attack.

Second, rapid and reliable identification and characterization of biological weapons necessitates adequate laboratory resources at the most likely points of treatment. There would have been less delay and debate over the identification of plague had Surat's New Civil Hospital laboratories been properly equipped to obtain and process larger numbers of sterile samples, perform rapid assessment assays, and send these samples on for further processing at national and international laboratories. It does not help to have state-of-the-art facilities in other cities and countries if there are insufficient local resources to obtain data properly in the first place.

Third, it is important to establish a working communication network between the local, national, and international agencies that may be involved in a future identification, characterization, and attribution process. Such a network could have prevented much of the delay and confusion over the identification of plague in Surat, especially if the key players had already established working relationships and all understood their respective roles. This kind of network can only be achieved through practice, for which ongoing disease surveillance would provide ample opportunities.

Fourth, protocols must be established for the rapid identification of pathogens. Most standards for the identification of infectious diseases are based upon ideal conditions: unlimited resources with which to examine a limited outbreak originating from a single-point source. This is not likely to be the case for a biological attack in a developing country, and it was certainly not the case for plague in India. Diagnostic criteria must be adapted to make reasonably safe determinations under conditions of limited time and resources. These adaptations should be linked to stochastic models and data from known outbreaks so that decision makers can balance the relative risks and benefits of these rapid determinations.

Fifth, attribution requires rapid and reliable contact tracing. As with the attribution of arson, so the attribution of biological weapons requires contextual data from their points of origin. Such points must be determined by tracing the contact histories of known cases. The same kind of information would be essential for surveillance containment efforts (that is, the targeted isolation and treatment of contacts as well as cases) at the early stages of disease control. Even if the ideals of surveillance containment are not feasible—as in the case of multiple sources or later-stage epidemics—the population must nevertheless be triaged for treatment and primary disease prevention. Contact tracing is essential for early control as well as attribution.

Sixth, public trust must be established before the outbreak occurs. Given the shortcomings of Surat's public services, city officials could not reasonably have expected the public to believe government accounts of the disease, to comply with government health messages, or to provide full and accurate information to authorities with whom they had no previous contact. It is notable that, in Surat, many people sought the services of the New Civil Hospital, and provided it with data about their locations and contacts. No other institution had the same history of service to the community, and no other officials had the same authority and credibility in a time of crisis. A pre-existing public-health infrastructure is essential for building public trust as well as surge capacity during a major epidemic.

Seventh, the need for transparency may exceed the need for security. This is especially the case for public identification of the disease. It was unlikely that the Indian authorities could have kept the plague a secret for long, and an earlier announcement could have given them the upper hand in the dissemination of accurate information. It is helpful if public messages can include examples of successful disease control in other parts of the world. For example, the United States saw 10 reported cases of human plague in 1993, nine of whom were successfully treated.[60] At present, all known bioweapons could be defended against with basic medical resources. These defenses could be compromised, however, by secrecy and undue alarm.

Finally, it should be emphasized that the challenges of biosecurity are not restricted to national borders: globalization entails the international movements of pathogens as well as people. Even before the advent of commercial air travel, steamships transported plague across the Asian continent, resulting in more than 15 million deaths between 1894 and 1901.[61] Much like the Indian plague of 1994, a pneumonic plague epidemic occurred in a city of migrant workers in the north of China in 1910–11 and spread by rail throughout Manchuria, with further impact in Russia and Japan.[62] All of these cases involved the amplification of epidemics in vulnerable populations, and all involved a more ready transmission of pathogens than of remedies across political borders.[63] These same lessons should be applied to the threat of biological weapons, which must always be considered within the context of a global human disease ecology.

Notes

1. Thomas Inglesby, Rita Grossman, and Tara O'Toole, "A Plague on Your City: Observations from TOPOFF," *Clinical Infectious Diseases* 32 (2001): 436–45; Department of Homeland Security, "Top Officials (TOPOFF) Exercise Series: TOPOFF2—After Action Summary Report for Public Release," December 19, 2003, <http://www.Housegov/etheridge/Topoff.doc>, accessed June 15, 2006; Department of Homeland Security, Office of the Inspector General, "A Review of the Top Officials 3 Exercise," OIG-06-7, November 2005, <http://www.dhs.gov/dhspublic/interweb/assetlibrary/OIG-06-07_NOV05.pdf>, accessed June 15, 2006; Thomas Inglesby et al., "Plague as a Biological Weapon: Medical and Public Health Management," *Journal of the American Medical Association* 283, no. 17 (2000): 2281–90; Ronald Atlas, "Bioterrorism: From Threat to Reality," *Annual Review of Microbiology*, 56 (2002): 167–85; Ronald Greenfield et al., "Bacterial Pathogens as Biological Weapons and Agents of Bioterrorism," *American Journal of the Medical Sciences*, 323, no. 6 (2002): 299–315.

2. Centers for Disease Control and Prevention, "Emergency Preparedness and Response: Bioterrorism Agents/Diseases by Category," May 21, 2006, <http://www.bt.cdc.gov/agent/agentlist-category.asp>, accessed June 15, 2006.

3. The most infamous historical example concerns the Japanese Imperial Army's experimental use of plague against Chinese citizens and Soviet prisoners during the Second World War. Reports suggest that these experiments produced haphazard results, but did inflict an undetermined number of casualties. See Jeanne Guillemin, *Biological Weapons: From the Invention of State-Sponsored Programs to Contemporary Bioterrorism* (New York: Columbia University Press, 2005), 84–97. See also Chapter 8 by Jeanne Guillemin in this volume.

4. Here, I am using the term "virulence" as it describes higher case fatality rates. For more information on the characteristics of the plague bacillus, see Robert Perry and Jacqueline Fetherstone, "*Yersinia pestis*—Etiologic Agent of the Plague," *Clinical Microbiology Reviews* 10, no. 1 (1997): 35–66.

5. Christopher Wills, *Yellow Fever Black Goddess: The Coevolution of People and Plagues* (Cambridge, MA: Perseus Publishing, 1996), 53–89.

6. "Confirmation" is defined by seropositivity: the presence of antibodies to plague-specific antigens. More technically, samples were determined to be seropositive by passive hemagglutination assay (PHA) for F1 antigens, conducted by the World Health Organization (WHO) investigative team (National Centers for Infectious Disease [NCID] for Surat samples). Suspected cases were determined based upon clinical presentation and staining characteristics of smear samples. The debate over "confirmed" and clinically "suspected" cases is addressed in the next section.

7. Human ecology has been variously labeled as cultural ecology and political ecology. I am expressly avoiding either term to distance myself from academic squabbles between their respective extremes: vulgar adaptationism and vulgar activism, and to use the best of their methods without subscribing to the worst of their agendae. For a sample of these approaches and a review of the debates between them see Hans Baer, ed., "Critical and Biocultural Approaches in Medical Anthropology: A Dialogue" (Special Issue), *Medical Anthropology Quarterly* 10, no. 4 (1996): 451–522. For an example of this chapter's approach see Ronald Barrett, Christopher Kuzawa, Thomas McDade, and George Armelagos, "Emerging and Re-Emerging Infectious Diseases: The Third Epidemiologic Transition," *Annual Review of Anthropology* 27 (1998): 247–71.

8. Pierre Camberlin, "Rainfall Anomalies in the Source Region of the Nile and their Connection with the Indian Summer Monsoon," *Journal of Climate* 10 (1997): 1380–92.

9. Rajiv Gupta, "Water and Energy Linkages for Groundwater Exploitation: A Case Study of Gujarat State, India," *Water Resources Development* 18, no. 1 (2002): 25–45.

10. H. M. Shavanand Swamy, Anajana Vyas, and Shipra Narang, *Transformation of Surat: From Plague to Second Cleanest City in India* (Delhi: All India Institute of Local Self Government, 1999), 1–20.

11. Vijay Saxena and T. Verghese, "The Ecology of Flea-Bitten Zoonotic Infection in Village Mamla, District Beed," *Current Science* 71, no. 10 (1996): 800–802.

12. I. J. Catanech, "The 'Globalization' of Disease? India and the Plague," *Journal of World History* 12, no. 1 (2001): 131–54; Michael McCormick, "Rats, Communications, and Plague: Toward an Ancient and Medieval Ecological History," *Journal of Interdisciplinary History* 34, no. 1 (2003): 1–25.

13. Saxena and Verghese, "The Ecology of Flea-Bitten Zoonotic Infection."

14. With the exception of Maharashtra, in which 485 (24.3 percent) of 1999 collected serum samples were tested, state samples were opportunistically acquired and their methods of collection were incompletely reported. Sampling and testing methods are addressed in the next section.

15. World Health Organization, *Plague in India: World Health Organization International Plague Investigation Team Report* (December 9, 1994), reproduced in Ghanshyam Shah, *Public Health and Urban Development: The Plague in Surat* (Delhi: Sage Publications, 1997), 277–90.

16. Perry and Fetherstone, "*Yersinia pestis.*"

17. Ibid.

18. G. S. Agarwal and H. V. Batra, "Passive Haemagglutination Tests for *Y. pestis* Infection in Surat Pneumonic Patients," *Current Science* 71, no. 10 (1996): 792–93.

19. Swamy, Vyas, and Narang, *Transformation of Surat.* The estimated proportion of patients by socioeconomic status and living conditions was based upon a household

survey of 301 registered cases at the New Civil Hospital. Ghanshyam Shah, *Public Health and Urban Development*, 38–39, 70.

20. Biswaroop Das, *Socio-Economic Study of Slums in Surat City* (Surat: Centre for Social Studies, 1994), 32–33, 83–91; Shah, *Public Health and Urban Development*, 112–13, 139–41.

21. Shah, *Public Health and Urban Development*, 70–73.

22. Shah, *Public Health and Urban Development*, 123–25. These figures are based upon a sample of 301 families with plague patients. A comparison with non-affected families from the same communities (n = 291) found a small but statistically insignificant difference in living area, rooms, and amenities. Unfortunately, however, this study does not give the distribution of exact household densities, nor does it account for the distribution of multiple cases within a given household.

23. Sarita Bahl, Sonia Kapoor, Priti Kumar, Pranay Lal, Tanvi Mishra, Amit Nair, and Atanu Sarkar, "Plague," in *Draft Dossier: Health and the Environment*, Centre for Science and Environment, <www.cseindia.org/programme/health/pdf/conf2006/aplague.pdf>, accessed June 21, 2006.

24. Bahl et al., "Plague."

25. Vijay Saxena and T. Verghese, "Observations on Urban Ecology of Surat and Bubonic Plague Transmission in the City," *Current Science* 71, no. 10 (1996): 803–5.

26. Shah, *Public Health and Urban Development*, 125–31. It should be noted, however, that only 18 percent of the patients from the 301 case families studied had come to Surat within the previous five years.

27. Ibid., 113–20.

28. Das, *Socio-economic Study of Slums in Surat*, 53–64. Some clustering according to subcaste and religious sect was also observed but not systematically distinguished. It is very difficult to measure and analyze these kinds of data.

29. Meera Kosambi, "Urbanization, Migration, and Commuter Flows in India with a Focus on Maharashtra State," in *Inequality, Mobility, and Urbanisation: China and India* (New Delhi: Indian Council of Social Science Research, 2000).

30. Lancy Lobo and Biswaroop Das, *Poor in Urban India: Life in the Slums of a Western Indian City* (New Delhi: Rawat, 2001).

31. Shah, *Public Health and Urban Development*, 142–51.

32. Pravin Sheth, "Surat Riots—1: Degeneration of a City," *Economic and Political Weekly* 28, no. 5 (1993): 151–52; Lancy Lobo and Paul D'Souza, "Surat Riots—2: Images of Violence," *Economic and Political Weekly* 28, no. 5 (1993): 152–54.

33. Ibid.

34. Biswaroop Das and Akash Acharya, personal communication, September 9, 2005.

35. Sheth, "Surat Riots—1."

36. Shah, *Public Health and Urban Development*, 142–54.

37. Ibid.

38. Sheth, "Surat Riots—1," 151–52.

39. Ira Klein, "Plague, Policy and Popular Unrest in British India," *Modern Asian Studies* 22, no. 4 (1988): 723–55.

40. Melisa Shah, *The Power of Stigma: The Plague in Surat, India*, unpublished thesis (Stanford, CA: Stanford University Department of Anthropological Sciences, 2006).

41. Arvind Susarla, *Plague in Surat, India*, unpublished thesis (Worcester, MA: Clark University Graduate School of Geography, 2006), excerpts available at <http://www.aag.org/HDGC/www/health/units/unit4/html/4bkground.html>, accessed June 15, 2006.

42. Shah, *The Plague in Surat*, 142–57.

43. Ibid.

44. World Health Organization, *Plague in India*.

45. Ibid.

46. Renu Bharadwaj, Anju Kagal, S. K. Deshpandey, S. A. Joshi, P. M. Kare, A. R. Junnarkar, and M. A. Padke, "Outbreak of Plague-like Illness Caused by *Pseudomonas pseudomallei* in Maharashtra, India," *The Lancet* 344, no. 8936 (1994): 1574. For a critical review of the controversies surrounding the identity of the pathogen, see Dileep Mavalankar, "Indian 'Plague' Epidemic: Unanswered Questions and Key Lessons," *Journal of the Royal Society of Medicine* 88 (1995): 547–51.

47. Agarwal and Batra, "Passive Haemagglutination Tests."

48. S. K. Panda et al., "The 1994 Plague Epidemic of India: Molecular Diagnosis and Characterization of *Yersinia pestis* Isolates from Surat and Beed," *Current Science* 71, no. 10 (1996): 794–99.

49. Ibid. See also S. Shivaji, N. Vijaya Bhanu, and R. K. Agarwal, "Identification of *Yersinia pestis* as the Causative Organism of Plague in India as Determined by 16S rDNA Sequencing and RAPD-based Genomic Fingerprinting," *FEMS Microbiology Letters* 189 (2000): 247–52.

50. Shah, *The Power of Stigma*.

51. Susarla, *Plague in Surat, India*.

52. Biswaroop Das, personal communication, September 9, 2005.

53. Swamy et al., *Transformation of Surat*.

54. Ibid. No data is available to support or disconfirm this claim, nor is there any available mention of which is the cleanest city in India (although Delhi would be a strategic guess).

55. Number of rats captured and flea indices from 1993 to 2004 are provided by the Surat Municipal Government.

56. Mean proportion of *P. vivax* among total identified malaria cases: 1990–94 = 0.36

(S.D. = 0.04); 1995–2004 = 0.50 (S.D. = 0.16). Pearson X^2 = 4.0 (df =1) p = 0.046. Source: Surat Municipal Government.

57. U.S. State Department, "Avian Influenza Update," <http://newdelhi.usembassy.gov/acsinfluenza.html>, accessed November 28, 2006.

58. Adrienne Mayer, *Greek Fire, Poisoned Arrows, and Scorpion Bombs: The History of Biological and Chemical Warfare in the Ancient World* (New York: Overlook Press, 2004).

59. Mavalankar, "Indian 'Plague' Epidemic."

60. Centers for Disease Control and Prevention, "Human Plague—United States, 1993–1994," *Morbidity and Mortality Weekly Report* 43, no. 13 (1994): 242–46.

61. M. Echenburg, "Pestis Redux: The Initial Years of the Third Bubonic Plague Pandemic, 1894–1901," *Journal of World History* 13, no. 2 (2002): 429–49.

62. M. Gamsa, "The Epidemic of Pneumonic Plague in Manchuria 1910–11," *Past & Present* 190, no. 1 (2006): 147–83.

63. For further discussion on the differential spread of pathogens and remedies, see P. Farmer, "Social Inequalities and Emerging Diseases," *Emerging Infectious Diseases* 2, no. 4 (1996): 259–69; C. F. Chyba, "Biological Security in a Changed World," *Science* 293, no. 5593 (2001): 2349.

CHAPTER FOUR

The Yellow Rain Affair

Lessons from a Discredited Allegation

MATTHEW S. MESELSON AND JULIAN PERRY ROBINSON

U.S. Secretary of State Alexander Haig, in a speech in West Berlin[1] in September 1981 and in a detailed report to the Congress the following March,[2] charged Soviet-backed Laotian and Vietnamese forces with waging toxin warfare against Hmong resistance fighters and their villages in Laos and against Khmer Rouge soldiers and villages in Cambodia. The charges were repeated with additional details in a further report to the Congress and to the member states of the United Nations in November 1982 by Haig's successor, Secretary of State George Shultz.[3]

The investigation on which the allegation was based, however, failed to employ reliable methods of witness interrogation or of forensic laboratory investigation; it was further marred by the dismissal and withholding of contrary evidence and a lack of independent review. When the evidence for toxin attacks or any other form of chemical/biological warfare (CBW) was subjected to more careful examination, it could not be confirmed or was discredited. In what became known as the "Yellow Rain" affair, these charges—that toxic substances called trichothecenes were used in CBW—were initially pressed vigorously by the U.S. government and, even when the allegations proved unsustainable, they were not withdrawn.

This chapter reviews all of the evidence adduced at the time that is now public, including a large body of material declassified and provided to us and others starting in 1986 under the Freedom of Information Act. The evidence supports explanations of the Yellow Rain events that involve no CBW weapons at all, beyond the use of riot-control agents. Focusing on the evidence rather than the politics of the affair, the chapter seeks lessons that could increase the accuracy and credibility of possible future assessments of alleged or suspected CBW. There is first a historical introduction and then each category of evidence is described and assessed in turn. In the concluding section, the principal lessons drawn from the Yellow Rain episode for investigations of CBW allegations concern the taking and confirmation of testimony from alleged witnesses, the conduct of forensic chemical analysis, and the importance of wide consultation and critical review.

The U.S. Allegations

The Haig and Shultz reports cited three main types of evidence in support of their allegations. First, Hmong villagers who had fled from Laos to refugee camps in Thailand and Khmer soldiers operating in the Thai-Cambodian border region claimed to have witnessed chemical attacks, including several that were said to have caused hundreds of deaths. Altogether, the two reports list some 400 alleged attacks between the summer of 1975 and June 1982, nearly two-thirds of them in Laos, most of the rest in Cambodia, and a few in Thailand near the Cambodian border. Second, samples of a yellowish material were turned in by people who claimed to have witnessed attacks and who stated that the samples were air-dropped poison; this was the so-called "Yellow Rain." A third type of evidence comprised chemical analyses reporting the presence of trichothecene mycotoxins, toxic substances made naturally, especially by fungi of the genus Fusarium, in environmental samples from sites of alleged chemical attack and in biomedical samples from individuals allegedly exposed. In addition, the Haig report cited an account given to U.S. Embassy personnel in Thailand by a Lao pilot who had defected and who, according to the report, had been "directly involved in chemical warfare."

The Hmong are an ethnic group inhabiting the highlands of South China, Thailand, Vietnam, and Laos. Starting in 1960, the CIA secretly recruited and supplied an indigenous Lao army, composed mainly of Hmong, to oppose the communist-led Pathet Lao, the North Vietnamese, and other Hmong who were allied with the Pathet Lao. After the U.S. departure from Vietnam in 1975, the Hmong who had been allied with the United States continued to resist Lao government control and relocation from their highland settlements to the lowland plains; in the late 1970s they came under heavy attack by the Pathet Lao and the Vietnamese air force and, in 1978, their Phu Bia Mountain stronghold fell to the Pathet Lao, leaving their villages exposed to continuing harassment and attack by Pathet Lao and Vietnamese ground and air forces. By 1983, tens of thousands of Hmong had fled from Laos across the Mekong into Thailand, where they were interned in refugee camps, the largest of which was at Ban Vinai.

Soldiers of the Khmer Rouge regime of Pol Pot and soldiers of the anti-communist Khmer People's National Liberation Front (KPNLF) also claimed to have experienced chemical attacks. They were fighting each other and both were fighting Vietnamese forces that had invaded Cambodia in December 1978. Most of the attacks alleged to have occurred in Cambodia were said to have taken place in the Thai border region, while most of the alleged attacks in Laos were claimed to have taken place around Phu Bia Mountain, about 80 km from the Thai frontier.

A telegram from the U.S. Embassy in Bangkok to Washington dated September 2, 1978, appears to have been the first to report Hmong accounts of lethal chemical attack. It cited interviews conducted by Embassy personnel with Hmong who had arrived recently from Laos, three of whom claimed they had witnessed Hmong fatalities due to what they said was poison gas delivered by small aircraft, including "rocket-fired smoke" and "blue or yellow spray." The telegram said that for several months the Embassy had heard reports from refugees claiming that poison gas was being used against the Hmong in Laos, but cautioned that the telegram was "based on refugee interviews and should therefore be regarded as raw information rather than confirmed fact."[4]

The earliest Khmer Rouge claims of chemical attacks of which we are aware were made over Radio Phnom Penh in November 1978 and alleged the use of "poisonous gas" artillery munitions by invading Vietnamese forces.[5] A note distributed in April 1980 by the Khmer Rouge diplomatic mission in Geneva claimed there had been some two dozen attacks by Vietnamese aircraft and artillery with "toxic chemicals" that had caused vomiting, dizziness, fever, and at least 455 deaths between July 1979 and March 1980. The alleged agent was described as having a "yellow colour" and as sticking to "leaves of the trees."[6]

As claims of chemical warfare continued to be made, the U.S. State Department dispatched a Foreign Service officer to Thailand to conduct interviews regarding the allegations. In June 1979, he and a U.S. Embassy consular official interviewed, through interpreters, 22 Hmong refugees who told of chemical attacks in Laos, some of which were said to have been associated with hundreds of deaths. Nineteen of the refugees told of a CBW agent that was yellowish; two handed in samples of vegetation with yellow spots about 3 millimeters in diameter.[7]

In October 1979, four U.S. Army medical and toxicological specialists went to refugee camps at Ban Vinai and elsewhere in Thailand.[8] There they completed 38 more interviews with Hmong who claimed they had witnessed or knew of attacks. The alleged agent was said to have been of various colors—red, green, black, white, blue, grey—but most often yellow. The Army interviewers also were given samples from an alleged attack: yellowish spots a few millimeters in diameter on pieces of bark from a village rooftop.[9] Over the next few years, samples of the yellowish alleged agent continued to be handed in to U.S. officials and to officials of other countries, including Australia, Canada, France, Sweden, Thailand, and the UK, by Hmong refugees and Khmer soldiers claiming them to have been collected from sites of chemical attack.

Throughout all the available interviews with Hmong refugees conducted by U.S. and Canadian officials, by UN investigators, and by relief agency and hospital personnel from January 1979 through June 1983, the alleged agent was most often said to have been yellowish and to have fallen like rain. As described in the Shultz report, "Usually the Hmong state that aircraft or helicopters spray a yellow rain-like material on their villages and crops." The U.S. assessment that the yellow-rain-like substance was a chemical-warfare agent was repeated in a 1985 article co-authored by Christopher Green, the CIA official in the Agency's Directorate of Intelligence who chaired the CBW/Toxin Use Working Group, an inter-agency body formed to coordinate U.S. investigations of the CBW allegations. According to the article, "Aerial attacks, usually by spray, dispersed yellow to yellow-brown liquid or semi-solid particles that fell and sometimes sounded like rain when striking thatched rooftops."[10]

Composition of the Alleged Agent

None of the alleged attacks was witnessed by a Western observer. The most tangible evidence bearing on the allegations consisted of the samples of alleged agent turned in by refugees and the laboratory analyses of these and other environmental samples, of blood and urine from alleged victims, and of tissues taken at autopsy from a Khmer Rouge soldier.

Samples of the alleged agent—the yellow spots and powders handed in by Hmong refugees and Khmer soldiers—first became available to U.S. investigators in 1979. But it was three more years before their principal component was correctly identified. In January 1982, a scientist at the UK Chemical Defence Establishment at Porton Down saw under a microscope that the principal component of a Yellow Rain sample was pollen.[11] This was found to be the case for all samples of the yellow alleged agent accumulated at Porton, some 30 in number. Soon afterward, the discovery of pollen in Yellow Rain samples was made independently in Australia,[12] Thailand,[13] and Canada.[14] The Porton finding was communicated to the United States and was confirmed with many additional samples at what was then called the Army Chemical Systems Laboratory (CSL), later named the Chemical Research and Development Command (CRDC), at the Edgewood Area of Aberdeen Proving Ground, Maryland. It was also confirmed at defense establishments in France and Sweden. Altogether, at least 100 samples of yellowish spots and powders from alleged attacks in Laos and Cambodia were examined under the microscope and, without exception, found to consist principally of pollen.

The presence of pollen in the samples of the alleged CBW agent that had been accumulated by the United States was first made public by Emory Sarver of CSL on November 29, 1982, during a State Department press briefing on the Shultz report.[15] The next day, in a second Washington press briefing,[16] an explanation for the presence of pollen in the Yellow Rain samples was given by Gary Crocker, a State Department intelligence officer who chaired the Assessments and Policy Support Sub-group of the CBW/Toxin Use Working Group, and by Sharon Watson, an intelligence analyst at what was then called the U.S. Army Medical Intelligence and Information Agency (MIIA), later the Armed Forces Medical Intelligence Center (AFMIC), at Fort Detrick, Maryland. It was Watson who, in 1981, had suggested that trichothecenes had been used and who was responsible for scientific and intelligence aspects of the subsequent MIIA/ AFMIC program under which biomedical samples collected in Southeast Asia were analyzed for trichothecenes by contractor laboratories.

Crocker is recorded as having said:

> It contains pollen, and not windborne pollen, but pollen that would be commercially collected or is collected, if you will, by insects, the type of thing you would get in a—a honey bee would take from flowers. And they are the particular size. It happens to be the right size to be retained in the body.

This was the first public suggestion that the pollen in Yellow Rain might have something to do with honeybees. Crocker's explanation was then amplified by Watson:

> Well I think I might just clarify a point, and that is the role of pollen in the mixture. The agent, as it comes down, is wet, and at this time the primary exposure appears to be through the skin, and the toxins are dissolved in the solvent, going through the skin very quickly. But as the agent dries, a secondary aerosol effect can be caused by kicking up this pollen-like dust that is of a particle size that will be retained in the bronchii of the lung. Now we've shown in studies with animals that the internasal LD-50 [the dose lethal to 50 percent of an exposed population] for the Trichothecenes is much lower than we would have expected, and that the Trichothecenes, if they come in contact with the mucous membrane, were very rapidly absorbed and are very toxic by this route. So if you could bring the compound into contact with the mucous membranes of the bronchii, then it's a very effective way of getting it across. So there are two different ways that the compound is absorbed. It's [a] very clever, clever mixture.

Even then, the theory announced by these two U.S. intelligence analysts could have been dismissed for a number of reasons, not the least of which was that the samples of Yellow Rain had no such tendency to disperse.

U.S. officials nevertheless continued to assert this explanation for the presence of pollen in the yellow spots and powders that they claimed to be an agent of toxin warfare. In a December 1982 address to the First Committee of the United Nations General Assembly, Kenneth Adelman, then U.S. Deputy Representative to the UN, declared: "We are now, however, able to isolate the components of yellow rain. . . . There is good evidence for the presence of commercially produced pollen as a carrier and to help ensure the retention of toxins in the human body."[17]

Starting in early 1983, however, the government's theory that the yellow spots and powders handed in by refugees were samples of a chemical warfare agent was being undermined by studies done at the Smithsonian Institution in Washington by Joan Nowicke, an authority on pollen identification. Both the U.S. Army and one of the present authors (MM) had brought her samples of the alleged agent, in the latter case including samples from alleged attacks provided by Australian and Canadian government scientists. Examining the samples under an electron microscope, Nowicke had found by mid-April 1983 that the several plant families represented in the samples are common in Southeast Asia. She also found that no two spots, even on the same leaf or rock, had the same mixture of pollen types. The tropical plant families represented in the pollen and the diversity between spots were attributes not to be expected for a chemical warfare agent made in the Soviet Union and dispersed from exploding munitions or spray tanks.[18]

The implausibility of the government's explanation of pollen in the alleged agent and questions regarding other aspects of its Yellow Rain investigation had caused one of us (MM), together with an MIT colleague with experience in scientific intelligence matters, to convene a workshop of government and university experts in diverse fields of potential relevance, including anthropology, botany, toxicology, and analytical chemistry, to review the allegations of toxin warfare in Southeast Asia. It was held during April 15–16, 1983, at the American Academy of Arts and Sciences in Cambridge, Massachusetts. The 35 participants included Joan Nowicke; David Jarzen, a Canadian pollen expert who had examined samples of the yellowish alleged agent obtained by Canadian investigators; Gary Crocker of the State Department; Emory Sarver of the U.S. Army Chemical Systems Laboratory; Joseph Rosen, a Rutgers University chemist who had reported finding trichothecenes in a sample of the alleged agent obtained by ABC News that was later found by Nowicke to be mainly pollen;[19] Amos Townsend, a retired U.S. Air Force doctor who had interviewed Hmong refugees about the alleged chemical attacks; Peter Ashton, a Harvard botanist who had studied bee pollination of Southeast Asian trees; and both of the present authors. By the end of the workshop, it seemed clear that the findings of Nowicke and of Jarzen meant that the samples had to be of natural origin and that, as Crocker had suggested, bees were somehow involved—but how?

As the workshop ended, Ashton, the Harvard botanist, suggested that we contact Thomas Seeley, a Yale zoology professor who had studied wild honey-bees in Thailand. Upon hearing our description of the suspected agent—yellow, pollen-laden spots 2–5 millimeters in diameter that were said to fall like rain—Seeley concluded that the State Department explanation was "not parsimonious" and that the yellow spots were bee feces.[20]

At the time, entomologists did not know whether tropical Asian honey-bees defecated individually or might do so collectively, producing showers that could have been mistaken by witnesses for sprays from aircraft. In order to address the question, Seeley, Pongthep Akratanakul (a Thai honeybee expert), and one of us (MM) conducted a field study in Thailand in March 1984. On one occasion, near Chiang Mai, we observed great numbers of wild honeybees suddenly leaving their nests, flying too high to be easily seen, and producing a shower of feces that lasted for several minutes and covered an area of an acre or more with hundreds of thousands of yellow spots indistinguishable in appearance from those handed in and described as "poison from the sky." While this was the most intense shower we encountered, we also observed lesser showers of wild honeybee feces in other parts of the country.[21]

Reporting our findings at the U.S. Embassy in Bangkok, we were told that the Embassy had requested and Washington had eventually agreed to the creation of a joint State-Defense CBW team to conduct a more systematic field investigation than had so far been done. One of the activities of the CBW Team was a field trip, in April 1984, together with Akratanakul, to corroborate our discovery of honeybee fecal showers. Their telegram to Washington reported showers that they observed, including one in which the team physician and their Hmong interpreter were caught, during which "the bees were seen flying approximately 40 to 50 feet above and passing over at a speed of approximately 20 mph," noting that the defecating bees were "seen only with difficulty." The telegram also reported that, "Dr. Akratanakul stated that he never noticed bee feces deposits in all his years of work until the present yellow rain controversy arose."[22] Both we and the CBW Team spoke on a number of occasions with Hmong refugees who said they had witnessed chemical attacks but who, when shown spots of honeybee feces on leaves, identified them as the alleged agent.

Further tests by U.S., British, Australian, Canadian, French, and Swedish government investigators of the yellowish samples of the alleged agent found that they were indistinguishable from the feces of wild Asian honeybees. This included not only the gross appearance of the samples but also the concentration and species distribution of pollen seen under the electron microscope and the results of various other laboratory tests. One of these tests, on the ABC News sample in which the Rutgers laboratory had reported the presence of trichothecenes, showed the pollen grains to be hollow shells, just like the pollen grains in feces taken directly from honeybees, from which the nutritive protein and lipid has been removed by the bee's digestive processes.[23] There was little room to doubt that what the Hmong had frequently mistaken as poison from the sky and which the Haig and Shultz reports, Crocker, Watson, and the 1985 article co-authored by the Chairman of the CBW/Toxin Use Working Group all asserted was a chemical warfare agent, was, in fact, the feces of Asian honeybees.

The finding that the yellowish materials that Hmong refugees and Khmer soldiers had repeatedly claimed to be a chemical warfare agent were in fact only honeybee feces showed that U.S. government investigators had, for years, given inadequate attention to possible natural explanations of the Yellow Rain. Moreover, it raised grave questions about the reliability of the interviews. If the Yellow Rain that was described and handed in by the alleged witnesses was honeybee feces, how could there have been some other substance delivered from the air simultaneously in sufficient quantity to cause the claimed effects that was neither observed nor sampled?

It could be argued that, among the minority of refugee accounts that are recorded as having described other kinds or colors of agent—white, red, black, or green—some describe actual chemical attacks. Yet the casualties described even in these accounts, if authentic, could be ascribed to natural disease or to the effects of blast or of inhalation or contact with materials released from rocket or artillery marker rounds, explosive munitions, riot control munitions, or phosphorus bombs and projectiles, all of which are known to have been in use at the time in Laos and Cambodia. Moreover, the widespread and long-standing misidentification by alleged witnesses of honeybee feces as a chemical warfare agent casts serious doubt on the entire body of interview evidence.

Could some of the Hmong and Cambodians have misinterpreted a natural phenomenon as a weapon of war? Unknown at the time of the first U.S. allegations of chemical warfare in Southeast Asia, a similar misidentification of honeybee feces as poison from the sky had occurred in China in 1976. As described in an article published in 1977 in the Chinese science journal *Kexue Tongbau*, drops of a viscous sticky liquid fell from the sky like rain in many regions of Jiangsu Province in August and September 1976. The showers usually lasted for a few minutes and generally extended over areas of up to an acre and sometimes considerably more. Upon drying, the drops formed yellowish spots a few millimeters in diameter. Local people called it "Hwang Yu" (Yellow Rain) and some of them said it was poison sprayed from aircraft and that they were afraid to consume food or water that might be contaminated with it. Investigating scientists from Nanjing University, however, found no clinical evidence of toxicity, nor is there any evidence that honeybee feces are toxic. Upon examining the yellowish material under a microscope, the Chinese scientists saw that it contained concentrated pollen and that the types of pollen were those produced by local plants. They concluded that the phenomenon resulted from mass flights of defecating honeybees.[24] The Chinese yellow rain first became known to Western investigators of Yellow Rain only in 1983, when the 1977 article was brought to the attention of scientists and officials at Porton by a British academic.[25]

What if the villagers of Jiangsu, like the Hmong in Laos who fled to Thailand and like the soldiers and villagers in Cambodia, had been under frequent attack by aircraft and artillery delivering explosives, napalm, phosphorus, riot-control agent, and smoke markers? And what if, instead of university scientists and village officials telling them that there was nothing to fear, they had been interviewed by apparently authoritative Westerners asking them to describe the poison attacks? Under these conditions, would not the mistaken beliefs of the people in Jiangsu have been repeated and greatly amplified? If so, is it possible that Hmong and Cambodian "witnesses" had mistakenly associated naturally occurring disease and battle injuries with showers of honeybee feces; that others were repeating unfounded rumor, even if sincerely believed, sometimes saying they had seen things they had only heard about; and that some said what they had been told to say by others, or what they thought would conform to the expectations of their questioners? These and other questions raised by the bee-feces findings were never seriously addressed by MIIA/AFMIC, by the CBW/Toxin Use Working Group, or in any of the commentaries holding that there had been chemical attacks.

Interview Evidence and the State-Defense CBW Team

Until 1983, nearly all interviews with alleged witnesses had been conducted in ways that fell far short of standards that would allow fact to be distinguished from rumor, misperception, miscommunication, or fabrication.[26] Testifying to a committee of the Congress on December 12, 1979, Army dermatologist Colonel Charles W. Lewis, leader of the Army team that had conducted interviews with Hmong refugees two months earlier, said that, "Our team attempted to be very selective in talking only with Hmongs who had either been direct witnesses of attacks or those who had been exposed to chemical agents themselves."[27] The team's ethnic Hmong interpreters selected only those refugees who said they had been eyewitnesses to chemical attacks, thereby excluding those who might have disputed the claims of chemical warfare. Colonel Lewis said that, "To achieve conformity in our results, we used a prepared questionnaire that we took with us." No attempt was made to avoid leading questions: the first two questions in the questionnaire were: "How was your health prior to this incident?" and "Where were you when it happened?"

Not until the arrival of the Joint State-Defense CBW Team in 1983 were appropriate efforts made to check the reliability of the interview claims of chemical attack.[28] The team consisted of an Army Chemical Corps officer, a military physician, a Foreign Service officer, a secretary, and two interpreters, one who spoke Hmong and one who spoke Khmer. It operated in Thailand for three years, from November 1983 until October 1986. The methods the team employed to test the truth of earlier allegations included standard investigatory procedures for ascertaining the accuracy of witness testimony. The team used double-checks, seeking out and re-interviewing refugees whose previous interviews had portrayed them as victims or witnesses of attacks. Using cross-checks, the team questioned other refugees who had also been present at the same time and place or approximate locale as the interviewee who alleged chemical attacks, in an effort to determine whether their accounts supported what others had said. The CBW team's interviews took place at Ban Vinai refugee camp in Thailand and elsewhere in Thailand and the Thai-Cambodian border region.

Characteristic of the careful approach taken by the CBW Team was a report telegraphed back to Washington in January 1984. The team re-interviewed a Hmong man who had said in an earlier interview that he had seen "with his own eyes" chemical attacks on a village in Laos, had witnessed six deaths, and had suffered chest pains, chills, and dizziness. The CBW Team asked him how, while he was a resistance fighter in the distant jungle, he could know so much about attacks on the village. He then changed his account to say that he "did not personally see the attacks but rather had received accounts of the attacks from others." In another example, the team was able to locate a Hmong woman previously interviewed by a British nurse. The woman reportedly said in the earlier interview that she had experienced a chemical attack and had become very ill from it. When interviewed by the CBW Team, however, the woman gave a different account: she confirmed that airplanes flew over her village every two or three days at high altitude but she denied ever having experienced chemical warfare. The team also interviewed a Hmong man who, when in a group with other Hmong, "told of gassing attacks but denied its reality when the interviewer talked to him alone outside."[29]

The CBW Team also questioned people who had not been contacted before. In May 1984 they interviewed a former resistance leader who had recently led a group of 93 other Hmong out of Laos to Thailand. He had commanded about 40 men and their families living since 1975 on the slope of Phu Bia Mountain, where the Haig and Shultz reports said that most of the attacks in Laos had occurred. However, as the CBW Team reported in a telegram to Washington in 1984, "he denied ever having experienced a CBW attack nor ever having seen any evidence of CBW use." When questioned why other Hmong refugees gave accounts of CBW attacks and he, a resident of Phu Bia for eight years, had seen nothing, he explained that as an educated man, he related what he saw and not what he felt, whereas other Hmong would relate what they heard and felt to be true.[30] A few days later, the team telegraphed to Washington their view that, "The question is not whether Hmong refugees lie but whether Hmong refugees are accurate reporters of reality. Generally, we have not found them to be so and believe that their stories must be supported by external and, if possible, objective means." In the same telegram, the CBW Team reported that "The present Ban Vinai camp leader has told every member of the team that he doesn't know whether the gassing stories result from chemical warfare or from bee feces but that he would like the team to find out."[31]

The CBW Team identified a further reason to question the reliability of interviews conducted by previous investigators. Many of the interviews conducted in 1979 by State Department personnel and by U.S. Army medical and toxin specialists specified the exact day of alleged attacks.[32] The problem with such precision is seen in a telegram that the CBW Team sent to Washington in April 1984. The telegram described an interview the team had conducted with three family groups from the same village in Laos whose houses were ten meters apart. The family members could not agree among themselves on the date of an alleged attack within a four-month period, nor on the location of a Yellow Rain incident to which they had testified earlier. The team recognized the obstacles to resolving such conflicting details: "The Hmong culture does not compartmentalize units of time as tightly as we who have broken our lives into seconds, minutes, hours and days. Their time blocks are by seasons and as a result any effort to confirm a specific date of a given incident is usually frustrated."[33] Earlier interviewers and interpreters appear thus to have led the Hmong to stipulate Western calendar dates to a misleading degree of false precision, and therefore may have elicited other erroneous testimony as well. Moreover, the unlikelihood that Hmong refugees could accurately specify the exact dates of chemical attacks calls into question the extraordinary assertion in the Haig report that intelligence information "indicates that military activity took place at the time and place of every incident reported to involve lethal chemical agents."

After working in Thailand for two years, in November 1985 the CBW Team telegraphed Washington their "conclusions to date." Their Sixth Quarterly Report stated that "Information regarding the use of 'yellow rain' against the Hmong in Laos remains too incomplete or implausible on which to base conclusions."[34] Despite its long and careful investigation, the negative conclusions of the CBW Team were never publicly acknowledged by the U.S. government and became known to us only from declassified telegrams obtained under the Freedom of Information Act.

Alleged Symptoms

The finding that many of the alleged witnesses had mistaken honeybee feces for an agent of chemical warfare inevitably raises questions about the reliability of their claimed association of specific medical symptoms with chemical attacks. The Haig report presents tables comparing symptoms claimed by alleged victims of chemical attack in Laos and in Cambodia with the symptoms its authors believed would result from trichothecene poisoning and with symptoms characteristic of six well-known chemical warfare agents. The report claims a significant match of symptoms with those expected of trichothecenes. No attempt was made to compare the listed symptoms with those that would be expected to result from natural afflictions, smoke inhalation, blast damage, or other battle injuries. The symptoms listed in the Haig report as most often reported for alleged chemical attacks in Laos—vomiting, diarrhea, hemorrhage, breathing difficulty, and skin irritation—are not unusual given the level of natural illness, dislocation, and battle casualties experienced by the Hmong. Moreover, instead of the common symptomology suggestive of trichothecene exposure claimed in the Haig report, there was wide variation between individuals in the particular constellation of symptoms they described, as may be seen in the State Department and Army interviews of 1979 and as is underscored in the Shultz report, which notes that "different symptoms are ascribed to men, women, children and animals."[35]

Symptoms ascribed to alleged chemical attack were repeatedly judged by experienced physicians on the scene to be of altogether different origin. In March 1981, for example, the U.S. Embassy's Regional Medical Officer examined purported Cambodian and Hmong victims, but he found no clear evidence to support CBW allegations.[36] The medical investigations of the U.S. State-Defense CBW Team in Thailand did not reveal any clear evidence of exposure to chemical attack: during the period December 1983–June 1984, it investigated 36 suspected chemical warfare attacks, but not one yielded confirmatory medical evidence. For example, on several occasions the team investigated claims that Khmer Rouge soldiers had been gassed in combat. In a typical instance, extensive medical workup on an alleged victim who had complained of dizziness, nausea, and vomiting blood yielded the conclusion that his "symptoms, which he reported to be due to 'toxic gas exposure' could be easily explained by the clinical course resulting from the blast effects alone."[37] In another case, the team's chemical and medical officers examined five patients in a Bangkok hospital who complained of dizziness, vomiting, chest pain, and temporary unconsciousness, which they attributed to chemical attacks. After examining them, however, the team "conclude[d] that their symptoms were as a result of battle fatigue, smoke inhalation, heat stress, or a combination of these effects."[38] A few days later, the CBW Team and a Royal Thai Navy physician examined four other patients complaining of the same symptoms. The CBW Team agreed with the Thai physician's diagnosis that "all four victims suffered smoke inhalation and there is insufficient clinical evidence to support a finding of chemical warfare."[39]

Regarding claims that KPNLF soldiers fighting the Vietnamese in the Thai-Cambodian border region had come under lethal chemical attack, General Sak Sutsakhan, Vice President of the KPNLF and Chief of its General Staff in April 1984, "denied that Vietnamese had used toxic chemicals so far" against his forces. He said, "The blast of big shells can damage your skin and make a lot of blood vessels explode, so you vomit blood. This must have happened to some of our soldiers. It is also possible that tear gas has been used." The *Bangkok Post* article quoting him also noted that "General Sutsakhan's assessment on toxins was confirmed by other KPNLF sources and medical teams at the border."[40]

From the first allegations of chemical warfare in Laos and Cambodia in 1976 to the conclusion of the work of the CBW Team in 1986, we know of no case in which diagnostic examination or autopsy provided clear evidence of exposure to biological or chemical warfare agents other than riot control agents. With only the claims of alleged victims, with little or no attention to the problems caused by leading questions, hearsay, and possible fabrication, and no adequate consideration given to the likely effects of natural illness and the effects of battle, the claims of medical evidence for chemical warfare are not sustainable.

AFMIC argued that CBW attacks had largely ceased by the time in 1983 that the CBW Team implemented its more trustworthy methods of investigation, but that earlier reports were nonetheless authentic.[41] However, a presumption that earlier reports were authentic but the later ones were not would imply a severe lack of reliability in the Hmong and Cambodian testimony generally, nor would it account for testimony like that of the Hmong resistance leader or the Ban Vinai camp leader described above. It also fails to take into account the fact that all of the symptoms claimed to have resulted from chemical attack could be, and in many cases were, judged by U.S. and Thai military medical examiners to be the result of natural illness and battle casualties. It is more likely that, aside from the use of riot-control agents, there never was any good evidence for chemical attacks, and that the conclusions reached starting in 1983 differ only because reliable methods of investigation were then instituted, both by the CBW Team and also, as discussed below, by laboratories seeking to corroborate the reports of trichothecenes in samples from alleged attacks.

The Trichothecene Analyses

The concentrations of trichothecenes said by the United States to have been found in samples from sites of alleged toxin attack in Laos and Cambodia are very low, ranging from a high of 143 parts per million of T-2 in a sample of the pollen-laden alleged agent, down to concentrations of only a few parts per billion in some samples of blood and urine. Formidable problems face the chemist seeking to detect a substance present in such tiny amounts in the sample to be analyzed. The problem is greatly compounded when, as in the environmental and biomedical materials from alleged attack sites, the sample is a complex mixture of substances, some of which may mimic the one being sought, thereby giving a false positive. False positives can also result from laboratory contamination, as may occur when the substance being tested for at trace levels is present in the laboratory in more substantial amounts, or when some of the substance present in one analytical run is carried over into a subsequent run. These difficulties can be avoided only by taking the most stringent precautions.[42] The avoidance of false positives in analyses of environmental or biomedical samples for trace amounts of trichothecenes requires highly discriminating analytical methods and the parallel analysis of matched control samples. It is particularly risky to conduct trace analysis in a laboratory that has handled substantial amounts of the substance for which trace analysis is being attempted. The risk is that minute amounts adhering to containers, equipment, or other surfaces may inadvertently and unpredictably enter at various steps in the preparation of a sample or in its analysis. Indeed, both CSL and Porton found that reliable analysis of trichothecenes required the use of new glassware for each analysis. Trace analysis should never be undertaken in a laboratory that has previously handled anything but trace amounts of the substance or any substance that could mimic it. An example of a "clean" laboratory, so far as trichothecenes are concerned, is the U.S. Army Chemical Systems Laboratory in Maryland. Another is that of the UK Chemical Defence Establishment at Porton Down. A further essential precaution is to analyze blanks—artificial samples not containing the substance of interest but prepared for analysis just as one would prepare an unknown sample—preferably before and after each analysis of an unknown. Finally, if high confidence is required, no report should be accepted as correct unless it is confirmed in an independent laboratory.

Essentially all of the analyses for trichothecenes on which the United States relied in making its charges of trichothecene warfare were done, starting in 1981, in a contractor laboratory at the University of Minnesota. The Haig and Shultz reports as well as a 1983 publication from the Minnesota laboratory state that trichothecenes were found only in biomedical and environmental samples from alleged attacks and not in controls.[43] The publication reported analyses of some 80 blood and urine samples from alleged victims, nearly 40 percent of them positive for trichothecenes. Important questions, however, were left unanswered. The number of controls, the manner and sequence in which they were analyzed, and the specific results were not adequately reported and, for most samples, not reported at all. The lack of satisfactory information regarding control analyses is all the more problematic because the Minnesota laboratory had previously done a great deal of work with substantial amounts of trichothecenes, having published more than twenty papers about such work during the four years before undertaking trace analysis of samples from the alleged Yellow Rain attacks. The specific trichothecenes with which that earlier work was done included the same ones which the Minnesota laboratory subsequently reported in environmental and biomedical samples from alleged attacks, principally T-2 and its catabolite, the trichothecene HT-2.

The possibility that the reports on which the United States relied in making its accusations had been compromised by false positives did not cause much concern until it became apparent that government laboratories in the United States (CSL) and the UK (Porton Down) were failing to confirm the presence of trichothecenes in any of the numerous environmental and biomedical samples from alleged attacks they analyzed, not even in samples that the Minnesota laboratory had reported positive. One of these, for example, was a yellow pollen—containing material alleged to have been sprayed by a twin-engined plane on the afternoon of March 13, 1981, near Phu Bia, in Laos. Known as sample C-168-81, it had been sent seven months later to the Minnesota laboratory which reported it to contain 143 parts per million of T-2 and 27 parts per million of DAS (another trichothecene), the highest trichothecene levels the Minnesota laboratory reported for any sample from an alleged attack. Even though CSL and Porton should have been able to detect even a few parts per million of T-2 or DAS in their portions of this sample, neither could confirm the Minnesota finding.

According to information provided by the Army to the U.S. Senate Committee on Foreign Relations in 1992, CSL had analyzed a total of 251 environmental samples from alleged attacks and had found no trichothecenes in any of them.[44] Neither were trichothecenes found in any of the approximately 50 environmental and 20 biomedical samples from alleged attacks that were analyzed at Porton during the period March 1982 to September 1984,[45] nor in the approximately 50 samples analyzed at the Swedish Research Institute of National Defense,[46] nor in samples analyzed at Centre d'Etudes du Bouchet, the French CBW defense research center.[47]

Defending the Yellow Rain allegations, AFMIC argued that the trichothecenes had decomposed during the time between the Minnesota analyses and those done at CSL and Porton.[48] But pure T-2 and DAS are stable; there appears to be no experimental evidence showing that they would decompose in environmental samples under the conditions in which they were kept at CSL and Porton. A problem of trichothecene instability does arise, but it does so in a manner that raises additional doubts about the reliability of reports of trichothecenes in blood and urine samples. Because of the long trek through Laos from most of the alleged attack sites to refugee camps in Thailand, the biomedical samples were taken from alleged victims weeks after their alleged exposure. A 1988 report from the U.S. Army Medical Research Institute of Infectious Diseases at Fort Detrick describes experiments measuring the amounts of T-2 and its catabolite HT-2 in blood and urine taken at various times after intravenous injection of monkeys with T-2.[49] The report concludes that disappearance of HT-2 "was so rapid that its detection in serum as an indicator of T-2 intoxication would be useful only within the first 6 hr [six hours] following exposure." Measurements of the amount of T-2 in blood 28 days after its administration to monkeys and studies of trichothecene metabolism at Porton pointed to a similar problem.[50]

There is yet further reason to question the claim that trichothecenes were associated with alleged attacks. An April 1987 report prepared by a member of the Collection and Requirements Division at AFMIC tabulates the findings communicated to AFMIC by the Minnesota laboratory for T-2 and HT-2 in blood and urine samples collected from 1981 through 1985 from 146 individuals identified as controls.[51] Of these controls, the report lists 24 as positive and therefore concludes that "the blood and urine samples from CW victims in Southeast Asia cannot be used as evidence that mycotoxins were used as CW agents."[52]

Thus, the claim of an association between alleged attacks and the presence of trichothecenes in environmental and biomedical samples is undermined by the lack of reliable information about the performance and outcome of control analyses; by the substantial risk of laboratory contamination; by the lack of later confirmation by CSL, Porton, and other defense laboratories; and by the problem of trichothecene decomposition *in vivo*. A thorough, independent, and objective investigation, including a forensic audit of the original records, might be able to determine whether the conclusion of the above report is correct. If it is, the most senior officials of the U.S. government had been gravely misinformed.

The Shultz report charged that T-2 had also been detected on the surface of a Soviet gas mask obtained near Kabul, Afghanistan, in 1981 and concluded that trichothecene weapons had been used there since at least 1980. Little more has appeared in public about this allegation. While it is now known that the USSR, in violation of the 1972 Biological and Toxin Weapons Convention, had a massive bioweapons development and production program, there is no evidence even from recent inquiries that the Soviet program extended to trichothecenes.[53] The State-Defense CBW Team spent two weeks in Pakistan in October 1985 to conduct an exploratory investigation, but found itself "unable to provide a scientifically sustainable conclusion regarding agent usage."[54]

Defector and Prisoner Debriefings and the Absence of Recovered Munitions

The Haig report also claimed that "One of the most complete descriptions of chemical warfare activities in the 1976–78 period came from a Lao pilot who was directly involved in chemical warfare" and who defected to Thailand where he was interrogated by U.S. Embassy personnel. According to the Haig report, the pilot described numerous missions on which he said that he fired rockets at Hmong targets, dispensing smoke of various colors which he "surmised" was poison. The report asserts that several Hmong accounts support the testimony of the Lao pilot, and cites one of these in which rockets dispensing red and green smoke fired by aircraft over a seven-day period in June 1979 caused the deaths of ten villagers by gassing and 30 by shrapnel.

However, the portrayal of the Lao pilot's account in the Haig report had already been undercut by a classified telegram to Washington from the U.S. Embassy in Bangkok. It stated that when the Lao pilot was re-interrogated, this time not by Embassy personnel but by a U.S. Air Force pilot, an entirely different conclusion was reached. The U.S. pilot, an Air Force major, reported in the telegram his conclusion that "It seems very unlikely that the rockets fired contained toxic [word illegible in available copy] CW agents. A rocket-delivered gas attack would require at least some sort of rudimentary knowledge of prevailing winds along with a few basic safety procedures. Although there have been no Hmong reports to verify the contention, the RO [reporting officer?] suspects that, based on the Lao pilot's description of the aerial detonation of the rocket, the weapon in question may have been a flechette round,"[55] that is, a munition discharging many small dart-like projectiles.

It might nevertheless be asked if other pilots flying other missions had engaged in chemical attacks like those alleged by the Lao pilot. If so, many spent and dud chemical munitions would have reached the ground, for more than half of the 60 interviews summarized in the Haig report cite rockets as the means of dissemination. In order to achieve the target effects claimed, some of the attacks would have had to involve firing very large numbers of rockets.[56] Nevertheless, not a single authenticated chemical munition was ever recovered, neither from Cambodia nor from Laos, where Hmong refugees had collected numerous samples of what they claimed to be the alleged agent itself.

Debriefings of Vietnamese soldiers who had fought in Laos and Cambodia during the same years in which the Haig and Shultz reports claimed that there had been hundreds of chemical attacks also failed to obtain any evidence for chemical warfare. A CIA case officer who served in Southeast Asia during 1981–83, now retired, recently wrote in an article cleared by the CIA for publication that "none of the hundreds of Vietnamese soldiers, both defectors and prisoners, that we debriefed over the course of my two-year tour ever provided us a shred of information about anything remotely resembling 'yellow rain.' We talked to Vietnamese soldiers—officers, NCOs, and privates—who had fought in battles where chemical weapons had supposedly been used. They all said they had no knowledge of Vietnamese possession or use of chemical or biological weapons." He and his fellow working-level case officers in the CIA Directorate of Operations, who were specifically tasked to collect information on the alleged use of CBW weapons in Southeast Asia, concluded from their investigations that there was "absolutely no credible evidence of the existence or use of such weapons" but that "our Directorate of Intelligence (DI) analysts and senior administration policymakers did not like the answer we gave them."[57]

Conclusion

The U.S. accusations appear to have been based on no credible evidence: without confirmation of a single alleged witness report, without confirmation of an association between trichothecenes and any alleged attacks, without any sample of the agent itself, without any recovered rocket or other munition, without any otherwise inexplicable claimed symptoms, and without any credible defector or prisoner testimony in all these years, counterfactual analysis leads to the conclusion that, except for riot-control agent, CBW weapons were not used in Laos or Cambodia.

The lessons to be learned from the Yellow Rain episode are straightforward: reliable procedures must be used to acquire and evaluate interview evidence, including the use of corroborative cross-checks and double-checks and careful avoidance of leading questions. Chemical identification of trace components must adhere to appropriate standards for forensic analysis, and results must be corroborated by an independent laboratory. Hypotheses must be subjected to wide consultation and objective criticism. Failure to apply these lessons, whether through incompetence or because of political exigencies and pressures, imperils the credibility of subsequent investigations of situations in which CBW weapons may actually have been used.

Notes

1. Alexander Haig, U.S. Secretary of State, address before the Berlin Press Association, West Berlin, September 13, 1981, "The Democratic Revolution and Its Future," *Current Policy* (Washington, DC: U.S. Department of State, Bureau of Public Affairs), no. 311.

2. U.S. Department of State, Special Report no. 98, "Chemical Warfare in Southeast Asia and Afghanistan," March 22, 1982.

3. U.S. Department of State, Special Report no. 104, "Chemical Warfare in Southeast Asia and Afghanistan: An Update," November 11, 1982.

4. Telegram No. 25420, U.S. Embassy Bangkok to Secretary of State, September 2, 1978, Subject: "Hmong Refugees Escape Description." Such reports had been noted in the Thai press as early as October 1976: see Grant Evans, *The Yellow Rainmakers* (London: Verso, 1983), 32–33.

5. AP from Bangkok, "Cambodia: Vietnam Using Poison Gas," *Washington Post*, November 8, 1978, A32; Radio Phnom Penh quoted from Bangkok in "Cambodia Charges Gas Attack," *Washington Post*, November 14, 1978.

6. Mission Permanente du Kampuchea Democratique, Geneva, "Chemicals Spreadings, Toxic Gas Shell Firings and Other Forms of Chemical Arm Using by the Vietnamese Troops in Kampuchea, July 1979—March 1980." See also Democratic Kampuchea, Permanent Mission to the United Nations in Geneva, "Crimes des Agresseurs Vietnamiens contre le Peuple du Kampuchea," November 1979; Democratic Kampuchea, Ministry of Information press release, November 14, 1979, distributed in UN document A/34/692–S/13631, November 16, 1979.

7. U.S. House of Representatives, Committee on Foreign Affairs, Hearing before the Subcommittee on Asian and Pacific Affairs, "Use of Chemical Agents in Southeast Asia Since the Vietnam War," 96th Cong., 1st sess., December 12, 1979.

8. Ibid.

9. A portion of this sample provided by one of the Army interviewers to MM for examination was found to consist largely of pollen.

10. C. J. Stahl, C. C. Green, and J. B. Farnum, "The Incident at Tuol Chrey: Pathologic and Toxicologic Examinations of a Casualty After Chemical Attack," *Journal of Forensic Science* 39, no. 2 (April 1985): 317–57.

11. Often referred to simply as "Porton," these Ministry of Defence laboratories are now a component of the Defence Science and Technology Laboratories, known as DSTL Porton Down.

12. H. D. Crone, "The Examination of 'Yellow Rain' Specimens Received at MRL in April 1982," Australian Defence Scientific Service, Materials Research Laboratories (MRL), Maribyrnong, Technical Report OCD 82/14, August 1982.

13. Samaniya Sukroongreung, Sompool Kritalugsana, Churiratana Nilakul, Kleophant Thakerngpol, and Pithaya Viriyanondha, "Examination of the Yellow Spot Samples from Thailand Border Close to Cambodia," *Siriraj Hospital Gazette* 34, no. 9 (September 1982): 643–47.

14. D. M. Jarzen, "Yellow Rain," *BIOME* 4, no. 1 (1983): 3, National Museum of Natural Sciences, Ottawa, Canada.

15. U.S. Department of State, "On-the-Record Briefing on Chemical Warfare in Afghanistan, Laos, and Kampuchea, Washington, DC, Monday, November 29, 1982, 2:30 p.m.," official transcript, pp. 19–20.

16. United States Information Agency (USIA), "Briefing: Robert Dean and Gary Crocker on 'Yellow Rain,' Washington, DC, November 30, 1982," official transcript.

17. U.S. Ambassador Kenneth Adelman, statement before the First Committee of the UN General Assembly, December 8, 1982, transcript distributed as a U.S. Information Service *Official Text* by the U.S. Embassy, London.

18. Joan W. Nowicke and Matthew Meselson, "Yellow Rain—A Palynological Analysis," *Nature* 309, no. 5965 (May 17–23, 1984): 205–6.

19. R. T. Rosen and J. D. Rosen, "Presence of Four Fusarium Mycotoxins and Synthetic Material in 'Yellow Rain.' Evidence for the Use of Chemical Weapons in Laos,"

Biomedical Mass Spectrometry 9, no. 10 (October 1982): 443–50; Nowicke and Meselson, "Yellow Rain."

20. Thomas Seeley, telephone conversation with P. Ashton and M. Meselson, April 16, 1983.

21. Thomas D. Seeley, Joan W. Nowicke, Matthew Meselson, Jeanne Guillemin, and Pongthep Akratanakul, "Yellow Rain," *Scientific American* 253, no. 3 (September 1985): 128–37.

22. Telegram No. 18465, U.S. Embassy Bangkok to Defense Intelligence Agency, Washington, April 9, 1984, subject: "CBW Sample TH-840322-1JR."

23. Seeley et al., "Yellow Rain," 135.

24. Chang Chung-ying, Chen Yu-ming, Chou Shu, and Li Min, "A Study of the Origin and the Pollen Analysis of 'Yellow Rains' in Northern Kiangsu," *Kexue Tongbao* 22, no. 9 (September 1977): 409–12.

25. Alastair Hay, "Yellow Rain: Fresh Support for Apian Origin," *Nature* 306 (November 3, 1983): 8.

26. Julian Robinson, Jeanne Guillemin, and Matthew Meselson, "Yellow Rain in Southeast Asia: The Story Collapses," *Foreign Policy* 68 (Fall 1987): 100–117.

27. Colonel Charles W. Lewis (U.S. Army Medical Corps), testimony before the House of Representatives Committee on Foreign Affairs, Subcommittee on Asian and Pacific Affairs, December 12, 1979, hearing on "Use of Chemical Agents in Southeast Asia since the Vietnam War."

28. The official name of the team was the Joint Department of State/Department of Defense Chemical Biological Warfare Investigative Field Team.

29. Telegram No. 00656, U.S. Embassy Bangkok to Defense Intelligence Agency Washington, January 5, 1984, subject: "Alleged Use of CBW/Yellow Rain Against Hmong."

30. Telegram No. 24354, U.S. Embassy Bangkok to Defense Intelligence Agency Washington, May 10, 1984, subject: "Interview Summaries of Hmong Refugees Regarding CBW."

31. Telegram 27244, U.S. Embassy Bangkok to Defense Intelligence Agency Washington, May 30, 1984, subject: "CBW Samples TH-840523-1DS Through 7DS."

32. U.S. House of Representatives, Committee on Foreign Affairs, Hearing before the Subcommittee on Asian and Pacific Affairs, "Use of Chemical Agents in Southeast Asia since the Vietnam War," 96th Cong., 1st sess., December 12, 1979.

33. Telegram No. 21367, U.S. Embassy Bangkok to Secretary of State, April 25, 1984, subject: "CBW Sample Report from Ban Vinai Interview Follow-up."

34. Telegram No. 67036, U.S. Embassy Bangkok to Secretary of State, November 15, 1985, subject: "Sixth Quarterly Report of CBW Field Team Chief."

35. Seeley et al., "Yellow Rain in Southeast Asia"; Robinson et al., "Yellow Rain."

36. U.S. Government Memorandum, Henry Wilde (Regional Medical Officer) to

file, March 18, 1981, subject: "Report on Visits to Democratic Kampuchea Hospitals."

37. Telegram No. 08848, U.S. Embassy Bangkok to Defense Intelligence Agency Washington, February 17, 1984, subject: "CBW Samples TH-840211-1MS/2MS and TH-840212-1MS/2MS."

38. Telegram No. 20177, U.S. Embassy Bangkok to Defense Intelligence Agency Washington, April 19, 1984, subject: "Alleged Chemical Attack at Ban Sa Ngae on 15 April 84."

39. Telegram No. 21018, U.S. Embassy Bangkok to Defense Intelligence Agency Washington, April 24, 1984, subject: "Alleged Chemical Attack at Ban Sa Ngae on 17–18 April 84."

40. General Sak Sutsakhan, quoted in the English-language *Bangkok Post*, in Telegram No. 21682, U.S. Embassy Bangkok to Secretary of State, April 26, 1984, subject: "Chief of KPNLF General Staff Comments on CBW."

41. Letter Report: "Yellow Rain: Separating Fact from Fiction," Dr. Sharon A. Watson, ACSI Task: 84:056, AFMIC-SA, Fort Detrick, Md., June 18, 1984, 45pp.

42. P. Begley, B. E. Foulger, P. D. Jeffery, R. M. Black, and R. W. Read, "Detection of Trace Levels of Trichothecenes in Human Blood Using Capillary Gas Chromatography—Electron-Capture Negative Ion Chemical Ionisation Mass Spectrometry," *Journal of Chromatography* 367 (1986): 87–101.

43. Chester J. Mirocha, Robert A. Pawlosky, Kajal Chatterjee, Sharon Watson, and Wallace Hayes, "Analysis for *Fusarium* Toxins in Various Samples Implicated in Biological Warfare in Southeast Asia," *Journal of the Association of Official Analytical Chemists* 66, no. 6 (1983): 1485–99. The first three authors were at the Department of Plant Pathology at the University of Minnesota. Watson was at AFMIC and Hayes at the Rohm and Haas Corporation.

44. Document received by MM from U.S. Senate Committee on Foreign Relations August 27, 1992, Archive of M. Meselson, Harvard University.

45. *House of Commons Official Report* 98, no. 117, Col. 92, written answers to questions, May 19, 1986; and personal communication, June 29, 1987.

46. Memorandum, November 10, 1985: Swedish studies of Yellow Rain, interview with Dr. Johann Santesson, Swedish National Defense Research Institute. Stockholm, October 24–26, 1985, Archive of M. Meselson, Harvard University.

47. Memorandum, July 22, 1986: French studies of Yellow Rain, interview with Ingenieur-General P. Y. Herve and staff of Direction des Researches, Etudes et Techniques, Paris, July 7, 1986, Archive of M. Meselson, Harvard University.

48. Letter Report: "Yellow Rain: Separating Fact from Fiction."

49. K. A. Mereish, J. G. Pace, S. M. Naseem, R. E. Dinterman, R. W. Wannemacher, Jr., and D. L. Bunner, "Toxicokinetics of T-2 Mycotoxin and Its Metabolites in Cynomolgus Monkeys," U.S. Army Medical Research Institute of Infectious Diseases, Fort

Detrick, interim report, December 30, 1988, available from DTIC (Defense Technical Information Center) as document ADA202775. A catabolite is a substance produced by the breakdown of a complex molecule into a simpler one in living organisms.

50. R. M. Black and C. D. Upshall, "Assessing the Danger," *Chemistry in Britain* (July 1988): 659–64.

51. Richard Torian, "Foreign Medical Material Exploitation Program Report: A Report on the Program to Assess the Meaning of Mycotoxin Detection in the Blood and Urine Samples in Individuals in Southeast Asia," Armed Forces Medical Intelligence Center (AFMIC), Fort Detrick, Md., April 1987, 15 pp.

52. If the Torian report is correct, it may nevertheless be that AFMIC did not inform the Minnesota laboratory that it had reported trichothecenes in control samples.

53. See, for example, Jonathan B. Tucker, "Biological Weapons in the Former Soviet Union: An Interview with Dr. Kenneth Alibek," *The Nonproliferation Review*, Spring–Summer 1999, 1–10.

54. Telegram No. 71462, U.S. Embassy Bangkok to Secretary of State, subject: "Trip Report: CBW Team Visit to Pakistan," December 9, 1985.

55. Telegram No. 05196, U.S. Embassy Bangkok to Defense Intelligence Agency Washington, "Pilot Debrief of Lao FAC Concerning Gas Attacks," January 27, 1981.

56. Animal experimentation indicates that, if inhaled as an aerosol, the lethal dose of T-2 is approximately equal to that of phosgene, a poison gas widely used in World War I. Military firing tables for phosgene munitions have typically prescribed expenditures of 7–70 grams of phosgene per square meter of target, depending on the weather, for 30 percent casualty rates. Deposited on the skin, even if present together with a solvent to enhance adsorption, T-2 is less lethal than mustard, the principal skin-attacking CW agent of World War I, while T-2 causes skin burns at about the same doses as does mustard, for which prescribed battlefield expenditures are similar to those for phosgene. Multi-ton quantities, therefore, would have been needed to secure the casualty levels claimed for many of the alleged attacks described in the Haig and Shultz reports.

57. Merle L. Pribbenow, "'Yellow Rain': Lessons from an Earlier WMD Controversy," *International Journal of Intelligence and Counterintelligence* 19 (2006): 737–45.

CHAPTER FIVE

"Yellow Rain" Biological Warfare Agent Use

Evidence and Remaining Questions

REBECCA KATZ

Reports in the late 1970s of alleged chemical and biological weapons (CBW) attacks in Southeast Asia and Afghanistan, collectively known as "Yellow Rain," sparked the first large-scale investigation conducted by the United States into allegations of CBW use. The official U.S. conclusion was that biological toxin weapons had been used in Southeast Asia and Afghanistan. However, these conclusions were met with skepticism by some and alternative explanations (as outlined in Chapter 4 in this volume by Meselson and Robinson). Based in part on underlying evidence released in December 2003, recent analysis of evidence from the Yellow Rain investigation supports the claim that CBW attacks occurred, yet questions still remain as to identification of the agent, characterization of the incident, and attribution of the attacks to a specific perpetrator.[1]

This chapter outlines the history behind the allegations of CBW use, details the U.S. government's investigation, and reviews the subsequent challenges to the U.S. conclusions. It presents findings derived from recently released evidence that clarify some of the debated issues.

The Yellow Rain investigation serves as an important case study for examining the challenges of proving or disproving use and assigning attribution in a CBW investigation. The ability to assess an allegation accurately has implications for monitoring compliance with international legal agreements, and also for victims, public health, and arms control. The case illuminates the short-comings intrinsic to investigations of CBW use, and demonstrates the need for the creation of standards for data acquisition and verification.

Initial Reports of "Yellow Rain"

In 1976, reports started trickling out from Laos that the Hmong, one of the country's ethnic minorities, were being attacked by the communist Pathet Lao and Vietnamese forces with chemical weapons (CW).[2] Descriptions of what the Hmong called "the chemi" or "medicine from the sky" often involved a helicopter or plane flying over a village and releasing a colored gas, which would precipitate on thatched roofs, leaves, clothes, and skin in a manner that looked, felt, and sounded like rain. The most commonly reported color was yellow, giving rise to the term "Yellow Rain" for these attacks. Reported symptoms included nausea, vomiting, diarrhea, difficulty breathing, rash, blisters, eye irritations, coughing, dizziness, headache, and convulsions.

In late 1978 and early 1979, Khmer Rouge resistance fighters in Cambodia and *mujahedin* resistance fighters in Afghanistan began describing similar CBW attacks and subsequent symptoms. The similarities between reports from Laos and Cambodia and those from Afghanistan raised suspicions that the same agent was being used, and it was noted that all three locations were linked in some manner to the Soviet Union. In Afghanistan, the Soviets were directly involved in the war, and in Laos and Cambodia, they supported Pathet Lao and Communist Vietnamese forces. However, the initial reports did not make it possible to identify a known chemical or biological agent that would account for the reported signs and symptoms.

The U.S. Government Investigation and Conclusion

The first official U.S. response to the allegations of CBW use in Southeast Asia was a 1978 démarche to Laos, Vietnam, and the Soviet Union. The démarche was based on press and refugee reports, and accused these nations of chemical or toxin weapons use against the Hmong. All three nations, however, denied any use of chemical or toxin agents.[3]

The U.S. government's investigation into the Yellow Rain allegations began in 1979 with an initial assessment conducted by an Army medical team. The investigation continued through the end of 1982 as a somewhat ad-hoc, informal effort operated in Southeast Asia by a Foreign Service officer, a defense attaché, and a physician with the International Rescue Committee. This team, with the assistance of non-governmental organization (NGO) volunteers and refugees from the affected countries, collected biomedical and environmental samples for laboratory analysis, acquired medical data on alleged victims, administered questionnaires regarding alleged attacks, and searched for other information that could confirm or refute aspects of the refugee reports. NGO volunteers and CIA officials collected similar samples, medical data, and questionnaires from locations in Afghanistan and refugee camps in Pakistan.

Concurrently, government analysts from the U.S. intelligence community and the Department of State conducted regular interagency meetings to make sense of the data being collected in the field and to try to match it with other intelligence findings. Government analysts in the Washington, DC area coordinated the analysis of environmental and biomedical samples collected from Thailand, Laos, Cambodia, and Afghanistan.

In 1983, a formal joint Department of Defense–Department of State investigative team was sent to Thailand. By that time, however, reports of attacks had dramatically declined, and the investigation had become tainted, as refugees learned that claiming to be chemical/toxin weapons victims increased their chances of being granted asylum in the United States.

Government officials in the United States divided the samples collected in Southeast Asia and Afghanistan. Biomedical samples were sent to the United States Army Medical Intelligence and Information Agency (USAMIIA), which forwarded them for analysis to select academic institutions with relevant experience. Environmental samples went to the Foreign Science Technology Center (FSTC), and were then sent on to government laboratories in Edgewood, Maryland.[4]

Intelligence analysts from USAMIIA and the CIA suspected that the agent causing the type of morbidity and mortality reported by the refugees might be a type of toxin, specifically trichothecene mycotoxin (T-2). This suspicion was based primarily on reports of hemorrhaging and skin irritation. At the beginning of the investigation, however, government laboratories did not have the capacity to detect small amounts of trichothecene mycotoxin in a biomedical

or environmental sample. Therefore, academic laboratories with proven analytic capabilities were utilized. Academics who had published papers on methodologies for detecting T-2 toxin, including Dr. Chester Mirocha at the University of Minnesota and Dr. Joseph Rosen at Rutgers University, were selected
to conduct the laboratory analysis on samples collected in the investigation.
Intermediaries were utilized so that the researchers were blind to the origin of
the samples.

In 1981, trichothecene mycotoxin was detected in an environmental sample
from Southeast Asia, and U.S. Secretary of State Alexander Haig announced
that physical evidence had been found, proving that mycotoxins supplied by
the Soviet Union were being used as a weapon against civilians and insurgents
in Southeast Asia and Afghanistan.[5] The U.S. Department of State officially reported in March 1982 that attacks using trichothecene mycotoxins had in fact
occurred in Southeast Asia, and in November 1982, the State Department released an updated report with stronger evidence of attacks and additional supporting mycotoxin analysis.[6] The reports contained estimates of the minimum
number of deaths from chemical or toxin warfare: 6,395 Hmong, 1,046 Khmer,
and 3,342 *mujahedin*.[7] These are numbers for which there is a name associated
with a victim, and do not include vague reports of entire villages being slaughtered.

At the time, the reports released by the Department of State considered
chemical and toxin weapons use in Southeast Asia and Afghanistan a certainty,
although there were varying degrees of confidence in identifying the specific
kinds of chemicals or toxins being used.[8] The reports described a number of
alleged events in detail, and included lists of regions where attacks were said
to have occurred, with up to 139 attacks in Cambodia, 248 in Laos, 56 in Afghanistan, and 5 in Thailand. The exact sites of the attacks were not stated, but
characteristics of the attacks, such as method, were reported in summary.

Laboratory results and finished intelligence were made public in the State
Department reports, but much of the underlying evidence in support of the
claims, including raw intelligence on attacks, weapons storage, defector reports,
clandestine reporting, and raw toxicology and medical reports, remained classified.

President Ronald Reagan formally reported to Congress in 1984 that the Soviets had "repeatedly violated their legal obligation under the Biological Weap-

ons Convention and customary international law as codified in the 1925 Geneva Protocol" through "their involvement in the production, transfer and use of toxins and other lethal chemical warfare agents that have been used in Laos, Cambodia and Afghanistan."[9] This became the official policy stance of the U.S. government and was used as such to influence ongoing arms control negotiations and other policies. At the same time, however, the Yellow Rain findings were being strongly debated in the press, academia, and within the halls of the State Department.

A New Body of Evidence

In December 2003, the Defense Intelligence Agency, in coordination with my doctoral research, declassified many of the documents relevant to the Yellow Rain investigation; analysis of these newly released documents is presented in the subsequent sections of this chapter. The documents include medical records, laboratory reports, diplomatic communications, internal memos, and protocols. While some of this information had been released over the past 25 years, much was never before made public. Newly available information includes detailed information about the toxicology sample analysis program and results, protocols for the investigation, and specific intelligence related to the investigated events. This allows for a more complete analysis of the evidence that informed the U.S. government assessment of characterization, identification, and attribution. The newly available evidence, as I argue below, supports the conclusion that a toxin weapon was used in Southeast Asia and Afghanistan, but leaves some questions, such as agent composition and intent, unanswered.[10]

Toxicology Sample Analysis and Challenges for
Identification and Characterization

Over 1,600 environmental and biomedical samples were collected from Southeast Asia and Afghanistan to determine if CBW attacks were taking place, and if so, to determine the composition of the agent and possibly the origin. The collection and analysis of the samples occurred primarily between 1981 and 1985. Many of the environmental samples said to have come from alleged attack sites were collected by third parties—the attack sites were considered to be in hostile territory and not accessible to Americans—and therefore there was no way to confirm the chain of custody of the samples. When possible, however, U.S. government officials collected the samples, and were able to document more precisely, and with greater reliability, the validity of the sample.

Biomedical samples were taken from alleged victims anywhere from days to months after exposure or illness. These samples consisted of blood, urine, hair, breast milk, and occasional autopsy tissue. There was a considerable time lag between collection of the sample and final analysis, with an average of 16 days between collection and being processed and entered into the government's analysis program, with samples then kept an average of almost 79 days in the laboratory before being analyzed.[11]

Environmental samples were sent to the government laboratories, where they were analyzed and tested for known chemical weapons. Nearly all of the tests for known chemical agents were negative; exceptions included two samples positive for the riot control agent orthochlorobenzalmalonitrile (CS gas), one for the riot control agent chloroacetophenone (CN), at least one sample positive for cyanide, and one positive for explosive TNT.

After the initial T-2 finding in 1981, all of the biomedical samples and some of the environmental samples were tested for trichothecene mycotoxins. All toxicology results for trichothecene mycotoxins were interpreted using the methodology adopted by the Armed Forces Medical Intelligence Center in the early 1980s that attempted to mitigate problems in the sample collection process and the inexperience of particular laboratories. For example, data from certain laboratories had to be confirmed by additional laboratories, due to unacceptably high false positives during quality control experiments, and samples that were older at the time of analysis were given less weight, as they were less likely to produce reliable results due to sample degradation.[12]

The final results of the sample analysis coordinated by AFMIC and conducted between 1980 and 1985 documents that Dr. Chester Mirocha of the University of Minnesota found five out of six environmental samples from alleged attack sites analyzed to be positive; Dr. Joseph Rosen of Rutgers University found one environmental sample to be positive. Of the environmental control samples analyzed by Mirocha, 29 out of 29 were negative. An additional 48 environmental samples sent to an Army laboratory were not analyzed in a timely fashion and degraded.[13] Additionally, three separate laboratories found T-2 in samples from a Soviet gas mask found in Kabul, Afghanistan. T-2 was found on leaves and rocks from Laos and Cambodia not commonly associated with mycotoxin growth, and no fungi were found on leaves that were positive for T-2. Additionally, Dr. Rosen found polyethylene glycol (PEG) in the positive environmental sample he analyzed, a substance not found in nature, but linked to CBW because when added to T-2, it could stabilize the agent and prepare it for dispersion.[14]

The biomedical sampling program analyzed samples from 146 individuals between 1981 and 1985. Toxicologists at five universities around the country conducted these analyses on a blind basis. Some, but not all, of the results were confirmed by multiple laboratories, as shown in the newly declassified data. Twenty-nine of these samples, from five sites in Cambodia and from seven named sites and five unnamed sites in Laos, were found to be positive for trichothecene mycotoxin. All biomedical control samples analyzed as part of the U.S. investigation were identified as negative.[15]

The biomedical samples contained multiple trichothecene compounds, in concentrations that were smaller than the levels believed by some to be necessary to cause significant morbidity and mortality.[16] However, the presence of these multiple compounds in even small amounts led scientists in the 1980s to believe that the trichothecenes found were consistent with CBW use, since it was thought at the time that multiple combinations of trichothecene compounds did not exist in nature.[17]

Problems

Many mistakes were made in the sample collection and analysis program that cast doubt on the validity of the findings. To prove a CBW attack today, the investigation would need to provide evidence of chain of custody of the samples, appropriately matched controls, good baseline surveillance to rule out naturally occurring contamination or disease, and replicability of laboratory results. During the Yellow Rain investigation, by contrast, sample handling and transport may have led to the deterioration of the samples, and it was almost impossible to confirm the chain of custody. Time delays between sample collection and analysis arose from lack of funds, time spent establishing capacity and analysis procedures, contract negotiations, technical problems at the laboratories, quality control testing, and difficulties transporting the samples from Southeast Asia to the laboratories.[18] The paucity of appropriate human controls made it difficult to rule out natural exposure through food or water consumption, as controls were not matched well by age, sex, or even ethnicity; only a limited effort was made to find controls that had similar environmental exposures and diets. Environmental controls from near the attack sites were hard to obtain so most controls came from safer—and less meaningful—locations.

Techniques for the toxicology analysis were in their infancy and, while capable, were not yet developed into tested international standards. The laboratories chosen for analysis were not reviewed or professionally evaluated for consistency and accuracy, mainly because there were so few toxicologists capable of conducting the analysis during the time of the investigation.

Additionally, there was a lack of understanding in the early 1980s about the natural levels of mycotoxins around the world, nor was there much knowledge about the levels of toxin needed to cause disease in humans. There were other types of mycotoxins that could have been in the samples and were consistent with the reported symptomology, but the knowledge did not exist to test for them.[19]

Improvements

Numerous advancements have been made in the understanding of mycotoxins in the past twenty years. Today, in part due to disagreements over the Yellow Rain analysis, professional guidelines and international standards have been established for the analysis of mycotoxins. Over 100 laboratories around the world have been certified as capable of conducting accurate and reliable analysis for mycotoxins. These laboratories meet the highest international standards and pass routine challenges. Laboratory methodologies are now standard, so that results of sample analysis from any of the approved laboratories can be considered reliable. The scientific community has also developed standards for sample collection and handling of mycotoxins to avoid contamination and degradation.

It is now known that mycotoxins are found all over the world, including Southeast Asia, although the details about naturally occurring levels are fragmentary at best. Multiple trichothecene compounds can be found in the same plant host in nature, particularly in environments where the diversity of trichothecene-producing species is much greater due to limited agricultural development.[20] We now know that the severity of the toxins can be compounded by host factors, such as malnutrition and infectious disease status, and conversely, that toxin exposure can increase vulnerability to microbial disease, exacerbate malnutrition, and interact synergistically with other toxins.[21] Thus even small quantities may have quite significant effects under some conditions.

Even with theses advances in knowledge, there are still many uncertainties surrounding mycotoxins. There continues to be a limited understanding of how mycotoxins affect humans, and it remains difficult to conduct research on risk assessments because of the dearth of epidemiological data.[22] Information about the naturally occurring levels and combinations of mycotoxins around the world, and particularly in Southeast Asia, is fragmentary. And although it is known that multiple compounds can exist together, the frequency, combinations, and locations of such compounds has not been well documented.

Assessment

With these issues, and lacking adequate data, it can be extremely difficult to identify the source of a trichothecene mycotoxin in an environmental or biological sample. It is thus almost impossible for chemical analyses alone to prove that a trichothecene was used deliberately in an act of war or terrorism.[23]

Improved understanding regarding trichothecene mycotoxins necessitates that the conclusions drawn during the Yellow Rain investigation around identification and characterization be revisited. Without appropriate controls and in the absence of good survey data on naturally occurring levels of trichothecenes in the areas of interest, it is impossible to determine conclusively whether the mycotoxins found in the samples from alleged attacks were of natural or unnatural origin. Because the integrity of many of the samples was compromised by delays and improper handling techniques, it is possible that low levels of toxin found in the samples were due to degradation prior to analysis.[24] The findings of trichothecenes in multiple combinations does not necessarily rule out natural occurrence, and while refugee testimony tended to link an intentional exposure mechanism with immediate illness, causal links cannot be drawn in the absence of reliable toxicology studies, or without finding trichothecene-filled munitions at the alleged attack sites.

Medical Records, Morbidity, and Mortality

U.S. investigators collected medical records on alleged victims to evaluate the claim that toxin or chemical weapons were being used against the population. Anyone who presented to the hospital at a refugee camp had a record created, and records on patients who either reported exposure to a chemical attack, or had symptoms consistent with other reports, were shared with U.S. government officials.[25] Other mechanisms for collecting medical information on alleged victims came from interviews with NGO medical personnel or U.S. government officials during intake sessions when the refugee entered the camps, or when alleged victims presented themselves to an official within the camp. U.S. government officials also met with some refugees immediately following their arrival in Thailand, before entering a detention center or a refugee camp. NGO and U.S. government officials interviewed others while they were still in Cambodia.

Refugees and resistance fighters reported a set of symptoms, some of which started immediately after a reported attack, and others that developed several days to weeks afterwards; approximately half of the symptoms developed within an hour of the reported event. These early symptoms most often involved the central nervous system, followed by gastrointestinal symptoms.[26] Due to possible cultural differences, interviewer misinterpretation, refugee confusion, and difficulties in determining causation, my analysis gives more weight to symptoms that developed within minutes to days of the reported attack, rather than weeks or months later.

Symptoms commonly reported in association with the alleged attacks include vomiting, diarrhea, respiratory pain, rash, blisters, coughing, dizziness, headache, and convulsions. Severe cases often included bloody vomiting and diarrhea, as well as other signs of hemorrhaging. It is important to note that the vomiting described by the refugees was often bloody, and at times projectile with bright red blood. Severe gastrointestinal symptoms often resulted in death. At least a third of all reports mention some type of eye irritation, including excessive tearing, swelling, and loss or blurring of vision. All of these symptoms are consistent with trichothecene poisoning, but many of the symptoms are also consistent with chemical weapons such as nerve agents, arsines, phosgene oxide, and riot control agents, such as the ones left behind in Southeast Asia by the United States after the Vietnam War.

Problems

The medical records themselves varied greatly in quality and completeness. Illness surveys for use by government official and non-medical NGO volunteers were designed so that the interviewee only had to check boxes. In most of the surveys, the majority of the form is left blank. Instead of conducting a population-based survey, witnesses and victims were found through word of mouth, referrals from the refugee camp's hospital personnel, and preliminary interviews performed during the United Nations registration process for all recent arrivals. While there were problems inherent in the questionnaires used to collect data—primarily the omission of important details and lack of specificity—NGO medical personnel found the process was useful for capturing specific data on medical symptomology and attack incidents.[27] No effort was made until very late in the investigation to collect medical records on similar populations from regions that did not report attacks.

Assessment

Thorough analysis of the symptoms reportedly associated with attacks show that it is highly improbable that any of the natural diseases consistent with the reported and observed symptomology could have occurred in multiple people at the same time.[28] None of the possible diseases associated with the symptoms were endemic to the regions, nor could they have produced epidemics that might have been confused with CBW attacks. Therefore, it seems probable that the morbidity and mortality reported by refugees, and observed by NGO medical personnel and U.S. government officials, was at least in part due to some type of exposure to a toxin or chemical.

Attack Data

Based on the newly released data, in combination with previously available information and reports, I compiled detailed information on 766 separate attacks alleged to have occurred in Laos, Cambodia, Thailand, and Afghanistan between 1975 and 1985. For each such attack, there is information on the exact site, the number of reported events, the date for each event, the reported method of attack and its color and smell, associated illness and death, the number and ages of people affected, the impact on animals and vegetation, and in some cases the results of sample analysis. These reports came from refugees, journalists, intelligence intercepts, defectors, resistance fighters, and medical professionals. The majority of reported attacks are clustered between 1978 and 1982, in locations consistent with locations of Hmong, Khmer, and *mujahedin* villages or resistance-group clusters. The locations of the alleged attacks were also consistently correlated with high elevations and in areas difficult to reach through conventional military methods, particularly since villages and intended targets were hard to find due to caves or thick jungle cover.[29]

Contrary to previous analyses, these attacks occurred in every month of the year, with the fewest number of attacks occurring during the wet summer months.[30] Almost no attacks were reported to have occurred on rainy days, a fact that can be logically explained due to increased cloud cover making it difficult to find villages from the air and the idea that rain might wash away or dilute any alleged agent.

Assessment

Much of the data related to reported attacks comes from accounts offered by refugees and defectors, who may have had ulterior motives behind their reporting that might lead one to question the validity of their accounts. On the other hand, the vast number of individuals who came forward with attack information, in addition to the vast geographic differences in the location of these refugees, the number of accounts from young children, and the similarities in reports from individuals interviewed separately all lend credibility to the accuracy of the data. Many occurred at the time of military movements in the region, as supported by signal intercepts and imagery, and at least a third of the reported attacks are corroborated by more than one source of information.

Intelligence Links and Attribution

Laos, Cambodia, and Afghanistan all had in common a link to the Soviet Union. In Laos, the Pathet Lao and Vietnamese forces were directly supported by the USSR; the Soviet-supported Vietnamese were the alleged offenders in Cambodia; and in Afghanistan, the Soviets were directly involved in the war. In addition to these coincidental involvements of the Soviets in alleged CW conflict areas and defector accounts of Soviet involvement with chemical weapons in Laos, there was strong intelligence linking a mycotoxin research lab in the Soviet Union with the application of yellow mist from helicopters in Afghanistan, with a laboratory in Cambodia, and with a yellow substance loaded into Pathet Lao planes in Laos.[31] Such evidence and circumstances lead to the very strong suspicion, although not proof, that if chemical/toxin weapons were used in Laos, Cambodia, and Afghanistan, the Soviet Union was the force behind it—providing agent and supervising use.

Other Investigations, Conclusions, and Controversy

The Yellow Rain investigation was primarily a U.S. government operation, although the United Nations and independent researchers also looked into the allegations. Additionally, several other nations conducted their own investigations, often in secret. Few of these nations went public with their findings, particularly during the time of the investigation, and even privately, most were wary of sharing information. Their findings, however, are significant in the overall Yellow Rain investigation, and would have significantly added to the international debate.

Individual Nations

Canada was the only other country besides the United States to declare its investigation and findings publicly. It published several documents pertaining to the investigation, and openly shared its methodologies and findings with the international community. Canada found trichothecene mycotoxin in samples from alleged attack sites, but it also found positive biomedical samples in 5 out of 250 controls from Thailand.[32] A thorough epidemiologic investigation led the Canadians to conclude that a 1982 attack on the Thai village of Ban Sa Tong resulted in the illness of 21 individuals, with the common source of the illness being the yellow powder that covered parts of the village. The symptoms were not consistent with an allergic response from pollen, which as discussed below is an alternative hypothesis for the origins of Yellow Rain.[33] They also reported that while natural trichothecene producers exist in Southeast Asia, the amount of trichothecenes found in environmental samples and the disease presentation in the victims was not consistent with a natural occurrence.[34] They did not go so far, however, as to conclude that the trichothecenes were from a weapon.

The British collected their own biomedical and environmental samples from attack sites in Laos and Cambodia, yet the findings from their studies are controversial. Officially, the British government concluded in 1982 that there was a strong presumption that mycotoxins were being used as a weapon in Southeast Asia, and that it was very unlikely that the findings of trichothecene mycotoxins in the samples were due to natural contamination.[35] More recent public statements about the UK's Yellow Rain findings contradict this statement and a 1986 report issued by the British government stated that the analysis of a number of

environmental and biomedical samples had yielded negative results for mycotoxins.[36] Some government officials who worked on the Yellow Rain investigation confirm this 1986 report and claim never to have found mycotoxins in the
samples.[37]

According to primarily U.S. government sources, France, West Germany,
and China all supported the Yellow Rain mycotoxin hypothesis, although none
went public with their findings.[38] Several other nations looked into Yellow Rain,
including Australia, Norway, Sweden, Denmark, Israel, South Africa, Japan, and
Thailand. According to the Asian Lawyers Legal Inquiry on Alleged Violations
of Human Rights in Kampuchea and Laos, The Royal Thai Army issued a report of findings regarding the use of chemicals in Kampuchea, and concluded
that attacks had, in fact, taken place.[39]

The UN Group of Experts and Other Investigations

In December 1980, acting upon the request of the United States, the United
Nations General Assembly passed Resolution 35/144C, authorizing the formation of the Group of Experts to investigate allegations of CBW use in Southeast
Asia and Afghanistan. Neither Laos nor Cambodia allowed the UN Group to
enter its territory, so the investigation was focused instead on interviewing alleged survivors in Thailand and Pakistan, and collecting some environmental
and biomedical samples for analysis. The investigation was reportedly marred
by the attitude of the Group of Experts toward the refugees, said to be insult-
ing and frustrating to those trying to share their experiences.[40] There were also
problems in that samples from the team's first trip to Thailand were tampered
with, rendering the analysis useless.[41]

The UN Group of Experts completed its investigation in December 1982.
Although the group heard accounts of attacks and found trichothecene mycotoxins in biomedical samples from alleged victims, there were logistical challenges, a lack of capacity to distinguish between natural and unnatural exposure to trichothecenes, and questions about the veracity of the statements given
by alleged victims. These difficulties led the UN group to state that it could not
prove that chemical or toxin attacks had taken place, but that "it could not disregard the circumstantial evidence suggestive of the possible use of some sort
of toxin chemical substance in some instances."[42]

Individual researchers also attempted to discern if Yellow Rain was indeed due to CBW attacks, or if there was another explanation. An alternative hypothesis proposed by Matthew Meselson and his colleagues suggested that the "Yellow Rain" reported by the Hmong and Khmer was actually a naturally occurring phenomenon involving swarms of Asian honeybees defecating en masse.[43] This hypothesis was reached after reviewing laboratory analysis of environmental samples for presence of pollen and conducting field investigations designed to search for evidence of bee-cleansing flights in Thailand. Details regarding the findings of this investigation and subsequent conclusions can be found in Chapter 4 of this volume by Meselson and Robinson.

Assessment

Writing in the *Wall Street Journal* about Yellow Rain, Paul Gigot recounted a joke then current in the diplomatic community: "What is the best way to keep an international secret? Answer—have the United Nations and the United States investigate it. The cautious UN won't find the answer and no one will believe the U.S."[44] An investigation into CBW use that intends to demonstrate violations of international law and sway international opinion may require multinational cooperation. Investigations performed by one nation alone might not be trusted in the international community, while investigations conducted by the UN may be subject to the politics of the conflict region. In the Yellow Rain investigation, multiple nations chose to perform their own separate investigations, in part because each nation may have felt the need to develop an independent assessment of the event. The effect, however, was to have multiple nations holding bits of evidence and not contributing findings into an overall global assessment of the allegations.

Investigative Challenges

The difficulty in reaching a conclusive finding on all aspects of the Yellow Rain investigation derives in part from the multiple challenges facing the U.S. investigative team. Many of the problems derived from confusion, trying things for the first time (given that this was the first investigation of this type by the United States), the state of technology, and a lack of organizational commitment. It is important to note that none of the errors in the investigation appear to have been made deliberately or with ill will.

In addition to the problems of sample handling, baseline data, and lack of appropriate sample controls, the Yellow Rain investigation faced other trials. One of the primary challenges of the investigation was timeliness. Long periods of time passed between the alleged exposure to an attack and presentation of the victim or other supporting evidence to the investigative team, from a few days in the best of circumstances to several weeks.

Further delays took place in the laboratories: a sample might be examined right away, or might be left waiting for months or even years. The problem was particularly acute in government labs, which often halted analysis due to lack of funding, or let the samples sit while a methodology was developed. The delays between collection and analysis are important because the ability to detect trichothecenes in small amounts greatly diminishes over time, particularly if the sample is not properly stored.[45] Even when the samples had been analyzed, there were questions about the reliability of the results, mostly due to the fact that laboratory analysis techniques at that time were less sophisticated than they are today. In addition, since so few labs in the United States had the capacity to perform accurate tests, it was difficult to replicate results in multiple laboratories.

The Yellow Rain investigators also struggled with maintaining a proper chain of custody between the collection site and the arrival of a sample in the United States. There was no way to document the validity of environmental samples brought out of Laos or Cambodia, or from exactly where they were taken. There is no documentation addressing how secure the samples were once in Bangkok, and the time samples spent on a plane in transport could not be accounted for by specific individuals.

Although future investigators might have been able to shed new light on the sample analysis program, the samples from the Yellow Rain investigation were destroyed. In fact, requests by government labs to destroy the biomedical and environmental samples began almost as soon as they were collected. By the end of the 1980s, all of the samples collected as part of the Yellow Rain sample analysis program had been destroyed, making further analysis impossible.

The collection of health data was impeded by several factors. Hostilities in the region made it difficult to reach alleged attack sites and communicate with surrounding populations. Formal protocols for field investigators were lacking and there were possible problems with interview techniques. Although officials in Southeast Asia repeatedly requested a questionnaire to guide interviews, it took over a year for a form to be developed by experts in Washington and transmitted back to the field.[46] This lack of coordination and overall confusion derived from interagency battles over who would be in charge of the investigation. The Department of State and Department of Defense fought over which would be in charge, and neither department ever informed the Ambassador and attaché office at the Embassy in Bangkok to treat the Yellow Rain investigation as a priority, so resources were kept to a minimum.[47] Eventually an interagency group led by the CIA was established to coordinate efforts and findings, establishing formal responsibilities for the investigation. In 1983, a Science and Technology Advisory Panel reviewed the interagency group and the investigation as a whole, and recommended that additional funding and personnel be dedicated to the investigation, but neither funding nor personnel was increased.

Funding was the most pressing concern for the duration of the investigation, and became the reason for its cessation in 1986. The lack of funding touched every aspect of the investigation, from the collection of intelligence and medical data to the transportation of samples and the laboratory analysis. Downtimes of two to three months occurred when agencies depleted their funds and had to find alternative monies either from other agencies or through internal reprogramming.[48] On several occasions, sample analysis at government labs was halted for months at a time due to lack of funds, making timely analysis impossible.

Conclusions

Taking into account the newly released evidence on Yellow Rain along with all the previously published and available data, it appears the evidence most strongly supports the hypothesis that CBW attacks occurred in Southeast Asia and Afghanistan. The evidence, however, is not strong enough to definitively answer questions regarding the composition of the agent, the intent of use, or whether the agent originated in the former Soviet Union. As a result, more than twenty-five years after the initial reports, there is still a vigorous debate over whether chemical/toxin weapons attacks ever occurred in Southeast Asia and Afghanistan during this time, and over who the perpetrators and suppliers of such attacks may have been.

One of the larger unresolved issues raised by the Yellow Rain investigation is the level to which it is important to coordinate with experts in academia and industry, particularly where government expertise is limited. During the Yellow Rain investigation, academic laboratories with proven analytic capabilities were utilized primarily because the government was not capable of performing the needed sample analysis in a timely and accurate fashion. Although government experts have identified biological, chemical, and toxin agents likely to be used in a CBW attack, and have focused much of their research effort on tools to address those agents, a CBW attack might involve an agent not on the list, or an agent for which the government has not developed analytical expertise. Therefore contingency plans should be in place for a rapid response that swiftly engages the best academic and industry experts for any suspected agent or chemical. Reaching out to the academic community ahead of time could improve the reliability of some sample analyses, and increase the credibility of those results with the greater public.

The Yellow Rain episode also suggests that non-governmental organizations can provide important information regarding allegations of CBW use. NGOs and individual physicians contributed to the Yellow Rain investigation; some viewed alleged CBW use to be both a criminal issue and a human rights violation, while for others, it became a personal crusade to figure out what was happening to affected refugees. NGO volunteers, particularly those who provide medical and refugee-relief services around the world, are often well informed about the health, welfare, and political situation of a target population. Some NGO workers, particularly in refugee camps, spend years or even a lifetime working with a specific population. Others, who arrive when situations are most acute, have vast refugee and disaster medical experience. Their expertise could be extremely valuable during a CBW investigation, when medical information and background data on the health of the population must be collected and culturally competent professionals are needed to make interviews with alleged victims more comprehensive and reliable.

Not all NGOs or their workers may be willing or able to assist in a CBW investigation to the same degree: NGOs have often distanced themselves from public involvement with CBW allegations. Any involvement in the investigation, whether political by nature or not, may risk being perceived as a political maneuver, regardless of an NGO's or an individual's intentions. A political reputation might inhibit the ability of an organization or person to operate in a given environment, preventing them from rendering assistance to a population in need. Given these obstacles, it is still important to try to obtain cooperation from the NGO community, because of the valuable expertise and credibility they can bring to a situation.

Lastly, Yellow Rain raises important questions about the collection of data that might be necessary for an attribution assessment. No definitive proof is yet available that conclusively answers questions about identification, characterization, or attribution of Yellow Rain. A former Soviet or Vietnamese official might have definitive knowledge of whether attacks occurred, and if so, the composition of the agent. Documentation might yet be found in closed Soviet archives. Such evidence may be the only way to settle the Yellow Rain questions. Improvements in data collection and the conduct of the investigation could, however, at least have narrowed the room for controversy.

It can be argued that all data collected in an investigation are useful in some fashion, but particular information is needed to make a political judgment and hold a nation or organization responsible. And while every investigation will be different, there are some pieces of evidence that should always be sought. The ability to differentiate between naturally occurring disease and morbidity and mortality from an intentional attack is essential. Investigators need good baseline data on the health of a population and ongoing surveillance to determine whether a disease is endemic or epidemic. Biomedical samples should be collected from both victims and well-matched controls, and environmental samples should be taken both from regions reported to be affected and from control areas. Analysis of the samples should be conducted as quickly as possible. Initial examination of samples should be conducted on site, followed by analysis in internationally certified laboratories. Whenever possible, samples should be analyzed simultaneously by several independent laboratories.

Medical records of alleged victims should be obtained. Culturally sensitive, non-leading questionnaires should be used to conduct timely interviews with witnesses and to make the interviews comprehensive and useful. Evidence to be collected should include any munitions fragments, affected vegetation, and affected animals in alleged attack regions, as airborne release of an agent will almost always affect more than just humans. Evidence of an actual weapon would greatly contribute to a successful investigation.

Seldom will an investigation into allegations of use be conducted in a perfect environment with perfect information. There will almost always be ambiguities that affect the ability of the investigator to reach an attribution assessment.

Given these inherent difficulties, policymakers will always have to determine how much evidence is sufficient in order to reach a decision on use, assign attribution, and enforce compliance.

Notes

The views expressed in this chapter are those of the author, and do not represent the official view of the Department of State or the United States Government.

1. Over 8,529 pages of U.S. government documents were declassified by the Defense Intelligence Agency (DIA) and released to the author through a Freedom of Information Act request on December 23, 2003. The declassification numbers in these notes are those assigned by DIA.

2. Sections of this chapter were previously published as part of the author's doctoral dissertation: Rebecca L. Katz, "Yellow Rain Revisited: Lesson Learned for the Investigation of Chemical and Biological Weapons Allegations," Princeton University, 2005.

3. Letter from Francis Terry McNamara, Acting Assistant Secretary for Public Affairs, to Thomas Bush, private citizen, October 1, 1981, reprinted in Hearing before the Subcommittee on Arms Control, Oceans, International Operations and Environment of the Committee on Foreign Relations, U.S. Senate, 97th Cong. 1st sess., " 'Yellow Rain' and Other Forms of Chemical and Biological Warfare in Asia," November 10, 1981; William Safire, "Essay: Yellow Rain," *New York Times,* December 13, 1979, A31.

4. The U.S. Army Medical Intelligence and Information Center (USAMIIA) was renamed the Armed Forces Medical Intelligence Center (AFMIC) in 1982. The Foreign Science Technology Center (FSTC) was renamed the United States Army National Ground Intelligence Center (NGIC) in 1995.

5. Bernard Gwertzman, "U.S. Says Data Show Toxin Use in Asia Conflict: Haig, in Berlin Speech, Suggests Pact Violation," *New York Times,* September 14, 1981, A1.

6. Department of State, "Chemical Warfare in Southeast Asia and Afghanistan, report to the Congress from Secretary of State Alexander M. Haig, Jr.," March 22, 1982, Special Report no. 98, cited hereafter as "Haig Report"; Department of State, "Chemical Warfare in Southeast Asia and Afghanistan: An Update," report to the Congress from Secretary of State George P. Shultz, November 1982, Special Report no. 104, cited hereafter as "Shultz Report."

7. Shultz Report.

8. Shultz Report; Haig Report; Department of State, "Reports of the Use of Chemical Weapons in Afghanistan, Laos and Kampuchea," Washington, DC, 1980; Department of State, "Update to the Compendium on the Reports of the Use of Chemical Weapons," Washington, DC, 1981.

9. U.S. President, President's Report to Congress, "Soviet Noncompliance with Arms Control Agreements," January 23, 1984, Washington, DC.

10. The full collection of these documents can be accessed in the supplemental documents of the following article: Rebecca Katz and Burton Singer, "Can an Attribution Assessment Be Made for Yellow Rain? Systematic Reanalysis in a Chemical and Biological Weapons Use Investigation," *Politics and the Life Sciences* 26(1) (August 24, 2007): 24–42. Available at <http://www.politicsandthelifesciences.org/contents/subscribers/contents-2007-3/poll-26-01-05_24-42_supplemental_documents/>.

11. Armed Forces Medical Intelligence Center (AFMIC), "Status Summary" (Handwritten tables), (undated), document declassified by DIA December 2003, Declassification no. 152651.

12. Armed Forces Medical Intelligence Center, Subject: Compilation of CW Use Data, July 5, 1985, declassified by DIA December 2003, Declassification Number 152534.

13. DIA/AFMIC Response to Questions from Senate Foreign Relations Committee, declassified by DIA December 2003, Declassification Number 159216.

14. R. T. Rosen and J. D. Rosen, "Presence of Four Fusarium, Mycotoxins and Synthetic Material in 'Yellow Rain': Evidence for Use of Chemical Weapons in Laos," *Biomed Mass Spectrom.* 9, no. 10 (1982): 443–50.

15. Confirmation of laboratory results was disputed in Julian Robinson, Jeanne Guillemin, and Matthew Meselson, "Yellow Rain: The Story Collapses," *Foreign Policy* no. 68 (Fall 1987): 100–117. Evidence of confirmation, however, is derived from the newly declassified documents.

16. L. Ember, "Yellow Rain," *Chemical & Engineering News*, January 9, 1984.

17. S. A. Watson, C. J. Mirocha, and A. W. Hayes, "Analysis for Trichothecenes in Samples from Southeast Asia Associatedwith 'Yellow Rain,'" *Fundam. Appl. Toxicol.* 4, 700–717.

18. Armed Forces Medical Intelligence Center, Timeline for Analysis, [undated], document declassified by DIA December 2003, Declassification Number 152651.

19. Council for Agricultural Science and Technology, *Mycotoxins: Risks in Plant, Animal, and Human Systems* (Ames, Iowa, 2003); H. Schiefer, "The Possible Use of Chemical Warfare Agents in Southeast Asia," *Conflict Quarterly* 3 (2003), 32–41.

20. Personal communication from A. Desjardins, United States Department of Agriculture, August 2003.

21. J. W. Bennet, M. Klich, "Mycotoxins," *Clinical Microbiology Reviews* 16 (2003): 497–516.

22. D. Sudakin, "Trichothecenes in the Environment: Relevance to Human Health," *Toxicology Letters* 143, no. 2 (2003): 97–107.

23. A. E. Desjardins, "Trichothecenes: From Yellow Rain to Green Wheat," *ASM News* 69, no. 4 (2003): 182–85.

24. Personal communication from C. Mirocha, July 2003.

25. Unfortunately, both sets of original medical records from the Ban Vinai refugee camp originally held by World Vision have disappeared. This disappearance was first noted when the United Nations team visited the camp and requested access to the hospital records.

26. A. Crossland, D. Hulcher, and R. Harruff, "Preliminary Report of Questionnaire: Evaluation of Hmong Accounts of Possible CW Activity in Laos," January 1984.

27. Crossland, Hulcher, and Harruff, "Preliminary Report of Questionnaire: Evaluation of Hmong Accounts of Possible CW Activity in Laos."

28. Katz, "Yellow Rain Revisited," chapter 5, discussion of analysis using differential diagnosis software to rule out natural occurrence of disease.

29. Katz, "Yellow Rain Revisited," chapter 5: discussion of attack data.

30. The fact that the reported attacks occurred at all seasons of the year is not consistent with the bee theory discussed in Robinson, Guillemin, and Meselson, "Yellow Rain: The Story Collapses"; the naturally occurring event of bees defecating en masse in a "Yellow Rain" only occurs during particular times of the year.

31. Personal communication from C. Green, November 2002 and July 2003; Armed Forces Medical Intelligence Center, 1984, "Yellow Rain—Separating Fact from Fiction," ACSI Task: 84-056, June 18, 1984, declassified by DIA December 2003, Declassification number 152651, pp. 58–102 (cited hereafter as AFMIC, "Yellow Rain").

32. AFMIC, "Yellow Rain"; G. R. Humphreys, and J. Dow, "An Epidemiological Investigation of Alleged CW/BW Incidents in SE Asia," prepared by Directorate of Preventive Medicine, Surgeon General Branch, National Defence Headquarters, Ottawa, 1982.

33. W. Kucewicz, "Canada's Other 'Yellow Rain' Findings," *Wall Street Journal*, August 25, 1986, section 1, p. 20.

34. Humphreys and Dow, "An Epidemiological Investigation of Alleged CW/BW Incidents in SE Asia."

35. AFMIC, "Yellow Rain"; Written Answer by Lord Belstead, Minister of State, Foreign and Commonwealth Office, to a Parliamentary Question by Lord Hylton, June 7, 1982, *Hansard*, Lords, vol. 431, col. 92, as cited in Elisa Harris, "Sverdlovsk and Yellow Rain: Two Cases of Soviet Noncompliance?" *International Security* 11, no. 4 (Spring 1987): 41–95.

36. House of Commons, Official Report, Parliamentary Debates (Hansard), vol. 98, no. 117, Written Answers to Questions, Monday May 19, 1986.

37. Thomas D. Inch, Oral Evidence Taken before the Foreign Affairs Committee, UK Parliament, June 18, 2003, <www.publications.parliament.uk/pa/cm200203/cmselect/cmfaff/uc813-iii/uc81302.htm>, accessed May 2, 2006; personal communication from T. D. Inch, July 13, 2006, London.

38. U.S. Congress, Senate Committee on Foreign Relations, 79, Statement by Ster-

ling Seagrave; Foreign Broadcast Information Service (FBIS), AFP: Thailand, "French Diplomats Cited on Mycotoxic Evidence," Hong Kong AFP in English, January 26, 1983; AFMIC, "Yellow Rain"; Asian-Lawyers Legal Inquiry Committee on Alleged Violations of Human Rights in Kampuchea and Laos, Bangkok, Thailand, June 4–11, 1982; personal communication from C. Green, February 2003.

39. Asian-Lawyers Legal Inquiry Committee on Alleged Violations of Human Rights in Kampuchea and Laos, Bangkok, Thailand, June 4–11, 1982.

40. U.S. Congress, Senate Committee on Foreign Relations, 106; J. Hamilton-Merritt, *Tragic Mountains: The Hmong, the Americans, and the Secret Wars for Laos, 1942–1992* (Bloomington: Indiana University Press, 1999), 436.

41. United Nations, *Citation of Chemical and Bacteriological (Biological) Weapons: Report of the Secretary General*, November 20, 1982, Agenda Item no. 42, A/36/613; personal communication from G. Crocker, winter 2002–3.

42. United Nations, *Chemical and Bacteriological (Biological) Weapons: Report of the Secretary General*, December 1, 1982, Agenda Item 54, A/37/259.

43. T. D. Seeley, J. W. Nowicke, M. Meselson, J. Guillemin, P. Akratanakul, "Yellow Rain," *Scientific American* 253, no. 3 (1985): 128–37.

44. Paul Gigot, "Is the United States Crying Wolf on Yellow Rain, or Is Everyone Else Ignoring Evidence?" *Wall Street Journal*, December 14, 1982.

45. Personal communication from C. Mirocha, July 2003; personal communication from A. Desjardins, United States Department of Agriculture, August 2003.

46. U.S. Defense Attaché Office Bangkok, message to Defense Intelligence Agency and others, subject: "Chemical Warfare," 290308Z January 1981, declassified document Number 152540; U.S. Army Medical Intelligence Information Agency, message to U.S. Defense Attaché Office Bangkok, subject: "Chemical Warfare," 191730Z January 1981, declassified document Number 152540; U.S. Defense Attaché Office Bangkok, message to USAMIIA and others, subject: "Chemical Warfare," 200200Z December 1980, Declassified document Number 152540.

47. Sterling Seagrave, "Yellow Rain's Year: 'Like Laughing at Guernica,'" *Wall Street Journal*, 1982, 30.

48. C. Stettner, Stettner Committee Report and Recommendations, CW/toxin sample analysis program, August 23, 1984, declassified April 2003.

CHAPTER SIX

False Allegations of U.S. Biological Weapons Use During the Korean War

MILTON LEITENBERG

The first charge that the United States had used biological weapons (BW) during the Korean War was made on May 8, 1951, by North Korea (the Democratic Republic of North Korea, or DPRK).[1] In a cable to the president of the United Nations Security Council, the DPRK's Minister of Foreign Affairs claimed that the United States had used BW between December 1950 and January 1951. In early 1952, the DPRK, China, and the USSR initiated a much larger campaign of BW allegations against the United States. U.S. government officials explicitly rejected the charges in absolute terms on repeated occasions. In fact, these biological warfare allegations were contrived and fraudulent, as documents obtained from former Soviet archives in January 1998 show, explicitly and in detail. Nevertheless, the propaganda campaign had wide international resonance at the time.

This chapter reviews the charges and then details the international response and its shortcomings and missed opportunities to rebut the charges. It offers a retrospective assessment of the charges, and draws lessons of the case for future potentially false or fabricated allegations. It is important to understand who was responsible for conceiving and carrying out these fabricated charges: the USSR, China, or both? Because the charges were concocted, the book's framework of "identification, characterization, and attribution" is applied in a somewhat modified manner. Since putative "evidence" was planted and publicized internationally, the credibility of that "evidence" is examined. Given that the DPRK, China, and the USSR refused to permit field investigation of the charges by any international body, the key question becomes: what might have been done at the time that could have more clearly rebutted the charges?

The Charges

The North Koreans charged in May 1951 that the United States had spread smallpox in North Korea.[2] Then, on February 22, 1952, Bak Hun Yung, North Korea's Foreign Minister, issued another official statement addressed to the UN Secretariat claiming that the United States had carried out air drops of infected insects of several kinds bearing plague, cholera, and other diseases over North Korean territory on two occasions in late January and on five days in mid-February 1952.[3] Two days later, Zhou Enlai, the Foreign Minister of the People's Republic of China (PRC), publicly endorsed the North Korean charges. On March 8, Zhou Enlai enlarged the accusations against the United States, charging that the United States had sent 448 aircraft on no fewer than 68 occasions between February 29 and March 5 into Northeast China to air-drop germ-carrying insects.[4]

As shown in a chronology in two Chinese government documents, on February 18, 1952, Marshal Nie Rongzhen, Head of the General Staff Department of the People's Liberation Army, had reported to the Military Affairs Committee (Mao Zedong, Zhu De, Liu Shaoqi, and Lin Biao) that the United States was dropping flies, fleas, and spiders infected with bacteria (a claim he repeated on February 28).[5] Mao replied to the first message: "Premier Zhou should pay more attention to it and handle it."[6]

The human diseases in the allegations were plague, anthrax, cholera, encephalitis, and a form of meningitis. The spread of animal and plant diseases was also alleged, including fowl septicemia and 11 incidents involving four different plant diseases. Eighteen different species of insects and arachnids (spiders and ticks), as well as some small rodents, were alleged to have been used as the disease vectors. Infected clams, paper and cloth packages, various kinds of earthenware, and metallic "leaflet bombs"—containers—were alleged to have been the dispersion media.[7] It was winter in the area, and the insects and some other materials were reportedly found on top of the snow. China and North

Korea both also claimed that the United States had carried out BW experiments on North Korean and Chinese People's Volunteers (CPV) prisoners of war.

The Chinese and North Korean governments made use of three commissions to buttress their allegations. The first was the International Association of Democratic Lawyers (hereafter referred to as the Lawyers' Commission).[8] It sent a delegation to North Korea (March 5–19, 1952) immediately after the main BW accusations were made, and then to China (March 20–31). Its first report, issued in Beijing on March 31, claimed that the United States had used chemical weapons as well as bacterial weapons. Its second report, issued in Beijing on April 2, charged the United States with violations of the Geneva Protocol of 1925 and the Genocide Convention of 1948. These reports—alleging twenty-two BW incidents—appear to have been intended as a formal war crimes indictment.[9]

The Chinese government's own investigating commission concluded with an even more explicit accusation of war crimes in a report issued April 7, 1952.[10] This commission had only been organized a few weeks earlier, on March 15, 1952. It appears that this body gathered all of the evidence (materials and testimony) that was considered by the third group to investigate, the International Scientific Commission for the Investigation of the Facts Concerning Bacterial Warfare in Korea and China (ISC). The ISC was convened by the communist-oriented World Peace Council because, averred the Chinese representative to the World Peace Council, neither the International Committee of the Red Cross (ICRC) nor the World Health Organization (WHO) were "sufficiently free from political influence to be capable of instituting an unbiased enquiry in the field."[11]

The ISC was chaired by Dr. Joseph Needham, a well-known British scientist who was also an avowed Marxist. Needham had headed the British Scientific Mission in China from 1942 to 1946, when he had served as an advisor to the Chinese Army (Kuomintang) Medical Administration, and had participated in an investigation of Japanese use of BW in China during World War II (discussed by Jeanne Guillemin in Chapter 8 in this volume). The ISC was present in North Korea and China from June 23 to August 31, 1952. It published a massive 330,000 word, 669-page volume in Beijing in 1952, with extensive background information on entomology, vectors, pathogens, epidemiology, and so forth. All this information was prepared by and presented to the ISC by the

Chinese commission. The ISC alleged fifty BW incidents, which were distinct from the 22 incidents reported by the Lawyers' Commission. By contrast, the Chinese media and the Chinese government reported over eleven hundred BW incidents.

The ISC report claimed that the United States had used organisms causing five human diseases: anthrax, plague, meningitis, cholera, and encephalitis (but not smallpox, which had been the first North Korean allegation in May 1951). It also alleged U.S. spread of an animal disease, fowl septicemia, along with eleven incidents of four different plant diseases involving soy beans and fruit trees. It claimed that the United States had used 18 species of arachnids as vectors, as well as infected clams, plant materials, and voles dying of plague. Among the alleged delivery systems were a World War II device of a type used by the Japanese, a pottery container, and non-explosive metal containers used for massive leaflet drops from the air.

Chinese testimony to the ISC alleged many "anomalies": in the location, the numbers, the seasons, or the combinations of insect species that were found. Chinese testimony reported by the ISC claimed that there had been no previous epidemics of disease X or Y, or no incidence of the disease at all in the area in question. However, the testimony reported few (in the tens) or no casualties at all, allegedly to avoid supplying intelligence to the United States.[12]

U.S. and International Response

The USSR pressed the Chinese and North Korean BW allegations against the United States at the United Nations in the General Assembly, in the Security Council, and in the UN Disarmament Commission. The U.S. and UN responses are examined here, including the denials made by U.S. and UN officials; the proposals for international investigation of the BW charges; and what actual U.S. BW policies and capabilities were at the time.

Denials by U.S. Government Officials

There apparently was no official U.S. response to the first North Korean allegation in May 1951. The United States did, however, issue denials within days of the North Korean and Chinese charges at the end of February 1952. The first denial was made by the U.S. Far East Command in Tokyo, on February

27, 1952.[13] On March 4, 1952, U.S. Secretary of State Dean Acheson stated "categorically and unequivocally that these charges are entirely false; the UN forces have not used, are not using, any sort of bacteriological warfare."[14] Secretary Acheson repeated his denial on March 11 and March 26, 1952. General Matthew Ridgeway, Commander of the UN military forces in Korea, also denied the charges in mid-March, adding, "These charges are evidently designed to conceal the Communists' inability to cope with the spread of epidemics which occur annually throughout China and North Korea and to care properly for the many victims."[15] In an address to the U.S. Congress on May 22, 1952, Ridgeway stated that "no element of the United Nations Command has employed either germ or gas warfare in any form at any time."[16]

These denials were repeated in various statements by members of the U.S. delegation to the United Nations from April to June 1952. There was also a denial by the U.S. Secretary of Defense before July 1, 1952. On March 14, 1953—after the Soviet representative to the UN introduced the bacterial warfare charges into the work of the UN Disarmament Commission—U.S. delegate Benjamin Cohen repeated the American denials.[17] When the Soviet delegation distributed the "confessions" of captured U.S. pilots in the UN General Assembly's First Committee (Disarmament and International Security), General Omar Bradley, Chairman of the U.S. Joint Chiefs of Staff, submitted a denial on March 25, 1953, seconded by the commanding officers of the Marine Air Wings to which the pilots had belonged.[18] On behalf of the United Nations, Secretary General Trygve Lie also denied the allegations.[19]

Proposals for International Investigation of the BW Charges

The U.S. government immediately requested, in the United Nations, an on-site investigation by a competent international organization. In his first statement on March 4, 1952, Acheson asked the accusing nations to permit an investigation by the International Committee of the Red Cross (ICRC), and a week later, Acheson requested the ICRC to conduct an investigation.[20] Within 24 hours, the ICRC applied to China and North Korea to request their cooperation. The government of India offered to assist. The ICRC proposed to send a small team composed of three Swiss members, two Indians, and a Pakistani. The ICRC sent the same request again on March 28 and on March 31. The last time, on April 10, it stated that if it received no reply by April 20, it would consider its proposal rejected, and having received no direct reply from China or North Korea, on April 30 the ICRC terminated its effort.[21] The only reply in a UN forum came on March 26, when the Soviet delegate rejected the ICRC offer. China did respond indirectly: in *New China News Agency* broadcasts in March and April, it called the ICRC "a most vicious and shameless accomplice and lackey of American imperialism."[22]

On three occasions during March 1952, UN Secretary General Trygve Lie transmitted an offer by the World Health Organization to assist North Korea and China to control disease epidemics in North Korea. After a month without replying, China and North Korea rejected the offer. By April 1952, several UN member states urged the United States to ask the UN to conduct its own investigation, and also to bring the issue to the UN Security Council, which the United States did in June–July 1952. In 1952, Indian Prime Minister Jawaharlal Nehru privately suggested to China that it accept an impartial investigation of its BW charges against the United States, but China did not reply. China claimed that the only purpose of an ICRC or WHO investigation would be the collection of intelligence to evaluate the effectiveness of germ warfare.[23]

In July 1952, the United States took the issue of an ICRC investigation to the UN Security Council. It submitted a draft resolution calling for the ICRC to carry out an investigation and to report to the UN. The Security Council vote was 10 in favor but the Soviet Union vetoed it.[24] The United States then submitted a second draft resolution which proposed that "the Security Council would conclude from the refusal of the governments and authorities making the charges to permit impartial investigation that these charges must be presumed to be without substance and false; and would condemn the practice of fabricating and disseminating such false charges." The vote was nine in favor, one abstention, but the resolution again fell to a Soviet veto. During extensive debate in the UN General Assembly and in the UN Disarmament Commissions in 1952 and 1953, various governments offered their opinions.[25] Throughout these debates, the USSR kept pressing the point that the United States had never ratified the Geneva Protocol—which prohibits the use of biological weapons—and repeatedly called on the United States to do so (the United States did not, however, ratify it until 1975).

The United States made one last attempt at the UN to obtain an investigation. On April 8, 1953, the Political Committee of the UN General Assembly approved a U.S. proposal to institute a commission of investigation. On April 23, the UN General Assembly accepted the U.S. proposal by a vote of 51 for, 5 against, and 4 abstaining. Representatives to the commission from Brazil, Egypt, Pakistan, Sweden, and Uruguay were proposed, and all reported their willingness to serve. However, due to the refusal of assistance from the PRC and North Korea, on July 28 the president of the UN General Assembly reported that the commission was unable to accomplish its task.

U.S. BW Policies and Capabilities at the Time of the Korean War

U.S. policy on BW use had been promulgated in NSC 62 on February 1, 1950, months before the Korean War began. It stated that "chemical, biological and radiological weapons will not be used by the United States except in retaliation."[26] This policy remained in force throughout the Korean War and was confirmed, word for word, in NSC 147, on April 2, 1953, which stated that it "appl[ied] to U.N. operations, 1952–1953."[27] These national policy determinations were, however, not publicly disclosed. The policy was not changed until March 15, 1956, when NSC 5062/1 permitted first use of chemical or biological weapons by U.S. military forces, but only with presidential approval.

Evidence that there was no violation of these NSC policies during the Korean War includes President Harry Truman's reply to a letter by Congressman Robert Kastenmeier dated July 25, 1969: "I wish to state categorically that I did not amend any Presidential order in force regarding biological weapons nor did I at any time give my approval to its use."[28] Supporting this conclusion is an affidavit that Brigadier General H. Hillyard, Secretary to the Joint Chiefs of Staff, provided as evidence during a trial in April 1959, stating that "after a diligent search no record or entry has been found to exist in the records of the Joint Chiefs of Staff which discloses that the President or any authority superior to the Secretary of Defense, acting at the discretion of the President, did therein at any time, either expressly or impliedly direct, authorize, consent to, or permit any Armed Force, or any element thereof, to use or employ any form of toxic chemical warfare or biological warfare during the period above stated."[29]

The historical record clearly shows that after 1945, the United States neither produced nor procured any biological munitions until the end of 1951. Then, the United States produced wheat rust, an anti-plant agent meant for use against the wheat crops of the USSR.[30] It cannot produce any human disease, and neither China nor North Korea ever alleged that the United States had dispersed this agent. The second BW agent that the United States produced was a human pathogen, but it was not ready until the end of 1954, long after the Korean War was over. It was for the organism *Brucella suis,* which produces the incapacitating disease brucellosis, but brucellosis was not one of the diseases that China or North Korea ever charged the United States with spreading.[31]

Assessment of the BW Allegations

The allegations do not stand up, scientifically or historically. First, historical documentation clearly demonstrates that all of the diseases that the Chinese and North Koreans alleged were introduced by the United States, including smallpox, were endemic to the area at the time. During the Korean War, units of the Chinese People's Volunteers and the Korean People's Army (KPA) routinely suffered from typhus, cholera, and dysentery. En route to North Korea, the CPV forces had transited Manchuria, an area in which plague had been endemic for many preceding centuries. United Nations forces, as well as North Korean and Chinese combatants, also suffered from the viral disease Korean Hemorrhagic Fever. In the late winter of 1950 and the early spring of 1951, smallpox and typhus were reported throughout Korea, both north and south.

The UN command responded with mass inoculations and heavy applications of DDT to individuals, and DDT aerial spraying to the countryside at large. The United Nations carried out a massive public-health and vaccination program during the Korean War. Eighteen million people were vaccinated against typhoid fever, 16 million against typhus, 15 million against smallpox, and 2 million against cholera. Mortality in the south due to these diseases was 15,000–30,000 per month (around 270,000 per year) before the vaccination campaign; after the vaccination campaign, it fell to just 40–70 per month (660 per year).[32]

In the north, thousands of Chinese healthcare workers were dispatched to the area behind the front lines, and Hungarian and East German volunteer hospital units also went to North Korea to handle the outbreaks. Soviet anti-epidemic teams had been working in Manchuria and North Korea from 1946 on, and a prominent Soviet anti-plague expert was stationed in North Korea prior to the outbreak of the Korean War.[33]

In photographs presented as evidence by Chinese authorities, some bacteria were erroneously identified while others were simply harmless, and none could be carried by insects, according to Dr. Rene Dubos, an eminent U.S. bacteriologist who had participated in the U.S. BW program during World War II.[34] Dr. C. H. Curran, the Chief Entomologist at the American Museum of Natural History, concurred.[35] It was also the wrong season for anyone to attempt insect-borne BW: it was winter in the area. The reports stated that insects were found on snow, but there they would simply freeze and die. Dr. Wu Lien-teh, probably the most eminent Chinese plague expert of the time, labeled the BW allegations a "long string of unfounded accusations," and attributed the named disease outbreaks in North Korea and China to wartime conditions and deficient public-health conditions.[36]

The assessment of three Canadian scientists was presented by a Canadian UN delegate during the mid-1952 UN General Assembly debate. They discounted the evidentiary value of the "anomalies" claimed by the Chinese, and attributed the entomological "novel discoveries" to a massive and probably unprecedented collection effort.[37] The UN representative from New Zealand presented the summation of an assessment by the President of the New Zealand Association of Scientific Workers, which disparaged the various allegations and the reports containing them. This was particularly noteworthy, as its parent association, the International Association of Scientific Workers, was a recognized Soviet front organization. The New Zealand delegate concluded that there was no indication that Needham's group had ever found any physical evidence in the places where bacterial weapons were said to have been used.[38] The Australian delegate presented the conclusion of a group of Australian scientists headed by Sir MacFarlane Burnett, who concluded that BW had never been used by UN forces in Korea.[39]

New research methodologies have recently helped disprove one of the Chinese allegations. In disclosures publicized in 1988, China had claimed to have "documented" four cases of anthrax it attributed to U.S. air drops. In 1990, however, a conference paper on anthrax by a Chinese scientist stated that industrial anthrax infections due to contaminated wool in Chinese knitting factories were routine.[40] Moreover, in 2002, analysis was carried out under U.S.-Chinese collaboration in the United States of some 200 samples of B. anthracis isolates from Chinese culture collections; it found all to be indigenous Chinese strains, even those identified by the Chinese as being from the alleged U.S. an-thrax attacks.[41]

A second reason to be skeptical of the allegations is that the two international commission reports have very little scientific credibility. Neither the Lawyers' Commission nor the ISC did any field investigations or analyses: both accepted as fact the evidence presented to them by Chinese government field staff, without any independent corroboration. Even the Commission members conceded as much. For example, the Swedish representative on the Commission reportedly said that, "the delegates implicitly believed the Chinese and North Korean accusations and evidence." The ISC chair, Dr. Needham, was asked what proof he had that the samples of plague bacillus he was shown actually came, as the Chinese said, from an unusual swarm of voles; he reportedly replied, "None. We accepted the word of the Chinese scientists. It is possible to maintain that the whole thing was a kind of patriotic conspiracy [but] I prefer to believe the Chinese were not acting parts."[42]

Neither China nor North Korea ever claimed to have shot down a U.S. aircraft containing the means of delivery for biological agents or any agents themselves, even though the Chinese claimed, for example, that a total of 955 sorties to drop BW over Northeast China were undertaken by 175 groups of U.S. aircraft between February 29 and March 31, 1952. Similarly, the Chinese claimed that the United States had spread BW over "70 cities and counties of Korea . . . on 804 occasions."[43] The Chinese obtained "confessions" of some 25 captured U.S. pilots which offered voluminous detail about the kinds of bombs and other containers allegedly dropped, the types of insects, the diseases they carried, and so forth, along with a great deal of communist rhetoric familiar from Chinese press reports with references to "imperialists" and "capitalistic Wall Street war mongers." The combination of rhetoric and excessive technical detail led nearly all objective observers to conclude that none of the "confessions" had been written by the pilots themselves. Not surprisingly, then, all of the confessions were renounced when the U.S. airmen returned to the United States. The Chinese authorities also touted supposed confessions from captured U.S. ground troops "admitting" that they had delivered BW in Korea by artillery—"epidemic germ shells"—a type of armament the United States did not have either then or for many years afterwards.[44]

Remarks to U.S. State Department officials by General Hoyt Vandenberg, then chief of the U.S. Air Force, responded to a Chinese allegation that U.S. air-craft had dropped insects over the city of Tsingtao. General Vandenberg stated that U.S. aircraft had no authority to fly over the area in question, that no such flights had been authorized, and that no U.S. planes flew over Tsingtao on re-connaissance.[45]

During the Korean War, Tibor Meray, a Hungarian war correspondent, had accepted the biological warfare charges, and wrote about them in dispatches and in books, but he later described his doubts on the "evidence" that had been provided to him in Korea. He stated that local staff at a Hungarian rural hospi-tal in North Korea said that Chinese soldiers had emplaced the "germ sachets"; they had not been dropped by U.S. airplanes.[46] He also recounted conversations in 1956 with "various Communists, Poles, Yugoslavs . . . who have recently spent some time in China [and who] have informed me that *some Chinese leaders* in the course of friendly conversations stated that they *considered the whole Korean war to have been a mistake* into which they had been pushed by Stalin. *And that they believed the accusations about germ warfare to have been without foundation.*"[47]

A third and overwhelmingly compelling reason to discount the allegations is that Soviet documents of the period described them as "fictitious." In the months following the death of Stalin on March 5, 1953, Nikita Khrushchev and Lavrenti Beria struggled for power. In the 1990s, Cold War historians would learn how the battle was fought in the Central Committee on proxy grounds over several substantive issues such as "the Doctors plot" and Beria's notions for future Soviet policies toward Germany. In 1998 a third such issue was revealed to be the Korean War BW allegations against the United States.

In January 1998, a dozen documents became available from former Soviet archives that provided explicit and detailed evidence on the Korean War BW charges.[48] The documents shed light on how the BW allegations were deliber-ately contrived—at least in part—by Chinese officials and Soviet advisors, and they identify several of the individuals involved in the process.[49] They reveal a number of telling details. For example, Soviet military advisors, together with North Korean personnel, created "false areas of exposure" prior to the arrival of the ISC members, using cholera bacteria obtained from corpses in China. "Sites of infection" were also created before the Lawyer's Commission arrived. Soviet advisors created "false plague regions," in which corpses were arranged and cholera and plague bacterial samples were supplied for the ISC investigation. To hurry the ISC out of viewing areas, Soviet advisors and North Korean personnel set off explosions close to them.

The documents reveal that the Soviet advisor "aided" in composing the initial 1951 North Korean accusation that the United States was spreading smallpox, because the North Koreans felt the BW allegations were needed to discredit the Americans. The same Soviet advisors reported in March 1952 to General Shtemenko, Chief of Staff of the Soviet Armed Forces, and to the Soviet General Staff, that there had been no outbreaks of plague and cholera in China and no examples of bacteriological weapons, and stated that if any were found, they would be sent to Moscow immediately. Soviet advisors informed Kim Il Sung that they had been unable to confirm any use of BW, and that they had disproved the Chinese charges that the United States was using poison gas. In addition, "[on] 22 February 1952, the DPRK received an intentionally false statement from the Chinese about the use of bacteriological weapons by the Americans."

Finally, the documents reveal, on April 21, 1953, Foreign Minister Molotov directed the Soviet ambassador at the UN to reduce his emphasis on the accusations. A Soviet cable to Mao of May 2, 1953, is particularly striking. It charges that: "The Soviet Government and the Central Committee of the CPSU were misled. The spread in the press of information about the use by the Americans of bacteriological weapons in Korea was based on false information. The accusations against the Americans were fictitious." The message recommended that the international anti-American campaign on the subject be dropped immediately.

It is possible that other Soviet documentation on the Korean War allegations might establish exactly whose idea the false allegations were—whether the USSR's or China's—and provide a more detailed understanding of the nature and degree of the technical assistance that Soviet advisers contributed. The available documents imply first a Chinese and then a North Korean initiative, with Soviet personnel as collaborators. After the appearance of the Lawyers' Commission reports in early April 1952, the United States learned that Soviet representatives in North Korea had "reprimanded the North Koreans and Chinese for failing to produce a better propaganda case on bacteriological warfare."[50] It is conceivable that there were different Soviet and Chinese bureaucratic initiatives at different times, with the Chinese taking greater responsibility after the initial 1951 events. These remain open questions until it is possible to understand more about the operations of the USSR Ministry of State Security at the time, its collaboration with analogous Chinese government organs, their elaboration of "active measures," and so forth. A clear chain in the allegations preceded the start of the Korean War, which included the release of BW-related disinformation concerning U.S. activities in the North Pacific region that charged that the United States was preparing to use BW, employing scientists who were major figures in the Japanese BW program, preparing relevant BW facilities in Japan, and producing biological weapons there for use in Korea.[51] Such pre-war charges would have been produced by the disinformation sections within the Soviet and Chinese intelligence agencies. However, the decision to charge the United States with using BW could only have been made in the context of the war. The unanswered question is the degree of consultation and cooperation between the USSR and China about propaganda in the period not covered by the documents.

Jung Chang and Jon Halliday assert that China was responsible for the false charges, arguing that "Mao used the issue to whip up hatred for the United States inside China."[52] When the brusque May 2, 1953, cable reached Mao, accusing China of misleading the Soviet leadership, "Mao was clearly taken aback, [and] he gave orders to end the war that very night."[53]

Western Speculation about Reasons Why the Korean War BW Allegations Were Made

It is notable that the Soviet documents confirm a simple explanation of the motivation of at least one of the accusing parties: the North Koreans intended to discredit the Americans with the allegations. For decades, the simplest explanation has always seemed the most sensible: that the BW allegations were part of the Soviet, Chinese, and North Korean war effort, meant to discredit the United States and to weaken international support for the UN intervention to reverse North Korea's invasion of South Korea. However, a long list of more disparate, complicated, and often contradictory reasons were suggested by senior U.S. government officials and academics over a period spanning 50 years. These include: to blame the United States for naturally occurring disease epidemics in North Korea and China during the war;[54] to provide tactical advantage for China and North Korea in the truce negotiations;[55] as propaganda to assist the World Peace Council, a Soviet front organization, in its annual mobilization campaign;[56] as Soviet anti-U.S. propaganda, with both domestic and international goals, "intended to confuse, to divide, to paralyze . . . [and] to isolate the free world from the United States";[57] to prepare the ground for Soviet use of BW against U.S. or allied forces in Korea;[58] as a proxy campaign to deter the United States from using nuclear weapons in the Korean War;[59] to prop up public support within China for the continuing war,[60] as a preventive public-health measure, to facilitate mass public-health mobilization campaigns in China; or a combination of several of these reasons.[61]

Lessons of the Case

The United States did not do as much as it could have to uncover and confirm relevant facts. U.S. intelligence agencies did try to identify who was responsible for carrying out the planting of evidence in the field in China.[62]

The CIA produced a Special Estimate in March 1952 titled "Communist Charges of US Use of Biological Warfare." It is remarkably bland and, perhaps due to its early provenance, contains far less information than is provided in the pages of this chapter. The one significant piece of information that it contained was:

> that the Chinese Communist Government may have established a small basic and applied laboratory BW research program. This program is probably carried out in three scientific institutes located in North China and Manchuria. . . . The Chinese BW program, intimately related to the CW program, is reported to be closely supervised and supported by the USSR. Non-Chinese are prominent in the research program. Soviet personnel participate as directors of the principal laboratories, and as many as 50 percent of the scientists and technicians are reportedly Soviet. In addition, 120 Japanese specialists from the Former Kwantung Army BW units have been integrated into the program by the Chinese Communists.[63]

No further information is available regarding the activities of the Soviet, Chinese, and Japanese personnel. Whether they played any role in depositing the biological materials in the field that the Chinese used as the basis for the allegations is unknown.

The Soviet documents that became available in 1998 do explain the role of Soviet military representatives in North Korea in concocting and placing false "evidence" in North Korea. The political culture of each of the three accusing countries—the USSR, China, and North Korea—was built on false and fabricated information, often elaborate, directed both to its own domestic public and to the international community. Chinese and North Korean officials sometimes claim, even now, that the United States used BW during the Korean War.[64] Current Chinese military historians who still think the Korean BW charges are correct apparently do so on the basis of the two internal Chinese military documents quoted earlier, not on the basis of the "evidence" of the insects, spiders, clams, and so on that the Chinese gave to the Needham Commission.[65]

The U.S. government missed one significant opportunity to diffuse the Soviet propaganda campaign: in pressing their charges in the UN debates, Soviet diplomats repeatedly pointed out that the United States was not a signatory to the 1925 Geneva Protocol. In 1943, however, President Roosevelt had declared that the United States would abide by the provisions of the Geneva Protocol and would not use chemical or biological weapons (CBW) except in retaliation. Under NSC 68, this remained official U.S. policy throughout the Korean War. However, U.S. government officials and diplomats never reiterated the 1943 U.S. statement nor publicly stated U.S. BW policy at any time during the Korean War.[66] On the contrary, Ambassadors Gross and Cohen described the Protocol as "obsolete" and "a paper promise," and pointed out that the USSR's own signature to the "no first use" provision of the Protocol was functionally nullified by its charges of U.S. use. Moreover, China and North Korea were not signatories either.

It is clear that some individuals in the U.S. government considered how to rebut the BW allegations, but they were all at low levels in various departments. None held a position of authority sufficient to mandate any particular course of action, and there is no available record of consideration of a meaningful analytical response by senior level officials. Their ideas varied widely in their potential utility. Some of the suggestions skirted close to what should have been done, while the purpose of others was purely rhetorical or symbolic.

Among the suggestions were to ask the UN Secretary-General to secretly dispatch Swedish or Indian medical officers, then serving with their national units in South Korea, to ascertain that UN forces had no chemical munitions.

Another suggestion was to investigate the possibility of filing an international libel action against the Soviet Union in the World Court or the UN.[67]

The first analysis within the U.S. government regarding the BW accusations was a Special Estimate prepared by the Central Intelligence Agency on March 27, 1952, quite soon after the 1952 accusations were made. It was a brief, 7-page document divided into four sections: "Facts Bearing on the Problem," "Possible Purposes of the Campaign," and two appendices, "Disease in the Korean Area" and "Communist BW Capabilities in the Korean Area."[68] A draft prepared seven days earlier, on March 18, included a third, longer appendix titled "The Propaganda Campaign." There is virtually nothing notable in the document except the report of astonishingly high mortality rates among North Korean and Chinese combat forces during the preceding year's—1951—epidemics, between 30 and 60 percent of those infected in the typhus, typhoid, and smallpox epidemics.[69]

By July 1, 1952, a special interdepartmental committee was established with the purpose of devising ways and means of refuting the BW allegations. As part of this effort, the Office of Public Information (OPI) in the Department of Defense compiled a package entitled "The Truth About BW" with copies of official letters, messages, and speeches by U.S. officials as well as officials of other governments, scientific opinions, press comments, and other background material. It was meant to be used as an official source by U.S. government officials for rebutting the Communist propaganda charges.[70]

In September 1952 British Prime Minister Winston Churchill requested the opinion of his WWII scientific adviser, Lord Cherwell, on the BW allegations. Cherwell's reply demolished the charges. He noted the simplicity of faking "evidence," but in regard to the Communist BW allegations he wrote "No normal mind would consider such suspect pieces of evidence as valid proof . . . these things are nonsense from a scientific point of view. . . . It is strange that the Communist propagandists should be so stupid as to allow allegations of this sort to be put forward when any competent biologist must know they are rubbish. It shows either that they are extremely ignorant or extremely careless in faking their evidence . . ."[71] But Cherwell did not suggest that the British government produce a public report explaining precisely what he told Churchill.

On September 17, 1952, the Department of State had decided to "concentrate on demonstrating that [the Needham Commission] is not an impartial commission" and to "try to find a basis for shooting holes in 'scientific find-ings'." Then, it would again seek "to create a genuinely impartial commission to investigate the BW charges."[72] Others, however, wondered "whether or not we do ourselves more harm than good by raising the issue and debating it ex-tensively."[73] As late as March 1953, Henry Cabot Lodge, U.S. ambassador to the UN, sought assistance from the White House in rebutting the BW charges.[74] One response was a proposal for creation of "an American Committee of 100 Against Soviet Germ Warfare Lies," which would request that the U.S. govern-ment "assist it in the scientific research necessary to refute the charges [and] expose the lies."[75]

This was much too late, and too diffuse, and by March and April 1953, the issue had died down. The only operational U.S. responses to the allegations were its blanket denials and requests for ICRC, WHO, and UN investigations. The U.S. government's initial response was the appropriate one: it requested an immediate investigation by an international agency, the International Red Cross. However, after that effort failed almost immediately, the United States did nothing for a full year. A second response was an offer from General Wey-land, the commander of the U.S. Far East Air Forces (FEAF) to permit Ambas-sador Lodge to reveal that FEAF had no biological warfare capability, though Weyland was not happy to do so.[76] Then, in the spring of 1953, it requested the UN investigation, which it must have expected would be rejected by China and North Korea. The U.S. government made no effort to produce a serious scien-tific analysis of the charges. Although such an effort would obviously have been hampered by lack of on-site access, it could have been useful.

A number of measures could have improved the process of identification, characterization, and attribution. An international investigatory group of emi-nent microbiologists, entomologists, and epidemiologists should have been convened. Pre-1949 data on the incidence of the diseases in question in China and North Korea could have been compiled, as could data for South Korea before and after immunization campaigns. Public-health data for Korea dur-ing the decades of Japanese occupation might have been available. Information on the insects, their geographical distributions and life cycles—particularly in South Korea—and their relations to specific pathogens could have been assem-bled and analyzed. Entomological and microbiological field sampling could have been carried out in South Korea. The report could also have articulated the standards and methodology proper to such an investigation. Even with limitations, all UN member states could have been given a scientific rebuttal of the charges. Although this would not have resolved the issue in an absolute sense, it would have meant that the Needham/ISC report was not left without a serious analytical rebuttal. However, no other quasi-governmental or non-governmental Western group ever investigated the Korean War BW allegations.

It is unquestionable that Soviet-bloc Cold War practices led to the false attributions of BW use during the "hot" Korean War. Because they were fabrications, there was no possibility that China or North Korea would allow an impartial expert investigation by the United Nations, the World Health Organization, the International Committee of the Red Cross, or any ad hoc group. The only other thing that could have been done, either under state sponsorship or by an independent scientific coalition of some sort, would have been an academic analytic exercise without recourse to field samples. These lessons of the Korean War case may well be needed in the future, if opponents seek once again to discredit one another in the international arena with fabricated allegations of BW use.

Notes

1. Portions of this chapter are adapted from Milton Leitenberg, "New Russian Evidence on the Korean War Biological Warfare Allegations: Background and Analysis," *Cold War International History Project Bulletin* no. 1 (Winter 1998): 185–200; and Milton Leitenberg, "Resolution of the Korean War Biological Warfare Allegations," *Critical Reviews in Microbiology* 24, no. 3 (Fall 1998): 169–94.

2. UN Security Council 1951, S/2142/Rev 1: Cablegram dated 8 May 1951 addressed to the President of the Security Council from the Minister for Foreign Affairs of the People's Democratic Republic of Korea, United Nations Security Council: Official Records, Supplement for 1 April through 30 June 1951.

3. Statement by North Korean Foreign Minister Bak Hun Yung to the UN Secretariat, in Anonymous, "Stop U.S. Germ Warfare!" (Beijing: Chinese People's Committee for World Peace, n.d. [probably 1952]). On the day before, the New China News Agency (NCNA) broadcast the charge of BW attacks between January 28 and February 17, 1952 against North Korea. Central Intelligence Agency, Board of National Estimates, "Memorandum for the Intelligence Advisory Committee. Subject SE-24, Communist Charges of US Use of Biological Weapons," March 18, 1952.

4. Zhou Enlai statements of February 24, 1952, and March 8, 1952, in Anonymous, "Stop U.S. Germ Warfare!" Once again, NCNA broadcast the charges two days earlier.

Central Intelligence Agency, Board of National Estimates, "Memorandum for the Intelligence Advisory Committee."

5. "Report on American Invaders Using Bacteria Weapons and Our Responsive Actions," February 28, 1952, *Selected Military Works of Nie Rongzhen* (Beijing: PLA Publishing House, n.d.).

6. "Comments on Nie Rongzhen's Report about Large-scale Airdropping of Insects Carrying Bacteria by Enemy in the Korean Battlefield, February 19, 1952," in *Anthology of Mao Zedong Since 1949*, vol. 3: *January 1952–December 1952* (Beijing: The Central Documents Publishing House, 1989).

7. UN Security Council, "Letter from the Permanent Representative of the Union of Soviet Socialist Republics, President of the Security Council, Dated June 30, 1952; Annexes I, II and III, International Association of Democratic Lawyers," S/2684/Add.1, June 30, 1952 (hereafter "USSR letter of June 30, 1952").

8. Ernest A. Gross, "Security Council Statement of July 1, 1952," *Department of State Bulletin*, July 28, 1952, 153–59. The most useful source for reference to original UN and U.S. documents dealing with the Korean War BW allegations are the endnotes in John Ellis Van Courtland Moon, "Biological Warfare Allegations: The Korean War Case," in R. A. Zilinskas, ed., *The Microbiologist and Biological Defense Research, Annual of the New York Academy of Sciences*, no. 666 (1992): 53–83.

9. USSR letter of June 30, 1952.

10. "Chinese Commission for Investigation of the American Crime of Germ Warfare," New China News Agency (NCNA), April 7, 1952.

11. *People's China*, April 16, 1952, supplement.

12. Indeed, Mao told members of Needham's commission, "Don't make too much of all this! They have tried using biochemical warfare, but it hasn't been too successful. What are all these uninfected insects they are dropping?" Jon Halliday and Bruce Cummings, *Korea: The Unknown War* (New York: Pantheon, 1988), 185.

13. A. M. Halpern, *Bacteriological Warfare Accusations in Two Asian Communist Propaganda Campaigns*, RAND RM-796 (Santa Monica, CA: RAND, 25 Apr 1952), 6–7.

14. Dean Acheson, *Department of State Bulletin* 26: 664 (1952), 427–28.

15. Matthew B. Ridgeway, "Report of the U.N. Command Operation in Korea: Forty-first Report. For the Period Mar. 1–15. 1952," *Department of State Bulletin* 26, no. 679 (1952): 1040. See also General Matthew B. Ridgeway, "A Report on the Far East," *Department of State Bulletin* 26, no. 676 (1952): 926.

16. See Halpern, *Bacteriological Warfare Accusations*, 6–7.

17. Benjamin V. Cohen, "U.S. Position on Germ Warfare, Statement on May 27, 1952 to the UN Disarmament Commission," *Department of State Bulletin* (June 9, 1952): 911–63.

18. See Halpern, *Bacteriological Warfare Accusations*, 6–7.

19. UN Security Council Official Records, Seventh Year, 590th meeting, and UN Document 5/2688.

20. La Comité Internationale de la Croix-Rouge, *La Comité International de la Croix Rouge and le Conflit de Corée, Recueil de Documents*, vol. II, January 1–June 20, 1952 (Geneva: International Committee of the Red Cross, 1952). The ICRC had experience in this area: during World War II, China had appealed to the ICRC to investigate its charges that Japan was employing BW in China. In 1952, the Red Cross societies of virtually all the Soviet-bloc states had sent direct appeals to the ICRC asking it to "take action against the U.S. atrocities" in Korea.

21. La Comité Internationale de la Croix-Rouge, *La Comité International de la Croix Rouge and le Conflit de Corée*, 84–109.

22. Quoted in Moon, "Biological Warfare Allegations," 69.

23. Anonymous, "Stop U.S. Germ Warfare!"

24. UN Security Council Official Records, Seventh Year, 590th Meeting, and UN Document S/2688.

25. The discussions in the General Assembly in this phase of the dispute are summarized in Jozef Goldblat, "Allegations of the Use of Bacteriological and Chemical Weapons in Korea and China," *CB Disarmament Negotiations 1920–1970* (Stockholm: Almqvist and Wiksell, 1971): 216–18.

26. "NSC 62: Chemical Warfare Policy," A Report to the National Security Council by the Secretary of Defense, February 1, 1950, Record Group 273, U.S. National Archives.

27. "NSC 147: Analysis of Possible Courses of Action in Korea," December 28, 1953.

28. Copy of President Truman's letter, July 25, 1969, supplied to the author by Representative Robert Kastenmeier in 1969.

29. Certificate, Brigadier General H. L. Hillyard, U.S. Army, Secretary of the Joint Chiefs of Staff, April 21, 1959, CCS 3260: Chemical, Biological etc.: 1959, RG 218: Records of the Joint Chiefs of Staff: Central Decimal File, Box 032, National Archives of the United States. This information was kindly supplied by the historian John van Courtland Moon, in a personal communication in 1998.

30. Eileen R. Choffnes, "Germs on the Loose," *Bulletin of the Atomic Scientists* 57 no. 2 (March–April 2001): 57–61. During the years 1951 to 1954, a small group of planners in the Air Force Operations Atomic (AFOAT) unit at U.S. Air Force headquarters in Washington kept optimistically pushing for a U.S. Air Force BW capability, only to be repeatedly blocked not only at the policy level but also by the delays in U.S. BW development. For a very useful guide to available declassified papers, see Conrad C. Crane, " 'No Practical Capabilities': American Biological and Chemical Warfare Programs During the Korean War," *Perspectives in Biology and Medicine,* 45:2 (Spring 2002): 241–49.

31. United States Department of the Army, *U.S. Army Activity in the U.S. Biological Warfare Program*, vol. 2, February 24, 1977.

32. Gross, "Security Council Statement of July 1, 1952," 157.

33. Information provided by U.S. CIA in 1999, and corroborated by a Russian plague expert in 2002 (personal communications).

34. A. M. Rosenthal, "Reds' Photographs on Germ Warfare Exposed as Fakes," *New York Times*, April 3, 1952.

35. Rosenthal, "Reds' Photographs on Germ Warfare Exposed as Fakes."

36. Dr. Wu Lien-teh, writing in the *Hong Kong Standard*, quoted in Henry R. Lieberman, "Chinese Scientist Scouts Germ Use: Plague Authority Says Enemy Charge Reflects No Credit on Red Army Doctors," *New York Times*, April 7, 1952. This reference was kindly supplied by Dr. Martin Furmanski.

37. UN Document, A/C. 1/SR. 591.

38. Ibid.

39. Ibid.

40. Shu Lin Dong, "Progress in the Control and Research of Anthrax in China," *Salisbury Medical Bulletin, Special Supplement: Proceedings of the International Workshop on Anthrax*, no. 68 (January 1990): 104–5.

41. Martin Hugh Jones, personal communication, 2002. Dr. Jones, Department of Veterinary Medicine, Louisiana State University, is one of the most prominent experts in anthrax and maintains one of the largest reference collections of anthrax cultures in the world.

42. G. P. Thompson, "Germ Warfare," *New Statesman and Nation* (December 5, 1953).

43. Anonymous, "Stop U.S. Germ Warfare!"

44. David Rees, *Korea: The Limited War* (Baltimore, MD: Penguin, 1964), 355–57, 360–63.

45. General Hoyt Vandenberg, cited in *Foreign Relations of the United States (FRUS), 1952–54*, March 19, 1952, 101.

46. Tibor Meray, "The Truth about Germ Warfare," *Franc-Tireur*, May 6–19, 1957. This series of twelve articles published in the Parisian daily was translated into English in 1999. See in particular pp. 25, 26, 27, 28, 51, and 52 of Meray's unpublished English-language translation (copy in my possession).

47. Meray, "The Truth about Germ Warfare" (emphasis added). According to an informant, a former senior Chinese diplomat said, "It was all bullshit." Personal communication, December 14, 1995.

48. The documents were not released through official channels, but since the documents reached the West, they have been authenticated through multiple independent contacts with Russian authorities (some of whom served at the time of the Korean War, and others in the Russian government in the 1990s). One fragmentary document is dated February 21, 1952; the remaining eleven date from April 13 to June 2, 1953, in the four

months following Stalin's death. The documents consist of reports to the Soviet Central Committee from members of the Soviet military mission in North Korea; messages to the Soviet ambassadors in North Korea and China directing them to transmit messages to Kim Il Sung and to Mao Zedong; the substance of those messages; and replies to Moscow by the same Soviet ambassadors. Translations of the twelve documents were published and described in detail in Leitenberg, "New Russian Evidence on the Korean War Biological Warfare Allegations: Background and Analysis"; and Leitenberg, "Resolution of the Korean War Biological Warfare Allegations."

49. Ibid.

50. U.S. Department of State, Office of Intelligence and Research, "Communist Bacteriological Warfare Propaganda," Special Paper 4, Washington, DC: June 16, 1952, 16.

51. Details are provided in Leitenberg, "New Russian Evidence on the Korean War Biological Warfare Allegations"; and Leitenberg, "Resolution of the Korean War Biological Warfare Allegations."

52. Jung Chang and Jon Halliday, *Mao: The Unknown Story* (London: Vintage, 2006), chapter 34, "Why Mao and Stalin Started the Korean War," pp. 371–95. In interviews with Chang and Halliday, Russian Generals Valentin Zozinov and Igor Selivanov denied that any biological warfare occurred in Korea, and Colonel Karpov of the Russian FSB confirmed the authenticity of the documents.

53. Chang and Halliday, *Mao*, 393.

54. Acheson, *Department of State Bulletin* 26: 664 (1952); and Matthew B. Ridgeway, "Report of the U.N. Command Operation in Korea. Forty-First Report."

55. Halpern, *Bacteriological Warfare Accusations in Two Asian Communist Propaganda Campaigns.*

56. U.S. Department of State, *Communist Bacteriological Warfare Propaganda*, OIR/CPI Special Paper no. 4, 16 (June 1952), unclassified.

57. Statements by Ernest A. Gross, "Need for Elimination of Germ Warfare," to the UN Security Council, June 18, 1952; and Gross, "Request for Impartial Investigation," to the UN Security Council, June 20, 1952, *Department of State Bulletin* (July 7, 1952): 32–37; statement by Ernest A. Gross, "The Soviet Germ Warfare Campaign: The Strategy of the Big Lie," to the UN Security Council, June 20, 1952; and Gross, Security Council Statement of July 3, 1952, *Department of State Bulletin* (July 28, 1952): 153–59.

58. Statement by Benjamin V. Cohen, "U.S. Position on Germ Warfare"; Statement by Ernest A. Gross, "Need for Elimination of Germ Warfare." Under-Secretary of State Robert Lovett also considered this to be a likely reason, as did General Mark Clark while serving in Korea.

59. Henry A. Kissinger, *Nuclear Weapons and Foreign Policy* (New York: Harper, 1957), 376; Alice Langley Hsieh, *Communist China's Strategy in the Nuclear Age* (Englewood Cliffs, NJ: Prentice Hall, 1962), 4; Mark A. Ryan, "Nuclear Weapons and Chinese

Allegations of Chemical Biological Warfare," *Chinese Attitudes Toward Nuclear Weapons: China and the United States During the Korean War* (Armonk, NY: M. E. Sharpe, 1989), 104–38.

60. William Stueck, *The Korean War: An International History* (Princeton, NJ: Princeton University Press, 1995).

61. David Rees, *Korea: The Limited War* (Baltimore: Penguin, 1964); Albert E. Cowdry, " 'Germ Warfare' and Public Health in the Korean Conflict," *Journal of the History of Medicine and Allied Sciences* 39 (April 1984): 153–72; Conrad Crane, "Chemical and Biological Warfare During the Korean War: Rhetoric and Reality," *Asian Perspective* 25, no. 3 (2001): 61–83; Ruth Rogaski, "Nature, Annihilation, and Modernity: China's Korean War Germ-Warfare Experience Reconsidered," *Journal of Asian Studies* 61, no. 2 (May 2002): 381–415.

62. In early 1999, the U.S. Central Intelligence Agency supplied the author with several pages of declassified information.

63. Central Intelligence Agency, "Special Estimate: Communist Charges of US Use of Biological Warfare," SE-24, March 25, 1952. Although labeled "Confidential" and therefore not technically classified, it proved impossible to obtain this document from the CIA since 1988 or to locate a copy in the National Archives. It was only obtained in July 2007 through the special intervention of a former CIA official.

64. Milton Leitenberg, "The Korean War Biological Weapon Allegations: Additional Information and Disclosures," *Asian Perspective* 24, no. 3 (2000): 159–72.

65. Personal communications, February 22, 1996 and March 18, 1996.

66. "Clearer Statement on Germ War Sought," *New York Times*, May 4, 1952; Thomas J. Hamilton, "United States Once Spurred Protocol It Now Fights on Germ War," *New York Times*, June 20, 1952; and Thomas J. Hamilton, "Germ-Warfare Canard Grows to Major Issue: Moscow, Which Spread the Story, May Hear More from the UN Assembly," *New York Times*, July 12, 1952. These references were kindly supplied by Dr. Martin Furmanski.

67. Edmund L. Taylor, Assistant Director, Office of Policy and Plans, U.S. Department of State, July 3, 1952.

68. Central Intelligence Agency, "Special Estimate: Communist Charges of US Use of Biological Warfare," SE-24, March 25, 1952.

69. Central Intelligence Agency, Board of National Estimates, "Memorandum for the Intelligence Advisory Committee."

70. "Report on Chemical and Biological Warfare Readiness," Office, Director of Administration, Office of the Secretary of Defense, Assistant for Special Security Programs, July 1, 1952, p. 29.

71. Lord Cherwell, Paymaster-General to Prime Minister, 24 September 1952, PREM 11/250 Communist Allegations of US Germ Warfare in Korea and China: Report to Prime Minister 1952.

72. Staff Meeting, Psychological Strategy Board, September 17, 1952. Referring to the "still unexplained . . . ridiculous nature of the BW charges" and their "insultingly unscientific basis" was a memo from Col. K. K. Hansen, State Department, re: "Evaluation of Communist Bacterial Warfare Charges," Psychological Strategy Board, May 15, 1952.

73. Charles R. Norberg, Memorandum: "Germ Warfare," Psychological Strategy Board, October 10, 1952. Apparently many U.S. embassies shared that view. Staff Study, Preliminary Analysis of the Communist BW Propaganda Campaign (PSB D-25), Psychological Strategy Board, June 3, 1952.

74. Ambassador Henry Cabot Lodge, Letter to "C.D." (C. D. Jackson, White House staff), March 12, 1953.

75. C. D. Jackson, Letter to President Dwight D. Eisenhower, April 21, 1953.

76. Crane, "'No Practical Capabilities,'" 2002, 242.

CHAPTER SEVEN

Cuban Allegations of U.S. Biological Warfare

False Allegations and
Their Impact on Attribution

RAYMOND A. ZILINSKAS

Although Cuba's achievements in biomedical research and applications since Fidel Castro came into power in 1959 have been truly impressive,[1] a less savory aspect of Cuban science should not be overlooked: Cuban officials, led by President Fidel Castro himself, have repeatedly subverted science for the political purpose of denigrating the United States. In particular, since 1962, the Cuban government has alleged that the U.S. government or its agents have caused at least 10 infectious disease outbreaks and one insect infestation that severely damaged Cuba's population or agriculture.

As outlined in the introductory chapter to this volume, attribution is a three-step process: to identify the existence of a biological event, to differentiate between a natural disease outbreak and a deliberately caused disease outbreak, and to determine the perpetrator of a deliberately caused disease outbreak. In this chapter, it can be seen that the Cuban government had already made its attributions; it claimed that all 10 disease outbreaks and the insect infestation were deliberately caused and, further, that the perpetrator in each case was the U.S. government.

Since the Cuban government has released no objective information to support its allegations, outside analysts have little basis for determining their veracity. This being so, an analyst who seeks to analyze the accuracy of the 11 Cuban allegations must research available epidemiological, epizootic, phytopathological, and other biological and medical data for clues as to how and why each event may have occurred. I undertook such an analysis, presented in a 1999 publication, and I concluded that all of the allegations were false; that analysis is the basis for this chapter.[2]

This chapter begins with a summary of each of the Cuban allegations that blamed infectious disease outbreaks and an insect infestation on the United States. The insect infestation differs from the others in that it was the only one officially presented to the international community by Cuba's having invoked a provision of the Biological and Toxin Weapons Convention (BWC). It thus is given added attention, including its negative impact on consultative meetings, one of the main compliance measures of the BWC. In the conclusion, I analyze the different implications of nations lodging erroneous versus false allegations and pose three different scenarios for how future allegations will be addressed by the international arms control community.

Cuba's Allegations

The 11 allegations are reviewed briefly in this section. In 1997, the Cuban government alleged that the United States had already, in 1962, deployed the Newcastle disease virus against its poultry industry. A more likely reason why a Newcastle disease occurred is that, due to poor manufacturing practices or lack of quality control, the Cuban manufacturer produced a faulty vaccine that contained virulent viruses that caused the outbreak.

On June 1, 1964, a communiqué issued over Fidel Castro's name accused the United States of having sent balloons carrying bacteriological cultures over Cuban territory.[3] No claim for damages was made. Since the Cubans have provided no information about this alleged event, it cannot be analyzed.

Cuba blamed African Swine Fever (ASF) outbreaks in 1971 and 1980 on the United States as part of what I call an "allegation package."[4] The outbreaks caused enormous damage to Cuban agriculture. The 1971 outbreak, for example, was controlled only after the Cuban government slaughtered over 740,554 pigs.[5] The 1980 outbreak led to the slaughter of 297,137 pigs.[6] The United States had nothing to do with either outbreak, however; the first was caused when a commercial aircraft that departed from a country in which ASF was endemic brought the virus to Cuba in contaminated meat.[7] The second time, the virus was imported by Haitian refugees who, together with their household animals, foundered on the Cuban coast as they were trying to sail to Florida.[8]

Devastating tobacco blue mold epidemics affected Cuba during 1979 and 1980. Castro stated that these epidemics destroyed 25 percent of Cuba's tobacco crop in 1979 and almost 90 percent in 1980. Cuban officials have frequently alleged, as part of the "allegation package," that the United States was responsible for introducing the blue mold disease into Cuba. However, blue mold spores probably arose from a primary inoculum source in the Caribbean region itself and were carried into Cuba by winds that prevail in the Caribbean Sea.[9]

Sugarcane rust disease affected many Caribbean countries, including Cuba, in 1979.[10] As part of its "allegation package," Cuban officials assert that the United States was responsible for the introduction of sugar cane rust. Rather than being an incident of biological warfare, however, the most likely explanation is that rust spores, which had been conveyed from the Cameroon Republic in west Africa to the Dominican Republic, subsequently spread by prevailing winds to other Caribbean countries, including Cuba.[11]

In 1980, dengue fever (DF) appeared in Cuba, and by the time the outbreak ended in 1981, 344,203 Cubans had contracted the disease. Of these, 10,312 developed dengue hemorrhagic fever (DHF), and 158 died. On July 26, 1981, as part of the "allegation package," Castro claimed that the CIA had introduced DF.[12] The most likely explanation for the outbreak, however, is that Cuban soldiers or health workers who had served in Africa or the Indochina peninsula, where DF is endemic, brought a DF virus strain endemic to those regions back to Cuba with them. (It bears noting that Cuba periodically has experienced DF outbreaks throughout its history; for example, particularly severe DF outbreaks occurred in 1977, 1997, and 2002. However, the United States has not been accused of causing them.)

Soon after Acute Hemorrhagic Conjunctivitis (AHC) was first reported in Cuba in 1981, the Cuban government alleged that it resulted from a U.S.-instigated biological attack.[13] The most likely explanation for the AHC outbreak is that Cuban soldiers or health workers had brought the AHC virus (as well as the DF virus in 1980), when they returned home after having served in African or Asian countries where the disease is endemic.

When epidemic optic and peripheral neuropathy first appeared in 1992, Cuban officials asserted that it was caused by "enemy action." In fact, it resulted from the lack of folic acid in the Cuban diet.[14] After the Cuban government provided vitamin supplements to its population in May 1993, the outbreak abated and then disappeared.[15]

In the beginning of 1997, the Cuban government alleged that the United States was responsible for having introduced the insect pest *Thrips palmi* (commonly called thrip or thrips) onto the island in 1996. Since this allegation had important international repercussions, it is discussed in detail below.

The Cuban government has continued indicting the United States as a biological aggressor since 1997. Most noteworthy, Cuban labor unions and other organizations brought suits in Cuban courts against the U.S. government twice, in 1999 and 2000, seeking damages for alleged attacks by the United States. The first was adjudicated in the plaintiffs' favor and awarded them $181 billion in damages.[16] The second suit, filed in January 2000, asked for $121 billion in damages.[17] Added to the 11 allegations discussed above, Cuba claimed that the United States carried out attacks that utilized or caused bovine nodular pseudodermatosis (1981), ulcerative mammalitis of cows (1989), black sigatoka of plantain (1990), black plant louse of citrus trees (1992), citrus leafminer of citrus trees (1993), rabbit viral disease (1993), borer worm of coffee (1995), varroasis of bees (1996), ulcerative disease of trout and tilapia (1996), and rice mite (1997).[18] The suit was adjudicated in plaintiffs' favor in April 2000. The U.S. government did not contest either suit.

In 2004, as part of its campaign to refute allegations made by certain Bush administration officials that Cuba supported a BW research and development program, the Cuban government invited the Center for Defense Information (CDI) to organize a visit to its biotechnological facilities.[19] A member of the CDI group, Jonathan Tucker, subsequently reported that Cuban government officials addressing the group had claimed that "more than a dozen covert releases of infectious-disease agents" had been "carried out by the CIA, beginning with Operation Mongoose during the 1960s."[20] Tucker further quoted the assertion of Jesús Bermúdez Cutiño, president of the Cuban Center on Studies for Defense Information, that: "Cuban scientists have proved that the strains responsible for these outbreaks had been artificially modified in the laboratory,

or were not indigenous to the Americas, indicating that they had been artificially introduced."[21] Neither Cutiño, nor any other Cuban officials, provided
the group with scientific data to back up these claims.

Thrips palmi Infestation

It is instructive to examine in detail Cuba's allegation on the cause of an
infestation by *Thrips palmi*, and the U.S. and international responses to this
allegation, because it was pursued by resorting to a compliance provision of
the BWC. Thrip is an insect that feeds on many types of agriculturally important plants in most regions of the world, including eggplant, cotton, cowpeas,
cucumbers, melons, soybean, sunflower, tobacco, and watermelons. Infested
plants are characterized by a silvered or bronzed appearance of the leaves,
stunted leaves and terminal shoots, and scarred and deformed fruit. Heavily
infested plants usually die.[22]

Thrip was detected for the first time in the Caribbean region in 1989, in
Martinique and Guadeloupe.[23] By 1992, thrips were infesting Antigua and Bar-
buda, Barbados, Dominica, the Dominican Republic, Grenada, Guadeloupe,
Haiti, Jamaica, Martinique, Puerto Rico, St. Lucia, St. Kitts and Nevis, Trinidad
and Tobago, and Venezuela.[24] Thrip was discovered for the first time in Cuba
in December 1996. The Cuban government soon thereafter began circulating
the story that an American aircraft had dispersed the pest over Cuban territory. Specifically, Cuba claimed that, on October 21, 1996, a U.S. S2R aircraft
had overflown Cuba's territory on its way to Colombia, where it was to aid
the effort to control illicit coca plant farming, in accordance with a flight plan
approved by the Cuban government (see Figure 7.1). A Cuban piloting a Fok-
ker-27 commercial aircraft owned by Cubana de Aviación was said to have observed the S2R intermittently release an unknown substance into the air "in the
form of a whitish or grayish mist."[25] Three months later, Thrip was recovered
from a field in the Matanzas province. By March 1997, thrips had spread over
9,000 hectares and was damaging 17 different crops in the provinces of Havana,
Matanzas, Pinar del Rio, and Cienfuegos.[26] The Cuban government instituted
an emergency program to control the pest, including the large-scale application
of pesticides, to little effect.

On December 26, 1996, the Cuban Ministry of Foreign Affairs asked the U.S.
Interest Section in Havana to clarify the S2R's actions. The United States ex-

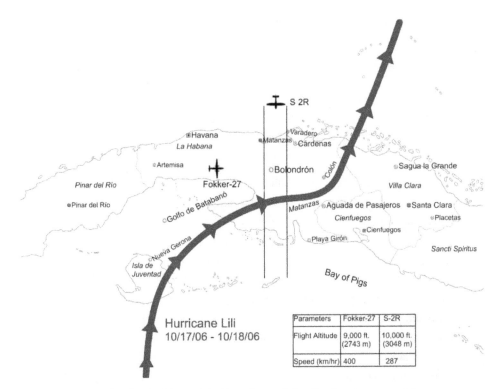

FIG. 7.1. Flight of United States S2R Aircraft over Cuba, October 21, 1996 and the
Path of Hurricane Lili, October 17–18, 1996. Source of information on the flight paths:
Granma International, "Cuba denounces US Biowarfare (Text of the Cuban report
given to the UN secretary-general)," *Granma International 1997*, International Edition
<http://southmovement.alphalink.com.au/countries/Cuba/biowar.htm>, accessed
April 3, 2007. Source for path of Hurricane Lili: UNISYS, "1996 Hurricane/Tropical
Data for Atlantic"; http://weather.unisys.com/hurricane/atlantic/1996/LILI/track.gif
(accessed September 11, 2007).

plained that the pilot of the S2R aircraft had seen the Cuban aircraft below him,
and that it had appeared to be climbing. To warn the Cuban aircraft of his presence, he had used the aircraft's smoke generator to generate smoke for visual
effect. The U.S. reply did not satisfy the Cuban government. Thus, on April 29,
1997, the Cuban government wrote the UN Secretary-General, claiming that,
"There is reliable evidence that Cuba has once again been the target of biological aggression."[27] It requested that its complaint be considered by a consultative
meeting of BWC state parties.

Two BWC articles address compliance concerns; of most relevance is Article V:

> The States Parties to this Convention undertake to consult one another and to cooperate in solving any problems which may arise in relation to the objective of, or in the application of the provisions of, the Convention. Consultation and cooperation pursuant to this article may also be undertaken through appropriate international procedures within the framework of the United Nations and in accordance with its Charter.

Article V's "undertaking to consult . . . and to cooperate" has been termed ambiguous and imprecise, and therefore attempts have been made to clarify it at review conferences of the BWC (held every five years).[28] At the first review conference of the BWC (known as RevCom1) in March 1980, the British delegation proposed that any state party could request that "a consultative meeting open to all State Parties be convened at the expert level."[29] This concept of a "consultative meeting" was refined at RevCom2 in 1986, RevCom3 in 1991, and RevCom4 in 1996. In the end, a mechanism was created that allowed for the rapid convening of a consultative meeting in the event that one or more state parties had concerns that another state party had violated the BWC; it further allowed for any of the involved parties, or the consultative meeting itself, to request specialized assistance to help resolve technical issues.

The 1997 consultative meeting has been covered in detail elsewhere,[30] as have the accusation made by the Cuban government and the defense by the U.S. government. Only aspects of the consultative meeting of direct relevance to this chapter are considered here. The consultative meeting was held August 25–27, 1997, in Geneva. Delegates appointed Ambassador Ian Soutar of the United Kingdom as the Chairman; he, together with six vice-chairmen (these were the representatives of Brazil, Canada, Iran, Netherlands, Nigeria, and Russia), formed the meeting's Bureau. The United States was represented by Ambassador Donald Mahley; Deputy Minister of Foreign Affairs Maria Florez represented Cuba. The United States and Cuba each made a formal presentation and took questions; each also distributed written materials to all members of the consultative meeting.[31] Ambassador Soutar then invited state parties to submit "observations" on the presentations, which the Bureau would consider when attempting to clarify and resolve issues related to the Cuban allegation.[32]

By the deadline of September 27, 1997, 11 states parties had offered observations. Australia, Canada, Denmark, Germany, Hungary, Japan, Netherlands, and New Zealand found no causal link between the U.S. overflight and the thrips infestation. Two others, China and Vietnam, argued that the technical complexity of the issue and the lack of detailed information made it impossible to reach a clear verdict. North Korea alone concluded that the U.S. aircraft had dispersed thrips over Cuba. Reflecting this lack of consensus, the "finding of fact" in the Bureau's report was inconclusive: "due inter alia to the technical complexity of the subject and the passage of time, it has not proved possible to reach a definitive conclusion with regard to the concerns raised by the Government of Cuba."[33]

Some years after the Consultative Meeting concluded, my research unearthed a Cuban publication that demonstrates the deliberate falseness of the Cuban government's thrip allegation.[34] Even before acquiring this publication, I had no doubts that Cuban agricultural scientists and workers were aware, before 1996, that thrips infestations were afflicting most if not all of the neighboring countries, and that they and the Cuban government knew that this insect would shortly invade Cuba. However, the publication evidences that in 1994, the Cuban government had already published a bulletin on *Thrips palmi Karny.* Among its contents, the bulletin informed Cuban agricultural workers that, although thrips had not so far been detected in Cuba, there was a need for them to be able to identify the insect as part of a defensive quarantine program against plant pests.[35] When thrips were recovered from a Cuban site for the first time, in December 1996, instead of accepting it as a natural, albeit unfortunate, event, the Cuban government chose once again to falsely attribute responsibility for the event to the Americans.

The Effects of Cuba's Thrip Allegation on the Biological and Toxin Weapons Convention

If the Cuban government had really believed that the United States was responsible for the thrips infestation, it would presumably have mobilized its substantial scientific and technical resources in agriculture, entomology, and biotechnology to craft a strong case, based on objective evidence, to support its allegation in the BWC proceeding. It might, for example, have invited foreign entomologists to examine lands infested by thrips, presented samples of the invading thrips to foreign entomological laboratories for analysis by classical and molecular methods, and demonstrated the method by which an aircraft piloted by a single individual would have been able to effect the release of viable thrips in the manner witnessed by a Cuban pilot. The Cuban government did none of the foregoing. The case presented by the Cubans in Geneva largely paralleled previous allegations in that no substantive evidence was made available to outsiders, but depended on conjecture and innuendos, such as that the United States had previously operated a BW program; that U.S. leaders hated Castro and would do anything to get rid of his government; and that the United States had perpetrated biological attacks on Cuba in the past.[36]

Even before the Bureau's final report was issued, Cuba's representative stated that, "her Government continues to adhere to the suspicions which had given rise to the original complaint."[37] The view of the U.S. government has not, as far as I am aware, been announced, but a Department of State official who was present called the proceeding, privately, "a charade."

Perhaps the consultative meeting's Bureau itself came to recognize the futility of its endeavors. As part of its final report it was concluded that "the experience of conducting this process of consultation had shown the importance of establishing as soon as possible an effective Protocol to strengthen the Convention which is being negotiated in the Ad Hoc Group."[38] To me this more than implies that, since the consultative meeting process did not generate a definitive answer to the question whether the United States had dispersed thrips over Cuba, a better procedure is needed to evaluate allegations of actions or events that appear to contravene the BWC. Of course, the Bureau could not foresee that negotiations to develop a Protocol to the BWC were to collapse in 2001 and are not likely to resume for the foreseeable future. As a result of this development, the only mechanism currently available outside the BWC for investigations is that proffered by the UN Secretary-General, which is discussed below.

I argue that this episode demonstrated that the consultative meeting process cannot make a determination whether a violation of the BWC has occurred, as claimed by a plaintiff government and denied by a defendant government, by relying only on the statements of those two governments. In the thrip case, the Cuban government chose to employ many of the words that it had previously used when voicing unofficial allegations of U.S. biological attacks; these words conveyed propaganda rather than objective evidence. Conversely, the United

States faced the difficult problem of proving the negative: once it had been accused of having caused an infestation and the accuser actually was experiencing an infestation that, in some ways, was consistent with assertions made by Cuba in its allegation, the United States had limited ability to defend itself persuasively in this type of forum.

This does not mean, however, that the United States could not have mounted a more effective defense. A two-pronged approach would have resulted in a stronger case. The first would have been to demonstrate convincingly the fact that the S2R aircraft flown over Cuba was so well camouflaged that its pilot had reason to generate smoke in order to be noticed by the Cuban pilot of the approaching aircraft. Instead, in the report distributed by the United States to consultative meeting participants, there are generic photos of an S2R aircraft painted in bright white with an orange stripe running along its side.[39] One photo shows the S2R flying over green fields and starkly standing out against the background. If these photos did guide consultative meeting participants, they would have seen no reason why such an aircraft needed to emit smoke for visualization. The second approach would have been to provide a more reasonable explanation for how thrips came to infest Cuba than that postulated in the report, which was that the insect was transported by wind from the Bahamas. However, the Bahamas government had at that time not reported that thrip infested its nation; furthermore, the prevailing winds tend to blow the other way, from Cuba to the Bahamas. A more reasonable explanation for thrips appearing in Cuba would have been that they were conveyed there by Hurricane Lili. After having crossed northern Venezuela and Jamaica, Lili moved across the Caribbean Sea and then over the middle of Cuba during October 17 and 18, 1996. It thus took nearly the same path as the U.S. S2R did three days later, but in the opposite direction. Hurricane Lili caused tremendous damage to large areas of Cuba, including the province of Matanzas where thrips supposedly were first recovered approximately three months later. It is reasonable to hypothesize that Hurricane Lili winds picked up thrips between October 14 and 16 in Venezuela or Jamaica, where they were endemic, and deposited them onto Cuba on October 17 or 18.

The consultative meeting process includes provisions for engaging experts on request by the involved parties or by the consultative meeting itself, but does not say how this might be implemented. Nevertheless, for the sake of discussion here, I posit a situation that engages experts and uses the thrip infestation as a hypothetical case study. I conjecture that the pest first arrived in Cuba in the middle of October 1996. When it became apparent in December, the Cuban government asked the Americans for an explanation. However, Cuba did not declare that the United States was responsible for the pest's introduction until April 1997. For unknown reasons, the Cuban government chose not to ask any international experts to investigate the pest's introduction, so this was not done. Conceivably, the United States at that time could have requested that Cuba admit foreign experts to investigate the thrip infestation, but did not do so. Perhaps the U.S. government from the first viewed the allegation as mere propaganda, and therefore did not wish to lend it any sense of legitimacy. Furthermore, it might have doubted whether foreign experts, even if allowed admittance, could discover anything meaningful because by then much time had passed and the infestation had spread over most of Cuba. (These same reasons would probably have persuaded the consultative committee, meeting three months later, not to send experts to Cuba, should the issue have arisen.) As can be realized from this hypothetical case, a meaningful investigation by experts of the thrip infestation could not have been done after Cuba made known its intent in April to pursue its allegation at a consultative meeting.

Of the many allegations made by the Cuban government, the thrip case was the only one that was propelled into the international arena by means of a consultative meeting. The Cuban government probably took this step knowing that its allegation would be discussed and considered but would be neither investigated nor resolved. Thus, the allegation itself was given full play to the Cuban government's internal and international political advantage, and with no risk that its falseness would be revealed. In my view, the August 1997 consultative meeting demonstrated that this mechanism does not work to settle allegations, because it depends on diplomats making judgments about scientific and technical developments or events, without having timely access to the requisite expertise.

Erroneous, False, and Authoritative Attributions

In some instances, the words "accuse" and "allege" on the one hand, and "attribute" on the other, will have about the same meaning to their users, but in other situations their meaning may differ greatly.[40] Illustrations of both can be found in what has become known as the "Yellow Rain" episode (see Chapter 4 by Meselson and Robinson and Chapter 5 by Katz in this volume). It provides a useful comparison to the way that the Cuban allegations, and U.S. and international responses to them, have unfolded.

In September 1981, U.S. Secretary of State Alexander Haig asserted publicly that the United States had conclusive evidence that chemical weapons in the form of mycotoxins had been used against the Hmong and Afghans. President Ronald Reagan repeated this assertion while addressing the UN Second Special Session on Disarmament on June 17, 1982, and further accused the Soviet Union of having violated the Geneva Protocol and the BWC by its activities in Laos, Vietnam, and Afghanistan. These statements, as well as U.S. Department of State reports of the time,[41] make clear that the U.S. allegations were in effect attributions: the United States had concluded that mycotoxins were the cause of disease among the Hmong, that the Vietnamese government had deliberately dispersed these mycotoxins over Hmong population centers, and that the Soviet Union had supplied the mycotoxins used in the attacks to the Vietnamese. The United States presented its allegations to the United Nations and strove to have them investigated.

In response to a UN General Assembly resolution in 1980, the UN Secretary-General established an expert group and charged it with investigating these allegations. The expert group began its investigation in April 1981, but its report, submitted to the Secretary-General on November 20, 1981, drew no conclusion as to whether chemical weapons had been used in Southeast Asia or in Afghanistan.[42] A second expert group that essentially repeated the investigation of the first, in early 1982, also reported inconclusive findings.[43] Neither expert group thus substantiated the U.S. allegations by making a judgment as to whether a chemical weapon had been used nor by corroborating the U.S. attributions.

Although numerous questions remain about the Yellow Rain episode, many analysts, myself included, believe that it did not occur as the U.S. government charged at the time but that instead its basis was a misunderstood or misinterpreted natural event. If this school of thought is correct—it probably will never be known for certain—then the U.S. government's allegation was erroneous. However, as discussed above, the United States was so certain of the correctness of its version of events that it willingly supported two international investigations of its allegations. I do not think this would happen if a government issued false allegations because an investigation might reveal the falseness of the allegation to the world.

The Cuban allegations also amount to attributions: the Cuban government has repeatedly held the United States responsible for ten disease outbreaks and an insect infestation in Cuba. However, unlike the Yellow Rain case, the Cuban government never requested the UN, the UN Secretary-General, or other outside authority to investigate any of the biological attacks it blamed on the United States.[44] Since it did not, although knowing that the Secretary-General had sent off expert groups to distant parts of the world to conduct investigations since 1982, one can only conclude that it refrained in order to avoid having an authoritative body investigate them.

The thrip case and the Yellow Rain case both seem to suggest that a nation cannot, by itself, make persuasive or authoritative attributions. An internationally recognized non-governmental organization, such as the Stockholm International Peace Research Institute, or intergovernmental organization, such as the International Centre for Genetic Engineering and Biotechnology, might be sufficiently trusted by all sides of a dispute to make such a determination. However, few if any such organizations possess the requisite technical expertise, equipment, supplies, and logistic and communications support. By a process of elimination it appears that the UN, or one of its specialized agencies, might be in the best position to investigate an allegation or suspicious event and then make an authoritative attribution; indeed, the UN already has a proven record in this regard, which brings us back to the Secretary-General.

To date, there has been no official attempt by the international community to investigate a biological event for the purpose of attribution, so I turn to the chemical field for surrogate cases. Between 1981 and 1992, two serving UN Secretary-Generals dispatched expert groups on twelve occasions to investigate alleged violations of the Geneva Protocol.[45] Of these occasions, two were the Yellow Rain investigations; eight investigations explored the alleged use of chemical weapons during the Iran-Iraq War (1980–88); one, in 1992, was requested by Armenia to clear itself of an allegation by Azerbaijan that Armenian forces had used chemical weapons; and another, also in 1992, was to investigate the alleged use of chemical weapons in Mozambique.

It is important to note that only two of the 12 investigations identified perpetrators. This means that a very high proportion of investigations conducted under the authority of the Secretary-General resulted in inconclusive attributions. For example, an investigation requested by Iran in 1984 stated its conclusion in passive voice: "The expert group concluded that chemical weapons in the form of aerial bombs containing mustard gas and tabun *had been used* against Iranian troops and civilians."[46] Similarly, when investigating two accusations by Iraq that Iran had used chemical weapons against its forces, in neither case did the expert groups actually identify the perpetrator; to wit, no report included an attribution such as "the Iranians did it." Rather, one report states that, "Iraqi forces have been affected by mustard gas and a pulmonary irritant, possibly phosgene. In the absence of conclusive evidence of the weapons used, it could not be determined how the injuries were caused."[47] A subsequent UN investigation of an Iraqi allegation had similar findings.[48] It thus is up to the reader to make the attribution, drawing conclusions as to whether the Iranians employed chemical weapons against Iraqi forces, or perhaps that the Iraqis had used them against their own troops as part of a ruse. Most readers probably would made their determination along the following lines: there are only two parties to the conflict, and since the soldiers of one side—Iraq—were affected by chemical weapons, the other side—Iran—must have been the perpetrator. Indeed, delegates from the United States, United Kingdom, and other countries at the Committee of Disarmament meetings in the late 1980s generally accepted that, at a late stage of the Iran-Iraq conflict, the Iranians decided to acquire and use chemical weapons after having repeatedly been subjected to chemical attacks by the Iraqis.

A definitive identification of a perpetrator of chemical attacks during the Iran-Iraq War was not made until strong evidence became available to UN investigators. This included testimony from a captured Iraqi pilot who twice had dropped chemical bombs on Iranian forces, as well as analysis of fragments of bombs used by the Iraqis in 1984, 1986, and 1987. With this evidence in hand, the expert groups identified perpetrators by writing clear statements of attribution, such as "chemical weapons have been used against Iranian positions by Iraqi forces."[49] They also referred to "repeated utilization of chemical bombs by Iraqi forces."[50] It can be seen from the investigations instigated by the UN Secretary-General that the level of certainty that an event actually occurred as alleged must be very high before an expert group is willing to make an attribution, that is, to identify a specific party as having been responsible for that event. It is safe to assume that, were the Secretary-General to dispatch an expert group at some future time to investigate a biological event, similar criteria would apply.

Five lessons may be drawn from the Secretary-General's 12 investigations that would be useful for guiding future investigations of alleged breaches of the BWC.[51] First, the Secretary-General's office should have a permanent fund that could be tapped at any time to pay for investigations, and a method for replenishing it as necessary. Second, this office needs access to a pool of neutral and capable investigators with periodically updated skills from which to form an expert group when needed. Third, any such expert group must be given immediate, secure access to the site of any alleged BW use; it must have free, unfettered access to victims and witnesses, and the services of qualified interpreters. Fourth, it must be supported by proper equipment and supplies, including communications. Fifth, the expert group must be able to send whatever samples it collects to capable reference laboratories while keeping chain-of-custody evidence intact.

It bears noting that this approach, to have the UN Secretary-General investigate possible violations of the BWC, was given special attention at the recently concluded Sixth Review conference of the BWC, held in November–December 2006. Its final report "notes that the Secretary-General's investigation mechanism, set out in A/44/561 and endorsed by the General Assembly in its resolution 45/57, represents an international institutional mechanism for investigating cases of alleged use of biological or toxin weapons."[52]

Looking Forward

As a result of the consultative meeting process having been thoroughly discredited by the procedures and results of the August 1997 consultative meeting, three scenarios can be foreseen for how future allegations of biological misconduct will play out.

First, nation A alleges that nation B has violated the BWC, and B knows that the allegation is correct. In this case, A presumably would want B's illegal actions to be revealed to the world, so it would request the Secretary-General to conduct an investigation. B will seek to hide its illegal actions, so it does not want an investigation, but if, for political reasons, B feels it must do something other than refusing investigation outright, it could request a consultative meeting as an alternative to the Secretary-General's investigation, with the aim of seeking to make sure its results will be inconclusive. Were this scenario to be realized, the issue of importance would be how to resolve any dispute between two state parties as to which course is to be followed, investigation or consultative meeting.

In a second scenario, nation A alleges that nation B has violated the BWC, but B knows that the allegation is erroneous. In this case, A would not know that its allegation is erroneous and therefore would proceed as if a violation had occurred and that B's perceived illegal actions should be revealed to the world. It accordingly would request the Secretary-General to conduct an investigation. Wishing to clear itself of the erroneous charge, B could follow Armenia's 1992 example and request the Secretary-General to investigate. In this case there would be no dispute, so the Secretary-General's investigation probably would be done.

Third, nation A alleges that nation B has violated the BWC, but the allegation is false. In this case, a situation much like that engineered by the Cuban government in 1997 would result: nation A would like to see its allegation be given wide play but would not want to have its falseness revealed. It therefore would request a consultative meeting, and then act to increase the probability that the meeting generates inconclusive findings. Nation B would wish to clear itself and to reveal the falseness of the charge, so it would request an investigation by the Secretary-General. This case would raise the same issue as the first scenario, namely, how to resolve a dispute as to which approach would be used.

As a general guideline, were a dispute described in scenarios one and three to occur, the most definitive approach should be chosen, which is an investigation by the Secretary-General. To this end, the Secretary-General could proceed with an investigation on his own authority, which he has the right to do according to both UN General Assembly and UN Security Council resolutions. But his hand would be strengthened if the Seventh Review Conference, to be held in 2011, were to codify this approach by adopting an appropriately worded politically binding resolution.

When I started my research for this paper, one of my working hypotheses was that the Cuban government had done a disservice to international biological arms control by having one of its false allegations addressed by a consultative meeting, because it revealed this compliance provision to be useless and, by doing so, weakened the BWC. I am not so certain any longer about this: now I tend to believe that the Cuban government did the international security community a favor by taking an action that revealed the consultative meeting process to be a sham before it was put to a really meaningful test, which it would have failed, with substantial negative consequences. What I mean by this is that the thrip infestation intrinsically had no implications for the operation of the BWC because it posed no real compliance concerns; the minor political issue brought to the forefront by the event had to do with misuse of one of its compliance provisions by Cuba to pursue a false allegation. However, in the event of a real and major violation of the BWC by a nation in the future, no one will be likely to suggest that a consultative meeting should address the violation, because the 1997 meeting demonstrated the futility of this approach. The parties involved having recognized that a BWC consultative meeting would have little or no chance of making an authoritative appraisal as to what occurred nor an attribution as to who was responsible, either the BWC's Article 6 would be invoked, making the UN Security Council responsible for investigating the alleged violation, or the Secretary-General would be requested to undertake the investigation. Either mechanism, if applied quickly and by a well-staffed, well-equipped team, would have a fair-to-middling probability of resolving the allegation to the satisfaction of the international community, something that a consultative meeting would have almost no chance of accomplishing.

Notes

1. Nuclear Threat Initiative, "Cuba Profile: Biological Overview," <http://www.nti.org/e_research/profiles/Cuba/Biological/3481_3482.html>, accessed October 8, 2006.

2. Raymond A. Zilinskas, "Cuban Allegations of Biological Warfare by the United States: Assessing the Evidence," *Critical Reviews in Microbiology* 25, no. 3 (1999): 173–227.

3. R. Eder, "Cuba Charges U.S. May Drop Germs," *New York Times*, June 2, 1965, A9.

4. Cuban authorities tend to lump four outbreaks that occurred in 1979–80—ASF, dengue fever, blue mold disease, and sugar cane rust—into one package of allegations, and give three explanations for why the United States is responsible for them. First,

these diseases appeared almost simultaneously, but such a simultaneous emergence of four different diseases could not have happened by accident or through the workings of natural forces; it could only have occurred because it was done deliberately by an enemy. Second, the pathogens that caused the four outbreaks had been extensively researched as part of the U.S. biological warfare program and that the results of this research was now being applied to attack Cuba. Third, the imperialistic U.S. government has an implacable hatred for the Cuban government and would use any means, including biological weapons, to bring it down.

5. Cuba, *Consultative Meeting of State Parties of the Convention on Biological Weapons Request by the Republic of Cuba: The Use of Biological Weapons by the United States of America Against Cuba* (Geneva: Government of Cuba, August 1997).

6. Cuba, *Consultative Meeting of State Parties on the CBW Request,* 1997.

7. Zilinskas, "Cuban Allegations of Biological Warfare by the United States."

8. F. Castro, "That This Country Can Never Be Threatened, Never Be Intimidated, to Give Up a Single One Of Its Principles," *Granma Weekly Review,* March 16, 1980.

9. G. B. Lucas, "The War Against Blue Mold," *Science* 210 (1980): 147–53; C. E. Main, "The Blue Mold Disease of Tobacco," 2005, <http://www.ces.ncsu.edu/depts/pp/bluemold/thedisease.php>, accessed October 23, 2006.

10. L. H. Purdy, S. V. Krupa, and J. L. Dean, "Introduction of Sugarcane Rust into the Americas and Its Spread to Florida," *Plant Disease* 69 (1985): 689–93.

11. L. H. Purdy, S. V. Krupa, and J. L. Dean, "Introduction of Sugarcane Rust into the Americas and Its Spread to Florida."

12. O. Johnston, "U.S. Rebuts Cuba, OKs Virus Control Aid," *Los Angeles Times,* July 28, 1981, 5; "Offer of Pesticide to Cuba Revealed," *Washington Post,* July 29, 1981:A25; V. Cohn, " 'Neglected' Dengue Fever Now Looms in Caribbean," *Washington Post,* August 4, 1981, A5.

13. Cuba, "Declaration by the Revolutionary Government of Cuba," September 9, 1981.

14. P. K. Thomas et al., "An Epidemic of Optic Neuropathy and Painful Sensory Neuropathy in Cuba: Clinical Aspects," *Journal of Neurology* 242, no. 10 (1995): 629–38.

15. Public Health Ministry of Cuba, "Public Health Ministry: Neuropathy Epidemic Controlled," Radio Broadcast at 17:00 GMT on September 10, 1993, *Havana Radio Rebelde Network.*

16. Granma, "Compensation Claim Against the United States: Pain Has No Price," 1999, <http://www.granma.cubaweb.com/cubademanda/ingles/demanda14-i.html>, accessed October 20, 2006; Juan O. Tamayo and Meg Laughlin, "Cuba Files $181 Billion Claim Against the U.S.," *Miami Herald,* June 2, 1999, <http://www.latinamericanstudies.org/us-cuba/181-claim.htm>, accessed January 10, 2007.

17. Raisa Paiges, "Lawsuit Against U.S. for Economic Damages: $121 Billion USD Demanded in Compensation," *Granma International*, April 10, 2000, <http://www. latinamericanstudies.org/us-cuba/lawsuit-damages.htm>, accessed January 10, 2007.

18. The names of diseases are as written by the Cubans.

19. The Center for Defense Information (CDI) is a non-governmental organization based in Washington, DC, that describes its objective as providing "expert analysis on various components of U.S. national security, international security and defense policy"; <http://www.cdi.org/about/index.cfm>, accessed March 23, 2007.

20. Jonathan B. Tucker, "Assessing the U.S. Bioweapons Allegations Against Cuba" (Washington, DC: Center for Defense Information, January 10, 2005), <http://www. wsicubaproject.org/cubanbiotech_05.cfm>, accessed March 26, 2007.

21. Tucker, "Assessing the U.S. Bioweapons Allegations Against Cuba."

22. K. Sakimura, L. M. Nakahara, and H. A. Denmark, "A Thrips, *Thrips palmi* Karny," Florida Department of Agriculture and Consumer Services, Division of Plant Industry, Entomology Circular no. 280, January 1986, <http://www.doacs.state.fl.us/pi/ enpp/ento/entcirc/ent280.pdf>, accessed January 1, 2007.

23. B. Denoyes, D. Bordat, H. de Bon, and P. Daly, "A New Pest of Vegetable Crops in Martinique: *Thrips palmi* Karny," *Agronomie Tropicale* 41 (1986): 167–68.

24. K. Sakimura, L. M. Nakahara, and H. A. Denmark, "A Thrips, *Thrips palmi* Karny."

25. Cuba, "Note verbale dated 28 April 1997 from the Permanent Mission of Cuba to the United Nations addressed to the Secretary-General," United Nations General Assembly document A/52/128.

26. N. Diaz, "FAO-Sponsored Project to Control 'Thrips palmi': Blight Introduced as Part of U.S. Biological Warfare Against Cuba," *Granma International*, December 8, 1997.

27. Cuba, "Note verbale dated 28 April 1997 from the Permanent Mission of Cuba to the United Nations addressed to the Secretary-General."

28. Nicholas A. Sims, *The Diplomacy of Biological Disarmament: Vicissitudes of a Treaty in Force, 1975–85* (New York: St. Martin's Press, 1988): 199–225.

29. Quoted in Nicholas A. Sims, *The Evolution of Biological Disarmament*, SIPRI Chemical and Biological Warfare Studies 19 (Solna, Sweden: Stockholm International Peace Research Institute, 2001): 32.

30. Ian Soutar, *Report to All State Parties to the Biological and Toxin Weapons Convention on the Results of the Formal Consultative Meeting of State Parties to the Biological and Toxin Weapons Convention held from 25–27 August 1997* (Geneva: United Kingdom Permanent Representation, 1997); Zilinskas, "Cuban Allegations of Biological Warfare by the United States"; Sims, *The Evolution of Biological Disarmament*.

31. The statements are reproduced in the formal report of the meeting: Formal Con-

sultative Meeting of State Parties to the Convention, *Report*, document BWC/CONS/1, Geneva, 27 August 1997; Cuba, "Note verbale dated 28 April 1997 from the Permanent Mission of Cuba to the United Nations addressed to the Secretary-General"; United States, *Documents in Support of United States Presentation Regarding Cuban BW Allegations, Geneva, Switzerland, 25 August 1997* (Geneva: United States Delegation, 1997).

32. Ian Soutar, *Report to All State Parties to the Biological and Toxin Weapons Convention*.

33. Ian Soutar, *Report to All State Parties to the Biological and Toxin Weapons Convention*, paragraph 7.

34. L. L. V. Moreno, *Guia Para el Diagnostico Entomologico, 1: Thrips palmi Karny (Thysanoptera: Thripidae)* (Havana: Instituto de Investigaciones de Sanidad Vegetal, 1998).

35. L. L. V. Moreno, *Guia Para el Diagnostico Entomologico, 1: Thrips palmi Karny*.

36. Formal Consultative Meeting of State Parties to the Convention, *Report*.

37. Soutar, *Report to All State Parties to the Biological and Toxin Weapons Convention*, paragraph 5.

38. Soutar, *Report to All State Parties to the Biological and Toxin Weapons Convention*, paragraph 7.

39. United States, *Documents in Support of United States Presentation Regarding Cuban BW Allegations*.

40. It is useful to define the words "accuse," "allege," and "attribute." To accuse is to charge unequivocally with a specified or implied wrong or fault, often in a condemnatory or indignant manner. To allege is to state or declare as if under oath positively and assuredly but without offering complete proof. To attribute is to explain as caused or brought about by, or to regard as occurring in consequence of or on account of. *Webster's Third New International Dictionary, Unabridged* (Merriam-Webster, 2002) <http://unabridged.merriam-webster.com>; accessed January 27, 2007.

41. U.S. Department of State, "Chemical Warfare in Southeast Asia and Afghanistan: Report to the Congress from Secretary of State Alexander M. Haig, Jr.," Special Report No. 98, March 22, 1982; U.S. Department of State, "Chemical Warfare in Southeast Asia and Afghanistan: An Update. Report from Secretary of State George P. Shultz," Special Report No. 104, November 1982.

42. United Nations General Assembly, "Chemical and Bacteriological (Biological) Weapons: Report of the Secretary-General," document A/36/613, November 20, 1981.

43. United Nations General Assembly, "Chemical and Bacteriological (Biological) Weapons: Report of the Secretary-General," document A/37/259, December 1, 1982.

44. The 1997 consultative meeting described above did not call on any kind of technical expertise or investigation.

45. J. B. Tucker and R. A. Zilinskas, "Assessing U.S. Proposals to Strengthen the

Biological Weapons Convention," *Arms Control Today* 32 (202): 10–14 <http://www.armscontrol.org/act/2002_04/tuczilapril02.asp>, accessed January 28, 2007.

46. United Nations Security Council, *Report of the Specialists Appointed by the Secretary-General to Investigate Allegations by the Islamic Republic of Iran Concerning the Use of Chemical Weapons*, document S/16433, March 26, 1984.

47. United Nations Security Council, *Report of the Specialists Dispatched by the Secretary-General to Investigate Allegations of the Use of Chemical Weapons in the Conflict Between Iran and Iraq*, document S/18852, May 8, 1987.

48. United Nations Security Council, *Report of the Mission Dispatched by the Secretary-General to Investigate Allegations of the Use of Chemical Weapons in the Conflict Between the Islamic Republic of Iran and Iraq*, document S/20063, July 25, 1988.

49. United Nations Security Council, *Report of the Mission Dispatched by the Secretary-General to Investigate Allegations of the Use of Chemical Weapons in the Conflict Between the Islamic Republic of Iran and Iraq*, document S/17911, March 12, 1986.

50. United Nations Security Council, *Report of the Mission Dispatched by the Secretary-General to Investigate Allegations of the Use of Chemical Weapons in the Conflict Between the Islamic Republic of Iran and Iraq*, document S/20060, July 20, 1988.

51. Tucker and Zilinskas, "Assessing U.S. Proposals to Strengthen the Biological Weapons Convention."

52. Sixth Review Conference of the States Parties to the Convention on the Prohibition of the Development, Production and Stockpiling of Bacteriological (Biological) and Toxin Weapons and on Their Destruction, *Final Document*, document number BWC/CONF.VI/6, Geneva, 2006.

CHAPTER EIGHT

Imperial Japan's Germ Warfare

The Suppression of Evidence at the Tokyo War Crimes Trial, 1946–1948

JEANNE GUILLEMIN

During the twentieth century, most of the world's major military powers—France, the Soviet Union, Imperial Japan, the United Kingdom, and the United States—covertly attempted to develop biological weapons (BW).[1] Among these now defunct national programs, that of Imperial Japan stands out as uniquely criminal, in two ways. First, its secret BW venture, based in occupied Manchuria and lasting from 1932 to 1945, relied extensively on inhumane medical experimentation, mainly involving captured Chinese men and also women and children. Second, Japanese military leaders actually conducted biological warfare against civilian populations. In the years 1940–43, Japan's military attacked Chinese cities and towns with plague, cholera, typhoid, dysentery, anthrax, glanders, and other lethal diseases. By some reckonings, the Japanese program, including recurring plague epidemics, caused hundreds of thousands of deaths and casualties.[2]

Immediately after the war, key Japanese leaders responsible for the BW program ought to have been indicted for these war crimes at the 1946–48 International Military Tribunal of the Far East (IMTFE), also known as the Tokyo war crimes trial. Instead, at this critical legal juncture, the United States withheld evidence concerning Japan's BW program, and the other victor nations posed no objection. As this chapter describes, there was no shortage of incriminating facts. First-hand testimony and medical and laboratory documents about

Japan's biological weapons emerged during the war and, after Japan's surrender, continued to circulate in diplomatic and intelligence channels. During the Tokyo war crimes trial, mainly for reasons of national security, American authorities chose not to present evidence for indictments of Japanese leaders for BW-related crimes. Further, in April 1947, U.S. officials secretly arranged to protect Major-General Ishii Shiro, the program's leader, and 18 other BW medical scientists from IMTFE prosecution, in exchange for their information about human experimentation and biological warfare.[3]

Historically, the IMTFE represents an important missed opportunity to impose legal safeguards for future civilians at risk from biological weapons. In 1948, an international legal precedent could have been established for prosecuting state leaders or other individuals in violation of the 1925 Geneva Protocol, which prohibits the use in war of biological and chemical weapons. An international legal precedent also could have been set for banning all state BW programs, which is the essence of the 1972 Biological and Toxin Weapons Convention (BWC). Following the IMTFE, unrestrained by any recognized criminalization of biological weapons, the United States, United Kingdom, France, and the Soviet Union, and also Israel, South Africa, and Iraq, pursued their secret BW programs, with destructive and destabilizing repercussions extending into this century.

The Nature of the Crimes: Japan's BW Program

The secrecy surrounding the crimes committed under the Japanese biological warfare program had eroded by the late 1970s, after the Western powers—the United States, United Kingdom, and France—had terminated their offensive biological weapons programs. In the 1980s and 1990s, Japanese and Western journalists and scholars began to expose the Japanese BW program, which, in turn, prompted some of its former BW scientists and military commanders to confess old crimes.[4] The enactment by the U.S. Congress of the Japanese Imperial Government Disclosure Act (P.L. 106-657) in 2000 resulted in the retrieval of over 100,000 pages of U.S. government documents which support many previous findings and further describe the organization and crimes of the Japanese BW program.[5]

Code named Unit 731, the program's center was a walled town with 70 buildings—including officer housing, a Buddhist temple, a brothel, prison blocks,
laboratories, an air field, and three crematoria—on six square kilometers near
the city of Harbin in Japanese-occupied Manchuria. Its other major division,
Unit 100, was in Changchun, also in Manchuria. After the start of the China
War in 1937, satellite facilities were created in Nanking, Singapore, Shanghai,
and elsewhere in China, French Indochina, and Burma. At Unit 731 and Unit
100 in particular, Japanese scientists experimented with anthrax, plague, cholera, typhus, and other diseases using human subjects, mostly Chinese and also
some Soviet, White Russian, and Mongolian captives rounded up by the Japanese Kwantung Army and its military police (the Kempetai) in Manchuria.[6]
The Japanese also conducted human experiments on the physiological effects
of freezing and high pressure. Captive men and "comfort women" were infected
with syphilis to investigate cures for the Japanese army.[7] Human vivisection
(with and without chloroform) was common. Captives were also used in field
tests of explosive germ bombs. Japanese policy was to execute any survivors. A
conservative estimate is that, at Unit 731 alone, 3,000 people died from medical
experiments.[8]

General Ishii's first experience with directing the Kwantung Army's use of
biological weapons was in 1939, against Soviet forces at the border shared by
Manchuria, Mongolia, and the Soviet Union, in a battle called the Nomonhan
Incident. After the Japanese defeat on August 30, Ishii organized saboteurs to
infect Soviet troops with typhus, paratyphus, cholera, and dysentery. Although
the outcome was inconclusive, General Ishii and Unit 731 received Kwantung
Army commendations for this effort.[9]

These commendations were followed by Ishii's increased involvement in
Kwantung Army campaigns, led by its new commander-in-chief, Umezu Yoshijiro, as part of the intensification of the China War.[10] In 1940, over the course
of five months, Ishii directed a number of disease attacks on the Chinese port
city of Ningpo and the surrounding area. Using planes for air drops and spies to
infiltrate enemy settlements, the Kwantung Army spread plague-infected fleas,
reportedly making a thousand people ill and causing 100 deaths. The Japanese
also sought to infect the area's water sources with typhoid and cholera germs.
Disease outbreaks caused alarm, particularly since plague was not endemic to

the area, but the subterfuge with which most attacks were conducted made it difficult to attribute them to the Japanese.

Wartime Accounts from China

In the summer and fall of 1941, General Ishii directed more BW attacks on central China, in Chekiang (Zhejiang) Province, Hunan Province, and Honan Province. Peter Z. King, director general of China's National Health Administration, assembled a report of all the attacks, starting with Ningpo, and this report became the basis for China's 1942 accusation that Japan had engaged in biological warfare.[11]

The attack on the city of Changteh (Changde), a commercial center of 50,000 people in Hunan Province already besieged by Japanese air attacks, was well documented and corroborated after the war by former Japanese BW scientists.[12] The causal link between a November 4 air drop and the outbreak that began in the city ten days later was identified at the time by Dr. Robert H. Pollitzer, an Austrian epidemiologist from the Chinese National Health Administration who had spent 20 years studying plague in China. Pollitzer noted that nearly all cases occurred in neighborhoods where suspicious grain and cotton had been air-dropped in profusion. He pointed out that plague was not endemic in Hunan Province or likely to have been communicated via any trade routes to the then-isolated Changteh. He reasoned that plague-infected fleas were the vectors and that the Japanese had added grain to attract rats as hosts to spread the disease. Pollitzer concluded that "the recent plague outbreak in Changteh was in causal connection with the aerial attack of November 4th."[13] He repeated his observations in an April 1942 medical journal article, co-authored with Dr. Robert Lim, head of the Chinese Red Cross.[14]

Dr. Won Kwei Chen, head of the Department of Laboratory Medicine of the Emergency Medical Service Training School in Kweiyang (Guiyang), concurred with Pollitzer and verified that plague was indeed the disease that eventually affected hundreds.[15] Dr. Chen's autopsy of a 28-year-old man who had fallen ill on November 23 confirmed the clinical diagnosis of plague. Six other fatal cases were confirmed by tissue culture. Dr. Chen documented five more suspected cases, for which tests revealed bacilli resembling those of plague.

China wanted the Allies and the wider world to respond to this new kind of Japanese aggression. In early 1942, the Chinese distributed the King report to the U.S., UK, and eight other embassies in Chungking. The document was then circulated among Allied officials and infectious disease experts, whose reactions were mixed.[16] The report was ultimately forwarded to the Allies' Pacific War Council, but the Americans and British were against raising public suspicions of Japanese biological warfare. At the time, both governments had begun their own covert BW quests. In July 1942, UK program scientists were in Scotland testing anthrax bombs for possible strategic use against Germany.[17] The United States, having laid the groundwork for an immense BW program, was intent on keeping the public from knowing about it.[18]

While the Chinese allegations of Japanese biological warfare were virtually ignored in the West, General Ishii was awarded his greatest opportunity to demonstrate the achievements of his program, in a scorched-earth campaign focused on Chekiang Province. In the April 1942 Doolittle air raid on Tokyo, the United States had relied on the Chekiang region southwest of Hangzhou, along the Zhejiang-Jiangxi Railway, as an escape route for its air crews; after the raid, downed U.S. pilots found refuge in its towns and villages. Late that summer, in retreat from the advancing Chinese army, the Japanese military destroyed railway lines and air bases in the area. In revenge for assistance to Americans, entire towns and villages were razed. An estimated 250,000 Chinese civilians in Chekiang were killed by bombings, artillery attacks, and mass executions.[19]

Biological weapons were also used in this campaign. General Umezu enlisted the aid of General Ishii and 300 of his trained staff to assist in the aerial spraying of germ agents and in infecting water supplies. The spread of cholera, dysentery, typhoid, plague, anthrax, glanders, and paratyphoid was intended to make the area uninhabitable, first for civilians and then for Chinese ground troops. Although it was difficult to distinguish the impact of germ warfare from that of conventional weapons, deaths from these disease attacks have been characterized as enormous, perhaps in the many thousands.[20] Interviews conducted in 2002 with Chinese survivors suggest that there were thousands of civilian casualties from anthrax and glanders alone.[21] Despite precautionary measures, Japan's own troops suffered an estimated 10,000 casualties and almost 2,000 deaths, most of them from cholera.[22] Although Ishii had more plans for germ warfare, these accidental casualties apparently affected his reputation and he directed no further mass BW attacks.

The International Military Tribunal
for the Far East (IMTFE)

In 1945, the United States led the way in criminal prosecution of defeated Axis leaders. On August 8, 1945, two days after the Hiroshima bombing, the Allies—the United States, the United Kingdom, the Soviet Union, and France—signed the London Agreement mandating the prosecution of war criminals by the International Military Tribunal (IMT) and outlining the tribunal's constitution, jurisdiction, and functions. The London Charter, based largely on rules for U.S. military commissions, became a model for the many World War II war crimes tribunals that followed in Europe, the Pacific, and Asia.

The common conceptual framework for the Nuremberg and Tokyo tribunals was that the Axis governments had criminally conspired to make aggressive war in a time of peace and that individuals among them bore responsibility for war crimes and crimes against humanity.[23] The crime of "war of aggression" referred not to the technical means by which war was carried out or the scope of destruction, but to the unprovoked nature of Axis military aggression. Generally, crimes against humanity referred to Axis assaults on civilians and prisoners-of-war.

The first Nuremberg tribunal was completed in less than a year, in October 1946, just before the Tokyo tribunal commenced. Its four judges (American, British, Soviet, and French) imposed death sentences on 11 of 22 accused high-level Nazi leaders. There were three life sentences and three acquittals for other defendants; with the rest of the accused were given sentences of 10 to 20 years. This first Nuremberg tribunal was followed by 12 other U.S. military tribunals to prosecute Nazi criminals, notably the "Doctors Trial," which held individual physicians accountable for crimes of mass extermination and forced human experimentation.

Neither the London Charter nor the later Tokyo Charter imposed technical rules of evidence; both allowed tribunal members the authority to evaluate and admit evidence as they saw fit.[24] The amount of documentary evidence available at the two tribunals differed significantly.[25] In Germany, despite Nazi efforts to destroy incriminating documents, many were discovered in duplicate throughout the Reich and quickly made available to prosecutors. On its part, the Japanese government efficiently organized the destruction of as much as

70 percent of the army's wartime records. After the war, Japanese officials were initially able to block access to sensitive files. Problems with translating the tens of thousands of documents that were eventually turned over to prosecutors further slowed the momentum of the IMTFE.

General Douglas MacArthur, in his capacity as Supreme Commander of the Allied Powers (SCAP) in the Pacific, exerted great control over the IMTFE—its charter, the appointment of judges, and who would be indicted. In opposition to Australia and other nations, MacArthur insisted that the emperor and his family be exempt from war crimes prosecution, lest the political infrastructure of Japan collapse and endanger U.S. occupying troops and the future of a democratic Japan as an American ally. The speculation that IMTFE revelations about the Japanese BW program might have destroyed the emperor's reputation has persisted as an explanation for the secrecy that the United States imposed in 1947.[26] The emperor, trained as a biologist, almost certainly understood the offensive objectives of Ishii's large venture; moreover, several members of the royal family had visited Unit 731 and were familiar with its research methods from the frequent lectures Ishii and others gave at medical centers.[27]

An alternative explanation for the U.S. suppression of Japanese BW evidence emerges from documents showing that U.S. government agencies in charge of decisions were consistently motivated by national security interests, and in particular, the military option to pursue a biological weapons capability. By March 1947, military intelligence (G-2) in Tokyo and the U.S. Army's Chemical Corps, which housed the U.S. biological weapons program, had convinced the Joint Chiefs of Staff and other high-level Washington officials that information about the Japanese biological weapons program was vital to national security.

Judges and prosecutorial teams from 11 victor nations participated in the IMTFE. Their national agendas and international alliances strongly influenced their contributions to the proceedings. The UK and Dominion judges from Canada, Australia, and New Zealand generally acted in concert with the United States, as did the judges from China and the Philippines. The judges from France, the Netherlands, and India disagreed with their colleagues on several fundamental issues, but only behind the scenes. In public, the judges and prosecutors from the 10 other nations followed the U.S. lead and acquiesced in decisions emanating from the office of SCAP.[28]

The Soviet Union was perhaps more familiar with the Japanese biological weapons program than any other foreign nation.[29] Before and during the war, its intelligence services had tracked information about Japanese BW activity. After the war, the Soviet Union was the first to gain concrete knowledge of the Japanese biological warfare program. In August 1945, after crossing the border to northern Manchuria, the Soviet military investigated the ruins of Unit 731 left by fleeing Japanese. Then, after searching among Japanese prisoners of war, it found and interrogated two dozen who had been affiliated with the BW program. Yet, for reasons that remain unclear, the USSR was complicit in the American decision not to introduce incriminating evidence about the Japanese program at the IMTFE.

Of all the nations at the tribunal, China had the most reason to pursue prosecution of Japanese biological weapons crimes, but the least latitude for independent initiative. Nationalist China's 1946–48 collusion in the suppression of evidence about Japanese biological weapons can be explained by its dependence on the United States, which was then supporting it in the violent, uncertain civil war against the Chinese communists. Rather than identifying atrocities involving biological weapons research and use, the Chinese argued for the prosecution of Japanese leaders on much broader charges: Japan's military invasions of China beginning as early as 1927, its occupation of Manchuria starting in 1932, and its brutality against Chinese civilians and captured soldiers. The IMTFE estimated, for example, that in 1937 Japanese forces invading the city of Nanking had murdered 300,000 Chinese. Even that atrocity received much less attention at the IMTFE than Japanese aggression in the Pacific, starting with the 1941 bombing of Pearl Harbor, and brutal treatment of Allied prisoners of war and civilians.[30]

The Tokyo war crimes trial began in May 1946, nearly 9 months after the Japanese surrender. As in Nuremberg in 1945, the Allies' intention was to indict only the highest-ranked officials and to move quickly to justice.

In early March 1946, before the trial commenced, Colonel Thomas Morrow, an American lawyer at the International Prosecution Section (IPS) of the IMTFE, noticed two articles in the U.S. Army's publication *Pacific Stars and Stripes* concerning interviews that Lieutenant Colonel Arvo Thompson, a biological weapons expert from the U.S. Army's Chemical Weapons Service (CWS) at Camp Detrick, had recently conducted with General Ishii. Although these articles emphasized Japanese defensive research, mention was made of plague experiments on humans and Ishii's invention of a porcelain BW bomb. Aware of China's 1942 accusations, Morrow alerted his boss, Joseph Keenan, the chief prosecutor for the IMTFE, who had been appointed by President Harry Truman. On Keenan's recommendation, Morrow immediately contacted the Tokyo office of G-2, where he met Thompson, who apparently had nothing significant to communicate.[31]

A week later, Morrow went to China as part of an investigatory IPS group aimed at advising the Chinese on their war crimes tribunals. His intention was to have Dr. King and other experts testify at the IMTFE. Also traveling in China was David Sutton, the American lawyer assisting the Chinese prosecutor, Che-chun Hsiang. Sutton interviewed Dr. King, Dr. Pollitzer, and Dr. Chen and obtained a copy of the King report. Sutton was unpersuaded. After returning to Tokyo in April, he advised Keenan that "no attempt be made to establish the use of bacteria warfare by the Japanese against China," although he mentioned that efforts were continuing in China to secure more evidence.[32] In May, Hsiang passed Sutton more evidence of Japanese BW, for example, first-hand testimony from Ishii's own staff.[33] As crafted by Sutton, though, the Chinese case presented that summer focused on the Rape of Nanking and similar atrocities committed by the Japanese army using conventional weapons. No other nation took up the issue of Japan's biological weapons program.

At the conclusion of the IMTFE, after two-and-a-half years, verdicts for 25 defendants were handed down.[34] Seven were sentenced to hang; 16 were sentenced to life imprisonment, including General Umezu; one defendant was sentenced to 20 years in prison and another to 7 years. The IMTFE lasted long enough to be affected by the communist victory in the Chinese civil war, Soviet expansion into Eastern Europe, and the intensifying Cold War antagonism between Moscow and Washington that would lead to an arms race of unprecedented dimensions.

Postwar Investigations and the Immunity Bargain

U.S. intelligence agencies played a major role in assessing the Japanese program. By May 1944, U.S. military intelligence had gathered a significant number of reports about the existence of Japan's BW program.[35] In addition, soon after the defeat of Japan, the United States engaged its scientists in investigating and assessing innovative Japanese weapons technology, just as it had done earlier in Germany.[36] The earliest U.S. mission to evaluate Japan's weapons, in November 1945, included five civilian and four military scientists, three from the Chemical Warfare Service (CWS).[37] After six weeks of interviews and site visits, U.S. investigators found little of scientific interest in Japan's chemical weapons program, which had been abandoned earlier in the war, or in its rudimentary attempt to develop nuclear weapons. Japan's biological weapons program was evaluated differently, in part because U.S. investigators sensed that the Japanese scientists they had interviewed were withholding important information. The conclusion, communicated to President Harry Truman, was that the Japanese program might contribute to American knowledge.

The U.S. BW program was then in crisis; its extensive wartime projects, including one to mass produce anthrax bombs, had been dismantled and most of its personnel had returned to civilian life.[38] Some within the military, especially at the Chemical Warfare Service, aggressively lobbied for the program's renewed expansion. Their argument, which would be refined over the next several years, was that biological weapons had a strategic potential similar to nuclear weapons and thus should be developed before the USSR seized the advantage.[39]

In May 1946, Lieutenant Colonel Thompson from CWS submitted his intelligence report based on his interviews with General Ishii. Ishii claimed that Japan's program had developed effective vaccines and curative sera for plague, typhoid, dysentery, and other diseases, as well as diagnostic sera and antigens and drugs, including penicillin.[40] Ishii also reported having done research on animal diseases, including anthrax and glanders, and on anticrop agents, but he denied that the program had an offensive component or engaged in human experimentation. Ishii's assertions of innocence were, however, contradicted by G-2 information from other sources, such as testimony from former BW program employees and earlier accounts from Japanese prisoners-of-war.[41]

Soviet Pressure to Share Information

In late 1946, Soviet representatives to the IMTFE began pressing their agenda regarding the Japanese BW program, which focused on murders of Soviet citizens and soldiers. They gave U.S. General Headquarters (GHQ) copies of signed affidavits by two Japanese BW scientists from Unit 731, Dr. Karasawa

Tomio and Major General Kawashima Kiyoshi, who had been captured by the Soviet military the previous year. Karasawa's affidavit described multiple germ attacks on Chinese civilians. It also described his participation in inhumane experiments on captives, perhaps the most credible evidence on this subject GHQ had seen. These and other Japanese informants in Soviet custody identified General Ishii as the program's leader and named two other Unit 731 officials, Colonel Ota Kiyoshi and Major Hinofuji Nobukazu, alleged then to be in Japan. The affidavits also implicated General Umezu Yoshijiro, who had been the Kwantung Army commander-in-chief from late 1939 to 1944, as an accomplice in Ishii's criminal activities. Among the 24 defendants already listed in 1946 were at least six former high-level Kwantung Army officials who had overseen General Ishii's program and might also have been held accountable. Unlike the others, Umezu had actually engaged in biological warfare; at USSR insistence, General Umezu was added to the list of IMFTE defendants. His BW-related activities were not specified, but the door remained open for the Soviet prosecutor to introduce evidence of those crimes.

On January 7, 1947, the International Prosecution Section informed G-2 that the senior Soviet prosecutor at the IMTFE, General A.N. Vasiliev, was impatiently requesting interviews with former Japanese BW scientists known to the Americans, to gain "evidence for war crimes" involving Soviet victims.[42] The response from Washington was guarded. The Americans and Soviets had worked well together at the Nuremberg tribunal, but a Cold War chill had begun to affect their relationship. Reflecting this, the climate at SCAP and GHQ in Tokyo was one of suspicion about Soviet intentions.[43]

On January 10, 1947, with little evidence in hand, G-2 reported that Japanese human experimentation data were "of the highest intelligence value."[44] Soon the facts the Americans were gathering about the Japanese program were put beyond the reach of any prosecutors. On March 5, 1947, the Joint Chiefs of Staff made the decision to put G-2 in charge of all information from the Japanese biological weapons scientists, mandating "the utmost secrecy . . . in order to protect the interests of the United States and to guard against embarrassment."[45] G-2 informed SCAP's Legal Section, which had accumulated a considerable file on the Japanese program, that its independent investigation of Ishii should be closed and that no prosecution of him would be possible without G-2 concurrence.[46]

After weeks of delay, in a March 20 communiqué, the U.S. Joint Chiefs of Staff finally agreed to let Soviet prosecutors interrogate Japanese scientists, within strict guidelines: U.S. monitors must be present, war crimes could not be discussed, and the Japanese were to be instructed beforehand not to reveal important information.[47]

Soviet pressure to meet with Japanese BW scientists spurred the Americans to expedite debriefings of Ishii and the other former BW medical scientists. On April 1, 1947, Dr. Norbert Fell, a Detrick division chief, arrived in Tokyo to conduct intensive interviews with Ishii and other scientists. An officer from CWS had already interviewed Colonel Ota and Major Hinofuji to ascertain whether they were anti-communist and favored the U.S. Occupation.[48] Soviet interrogations of the Japanese scientists were put off until late May, after Fell's interviews were completed. The Soviet prosecutors probably learned little from their interrogations, full records of which have yet to surface from either U.S. or USSR archives.

The Immunity Bargain

In the immediate postwar period, the U.S. government had the authority to make decisions regarding leniency and exemptions from war crimes prosecution, particularly on the basis of national security objectives. For example, Joint Chiefs of Staff directive 1067 for German occupation ordered U.S. authorities to arrest Nazi war criminals and those who abetted them, but left a loophole for individuals who might be "useful for intelligence or other military reasons."[49] Deals were struck with Nazi Germany's weapons scientists in return for amnesty, immigration, and U.S. defense employment.[50] This same exemption was applied to postwar Japan, through the JCS and the State-War-Navy Coordinating Committee (SWNCC), a national political-military group created in 1944. In July 1946, SWNCC directive 216/1 allowed local military commanders to withhold intelligence information that might jeopardize or prejudice U.S. relations with a foreign government. In approving this directive, the JCS put SWNCC in charge of adjudicating all intelligence requests, whether from the military or the Department of State. Thus SWNCC became a crucial decision maker in the U.S. immunity bargain with Japanese BW scientists.[51]

Once Dr. Fell's debriefings began, General Ishii and a dozen or so of his former colleagues began offering promises of important documents on experiments and disease attacks in exchange for immunity from war-crimes prosecution. On April 29, 1947, Dr. Fell met with three former Japanese BW scientists to discuss broadening the network of informants. The meeting report describes the request from their spokesman, Naito Ryoichi, and Fell's response:

> We are afraid some of us will be prosecuted as war criminals. . . . If you can give us documentary immunity, probably we can get anything [from other BW scientists]. The Japanese were assured that war crimes were not involved, and Dr. Fell checked the outline submitted earlier and instructed on those points on which more information was needed.[52]

Fell could hardly have made this commitment without General MacArthur's assent. Just days later, on May 5, MacArthur radioed a memo to Washington stating that the Japanese BW scientists should be exempt from prosecution at the trial.[53]

The receipt of MacArthur's statement, along with a report from Fell also advising immunity, divided members of SWNCC.[54] Its subcommittee on biological weapons was strongly in favor of immunity; a dominant member was Major General Alden Waitt, Chief of the Chemical Corps (formerly CWS), who wanted the BW program that was under his command to continue and thrive. The SWNCC representative from the Department of State, Richard A. Feary, who was not a BW subcommittee member, disputed the necessity of a written agreement. He also warned of a great public outcry should such a bargain become known outside intelligence circles. At that time, seven defendants at the Doctors Trial in Nuremberg were on trial for war crimes similar to those committed by Ishii and his BW scientists.

To protect the Japanese BW war criminals from prosecution would make the United States complicit in obstructing justice, as SWNCC was aware. In August 1947 the SWNCC subcommittee articulated its rationale for an immunity bargain: "The value to the U.S. of Japanese BW data is of such importance to national security as to far outweigh the value accruing from 'war crimes' prosecution."[55] The prosecution of anyone for BW-related war crimes, the argument went, risked revealing important weapons information to the USSR, which could endanger U.S. national security. President Harry Truman, his chief advisor Admiral William Leahy, or another high-level authority advised of SWNCC's dilemma must have favored approval of the immunity bargain, or at least chose not to forbid it, but no record of such a decision has been found.

Instead, the U.S. government left Camp Detrick scientists with the responsibility of fulfilling the terms of the immunity bargain; that is, they would gather the military intelligence data which was unavailable for prosecution purposes.

By March 1948, SWNCC concluded that, since the taking of evidence at the IMTFE had ended, the Japanese immunity bargain had become a *fait accompli* that no longer needed a signed agreement. A SWNCC cable on March 11, 1948, to the JCS recommended that a message be sent to General MacArthur advising him that, since the Detrick scientists were satisfied with the information received, the bargain had been fulfilled.[56] On March 13, a JCS message to that effect was sent to MacArthur.[57]

The scientific and technical yield from the Japanese scientists was disappointing, as might have been predicted from careful analysis of existing attack data (which showed their consistently crude methods) and of general information about Japanese medical science. The information on Japanese human experimentation, although voluminous and highly detailed, was disorganized and fragmentary.[58] The Japanese BW program was also technically far behind the United States and the United Kingdom in generating fine aerosols or engineering effective BW bombs.

Organizationally, though, the U.S. BW program gained greatly from the immunity bargain. First and foremost, the agreement gave the United States the military option of a strategic weapons program that might otherwise have been considered illegal, as, in fact, it became a quarter century later, when the 1972 Biological and Toxin Weapons Convention came into force. Instead of public documentation of the consequences of BW use, the secret immunity deal prevented worldwide attention, then riveted on photographs of Hiroshima and Nagasaki victims, from being focused on another new weapon of mass destruction, one that harkened back to the medieval Black Death.

After the Soviet Union tested its first atomic bomb in August 1949, the JCS, the Chemical Corps, and other Washington advocates of a U.S. BW capability argued that the USSR would turn next to biological weapons.[59] This threat and the promise of strategic biological weapons capability guaranteed life to the U.S. secret germ warfare program for another two decades.

The IMTFE Aftermath

In July 1947, when General Umezu's case was heard by the IMFTE, the Soviet prosecutor let pass the opportunity for introducing evidence relating to BW crimes. Umezu, indicted and found guilty on five charges relating to waging a war of aggression, was acquitted on another charge, authorizing or permitting atrocities, that could have linked him to biological weapons. Umezu died in Sugamo prison in 1949. In 1955, other war criminals still in prison were paroled, as Japan hastened to bury its wartime past.[60] After a comfortable retirement on his military pension, General Ishii passed away in 1959. Naito and other former BW scientists went on to successful careers in business or Japanese medical research and public-health administration in which, individually and collectively, they generated an astounding post-war record of ethical violations that jeopardized and cost lives.[61]

Immediately after the IMTFE concluded, the judges from India, the Netherlands, and France expressed dissatisfaction with the tribunal, and particularly with MacArthur's protection of Emperor Hirohito.[62] None mentioned the Japanese biological weapons program or its crimes.

The USSR also openly criticized U.S. "imperialist policy" that allowed Japanese reactionaries and the emperor to escape prosecution.[63] It then went further and conducted its own war-crimes trial of Japanese BW program officials. In the Soviet far-eastern city of Khabarovsk, on December 25–31, 1949, the Soviet Union tried 12 Japanese officials from Unit 731, Unit 100, and elsewhere, who had been captured in 1945 when the USSR overran Manchuria.[64] Representatives from the newly victorious People's Republic of China attended and joined in the criticism, although the Soviet prosecution focused on Japanese aggression against the USSR. It condemned Japanese leaders for employing "a criminal means of mass extermination of human beings—the weapon of bacteriological warfare."[65] The 12 defendants were found guilty and sentenced to 2 to 25 years of imprisonment. In 1956, the sentences still being served were commuted by the USSR as a conciliatory gesture toward Japan.

The USSR found little audience for the Khabarovsk trial outside the Soviet Union and Japan, despite daily press releases to the West. In Tokyo, December protests over Soviet delays in returning hundreds of thousands of Japanese prisoners-of-war overshadowed the trial's horrific testimony. Authorities in the West dismissed the tribunal, a transcript of which was published in English in 1950, as Soviet propaganda.[66] Nevertheless, nearly all of the Khabarovsk testimony was later corroborated by reliable sources.

Decades later, the legal import of the Japanese BW program emerged again. In 2002, in response to a law suit brought by 180 Chinese BW survivors and the families of victims, a court gave Japan's first official acknowledgment that it had used biological weapons against the Chinese. The plaintiffs were, however, denied the compensation and apology they sought.[67] The Japanese government, silent on the issue, has resisted opening its archives on Ishii's program and the IMTFE.

Continuing Legal Impact

The Tokyo war crimes trial has been more criticized than praised for its procedures and results.[68] From the perspective of the history of biological weapons, its major shortcoming consists of what did not happen: evidence was not made public, attribution was not established, and criminals were not prosecuted. The shortfall in legal restraints against biological weapons which began at the IMTFE continues today, leaving the rapidly advancing field of biotechnology open to exploitation for hostile purposes. The 1972 Biological and Toxin Weapons Convention bans BW programs, but it lacks the organizational power to effect compliance with its national-level legal requirements. Article IV of the BWC requires each state party to prohibit the development, production, acquisition, or stockpiling of biological weapons on its own territory or anywhere it has jurisdiction or control. Nearly half of the 151 BWC states parties have yet to do so; most of these are in destabilized areas of the Middle East, Africa, and Pacific Asia.[69]

Limited in its applicability, domestic legislation by itself cannot substitute for international criminal law, which codifies the principle of universal condemnation. A treaty to establish international criminal law—such as that prohibiting torture, aircraft hijacking, and several other crimes—should be created to prohibit the use and programmatic development or possession of biological and chemical weapons, no matter where the perpetrator, a modern-day Ishii or a terrorist, seeks refuge.[70]

The question remains what legal forum could now provide a fair hearing for alleged violations of laws against biological weapons. Culpability for apartheid South Africa's biological and chemical weapons program was only imperfectly adjudicated through hearings before the Truth and Reconciliation Commission and in two protracted civil suits.[71] The International Criminal Court, a likely forum for the prosecution of BW crimes, is at present awkwardly positioned for judgment. Article 8 on war crimes of the 1998 Rome Statute of the International Criminal Court incorporates language from the 1925 Geneva Protocol referring to sanctions against "employing poison weapons," but it leaves out the "bacteriological weapons" also banned by the Protocol.[72]

In sum, the suppression of evidence at the IMFTE of Imperial Japan's biological weapons—evidence that might have helped establish precedents—left a legal void that subsequent international and national laws have yet to fill.

Notes

1. Jeanne Guillemin, *Biological Weapons: From the Invention of State-sponsored Programs to Contemporary Bioterrorism* (New York: Columbia University Press, 2005). Although Germany had used anthrax and glanders in sabotage against pack animals of the Allies in World War I, Adolf Hitler's aversion to biological weapons kept Nazi medical scientists from developing them later.

2. Sheldon H. Harris, *Factories of Death: Japanese Biological Warfare 1932–45 and the American Cover-up* (New York: Routledge, 2002), 78–79.

3. Names of historical Japanese figures are presented family name first (Ishii Umezu).

4. "A Bruise—Terror of the 731 Corps," Tokyo Broadcasting System, November 2, 1976, Yoshinaga Haruko, producer; Tsuneishi Kei-ichi, *The Germ Warfare Unit That Disappeared* (Tokyo: Kai-mei-sha Publishers, 1981); John W. Powell, "Japan's Germ Warfare: The U.S. Cover-up of a War Crime," *The Bulletin of Concerned Asian Scholars* 12, no. 4 (1980): 2–17; Robert Gomer, John W. Powell, and Bert V. A. Röling, "Japan's Biological Weapons: 1930–1945," *The Bulletin of the Atomic Scientists*, October 1981, 43–53; and Peter Williams and David Wallace, *Unit 731: The Japanese Army's Secret of Secrets* (London: Hodder & Stoughton, 1989).

5. Edward Drea et al., *Researching Japanese War Crimes: Introductory Essays* (Washington, DC: National Archives and Records Administration [NARA] for the Nazi War Crimes and Japanese Imperial Government Records Interagency Working Group, 2006), 89–99. No new documentation has been found regarding the immunity bargain between the United States and General Ishii.

6. After the war, accusations of Japanese experiments on Allied prisoners arose but still lack substantive evidence. Harris, *Factories of Death*, 151–62.

7. Hal Gold, *Unit 731 Testimony* (Rutland, VT: Tuttle Publishing, 1996), 159–66.

8. *Materials on the Trial of Former Servicemen of the Japanese Army Charged with Manufacturing and Employing Bacteriological Weapons* (Moscow: Foreign Languages Publishing House, 1950), 431–34.

9. Tsuneishi, *The Germ Warfare Unit That Disappeared*, 36–37.

10. For a concise summary incorporating recently available diaries and testimony, see Harris, *Factories of Death*, 99–107.

11. P. Z. King, "Japanese Attempt at Bacterial Warfare in China," report forwarded to Professor H. K. Meyer, from A. W. Welsh, 15 December 1942, Appendix 1, HRS 14, Sheldon H. Harris Collection, University of California, Berkeley.

12. *Materials on the Trial*, 24.

13. P. Z. King, "Japanese Attempt," 3.

14. "Bacterial Warfare," *Medical Record* 155 (8): 269, 15 April 1942. Pollitzer later wrote the classic monograph *Plague* (Geneva: World Health Organization [WHO], 1954).

15. W. K. Chen, "Report of Plague in Changteh, Hunan," Dec. 12, 1941. David Nelson Sutton Collection, University of Richmond Law Library, Folder 17.

16. Theodor Rosebury, *Peace or Pestilence* (New York: McGraw-Hill, 1949), 109–10. Rosebury, in 1942 a division head at Camp Detrick, thought the accusations had some credibility, but describes George Merck, in charge of U.S. BW efforts, as dismissing them entirely.

17. Brian Balmer, *Britain and Biological Warfare: Expert Advice and Science Policy, 1930–65* (New York: Palgrave, 2001), 41.

18. Leo P. Brophy, Wyndham B. Miles, and Rexmond C. Cochrane, *The Chemical Warfare Service: From Laboratory to Field* (Washington, DC: Office of the Chief of Military History, U.S. Army, 1959), 103.

19. Carroll V. Glines, *The Doolittle Raid: America's Daring First Strike Against Japan* (Atglen, PA: Schiffer Military/Aviation History, 1991), 150–53.

20. Williams and Wallace, *Unit 731*, 69; Harris, *Factories of Death*, 147.

21. Li Xiofang, *Blood-weeping Accusations: Records of Anthrax Victims* (Beijing: CCP Press, 2005).

22. *Materials*, 309, 353–55.

23. R. John Pritchard, "The International Military Tribunal for the Far East and Its Contemporary Resonances: A General Preface to the Collection," in R. John Pritchard, ed., *The Tokyo Major War Crimes Trial: The Complete Transcripts of the Proceedings of the International Military Tribunal for the Far East* (Lewiston, NY: Edwin Mellen Press, 1998), vol. 99, xvii–lxviii.

24. Evan J. Wallach, "The Procedural and Evidentiary Rules of the Post World War II War Crimes Trials: Did They Provide an Outline for International Legal Procedure?" *Columbia Journal of Transnational Law* 37 (1999): 851–83.

25. Edward Drea, "Introduction," in Drea et al., *Researching Japanese War Crimes*, 3–20, 9–11.

26. Marius B. Jansen, *The Making of Modern Japan* (Cambridge, MA: Harvard University Press, 2000), 668–69.

27. Harris, *Factories of Death*, 188–98.

28. On the acquiescence of IMTFE victor nations to the American agenda, see Peter

Calvacoressi, Guy Wint, and John Pritchard, *Total War: The Causes and Courses of the Second World War* (New York: Pantheon, 1989), 1201–6.

29. Williams and Wallace, *Unit 731*, 180–89.

30. Takashi Yoshido, *The Making of the Rape of Nanking* (New York: Oxford University Press, 2006), reviews the recent controversy regarding the history of that atrocity.

31. To Mr. Joseph B. Keenan, Chief of Counsel, from Col. Thomas H. Morrow, Report Assignment "B," 8 March 1946, GHQ, SCAP, IPS, U.S. National Archives.

32. To Mr. Joseph B. Keenan from David Nelson Sutton, Subject: Bacteria Warfare, 25 April 1946. David Nelson Sutton Collection, Folder 13. This letter accompanied Sutton's summary "Report From China. Bacteria Warfare."

33. On May 11, 1946, Hsiang sent Sutton "Testimony regarding crimes committed by a Japanese Force," an in-depth interview with a former Ishii official about the BW facility built post-1937 in Nanking (David Nelson Sutton Collection, Folder 17). In July 1946, at an IMTFE hearing, Sutton inadvertently mentioned Ishii's Chekiang campaign division, and then quickly retreated from the subject. Williams and Wallace, *Unit 731*, 173–76.

34. Two defendants died during the tribunal; another was declared mentally unfit to be tried.

35. Harris, *Factories of Death*, 164–72; Drea et al., *Researching Japanese War Crimes*, 91–99.

36. Samuel Goudsmit, *Alsos* (Los Angeles: Tomash, 1983); John Gimbel, *Science, Technology and Reparations: Exploitation and Plunder in Postwar Germany* (Stanford, CA: Stanford University Press, 1990).

37. R. W. Home and Morris F. Low, "Postwar Scientific Intelligence Missions to Japan," *Isis* 84 (1993): 527–37. In September 1946, the name of the Chemical Warfare Service was changed to the Chemical Corps. In 1956, the center of the U.S. BW program, Camp Detrick, was renamed Fort Detrick.

38. Rexmond C. Cochrane, *Biological Warfare Research in the United States*, vol. II, part D, XXII (1 July 1940–15 August 1945) (Washington, DC: Office of Chief, Chemical Corps, 1947), 452–88.

39. William M. Creasey, "Presentation to the Secretary of Defense's Ad Hoc Committee on CEBAR," 24 February 1950, Joint Chief of Staff Files.

40. A. T. Thompson, "Report on Japanese Biological Warfare (BW) Activities, Army Service Forces, Camp Detrick, Maryland," 31 May 1946, Fort Detrick Archives, Supplement 3e.

41. Harris, *Factories of Death*, 175–77.

42. Memorandum, "USSR Request to Interrogate," March 27, 1947, General Headquarters, Military Intelligence Section, Far East Command, National Security Archive, George Washington University, Chemical and Biological Warfare Collection.

43. Williams and Wallace, *Unit 731*, 184–85.

44. Summary of Information, Subject Ishii, Shiro, January 10, 1947, Document 41, U.S. Army Intelligence and Security Command Archive, Fort Meade, Maryland.

45. State-War-Navy Coordinating Committee (SWNCC) 351/1, March 5, 1947. Record Group 3331, Box 1434.20, Case 330, U.S. National Archives.

46. Thomas Haycraft, *Plague, Politics, and Policy: The Decision to Grant Immunity to Suspected Japanese Biological Warfare War Criminals*, Master's thesis submitted to the U.S. Joint Military Intelligence College, August 1999, 58–59.

47. "Soviet Interrogation of Japanese General Ishii, Colonels Kikushi and Ota on the Subject of Biological Warfare Is Permitted on Several Conditions," War Department Cable 9446, MacArthur from Joint Chiefs of Staff, 20 March, 1947, Chemical and Biological Warfare Collection, National Security Archive, George Washington University.

48. "Interrogation of Dr. Kiyoshi Ota, re: Bacteriological Warfare" GHQ, U.S. Army Forces, Pacific, Office of the Chief Chemical Officer, 2 December, 1946, RG 319 ACSI, MFB, WNA.

49. Frank M. Buscher, *The U.S. War Crimes Trial Program in Germany, 1946–1955* (New York: Greenwood Press, 1989), 19.

50. Linda Hunt, *Secret Agenda: The United States Government, Nazi Scientists, and Project Paperclip, 1944–1990* (New York: St. Martin's Press, 1991).

51. Haycraft, *Plague, Politics, and Policy*, 49–50.

52. Norbert E. Fell, Chief, Field Division, to Assistant Chief of Staff. G-2, GHQ, Far East Command, through Technical Director, Camp Detrick, 24 June, 1947, memo on meetings on April 26, 29, and 30, and May 1, 1947, 2.

53. Julian Perry Robinson, *The Problem of Chemical and Biological Warfare*, vol. 1: *The Rise of CB Weapons* (New York: Humanities Press, 1971), 217–20.

54. Haycraft, *Plague, Politics, and Policy*, 62–68.

55. SFE 188/2, State-War-Navy Coordinating Committee for the Far East, August 1, 1947, RG 153, MFB, U.S. National Archives.

56. SFE 188/5, Note by the Secretary, March 11, 1948, Record Group 165, Entry 468, Box 628, State-War-Navy Coordinating Committee for the Far East, WCC 351, U. S. National Archives. Under the National Security Act of 1947, the committee's name changed to SANACC (State-Army-Navy-Air Corps Committee) but its function remained the same; Haycraft, "Plague, Politics, and Policy," 48.

57. Joint Chiefs of Staff to MacArthur, March 13, 1948, Outgoing Classified Message, Record Group 153, Entry 145, Box 73, 107-0, U. S. National Archives.

58. Norman N. Covert, "Response to Inquiries on Japanese BW Program," May 5, 1982, Fort Detrick Archives.

59. Study by the Joint Advanced Study Committee on Biological Warfare. JCS, 1837/26, September 7, 1951, 290, U.S. National Archives.

60. On differences between Japan and Germany regarding war crimes prosecution,

see Ian Buruma, *The Wages of Guilt: Memories of War in Germany and Japan* (New York: Penguin, 1994).

61. Harris, *Factories of Death*, 337–44.

62. The Tokyo Judgment, The International Military Tribunal for the Far East (I.M.T.F.E.), April 29, 1946–12 November 1948, vol. 1: *Judgment*, B. V. A. Röling and C. F. Rüter, eds. (Amsterdam: APA-University Press Amsterdam BV, 1977), 385–438; vol. 2: *Judgment of the Member from India, Opinion of the Member from the Netherlands*, 973–87.

63. Philip R. Piccigallo, *The Japanese on Trial: Allied War Crime Operations in the East* (Austin: University of Texas Press, 1979), 142–57.

64. *Materials on the Trial.*

65. *Materials on the Trial*, 9.

66. Williams and Wallace, *Unit 731*, 227–32.

67. "Japanese Court Rejects Germ Warfare Damages," *International Herald Tribune*, July 20, 2005 <http://www.iht.com/articles/2005/07/19/news/japan.php>.

68. Richard H. Minear, *Victors' Justice: The Tokyo War Crimes Trial* (Princeton, NJ: Princeton University Press, 1971), 160–66; Tim Maga, *Judgment at Tokyo: The Japanese War Crimes Trials* (Lexington, KY: The University Press of Kentucky, 2001); Yuma Totani, *The Tokyo War Crimes Trial: Historiography, Misunderstandings, and Revisions (Japan)* (dissertation, University of California, Berkeley, 2005), 421–34.

69. Angela Woodward, *Time to Lay Down the Law: National Legislation to Enforce the BWC* (London: VERTIC [The Verification Research, Training and Information Centre], 2003), 13.

70. Matthew Meselson and Julian Perry Robinson, "Draft Convention to Prohibit Biological and Chemical Weapons Under International Criminal Law," in R. Yepes-Enríquez and L. Tabassi, eds., *Treaty Enforcement and International Cooperation in Criminal Matters* (The Hague: OPCW, 2002), 457–69.

71. Chandré Gould and Peter Folb, *Project Coast: Apartheid's Chemical and Biological Warfare Program* (Geneva: United Nations Institute for Disarmament Research, 2002).

72. William A. Schabas, *An Introduction to the International Criminal Court* (New York: Cambridge University Press, 2004), 305.

CHAPTER NINE

A Quantitative Overview of Biological Weapons

Identification, Characterization, and Attribution

GARY ACKERMAN AND VICTOR ASAL

In addition to the close case-study approach utilized in much of this volume, the analysis of questions surrounding biological weapons (BW) events can be augmented by a view through the lens of quantitative social science methods. This approach allows for the identification of prospective trends and common features across geographically and temporally different events. This chapter explores how comparative quantitative analysis can reveal new insights related to identification of biological agents, characterization of intentionality of an outbreak, and attribution to specific perpetrators.

We recognize at the outset that the past is not a perfect guide to future behavior. Behavioral discontinuities, formally complex dynamics, and other nonlinear changes in perpetrators, technologies, and the global environment can cause radical departures from previous trends. For example, the availability of commercial microbiology "kits" has dramatically reduced the level of skill required to perform sophisticated microbiological techniques, including some of those required for the preparation of weapons-grade biological materials. As a result, where most past biological weapons events have been relatively limited in scope, future biological weapons attacks may have far greater impact on public health, the economy, and other foundations of society. Indeed, it is by extrapolating from naturally occurring disease epidemics and other forms of mass-casualty warfare and terrorism that defense planners have come to attach considerable significance to studying the characteristics of potential future uses of biological weapons. Yet, for every discontinuity, there may also be long periods of repeating patterns or consistent trends. With little other concrete guidance as to the future shape of biological warfare, the empirical record can help guide our understanding of what may occur, if we also keep in mind the potential for innovation and surprise.

In this chapter, first, we explain how we determined which cases to include in our analysis. (Cases are detailed in Table 9.1.) Then, we explore various aspects of identification of episodes as biological weapons events; characterization of them as intentional attacks (or not); and attribution of attacks to specific perpetrators. The chapter ends with some conclusions about the relative usefulness of quantitative and qualitative analysis for guidance in assessing and responding to future BW allegations.

Data and Characterization Issues: The Universe of Cases

Decisions about how to code or characterize incidents help us bound the subject of investigation so we can do a comparative analytical overview of biological weapons incidents. The study, however, is hampered by significant gaps in the data and historical record. To be sure, there are several reported cases of the use of biological agents as weapons before the twentieth century, extending as far back as ancient Greece. The Carthaginian general Hannibal is said to have ordered venomous snakes to be catapulted onto enemy ships in 190 B.C.E. Leprosy was reportedly spread by contaminated wine by the Spanish in Italy in 1495. A Polish artillery general in 1650 launched spheres filled with saliva from rabid dogs. Several reports claimed the intentional spread of smallpox by British military forces in the United States in the eighteenth century and by Confederate forces in the nineteenth century. However, lacunae in historical sources before the twentieth century make this record unlikely to be comprehensive or even representative. Moreover, the lack of systematic epidemiology prior to this period precludes even the possibility of independently confirming the etiology and sequelae of the illnesses described in these anecdotes. Therefore our study examines only events alleged to have occurred after 1900, with the aim of providing a comprehensive, verifiable, and detailed dataset.

The next decision about the universe of cases concerns the nature of what should be considered a biological agent. Some toxic organic chemicals are derived from living organisms (such as ricin and snake venom), but are not in themselves regarded as ever having been alive; the question is whether to classify these as chemical or as biological weapons. Many organizations continue to include such toxins under the rubric of biological weapons. Therefore, for the sake of inclusiveness, this study includes as biological weapons those toxins directly derived from living organisms, in addition to any microorganisms that cause illness.[1]

An important consideration is the threshold defining a biological weapon incident for inclusion. Some consideration of failed and foiled attempts to use biological weapons might prove illuminating. However, completely unrealized plots or attempts at acquisition are not included, and cases of possession of biological weapons are included only where there is some indication of how the agent was meant to be delivered. Foiled and failed attempts were utilized to derive general data, but since the criteria for evaluating such events can differ substantially from those used in examining events that did actually cause illness, unsuccessful attempts were excluded from most of our analyses of identification, characterization, and attribution.

The scale of incident is another criterion for inclusion. Acts of contamination during times of conflict have been frequently reported, including the contamination of drinking water in wells or ponds with animal carcasses, human bodies, sewage, or other potentially hazardous substances, as well as the use of biologically active substances to exacerbate wounds (for example, the Viet-Cong reportedly smeared punji sticks with excrement during the Vietnam War, and there are claims that the al-Aqsa Martyrs' brigade included HIV-infected blood in some of their bombs during the Second Intifadah). Although such tactics may have been in fairly common use throughout the history of warfare, they almost always reflect low levels of technical sophistication and little understanding of biological weapons. Moreover, the very ubiquity of such tactics throughout the history of warfare makes it almost impossible to obtain any significant detail on the effects or effectiveness of such tactics in the context of the general death and destruction of the conflicts within which they were used. Such low-level contamination incidents are therefore not counted here as true uses of biological weapons. Similar reasoning influenced the decision to exclude almost all small-scale biocrimes from analysis: crimes in which no political or ideological motive underlies the use of biological agents to cause harm, and in which only small-scale use is asserted, appeared to be a separate species of event that is less relevant in helping to understand the large-scale use of biological weapons. For instance, the many cases of spousal murder using castor beans (the source of ricin) or the intentional infection of sexual partners with HIV were excluded from analysis, except one case that had large-scale consequences.[2]

Within these parameters, the authors compiled information on any incidents involving at least the allegation of biological weapons use, irrespective of the source of the allegation or whether the alleged perpetrator was a state or a non-state actor. Data sources varied. For incidents alleged to have occurred before the latter half of the twentieth century, the authors relied mainly on historical reports, which were obtained from secondary sources that trace the general history of biological warfare[3] and from works describing particular historical episodes.[4] More recent cases were identified using both secondary and primary sources, including media reports and court cases. There are potential selection biases in the recording of biological weapons incidents, including greater media coverage of events happening within the English-speaking world. To address selection biases, the authors examined as many different sources as possible. Disinformation campaigns conducted by states may also raise the profile of some alleged incidents over others. The discussion of identification, characterization, and attribution below seeks to address issues of purposeful misinformation.[5] The authors examined occurrences of biological warfare or bioterrorism within the wider context of interstate warfare,[6] and international non-state terrorism,[7] respectively.

Table 9.1 provides a summary of information on 31 biological incidents occurring between 1900 and 2004; it is based on a more detailed, coded version of the data, available from the authors. The table lists the date and country where an occurrence was alleged, the infectious agent involved, basic morbidity and mortality figures (where available), the alleged perpetrator and purported motive, a brief description of the allegation, and the extent to which aspects of it have been confirmed (criteria for confirmation are discussed below). The authors also collected data for each incident, where available, on the duration of the outbreak, the countries affected, the primary source of the allegation, the rate of infection, and estimates of the scale of the economic and social consequences of the outbreak.

TABLE 9.1

31 Alleged Biological Weapons Episodes Since 1900

	Date, agent, and locus of alleged incident	Alleged perpetrator and purported motive or context	Description of allegation	Human morbidity and mortality	Confirmation of identification, characterization, attribution
1	1910 Botulinum toxin Northern Mexico	Supporters of Pancho Villa Mexican Revolution	Author William Burroughs describes Mexican rebels burying canteens filled with green beans and rotting pork to produce botulinum toxin and placing the resulting culture in food and on thorn bushes[8]	Unknown	None
2	1916–1918 *Bacillus anthracis,* glanders United States, Argentina, Romania	Germany World War I	The United States military and others claimed that German agents used anthrax and glanders bacteria to infect livestock (sheep in Romania, mules in Argentina, horses in the United States) and feed for export to Allied forces	Unknown	None[9]
3	1939 Typhoid bacteria (*S. Typhi*) Russia	Japan Interstate conflict preceding World War II	Surviving Japanese records suggest that Japanese troops poisoned Soviet water supplies with intestinal typhoid bacteria along the former Mongolian border[10]	2,000 infections	None
4	1940–1942 Plague (*Y. Pestis*) Manchuria, China	Japan World War II (suppress Chinese)	Japanese forces are alleged to have air-dropped ceramic globes filled with rice and wheat mixed with plague-carrying fleas over China and Manchuria, allegedly causing the 1940 plague epidemic in China	Outbreak estimated to have resulted in as many as 300,000 deaths	ID confirmed (1945); characterization confirmed (1945); attribution confirmed (1945); independent confirmation[11]
5	1942 Tularemia (*F. Tularensis*) Volga Basin, Soviet Union	Soviet Union World War II	Ken Alibek, a former senior Soviet bioweaponeer, alleges that the Russians spread tularemia among German troops on the Eastern front[12]	Around 10,000 infections	None
6	May 1942 Botulinum toxin Czech Republic	Czech Republic World War II	Alvin Pappenheimer quotes Paul Fildes, a British microbiologist who worked at Porton Down during World War II, asserting that modified grenades filled with botulinum toxin produced by the British Secret Service were used by Czech partisans to assassinate Reinhard Heydrich[13]	1 person affected, hospitalized and died	None

	Date, agent, and locus of alleged incident	Alleged perpetrator and purported motive or context	Description of allegation	Human morbidity and mortality	Confirmation of identification, characterization, attribution
7	May 1948 Typhoid bacteria Acre, Egypt	Israel 1948 Arab-Israeli War	Egyptian Ministry of Defense and, later, Israeli historians, contend that Israeli soldiers contaminated Acre's water supply[14]	Unknown	ID only confirmed (1948)
8	January 1952 *Synadenium grantii* (African milk brush plant) Kenya	Mau Mau Anti-colonial insurgency against British	British authorities accused anti-British Mau Mau insurgents of inserting the latex of the African milk bush plant into incisions cut into the skin of 33 cattle	None (anti-animal event)	ID confirmed (1953); characterization confirmed (1953); independent confirmation[15]
9	1952 Unspecified agent North Korea	United States Korean War	During the Korean War, China and North Korea claimed that U.S. forces air-dropped fomites (objects or substances capable of absorbing and transferring infectious organisms) and live insects to cause disease	Unknown	Allegation disproved[16]
10	1957–1965 Influenza, tuberculosis, measles, smallpox Mato Grosso, Bahia State, and Amazon Basin, Brazil	Brazil's Indian Protection Service (now Fundacao Nacional do Indio—National Foundation for Indians) Genocide	A 1968 report issued by Brazil's Attorney General claimed that Brazil's Indian Protection Service spread various diseases using fomites and human contact as part of a campaign of genocide against native Brazilian Amerindian tribes	Unknown	None[17]
11	1960s–1970s Newcastle Disease Virus; African Swine Fever; *Thrips palmi* Cuba	United States Undermining Cuban agriculture	Cuba maintains that on several occasions, the United States introduced agricultural diseases and pests into Cuba using various methods, such as air-drops	None (anti-crop and anti-animal events)	Allegation disproved[18]
12	1964–1966 Shigella (*S. dysenteriae*), Typhoid Fever (*S. Typhi*) Japan	Mitsuru Suzuki Unknown personal motives: possible revenge for treatment as a medical resident	Dr. Suzuki was arrested for contaminating food to infect up to hundreds of people with typhoid and dysentery	200–412 infections and up to 12 deaths (reports vary)	ID confirmed (1966); characterization confirmed (1966); attribution confirmed (1966)[19]

TABLE 9.1—cont.

31 Alleged Biological Weapons Episodes Since 1900

	Date, agent, and locus of alleged incident	Alleged perpetrator and purported motive or context	Description of allegation	Human morbidity and mortality	Confirmation of identification, characterization, attribution
13	January 1972 Typhoid cultures (*S. Typhi*) Chicago, IL, St. Louis, MO, other U.S. cities (planned targets)	R.I.S.E. Destroy mankind	Radical ecological group R.I.S.E. were arrested in Chicago with 30–40 kg of typhoid cultures which they intended to release into the water supplies of midwestern U.S. cities[20]	N/A	N/A—foiled attempt
14	1976 *Vibrio cholerae* Mozambique	Rhodesia Rhodesian civil war	Former Rhodesian intelligence operative Henrik Ellert claims that the Selous Scouts, a special forces regiment of the Rhodesian army, introduced bacterial cultures into the water supply of a town in Tete province, Mozambique, in an attempt to kill Rhodesian rebels. Mangold and Goldberg[21] allege that Rhodesian military forces experimented with cholera to contaminate the Ruya River near the Mozambique border in 1976	Unknown	None
15	1978 Ricin London, United Kingdom	Soviet Union Assassination of dissident	The United States contends that Soviet-sponsored assassins stabbed Bulgarian exile Georgi Markov with an umbrella that injected him with a ricin-filled pellet. (There are descriptions of several similar events occurring around the same time in the United States and elsewhere, but these are highly speculative.)	1 person affected, hospitalized and died	ID confirmed (1978); characterization confirmed (1978)[22]
16	1978–1980 Anthrax Gutu, Chilimanzi, Masvingo, and Mberengwa Tribal Trust Lands in Zimbabwe	Rhodesian military Rhodesian civil war	Several individuals have speculated that a large anthrax epidemic during the Rhodesian civil war might have been intentionally introduced by government forces, possibly by spreading an aerosol of anthrax spores from aircraft[23]	10,738 infections and at least 182 deaths	ID confirmed (1979–1980)[24]
17	1981 Tricothecene mycotoxins Cambodia, Laos	Soviet Union and Vietnam Interstate conflict	The United States accused the former Soviet Union and Vietnam of spreading tricothecene mycotoxins from aircraft, forming so-called "Yellow Rain"	Unknown	Disproved[25]

	Date, agent, and locus of alleged incident	Alleged perpetrator and purported motive or context	Description of allegation	Human morbidity and mortality	Confirmation of identification, characterization, attribution
18	January–September 1984 *Salmonella typhimurium* Wasco County, OR, United States	Rajneeshee cult Cult members sought to influence local elections	Members of the Rajneeshee cult were convicted of contaminating produce, restaurant salad bars, water, and a local court house	Approximately 778 infections and no deaths	ID confirmed (1984); characterization confirmed (1985); attribution confirmed (1985)[26]
19	1980–1989 Tricothecene mycotoxins; glanders Afghanistan	Soviet Union Suppression of insurgency	The United States alleged that Soviet Ilyushin-28 bombers based in southern Russia attacked Afghan mujahideen with biological weapons[27]	Unknown	None
20	May–June 1989 Botulinum toxin Swaziland	South Africa Elimination of regime opponents	Court documents describe South African security forces using contaminated cans of beer to kill Knox Dhlamini, an ANC operative in Swaziland	1 person affected, hospitalized and died	ID confirmed (1999); characterization confirmed (1999); attribution confirmed (1999)[28]
21	August 1989 *Vibrio cholerae* Windhoek, Namibia	South Africa Elimination of regime opponents	Court testimony reveals that South African agents emptied bottles containing cholera organisms into the water supply of a Namibian refugee camp. This attack had no effect, probably due to the water's high chlorine content.[29]	None (failed attempt)	ID—N/A; characterization confirmed (2002); attribution confirmed (2002)
22	1989 *Ceratitis capitata* (Mediterranean fruit fly) Los Angeles, CA, area, United States	The "Breeders" cult To halt aerial pesticide spraying of crops	Anonymous members of a group calling themselves the "Breeders" claimed that they had spread the Medfly throughout Southern California, thus causing an infestation that affected California's fruit crops	none (anti-crop event)	ID confirmed (1989)[30]
23	1990–1995 Botulinum toxin; *Bacillus anthracis* Japan	Aum Shinrikyo cult To fulfill an apocalyptic prophecy	Cult members allegedly used various devices to make at least 7 attempts to disseminate biological agents against various organs of Japanese government and civilians and U.S. bases in Japan[31]	None (failed attempt)	ID—N/A; characterization confirmed (1995); attribution confirmed (1995)

TABLE 9.1—cont.

31 Alleged Biological Weapons Episodes Since 1900

	Date, agent, and locus of alleged incident	Alleged perpetrator and purported motive or context	Description of allegation	Human morbidity and mortality	Confirmation of identification, characterization, attribution
24	1993 Unknown biological agent Myanmar	Myanmar (SLORC government) Elimination of regime opponents	Karen rebels claim that outbreaks of intestinal disease resulted after SLORC aircraft dropped parachute-and-balloon devices that may have contained bacterial cultures[32]	Unknown	None
25	1995 Ricin Minnesota, United States	Minnesota Patriots' Council Anti-government (probably to kill local law enforcement officials)	Four members of a right-wing militia group in the United States were arrested for being in possession of the toxin ricin[33]	N/A	N/A—foiled attempt
26	January 1995 Unknown biological agent Japan	Aum Shinrikyo cult Unknown motive (perhaps for testing purposes)	Cult leaders may have used biological agents on dissident members. This included mixing biological agents in their food.[34]	Unknown	None
27	January 1995 Hepatitis	Afghani warlord To end Russian occupation	The Center for Policy Studies in Russia claimed that an Afghani warlord operating in Tajikistan washed or injected various melons with urine that contained hepatitis acquired from a nurse and thereafter sold the items at low prices to Russian troops of the 201st division in Tajikistan. It was reported that the troops became infected with hepatitis as a result of this contact.[35]	Unknown	None
28	August 1997 Rabbit Hemorrhagic Disease New Zealand	Farmer Destroy an agricultural pest	Infected captive rabbits, then liquidized them in a blender and poured the virus-laden liquid onto vegetables which were subsequently distributed to the wild rabbit population	Unknown	ID confirmed (1997); characterization confirmed (1997)[36]

Date, agent, and locus of alleged incident	Alleged perpetrator and purported motive or context	Description of allegation	Human morbidity and mortality	Confirmation of identification, characterization, attribution
29 May 2000 *Salmonella typhimurium* Southern Israel	Palestinians Israeli-Palestinian conflict	Inspectors from the Israeli Agricultural Development Authority confiscated a machine which was allegedly being used by Palestinians to place counterfeit stamps on expired and salmonella-ridden eggs to be sold in Israel	Unknown	ID confirmed (2000); characterization confirmed (2000)[37]
30 September–October 2001 Anthrax New York, Washington, DC, Boca Raton, FL, and elsewhere in eastern United States	Unknown agent Unknown motive	Letters containing anthrax spores and threatening notes were mailed to prominent politicians and media outlets	22 infections, 12 hospitalizations, 5 deaths	ID confirmed (2001); characterization confirmed (2001)[38]
31 October 2003–February 2004 Ricin Greenville, SC, and Washington, DC, United States	Unknown agent Ostensibly to protest federal trucking regulations	Three letters laced with ricin were sent to government offices in the United States	None	ID confirmed (2003–2004); characterization confirmed (2003–2004)[39]

NOTE: No significant incidents have been reported since 2004.

Each case of an alleged BW event was coded to make it amenable to quantitative analysis. Coding requires a definition of what constitutes a separate use of biological weapons. In certain cases, as with the 2001 "anthrax letter" attacks in the United States, multiple locations were attacked within a short period of time, presumably by the same perpetrator(s). In others, the same target was allegedly exposed to a series of biological attacks by the perpetrator, as in the case of Japanese use of plague against the Chinese in 1940–42. Because of the difficulty inherent in disaggregating such compound cases, especially the more historically remote ones, this stage in the analysis uses a more inclusive measure, that of a "biological attack episode." A biological attack episode, as used here, consists of the same perpetrator or group of perpetrators exhibiting similar biological attack behavior within a limited or continuous period of time using the same disease-causing agent(s). Thus, the anthrax letters are treated as one biological attack episode, as are the activities of the Rajneeshees, and many of the activities of the Japanese in China during World War II.

A second coding issue concerns confirmation of identification, characterization, and attribution. The most demanding measure of confirmation of an agent would be independent, definitive, peer-reviewed laboratory analysis, but such a criterion is unlikely to be met in most cases. Therefore, the identification, characterization, or attribution of an alleged biological weapons event is regarded as having been confirmed by one or more of the following: a court of law issues a finding of fact to this effect (a national court, in the case of non-state actors, or in an international court such as the International Court of Justice in the Hague, in the case of state actors); public, uncoerced, and, where applicable, official admission by the alleged perpetrator of complicity in the incident; the results of rigorous scientific investigation subject to peer review; or overwhelming scholarly consensus based on documentary or independently validated oral evidence.

Identification of Biological Weapons Episodes

The identification of a biological weapons episode, as we define it here, consists of determining whether a disease event actually occurred as a result of a specific agent and involves two distinct steps: first, identifying the agent involved and second, determining whether the identified agent caused actual disease. In practical terms, the process of identification presents some problems. The first problem concerns establishing whether the event occurred at all. Usually this means investigating whether a disease event actually occurred in the time and place of the alleged attack and whether the details of the allegation match those of an independently recorded event, especially in terms of the type of agent involved and morbidity and mortality figures. The second problem relates to identifying biological weapons events that have never been reported. The only solution is to recognize the potential existence of unreported use of biological weapons and to proceed, according to the data that is available, with the most comprehensive list possible of alleged or suspected biological attack events. As new sources become available (for example, through deathbed confessions or official document declassification), new events might be added to the record presented in Table 9.1.

According to the data we have and the characterization parameters described above, there have been 31 episodes involving biological weapons since 1900. Only two foiled attempts and two failed attempts met our criteria; the remaining 27 episodes are events that are alleged to have occurred, to have involved biological weapons, and to have had a degree of success in causing illness or at least the potential for causing illness.[40] What is immediately apparent is that—even assuming that every single episode actually occurred as alleged—the use of biological weapons as we have described it is an extremely rare event relative to other methods of conflict. In only 17 of these biological weapons attack episodes were the perpetrators representing either states or nations in a military campaign, and therefore only just over half the alleged episodes can be considered cases of biological warfare, in the sense of interstate war.

Bio-attacks by non-state actors are just as infrequent. Roughly 70,000 recorded cases of terrorism between 1970 and 2004 are captured in the Global Terrorism Database.[41] During this period, only 43 bioterrorist incidents (represented by 14 of the 31 episodes in Table 9.1) involving the use of BW have been recorded.[42] This represents a minuscule frequency of around 0.0006%, or 1 in 1,600. As Figure 9.1 shows, the number of alleged biological weapons events has increased over the decades. A number of factors could explain this rise, from an increase in the actual number of attack episodes, to better reporting of events, to more numerous allegations stemming from an increased perception of their utility.

Applying several standard epidemiological measures, a series of tables de-

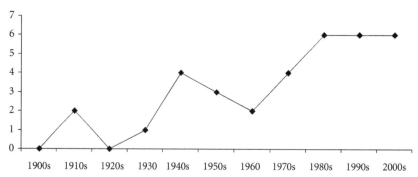

F I G . 9.1. Frequency of Alleged Episodes by Decade. 2000–2010 projected, based on 2000–2005 data.

pict frequencies, in each case where these are known, for the type of biological agent involved (Table 9.2), the recorded rate of infection (or onset of illness in the case of toxins) (Table 9.3), and human morbidity and mortality (Table 9.4). (Data is drawn from the more detailed, coded version of Table 9.1 that is available from the authors.)

From these tables, a number of preliminary observations can be made. First, it appears that bacteria feature far more prominently in alleged biological weapons attacks than viruses. Second, the rate of infection (where known) has tended to be rapid; rarely are there lengthy delays between the supposed use of the agent and its reported effects. Third, morbidity and mortality figures are only available for a little less than half of the episodes of alleged biological weapons use. Considering those cases where the numbers of infections or deaths are mentioned in the sources, one sees that the frequency distributions are extremely skewed, with very large tails.[43] Thus, although the average efficacy (1,834.38 human infections per incident) and deadliness (25,016.33 human deaths per incident) of biological weapons attacks appears at first very high, these averages depend on one or two incidents which, if discounted, would drastically reduce these figures. We therefore revisit these numbers later. Fourth, there is a wide geographic dispersion of alleged events; the loci of alleged incidents are spread almost evenly across several continents, with one notable exception. The United States of America has been the site of far more alleged biological incidents than any other country, a statistic which echoes its relative prominence as both a party to interstate conflict and a target of non-state terrorism since 1900.[44]

TABLE 9.2

Agent Type of Alleged Episodes

Type of biological agent	Frequency	Percent
Bacteria	13	46.43
Virus	3	10.71
Bacteria and virus	1	3.57
Toxin	8	28.57
Toxin and bacteria	2	7.14

NOTE: Excludes 4 failed or foiled attempts.

TABLE 9.3

Recorded Rate of Infection for Alleged Episodes

Relative rate of infection	Frequency	Percent
None	5	16.13
Slow (months or longer)	1	3.23
Moderate (within weeks)	5	16.13
Rapid (within days)	10	32.26
Unknown	10	32.26

TABLE 9.4

Human Morbidity and Mortality of Alleged Episodes
(excluding failed and foiled attempts)

Number of infections	Frequency	Percent	Number of deaths	Frequency	Percent
0	4	14.81	0	5	19
1	3	11.11	1	3	11
22	1	3.7	5	1	4
306	1	3.7	6	1	4
778	1	3.7	182	1	4
2,000	1	3.7	300,000	1	4
10,000	1	3.7	Unknown	15	56
10,738	1	3.7			
Unknown	14	51.85			
TOTALS	27	100	TOTALS	27	100

NOTE: For cases where sources differ on morbidity and mortality, the average of the reported figures has been used.

The data in Tables 9.2 though 9.4 represents in one sense a "worst-case sce-nario," if it were to be confirmed that every allegation and every alleged conse-quence of biological weapons use actually occurred. Looking only at those epi-sodes where the occurrence of the biological event and agent can be confirmed, the overall picture in terms of the shape of frequency distributions remains

TABLE 9.5

Time to Identification (only episodes where disease events or non-events have been confirmed)

Years	Frequency	Percent
<1	8	50.00
1	2	12.5
2	1	6.25
4	1	6.25
5	1	6.25
≥10	2	12.5
Unknown	1	6.25

largely the same. In only 16 of the 31 episodes was there confirmation, with 13 episodes where a disease event occurred and 3 conclusively refuted. Looking only at these 16 cases, bacteria still predominates as the type of agent used, followed by toxins; a rapid spread of effects is still most common; and neither the morbidity nor the mortality rates change substantially (in fact, these rates are now 1,316.22 and 30,019.5 respectively as a result of those 13 episodes where a disease event occurred—a function of considering fewer incidents with casualties).

While the basic epidemiological features do not alter dramatically when one only looks at confirmed incidents, Table 9.5 reveals information relating to the likelihood of identification (confirming that a disease event has occurred). First, the table shows that half of the events that are confirmed are done so within one year of the allegation. Thus, half of the events that were ultimately confirmed took longer than a year to confirm; some episodes were only confirmed as having occurred several years afterwards.[45] Only 13 of 27 episodes (48 percent) were ultimately confirmed, while 3 were conclusively refuted. This implies that once there is some delay (more than a year) in the conclusive identification of alleged BW incidents, achieving any kind of certainty in future attribution is likely to become a fairly drawn-out process. In the absence of an increased capability in this area, this may mean that, especially from a military and foreign-policy standpoint, states may not be able to mount a rapid political response to a covert BW incident.

Second, there is a statistically significant relationship (not shown in a table) between confirmation and the locus of an alleged event being in the United

States.[46] This is readily explained by the well-developed U.S. epidemiological capability and its active media which can maintain the political salience of any event until it is resolved.[47] A third notable feature concerns the percentage of alleged biological weapons episodes whose occurrence has been confirmed over time. While not quite reaching statistical significance, there are indications that, over time, a greater percentage of allegations have become linked to disease events that are subsequently confirmed. This suggests that we are getting better at biological event identification, probably as a result of the widespread adoption of modern epidemiological techniques and the advent of global disease surveillance through organizations such as the WHO. If this trend continues, it might mitigate some of the limitations on political capacity for responding to BW events.

Characterization

To characterize biological weapons events, we examine allegations that have been linked to an actual disease event to assess whether the disease was the result of an intentional or a natural act. In other words, how many of the cases of accusation reflect an actual biological attack? We include in our discussion of characterization the two "failed attempts" that were excluded from the analysis of identification, since delivery mechanism and intended target type are instructive for these incidents as well, even though no disease occurred. There were 13 episodes in which characterization was successful. Twelve were characterized as intentional; one case, that of Cuban allegations of U.S. BW attack, was disproved at the characterization stage. The remaining cases are still unresolved.

As Figure 9.2 shows, among alleged cases, food and water contamination predominate as the delivery types, followed by aerosol delivery. The majority of alleged attack episodes (26) have been directed against human beings rather than animals or crops(3 and 1 respectively; 1 is counted as unknown).

Our data shows that most allegations of biological weapons use (approximately 60 percent) are made by states, almost 30 percent by individuals, and only 10 percent by sub-state groups. The United States alone accounts for half the allegations made by states.[48] Of the 16 incidents alleged in the period 1946–

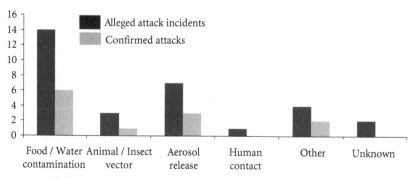

FIG.9.2. Delivery Type of Alleged and Confirmed Attacks

89, roughly corresponding to the Cold War, 11 were alleged by states, 6 of these by the United States and its allies, and 2 by allies of the USSR. Three of the 6 allegations made by the United States and its allies were directed toward the Soviet bloc, while both allegations made by allies of the USSR were directed against the United States.

Of the 31 alleged biological weapons episodes, 12 were characterized as intentional, 1 as naturally occurring, and the others are unresolved. How do these numbers change when we look just at those 12 events that were subsequently confirmed as actual biological weapons attacks? Confirmed attacks share a similar distribution of delivery mechanism (see Figure 9.2) and target type with the larger set of alleged biological attack episodes.[49] In contrast to alleged attack episodes, however, the 12 subsequently confirmed attacks are overwhelmingly those alleged by states (10), while individuals were the information source for only a single attack.[50] The United States is the source for almost half of the allegations of subsequently confirmed attacks, roughly similar to its share of allegations overall. Most of the allegations made by individuals or sub-state groups remain unconfirmed, perhaps because of a lower validity of sources in this context, or because resource constraints on non-state actors limit their ability to uncover confirmatory evidence where the issue is not taken up by states. Many of the investigative resources required for confirmation (such as laboratories, large epidemiological studies, and national intelligence assets) are most likely to be possessed or controlled by states; the failure to confirm some incidents alleged by individuals or non-state actors may be due to the reluctance of state parties to devote substantial resources toward investigating allegations that they themselves have not asserted.

Comparing epidemiological data for allegations to that for the 12 confirmed attacks, in many areas the results do not change: the United States (3 confirmed attacks) and Japan (2 confirmed attacks) remain the most common geographical loci; bacteria (6 cases) and toxins (5 cases) are still the 2 leading types of biological weapon used; and the effects of the attacks are still predominantly rapid (6 of 8 known cases). The small sample size and possible interactions between these variables mean that definitive conclusions cannot be drawn, but these features seem to be prominent in all episodes involving biological weapons, both alleged and confirmed.

Turning to data on morbidity and mortality and comparing the 12 confirmed attacks to all alleged attacks, the average number of infections in confirmed attacks is lower, at 123.11 per incident. Nearly all (98 percent, or 1,084) of the 1,108 total infections stem from just two incidents (the Rajneeshees and Dr. Suzuki); these two attacks together, though, accounted for at most 12 fatalities. The average number of deaths from confirmed biological attacks is still extremely high at 30,001.3 deaths per incident, but this average is so high almost entirely because of the 300,000 deaths from plague attributed to Japanese actions in the 1930s and 1940s in China. While both the occurrence of the plague event and the Japanese attempts to conduct biological attacks in China have been confirmed, there is still uncertainty over exactly how many Chinese deaths from plague resulted from the Japanese attacks. Apart from this episode, mortality resulting from confirmed biological attacks drops dramatically, to just 1.4 deaths per incident.

In the vast majority of cases, therefore, biological weapons have not proven to be a particularly lethal means of warfare, despite the aura of dread they evoke. These relatively low mortality and morbidity rates for biological weapons may, however, appear less reassuring when one considers that biological weapons have never been used in the modern age by a technically advanced actor that has succeeded in weaponizing an agent as an aerosol in order to expose a large number of victims. The delivery methods used thus far have been crude. Japan's airborne release over Chinese territory of rice and wheat carrying plague-infected fleas comes closest to the optimal dissemination mechanism and, indeed, this is the case that appears to have resulted in the highest number of deaths by far. Some idea of the increase in scope and efficiency of modern biological weapons programs, compared to many of the historical cases listed in Table 9.1, can be gained from the example of the Soviet Union's biological weapons program, which produced hundreds of tons of weaponized *Bacillus anthracis*. An accidental release of a limited number of these spores from a facility in Sverdlovsk in April 1979 killed at least 66 people.[51]

The percentage of alleged episodes either confirmed or disproved as attacks shows some increase over time; this suggests (but does not prove) that characterization of the intentionality of biological events may be getting easier.[52] The delay between the occurrence of the alleged episode and its subsequent characterization, and the delay between confirmation of identification of the agent and characterization, show an interesting phenomenon: in almost all cases where characterization as an attack (or not) was confirmed, the date of confirmation of characterization is the same as the date of confirmation of identification.[53] In other words, for those cases which have been confirmed as attacks, this confirmation as an attack comes almost immediately after identification. This factor may mitigate the relatively long delays with many cases of identification discussed above.

To derive principles for discerning between unintentional and intentional biological events, it would help to compare large numbers of known natural disease outbreaks with large numbers of known biological attacks to identify observable and statistically consistent differences between each type, which could serve as indicators to apply to a suspect biological event in order to help determine whether it was intentionally caused. Unfortunately, comprehensive longitudinal data of the type and form appropriate for such an effort does not yet exist; therefore, a quantitative comparison using statistical methods is currently impractical.

However, even a cursory qualitative comparison relying on small samples reveals two important points. First, the frequency, scope, and effects of naturally occurring biological outbreaks are far greater than those of alleged or confirmed biological attacks. Second, even taking into account some of the features described above (such as the prevalence of bacterial and toxin over viral agents), standard epidemiological measures at the macro-scale—such as morbidity and mortality, locus of infection, and rate of spread—are unlikely in most cases to help characterize an event definitively as an attack.[54] Thus we must probably look elsewhere for solutions to the problem of characterization of an outbreak as intentional or not. The sparseness of the historical record means that, at this stage, insights regarding characterization of biological events are more likely to be derived from the close case study of individual incidents, as in the other chapters in this volume.

Attribution of Biological Weapons Events to a Specific Perpetrator

Attribution involves determining the identity of the perpetrator, once the occurrence of an attack has been confirmed. Since this process often involves confirming or refuting the culpability of the governments of states, it is likely to be the most politically charged aspect of investigating an alleged biological weapons event.

Of the 31 alleged biological weapons episodes examined in this study, perpetrators have been named for 29 of them (all but the U.S. cases of letters contaminated with anthrax spores and and with ricin).[55] As Table 9.1 shows, the perpetrators represent a mix of actors and motives, including states involved in wars or in suppressing internal dissent, substate groups in conflict with their own government or with other groups, and individuals with their own agendas. However, in only 6 (20.7 percent) of the 29 episodes of alleged or attempted use has the perpetrator's guilt been established definitively.[56]

Figure 9.3 displays the distribution of perpetrator types and Figure 9.4 the motive types for the sets of alleged and of confirmed biological weapons perpetrators. Motives were coded into six broad categories. In terms of both alleged and confirmed perpetrators, states have been responsible for most biological attacks, although the differences for the confirmed set are marginal. The most common motives for the use of biological weapons involve interstate conflict or the efforts of governments, or elements within those governments, to suppress internal challenges to their power and authority. Although interstate conflict is the presumed motive in nine biological weapons incidents, in only one of these cases (Japan's use of biological weapons against Chinese civilians before and during the Second World War) was attribution to a specific perpetrator ultimately confirmed. All of the confirmed biological weapons attacks since 1990 have been carried out by non-state actors. This may indicate a shift from previous patterns.

When looking at the percentage of perpetrators confirmed as a function of

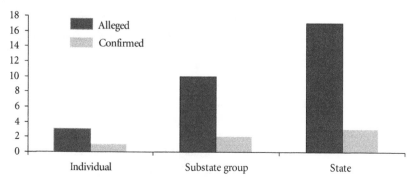

FIG. 9.3. Perpetrator Type (where known) for Alleged and Confirmed BW Episodes

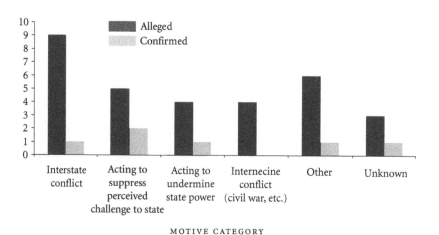

MOTIVE CATEGORY

FIG. 9.4. Perpetrator Motive (Alleged and Confirmed BW Episodes)

time, there is no evidence that capabilities are improving with respect to confirming the perpetrators of biological attacks. In all six cases where attribution was confirmed, this occurred at the same time as the confirmation of characterization.

Statistical Analysis and Biological Weapons Investigation

Part of the purpose of this chapter was to see whether quantitative analysis of the historical record can help with the identification, characterization, and attribution of biological weapons events. Few of the relationships explored yielded statistical significance. A variety of techniques failed to reveal any robust relationships between dependent and independent variables. At this stage, therefore, quantitative analysis offers only limited clues to improving the understanding and practice of identification, characterization, and attribution of biological weapons events. The close study of individual cases of alleged biological weapons use, an effort ably undertaken in the other chapters in this volume, may be more fruitful.

Our attempts to compare and analyze historical cases of biological weapons allegations and use have yielded several interesting descriptive observations. These include the prevalence of bacterial weapons and the rapid spread of disease effects in both alleged and confirmed attacks; the greater rate of confirming alleged events that took place in the United States; the somewhat misleading picture of morbidity and mortality in the historical record; and the observation that perhaps we are becoming more adroit at identification and characterization, but not attribution. The comparative approach undertaken here does offer a measure of performance. Figure 9.5 displays a curve describing performance as a function of the percentage of the total number of past allegations that has been confirmed at each stage of analysis (identification of the biological agent, characterization as an intentional attack, and attribution to a specific perpetrator). Independent confirmation denotes those cases where more than one of the confirmation criteria was met, for example, where a court of law and independent scientific evidence came to the same conclusion. The curve displays a decrease in the ability to confirm each successive stage of event analysis, with attribution being confirmed in only 6 of cases and independent confirmation being present in only two.

Using this measure of performance, the policy aim for those seeking to

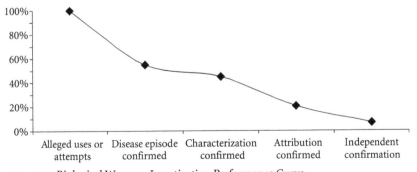

FIG. 9.5. Biological Weapons Investigation Performance Curve

improve performance then becomes to flatten out the curve as far as possible, representing a higher percentage of the identification, characterization, and attribution of biological weapons events being confirmed. Performance curves could, for instance, be used to compare the efficacy of new policies or techniques for identifying, characterizing, and attributing biological weapons events by constructing separate curves for a set period of time prior to and subsequent to the introduction of the new policies or techniques. Alternative measures could also be employed, such as depicting the delay between the time of occurrence of the alleged event and the subsequent confirmation of identification, characterization, or attribution.

Looking only at cases where identification is confirmed, the delay between the event itself and identification is an average of 2.4 years, with delay of more than a year in almost half of cases. However, once success is achieved in confirming identification, subsequent confirmation of characterization and attribution occurs either in short order or not at all. This can complicate the political response to allegations of BW use. A substantial delay in confirming (or disproving) BW allegations decreases the likelihood of success; hence it decreases the value of measures to prevent or deter future BW events by a perpetrator: by the time the allegations are confirmed, the perpetrator may have done further damage. So, in addition to a need to increase attribution capabilities generally, there is a need to increase the speed with which we can confirm such allegations.

Conclusions

The small sample size and the lack of detail surrounding many alleged incidents have made it impossible to derive statistical significance for several hypothesized relationships. Thus the best source of insights into identification, characterization, and attribution of biological weapons events remains in-depth empirical case studies such as those undertaken in this volume.

Quantitative historical data about BW does, however, emphasize the need to avoid being led astray by innuendo and false allegations. The relative rarity of BW attacks means that any conclusions drawn from historical data are extremely sensitive to the accuracy of the historical account. Accurate identification, characterization, and attribution, both in terms of whether a BW attack has in fact occurred and who has perpetrated it, therefore becomes a vital component in any analysis of BW events. The correct determination of identification, characterization, and attribution can serve to guide preparation and response measures, as well as to calibrate reactions to any future BW events appropriately. The historical record is an instructive, if imperfect, guide.

Notes

1. Almost all incidents involving pharmaceuticals, even those pharmaceuticals whose origins are organic compounds, are treated as being on the chemical side of the divide separating chemical and biological agents, and thus are excluded.

2. It was therefore decided to include the case of Dr. Mitsuru Suzuki, a Japanese physician who intentionally infected up to 400 of his patients with dysentery and typhoid fever, because this constituted a large-scale use of biological agent and because his motives, although not clearly known, may have included politically oriented resentment against his society.

3. For example, see Jeffrey K. Smart, "History of Chemical and Biological Warfare: An American Perspective," in Frederick R. Sidell, Ernest T. Takafuji, David R. Franz, eds., *Medical Aspects of Chemical and Biological Warfare* (Washington, DC: Borden Institute, Walter Reed Army Medical Center 1997); Eric Croddy, Clarisa Perez-Armendariz, and John Hart, *Chemical and Biological Warfare: A Comprehensive Survey for the Concerned Citizen* (New York: Springer, 2001).

4. For example, see Hal Gold, *Unit 731 Testimony* (Singapore: Yenbooks, 1996).

5. The authors initially intended to collect data on natural disease outbreaks in order to provide a comparative context, but there is no comprehensive, longitudinal dataset against which to compare alleged or actual biological attacks.

6. Correlates of War (COW) Inter-State War Data, 1816–1997 (v3.0); see also Meredith Reid Sarkees, "The Correlates of War Data on War: An Update to 1997," *Conflict Management and Peace Science* 18, no. 1 (2000): 123–44.

7. Edward F. Mickolus, *International Terrorism: Attributes of Terrorist Events, 1968–2004* (ITERATE 3-4) (Computer file) (Dunn Loring, VA: Vinyard Software [producer and distributor], 2006).

8. Benjamin Weissman, "Dream Control," *Los Angeles Times Book Review*, June 18, 1995, 15; Uncle Fester, *Silent Death*, rev. and exp. 2nd ed. (Port Townsend, WA: Loompanics Unlimited, 1997), 93, as cited in W. Seth Carus, *Bioterrorism and Biocrimes: The Illicit Use of Biological Agents in the 20th Century*, Working Paper (Washington, DC: Center for Counterproliferation Research, 1998): 103–4.

9. No allied source has confirmed that cases of disease were tied to the sabotage

efforts. The Argentinian saboteurs clearly thought that they were being effective, but Mark Wheelis remains skeptical. Author correspondence with Mark Wheelis, October 5, 2006.

10. Gold, *Unit 731*, 64.

11. Confirmation was obtained at the close of the war in the Pacific when Japanese BW personnel were taken into custody by American investigators. See "Warfare: Chemical and Biological Weapons," Stephen Garrard Post, ed., *Encyclopedia of Bioethics* (London: Macmillan Reference Books, 1995): 2545; for firsthand testimony, "Unit 731: Japan's biological force," Radio Broadcast on BBC2, February 3, 2002, transcript found at <http://news.bbc.co.uk/2/hi/programmes/correspondent/1796044.stm>, accessed October 10, 2006.

12. K. Alibek and S. Handelman, *Biohazard: The Chilling True Story of the Largest Covert Biological Weapons Program in the World—Told from the Inside by the Man Who Ran It* (New York: Random House, 1999): 4.

13. J. A. Poupard, L. A. Miller, "History of Biological Warfare: Catapults to Capsomeres," *Ann N Y Acad Sci* 666 (1992): 9–20.

14. Avner Cohen, "Israel and Chemical/Biological Weapons: History, Deterrence, and Arms Control," *The Nonproliferation Review* 8 (Fall–Winter 2001): 29–30, quoting Dr. Uri Milstein, an Israeli military historian. See also Sara Leibovitz-Dar, "Haydakim Besherut Hamedinah" (Microbes in state service), *Hadashot*, August 13, 1993: 6–10.

15. P. W. Thorold, "Suspected Malicious Poisoning," *Journal of the South African Veterinary Medical Association* 24 (1953): 215–17; and S. W. Carus, *Bioterrorism and Biocrimes* (LaVergne TN: Lightning Source, Inc., 2002).

16. See Chapter 6 by Milton Leitenberg in this volume.

17. There has been no formal admission by the Brazilian government nor independent confirmation that a BW event occurred.

18. See Chapter 7 by Raymond Zilinskas in the current volume.

19. Hamid Mohtadi and Antu Murshid, *A Global Chronology of Incidents of Chemical, Biological, Radioactive and Nuclear Attacks: 1950–2005*, July 2006, <http://www.fpd.umn.edu/files/GlobalChron.pdf>, accessed December 20, 2006.

20. Seth Carus, "R.I.S.E. (1972)," in Jonathan Tucker, ed., *Toxic Terror: Assessing Terrorist Use of Chemical and Biological Weapons* (Cambridge, MA: The MIT Press, 2000): 55–70.

21. Tom Mangold and Jeff Goldberg, *Plague Wars: The Terrifying Reality of Biological Warfare* (New York: St. Martin's Press, 1999): 223.

22. Post-mortem examination revealed the presence of a pellet containing traces of ricin.

23. See, for example, Meryl Nass, "Anthrax Epizootic in Zimbabwe, 1978–1980: Due to Deliberate Spread?" *PSR Quarterly* 2 (1992): 198–209.

24. The anthrax outbreak was confirmed, but teams of international experts investigating the incident were unable to determine conclusively whether or not the outbreak was the result of intentional or natural causes.

25. See Chapters 4 by Matthew Meselson and Julian Robinson and 5 by Rebecca Katz in this volume. Even though there is no evidence of the use of mycotoxins, the possibility of other agents (such as chemical weapons) has not been ruled out; the United States continues to claim that the incident was an attack, while others claim it was not. Therefore characterization and attribution for this incident are coded as still disputed.

26. Seth Carus, "Rajneeshees (1984)," in Tucker, *Toxic Terror*, 115–38.

27. George Shultz, *Chemical Warfare in Southeast Asia and Afghanistan: An Update*, U.S. Department of State Special Report no. 104, November 1982; Stuart J. D. Schwartzstein, "Chemical Warfare in Afghanistan: An Independent Assessment," *World Affairs* 145, no. 3 (1982): 267.

28. Hooggeregshof, *Die Staat teen Wouter Basson, Akte van Beskulding* (Indictment) (1999), 196, 241–43.

29. Centre for Conflict Resolution, *Basson Trial: Weekly Summaries of Court Proceedings*, October 1999–April 2002, testimony of Pieter Botes, <http://ccrweb.ccr.uct.ac.za/archive/cbw/cbw_index.html>, accessed on December 20, 2006.

30. John Johnson, "Female Medfly Found in Sun Valley Close to Area Targeted Earlier," *Los Angeles Times*, January 4, 1990, B3.

31. "Chronology of Aum Shinrikyo's CBW Activities," Center for Nonproliferation Studies, March 13, 2001, <http://cns.miis.edu/pubs/reports/pdfs/aum_chrn.pdf>, accessed on March 29, 2006.

32. Mark Wheelis, "A Short History of Biological Warfare and Weapons," in M. I. Chevrier, K. Chomiczewski, M. R. Dando, H. Garrigue, G. Granasztoi, and G. S. Pearson, eds., *The Implementation of Legally Binding Measures to Strengthen the Biological and Toxin Weapons Convention* (London: Springer 2004), 23.

33. Jonathan B. Tucker and Jason Pate, "Minnesota Patriots Council (1991)," in Tucker, *Toxic Terror*, 159–84.

34. "Sources Say Aum Fed Germ-Laced Meals to Cult Dissidents," *Kyodo* in English (18 June 1995).

35. "Yevstigneyev on Russian Biological Weapons," *Yaderny Kontrol* no. 11 (Summer 1999).

36. Mohtadi and Murshid, *A Global Chronology*.

37. "Counterfeit Stamps put on Diseased Eggs," *Ha'Aretz* (May 23, 2000).

38. Ralph R. Frerichs, *Disease Detectives: American Anthrax Outbreak of 2001*, University of California at Los Angeles, Department of Epidemiology, School of Public Health, <http://www.ph.ucla.edu/epi/Bioter/detect/antdetect_intro.html>, accessed on December 20, 2006.

39. Mohtadi and Murshid, *A Global Chronology.*

40. The Aum Shinrikyo (1990–95) and Namibia (1989) episodes in Table 9.1 are therefore recorded as "failed attempts," since Aum Shinrikyo did not have viable disease-causing organisms and the chlorine in the water supply in the Namibia episode is believed to have neutralized the cholera organisms, thus precluding any possibility of disease. On the other hand, the ricin letters of 2003–4 are coded as an "actual use," albeit one without injuries, because according to available information the ricin was capable of causing harm if ingested or inhaled. As shown in Table 9.1, the two foiled attempts are the 1972 attempt by R.I.S.E. to infect American water supplies with typhoid and the Minnesota Patriots' Council's ricin plot in 1995.

41. The Global Terrorism Database is a comprehensive collection of records of terrorist attacks, with information on both domestic and international terrorism. Gary LaFree and Laura Dugan, *Global Terrorism Database,* National Consortium for the Study of Terrorism and Responses to Terrorism (University of Maryland, 2006).

42. *Monterey Weapons of Mass Destruction Terrorism Database,* Monterey Terrorism Research and Education Program, Monterey Institute of International Studies (MIIS) (Monterey, CA: MIIS, 2006), as accessed at: <http://www.cns.miis.edu/db/wmdt/index. htm>.

43. The reason for the apparent discrepancy (the maximum number of deaths exceeds the maximum number of infections) is that the former includes 300,000 deaths attributed to Japanese dissemination of plague amongst the Chinese population during World War II, but there is no corresponding estimate of the number of infections.

44. Six attacks have been alleged on territory of the United States; three in Japan, and one each in Afghanistan; Brazil; Cambodia; China; Cuba; Czech Republic; Egypt; France; Israel; Kenya; Mexico; Mozambique; Myanmar; Namibia; New Zealand; North Korea; Russian Federation; Swaziland; Tajikistan; USSR; United Kingdom; and Zimbabwe. A further contributing factor to the prominence of the United States in the sample may be the relatively high level of public reporting in the media as compared with many other countries.

45. For example, in the South African cases, the alleged attacks only came to light during the Truth and Reconciliation process following the dismantling of apartheid.

46. Pearson chi-squared(1) = 2.8356 Pr = 0.092; Likelihood-ratio chi-squared(1) = 4.1996 Pr = 0.040.

47. Statistical significance could not be established for other countries, owing to the small samples involved. Reporting effects and biases cannot be ruled out as accounting for the prominence in the dataset of the United States.

48. The United States made 9 of the 18 recorded allegations by states. The only other country to make more than one allegation is Japan, which made two.

49. Target types alleged were human, 26; animal, 3; and crops, 1; similar proportions were reflected in the confirmed attacks (10, 2, and none, respectively).

50. The original source of the allegation of the remaining confirmed attack episode, that of the Japanese against the Chinese in 1940–42, is unknown; it is believed that Chinese doctors treating the outbreaks may have been the first to announce publicly that they might not be natural in origin.

51. Croddy, Perez-Armendariz, and Hart, *Chemical and Biological Warfare*, 233–34. See also Chapter 10 in this volume by Elisa Harris.

52. The relationship is almost, but not quite, statistically significant.

53. Of the original set of 27 episodes, occurrence or non-occurrence of a biological event was confirmed in 16 events; in 13 of these 16, it was confirmed that a disease event had occurred. In only 12 of the original 31 episodes has characterization as an attack been confirmed. In the case of the Rajneeshees, confirmation that the event was an attack occurred in 1985, one year after confirmation of the occurrence of a biological episode.

54. Obviously, the features of certain cases will make characterization much easier, such as a disease that is not endemic to a region with no discernible natural etiology. In another example, the anthrax letter attacks of 2001 involved a form of disease (inhalational anthrax) that had not been seen in the United States for almost 25 years.

55. The 2001 case of the anthrax letter attacks in the United States lacks a named suspect, but investigators have on numerous occasions categorized the perpetrator as an individual. See Chapter 2 by Leonard Cole in this volume.

56. This excludes the two foiled plots, where by definition attribution is not in question.

PART II

Policy and Scholarly Implications

CHAPTER TEN

U.S. Efforts to Investigate and Attribute the Use of Biological Weapons

ELISA D. HARRIS

On several occasions over the past half century, the U.S. government has had to address the issue of biological weapons use. In two of those instances, during the Korean War and in Cuba repeatedly since the 1960s, the United States itself was the target of allegations of having used biological weapons. In another case, that of Yellow Rain, the U.S. government was the accuser against the Soviet Union and its allies in Southeast Asia and Afghanistan. And in a fourth, the 2001 mailings of *Bacillus anthracis* spores in Florida, New York, and Washington, DC, U.S. citizens were the victims. In each of these cases, U.S. officials have confronted different aspects of the biological weapons attribution problem.

This chapter begins by discussing the existing legal basis for U.S. efforts to attribute the use of biological weapons. It then turns to each of the cases noted above, focusing in particular on how the United States investigated the allegations, including the strengths and weaknesses of the U.S. approach to each. It concludes by considering lessons from these experiences for future efforts to identify, characterize, and attribute the use of biological weapons.

Legal Underpinnings of U.S. Attribution Policy

Following the use of chemical weapons by Iraq, and allegedly Iran, in the 1980s, the U.S. Congress passed legislation requiring the president to make a formal determination, and to report to the Congress, in cases where there is evidence of the possible use of biological or chemical weapons by a foreign government against either another country or its own population. As outlined in the Chemical and Biological Weapons Control and Warfare Elimination Act of 1991, the president is required to make this determination within 60 days of receiving "persuasive" information indicating "the substantial possibility" that a foreign government has made "substantial preparations to use or has used" biological or chemical weapons. The law lists various factors that are to be considered in making a use determination, including physical and circumstantial evidence; information from the alleged victims, witnesses, and independent observers; the availability of the weapons concerned to the purported user; official and unofficial statements bearing on the issue; and the willingness of the purported user to permit an investigation by the United Nations Secretary-General or other legitimate outside parties.

The law also requires the president to terminate U.S. foreign assistance (except humanitarian and agricultural items), arms sales, and licenses, and to deny U.S. credits and certain national security exports to foreign governments that the president determines have used biological or chemical weapons. If the foreign government does not both end the use and allow verification by the UN or other international observers, the president is required to impose additional sanctions that affect multilateral development bank loans and U.S. bank loans or credits, imports, exports, diplomatic relations, and aviation to and from the United States. The United States has not made a use determination under these provisions since they first became law in October 1991.[1]

Internationally, U.S. efforts to investigate and attribute the use of biological weapons can draw on a variety of procedures developed under the Biological and Toxin Weapons Convention (BWC), the Chemical Weapons Convention (CWC), and by the United Nations, as Jonathan Tucker writes in Chapter 12 in this volume. Under Article VI of the BWC, any state party has the right to lodge a complaint with the United Nations Security Council if it believes that another state party is in violation of its obligations. Each state party is obligated under Article VI to cooperate in carrying out any investigation that the Security Council may undertake. The United States has never invoked Article VI and lodged a formal complaint against another state party, although it apparently considered doing so early in the Yellow Rain investigation.

Under Article V of the BWC, states parties undertake an obligation to consult one another and to cooperate in solving any problem that may arise in relation to implementation of the Convention. Although these consultations can be undertaken on a bilateral or multilateral basis, successive review conferences for the treaty have focused on elaborating procedures for carrying out such consultations multilaterally. The United States has never invoked these multilateral Article V procedures but, as discussed below, it has been the subject of a consultative meeting pursuant to a request by Cuba, another state party to the BWC.

Because the Chemical Weapons Convention applies to toxins, its very detailed procedures for investigating allegations of use are relevant to at least some concerns in the biological weapons area. They include procedures under Article IX for short-notice challenge inspections of allegations of use and under Article X for an investigation of requests for assistance from State Parties threatened or attacked with toxins or chemical weapons. Neither of these provisions has ever been invoked by the United States or by another state party against the United States since the CWC's entry into force in April 1997.

Finally, as discussed in the Tucker chapter, broad authority to investigate allegations of the use of biological weapons also resides in the United Nations. Under Article 99 of the UN Charter, the secretary-general has the right to bring any matter that threatens international peace and security to the attention of the UN Security Council. This provided the legal basis for the UN's efforts in 1981 and early 1982 to investigate the U.S. Yellow Rain allegations. Because of the inconclusive nature of those investigations, however, the United States and other countries sought more specific authority, under Resolution 37/98D of December 1982, for the UN Secretary-General to investigate, with the assistance of qualified experts, any allegations of biological or chemical weapons use brought to him by any UN member state. This authority has never been used by the United States to investigate the use of biological weapons.[2]

Allegations of U.S. BW Use in the Korean War

For a brief period in the spring of 1951 and on repeated occasions in early 1952, China, North Korea, and the Soviet Union accused the United States of carrying out biological warfare (BW) attacks in China and North Korea.[3] The descriptions of the U.S. attacks bore a close resemblance to publicly available information about Japan's use of biological weapons during World War II, alleging, for example, the use not only of anti-personnel agents such as *Bacillus anthracis*, *Vibrio cholerae*, and *Yersinia pestis* but also the dissemination of various plant and animal diseases using insects, arachnids, and small rodents. Some of the charges also linked U.S. BW activities with those of Japan in another way, claiming that the U.S. weapons were being produced with help from General Ishii and other Japanese war criminals of Unit 731 whom the United States had shielded from prosecution.[4]

Two international commissions were utilized by North Korea and China to investigate the attacks: the International Association of Democratic Lawyers and the International Scientific Commission for the Investigation of the Facts Concerning Bacteriological Warfare in Korea and China. After visiting North Korea and China, both commissions issued reports affirming the allegations against the United States, although neither ever conducted a field investigation of its own. Instead, both received testimony and samples from alleged attacks and accepted them as fact, with no independent confirmation. In addition, neither commission sought to determine whether the diseases being reported could be attributed to natural causes, although they were endemic in the areas in which North Korean and Chinese troops were moving or operating.

The United States did not respond to the first round of BW charges in 1951, which it later characterized as a "minor campaign" designed to justify the breakdown of sanitation and medical facilities in North Korea.[5] But if the 1951 accusations were viewed as largely meant for domestic consumption, the new round of charges in 1952 were seen as part of a broader, world-wide hate campaign against the United States.[6] "Propaganda of this type is itself a horror weapon," wrote one U.S. official in August 1952. "It is an attack not only against the United States, but against the very structure of human civilization."[7]

The new charges were quickly denied by top U.S. civilian and military officials, including the Secretary of State, the Ambassador to the United Nations, the U.S. Commander of UN Forces in Korea, and the Chairman of the U.S. Joint Chiefs of Staff. In early March 1952, Secretary of State Dean Acheson stated "categorically" and "unequivocally" that the charges were false, arguing that they were designed to cover up the Communist countries' own inability to care for the health of their citizens. In the same statement, Acheson also called for an impartial international investigation by a body such as the International Committee of the Red Cross (ICRC).[8] One week later, Acheson sent a formal request to the ICRC, pledging to give the agency's investigators full access to all information available on the UN side. Neither North Korea nor China ever responded directly to the ICRC's requests to conduct such an investigation.

In June 1952, the United States took the BW issue to the UN, submitting a Security Council resolution that called upon the ICRC to investigate the charges and report back. In another Security Council resolution submitted the following month, the United States declared that the BW charges were clearly false, since the accusing governments had refused to allow an impartial international investigation. Both resolutions received overwhelmingly affirmative votes, but were vetoed by the Soviet Union.[9]

Having been thwarted by Moscow in the Security Council, the United States tried another tack; in the UN Political Committee in early April 1953, it called for the establishment of a commission of investigation. The day before the U.S. proposal, the Soviet Union offered to drop the BW charges if the United States abandoned its effort to secure a UN investigation. The United States, however, refused the Soviet offer, and its proposal for a commission of investigation was approved by the UN General Assembly later that month. Yet, like the ICRC, the UN commission was unable to carry out its charge because North Korea and China would not cooperate.[10]

In addition to seeking an international investigation, the United States also considered a number of other options for countering what it saw as a Communist propaganda effort. Much of the analysis of the charges and discussion of possible U.S. responses was done in the Psychological Strategy Board, an interagency body comprising the Under Secretary of State, the Deputy Secretary of Defense, and the Director of Central Intelligence (or their designated representatives). One option proposed in March 1952 was for the President to offer to provide North Korea and China, either directly or through the ICRC, teams of medical workers equipped with vaccines and other supplies to combat the alleged outbreaks. Such an offer, it was argued, would place the Communists in an untenable position, as they would be forced either to refuse the aid and thus be seen as condoning the suffering of their citizens, or to accept the aid and undercut their own efforts to portray the United States as a ruthless aggressor.[11] Another recommendation the Board made in August 1952 was to consider filing an international libel action against the Soviet Union in the World Court or the United Nations.[12] In April 1953, a senior White House aide to President Dwight Eisenhower proposed the creation of an "American Committee of 100 Against Soviet Germ Warfare Lies." This committee, which would include eminent scientists, jurists, and others, would establish affiliated chapters around the world and would work with the U.S. government to refute the charges on scientific grounds and expose the Communist lies.[13]

These U.S. proposals were clearly designed for propaganda purposes. In the end, however, none were implemented, perhaps because of concerns that to do so would only keep the Communist BW propaganda campaign alive. Many U.S. missions abroad had expressed this concern in April 1952 in response to a Department of State circular on the impact of the germ warfare charges in various regions.[14] The United States also never released a detailed scientific rebuttal, which, as Leitenberg discusses in Chapter 6 in this volume, could have shown that the disease agents and insects in the photographs offered as evidence of the charges were misidentified or were harmless, that the diseases were endemic in the areas in question, and that none of the bacteria involved in the claims could be carried by insects. The closest the United States seems to have come is to produce, in the summer of 1952, a package entitled "The Truth about BW," which contained copies of letters, messages, and texts of speeches by officials from the U.S. and other governments, comments from reputable scientists and the press, and other relevant materials.[15]

Whether a report refuting the scientific evidence or even an international investigation could have definitively identified both the "nature and extent" of the epidemics in North Korea and China and "the real cause," as Secretary Acheson put it in his letter to the ICRC in March 1952, is, nevertheless, an open question.[16] Nearly fifty years after the Korean War, documents from the Russian Presidential Archives revealed that North Korea had fabricated at least some of the evidence, with assistance from the Soviet Union and China.[17] This included creating false areas of exposure and infecting prisoners with naturally occurring plague and cholera bacteria. An international investigation might well have identified the causative agents present in North Korea and China. But conclusive evidence that the outbreaks were natural in origin and had been falsely attributed to the United States only became available many years later with the publication of the Soviet documents and with the analysis of isolates from alleged anthrax victims, which showed that the strain was indigenous to Asia and not from the U.S. BW program.[18] Nevertheless, none of the three countries has ever withdrawn the charges, and North Korea continues to reiterate them publicly.[19]

Cuban Biological Weapons Allegations
Against the United States

Since 1964, Cuba has accused the United States of having caused more than twenty disease outbreaks among its population, livestock, and plants.[20] With one exception, all of the charges were made after widely publicized hearings in the U.S. Congress in 1975 revealed that the Central Intelligence Agency (CIA) had a secret program in the 1960s to develop biological agents and delivery systems for use in assassinating foreign leaders, and that Cuban President Fidel Castro had been one of the targets of the CIA effort.[21] Many of Cuba's BW allegations were first raised in a speech by Castro in July 1981 that also discussed the assassination attempts.[22] In the succeeding quarter-century, Cuba has never lodged a complaint with the UN Security Council, as it could do under Article VI of the BWC, and it has invoked the Article V consultative procedures only once, in conjunction with its 1997 *Thrips palmi* charges. The United States has ignored most of the Cuban allegations, responding only to *Thrips palmi* and an earlier dengue hemorrhagic fever (DHF) charge.[23]

In his speech in July 1981, Fidel Castro linked the CIA to a DHF epidemic that was then spreading through Cuba. The United States responded immediately that the charges were "totally without foundation," pointing out that it had just approved an emergency request from the Pan American Health Organization (PAHO) for the shipment of 300 tons of pesticide to help eliminate the mosquitoes that carried the disease.[24] Two months later, the deputy U.S. representative to the United Nations publicly reiterated these points, declaring that Castro knew the real origins of the disease, since Cuban health officials had previously told PAHO, U.S. diplomats in Havana, and others that it had been introduced into Cuba by Cuban troops returning from Angola.[25]

Following further Cuban DHF accusations in the fall of 1984, the United States sent a brief diplomatic note to the Cuban government "vigorously" protesting the Cuban "falsehoods." A much more detailed U.S. note was sent in April 1985 after receiving Cuba's response. In it, the United States rebutted Cuba's claims that DHF had appeared in Cuba before any other country, that no Southeast Asian or African country with whom Cuba had relations had experienced the disease at the time of Cuba's outbreak, and that the disease could not have been brought into the country by Cubans. The United States also pointed out that a former Cuban Ministry of Health official had reported that President Castro himself had admitted in a private meeting with leaders of Cuba's mosquito eradication program that the government had not paid sufficient attention to the disease and was thus responsible for the epidemic. The U.S. note echoed this theme, arguing that the epidemic had spread because of Havana's failure to promptly and effectively eradicate the mosquitoes after the disease was brought into the country by Cuban forces returning from Southeast Asia or Africa. The United States took the unusual step of releasing the texts of these diplomatic exchanges in December 1985 after the Cuban-backed Sandinista government in Nicaragua reiterated the Cuban DHF charges.[26] The United States never, however, requested an isolate or any other physical evidence from the 1981 outbreak from Cuba, nor did it take any other steps to try to characterize the event or attribute its source.[27]

The *Thrips palmi* case began in December 1996 with a diplomatic note from Cuba expressing concern over the release of an unknown substance from a Department of State narcotics crop eradication plane during an authorized overflight of the island two months earlier. The U.S. response in February 1997 stated that the pilot had released smoke to alert a Cuban commercial airliner flying below him to the presence of the Department of State plane. In May 1997, after Cuba submitted a report to the UN Secretary-General accusing the United States of intentionally releasing *Thrips palmi* during the October overflight, the United States issued a statement "categorically" denying the Cuban charges and describing them as "deliberate disinformation." The United States also reiterated publicly its earlier explanation for the release of smoke from the Department of State aircraft and described changes that had been made to the plane's aerosol spraying system that rendered it incapable of releasing Thrips.[28]

The United States elaborated on its position at the BWC consultative meeting convened at Cuba's request in August 1997, providing both an oral presentation and a package of supporting photographs and other documents. The U.S. presentation focused on two issues: the configuration and actions of the U.S.

aircraft, and the nature of *Thrips palmi* and related plant pests. For the first issue, the United States used photographs and diagrams of the plane as well as copies of its maintenance and fuel records to show that the plane's aerosol spray tank had been reconfigured to carry extra fuel and was therefore incapable of dispensing insects or an aerosol. It also provided a detailed explanation of how and why smoke had been released from the Department of State plane's underbelly, pointing out that smoke generators are standard equipment in such aircraft and that it was used in this particular instance to signal the U.S. plane's position so as to ensure the safety of both the U.S. plane and the Cuban airliner flying below it. For the second issue, the United States used scientific data on the natural spread of Thrips in the countries surrounding Cuba prior to 1996, and on how Thrips and similar plant pests can travel long distances on air currents and in ships or planes, to refute Cuban claims that the Thrips infestation could not have been natural in origin and therefore must have been started by the United States.[29]

One technical issue that was not addressed by the United States in its presentation at the consultative meeting was the feasibility of dispersing live insects or their eggs from an aerosol spraying system that had been designed to release liquids. The United States also never requested an independent investigation on Cuban soil of the Thrips charges, or insisted that Cuba provide samples of the insect to an impartial authority. Genetic sequencing of samples collected by international inspectors or provided by Cuba would have revealed whether the Cuban outbreak had been caused by the same variety of Thrips that already was circulating in the Caribbean and was naturally occurring.[30]

U.S. Yellow Rain Allegations Against the Soviet Union and Its Allies

The United States began to pursue reports of chemical and biological attacks in Southeast Asia and Afghanistan in 1978, but it was not until early in the Reagan administration that Yellow Rain became a prominent issue.[31] It emerged at the same time as reports of an anthrax outbreak near a military facility in the Soviet city of Sverdlovsk, and amidst growing U.S. concerns that the Soviet Union was maintaining an illegal biological weapons program in violation of the BWC. All three countries from which the Yellow Rain reports emerged—Laos, Cambodia, and Afghanistan—had Soviet troops or advisors on their soil. All three countries accused by the United States in the Yellow Rain attacks—Laos, Cambodia, and the Soviet Union—denied the charges.

The initial U.S. field investigation in Southeast Asia was carried out by two officials at the U.S. embassy in Bangkok, who in June 1979 interviewed 22 refugees from alleged chemical attacks in Laos. In September, four U.S. Army medical personnel were sent to Thailand. They concluded, based on 38 additional interviews, that unidentified chemical agents had been used, but a sample they brought back tested negative for known chemical agents. Then in mid-1981, a leaf and stem obtained from an alleged attack area in Cambodia the previous March reportedly tested positive for tricothecene mycotoxins.[32] Secretary of State Alexander Haig announced the discovery in West Berlin in September 1981 and attributed the mycotoxin attacks to the Soviet Union and its allies.[33] Two months later, Richard Burt, the Director of Politico-Military Affairs at the Department of State, announced that the United States had a "smoking gun," four separate pieces of physical evidence containing mycotoxins.[34]

In January 1982, President Ronald Reagan determined (in National Security Decision Directive 18) that the United States would intensify its public-information campaign at the UN to expose Soviet chemical and biological weapons use. He also agreed to consider taking the Yellow Rain issue to the UN Security Council as provided under Article V of the BWC and, as an ultimate step, withdrawing from the treaty.[35] In the end, the latter two steps were never taken, but it is noteworthy that they were even considered.

Throughout 1982, the United States pressed its case against the Soviet Union and its allies for using mycotoxins in Southeast Asia and Afghanistan, elaborating the charges in the Haig Report in March, in President Reagan's speech at the UN Special Session on Disarmament in June, and in the Shultz Report in November. Both the Haig Report and the Shultz Report were declassified versions of Special National Intelligence estimates on Yellow Rain that had been prepared by the intelligence community. Three types of evidence were outlined in the U.S. reports to support the charges: reports from refugees, defectors, and various individuals who had conducted investigations in the areas concerned; scientific evidence derived from samples from the environment and alleged victims; and other information from documentary and intelligence sources.

(This evidence is discussed in detail in the two Yellow Rain chapters that appear elsewhere in this volume.)

For much of the early 1980s, the U.S. investigation in Southeast Asia was ad hoc and informal, involving a Foreign Service officer and a defense attaché in the Bangkok embassy and a handful of medical personnel from non-governmental organizations (NGOs). Because of Thai sensitivities, U.S. personnel were precluded during the early 1980s from collecting evidence of Yellow Rain attacks during the week, and were forced to visit refugee camps and obtain samples on their own time on weekends. The U.S. Embassy provided no financial or other support for their effort, having never been told that the investigation was a priority.[36] In November 1983, a joint State/Defense chemical and biological weapons team finally was sent to Thailand to investigate full time. As Meselson and Robinson relate in their chapter, the new team found the information on the use of Yellow Rain "too incomplete or implausible" to reach any conclusions.

In Washington, overall management of the Yellow Rain investigation was the responsibility of low or mid-level intelligence analysts—from the U.S. Army Foreign Science and Technology Center, the U.S. Army Medical Intelligence Information Agency, the Department of State's Bureau of Intelligence and Research, and the Central Intelligence Agency—instead of senior policy officials. As a result, much more attention was focused on intelligence collection than on ensuring a scientifically and therefore politically credible case.[37]

In a memo on the Yellow Rain investigation written over a year before the Haig announcement, a senior Army medical officer emphasized the need to examine not only alleged victims but also controls, to establish baseline data. The memo pointed out that this would require separate laboratory and epidemiological studies for each group as well as separate interview questionnaires.[38] Much of this, however, was not done. Biomedical control samples were taken from healthy individuals with little attempt to match the age, sex, ethnicity, environmental exposures, or diet of alleged victims. Environmental control samples were not collected at the same time of year or in the same area as those from alleged attacks.[39] Interviews were conducted only with alleged victims or others said to have knowledge of attacks. Often the interviewees were pre-selected by translators or leaders in the refugee camps. U.S. and other interviewers made clear that they were looking for information about attacks and asked leading questions.[40] Only after the arrival of the joint State/Defense team in November 1983 were appropriately matched control samples obtained, proper interview methods used, and reports of alleged attacks double-checked and cross-checked for reliability.

The policy community's lack of attention to the Yellow Rain investigation also meant that turf battles within the intelligence community over who was in charge were not resolved. This led not only to confusion but also to critical delays in providing guidance and support to the field in the early years of the investigation. The Army medical team that visited Thailand in September 1979 had recommended that a formal questionnaire be developed for use in interviewing refugees. A request for a questionnaire also followed later from the two-person team in the U.S. embassy in Bangkok. More than a year passed, however, before this was provided.[41] Despite requests for guidance, formal protocols outlining how to collect and handle samples were never provided to the team in the field.[42]

The U.S. investigation also suffered from persistent shortages in personnel and funding. This had serious implications for the most important element of the U.S. investigation, the collection and analysis of samples from alleged attacks. Until November 1983, the collection effort was the responsibility of the two U.S. embassy officials in Bangkok working part-time, supplemented by NGO personnel. Because there was no funding for the embassy team's work, the two officials had to "borrow cars, beg rides in the country, and use jungle buses and oxcarts" to get to the refugee camps.[43] They had to convince commercial airline pilots to transport the samples back to Washington in airplane cockpit refrigerators. Some samples were lost due to breakage; the reliability of others was called into question because of concerns about deterioration in transit. Once a sample reached the United States, an average of 79 additional days passed before it was analyzed. Delays were a particular problem in government labs, which had neither sufficient administrative personnel to process samples nor adequate funding for the analysis. In 1983, a CIA advisory panel reviewing the arrangements for handling samples called for increased personnel and funding, but this was never implemented.[44]

Personnel and funding shortfalls also affected the U.S. investigation in another way. Until the arrival of the State/Defense team in 1983, the U.S. investigation in Southeast Asia was handled by people who had no background in chemical or biological weapons or in forensic investigations. Moreover, neither the people in the field nor the analysts in Washington had any training in epidemiology.[45] This lack of expertise may help explain some of the other U.S. missteps, such as the decision to rely upon one outside lab for most of the sample analysis, instead of dividing each sample and having it analyzed by at least two labs;[46] the failure to obtain professional review of the consistency and accuracy of any of the labs chosen to analyze samples; and, perhaps most astonishing, the decision to destroy all of the Yellow Rain samples in the 1980s.

One other weakness in the U.S. Yellow Rain investigation must also be noted: the inability to validate the chain of custody of many of the samples. As far as is known, all six of the environmental samples that the United States said tested positive for mycotoxins were provided by alleged victims.[47] But the United States had no means of verifying the validity either of the samples themselves or of the information about where they had been obtained. Chain-of-custody questions also arise for the period the environmental samples were in storage in Bangkok and in transit to the United States. The only sample from Afghanistan said to test positive for mycotoxins, a gas mask acquired in Kabul, was also reported to have chain-of-custody problems.[48]

As this discussion and the more detailed analyses in this volume's other chapters on Yellow Rain have shown, much of the original U.S. government evidence for the use of mycotoxins in Southeast Asia and Afghanistan has been discredited by subsequent information from other U.S. government sources, foreign governments, and independent experts. The reports of alleged attacks have been called into question because of methodological problems in the interviews with refugees as well as doubts about the reliability or interpretation of defector information. The scientific evidence at the heart of the U.S. case has also been gravely weakened by the discovery that the yellow material in environmental samples from alleged attacks was actually the feces of Southeast Asian honeybees, by the absence of confirmatory analysis from other labs for the biomedical samples the United States said tested positive for mycotoxins, and by the failure to collect and analyze appropriate control samples in order to rule out natural sources for the mycotoxins. The documentary and publicly available intelligence information concerning Soviet research on mycotoxins and the activities of Soviet advisors in the countries concerned has been shown to be largely circumstantial.[49]

In 1986, a Defense Science Board Study reportedly warned that there was no evidence to support the U.S. charge of toxin warfare in Afghanistan, although it stood by those for Southeast Asia.[50] In 1994, an assessment of the U.S. investigation in Southeast Asia by three Army scientists characterized the Yellow Rain evidence as "weak, unconfirmed, and based on classified sources not releasable to the public." The U.S. investigation, they concluded, was "a prime example of how not to conduct an investigation of allegations of chemical warfare."[51] In 2005, a Department of State Case Study on Yellow Rain concluded that "while the evidence most strongly supports the hypothesis that chemical/toxin attacks occurred in Southeast Asia and Afghanistan, the scientific evidence is not strong enough to answer with certainty questions regarding the composition of the agent, the intent of use, or whether the agent originated in the former Soviet Union."[52] In short, the U.S. identification of mycotoxins as the lethal agent, the U.S. characterization of the illnesses reported in Southeast Asia and Afghanistan as the result of intentional attacks, and the U.S. attribution of these mycotoxin attacks to the Soviet Union and its allies have all been undermined.

The Dissemination of Anthrax Spores in the U.S. Mail

In the fall of 2001, shortly after the terrorist attacks in New York and Washington, seventeen people became ill and another five died following exposure to *Bacillus anthracis* spores that had been put in letters and sent through the U.S. mail.[53] Based on the distribution of the victims, it is clear that at least seven letters with anthrax bacteria were mailed; five were sent to various media outlets—American Media, Inc., in Florida, and the *New York Post*, ABC News, NBC News, and CBS News in New York—on September 18, 2001, and two others to the U.S. Senate—Senator Thomas Daschle and Senator Patrick Leahy—on October 9. Of these, only the letters to NBC News, the *New York Post*, and the two senators were recovered. All of the letters contained the Ames strain of anthrax bacteria. But there appeared to be a difference between the material in the two sets of letters. The *New York Post* material was "clumpy and rugged," according to Major General John Parker of the U.S. Army Medical Research and Material Command, while the material in the Daschle letter was "fine and floaty."[54]

The characterization of the Daschle material as "floaty" quickly led to reports that the anthrax spores had been treated with chemical additives and had been produced using sophisticated technology. This view was reinforced following the discovery of the Leahy letter, whose anthrax spores also aerosolized easily. In late October 2001, White House Chief of Staff Andrew Card said: "This anthrax has been milled. It may have additives to it."[55] Army officials announced they had found silica in the material.[56] The *New Yorker* reported that an "anti-cling" substance had been added.[57] CNN claimed that an "unusual coating" had been found on the spores.[58]

All of these reports proved to be wrong. In the fall of 2002, the Federal Bureau of Investigation (FBI) reportedly told Congress that no additives had been found in the anthrax spores and that the particles were not a uniform size.[59] Four years later, in an article in a peer-reviewed microbiology journal, a member of the FBI investigative team wrote of "the widely circulated misconception" that the anthrax spores had been produced using additives and sophisticated engineering techniques like those found in military BW agent production. The author stated that the powder in the letters was "comprised simply of spores purified to different extents," and suggested that differences between the media letters and the Senate letters may have reflected different handling conditions, such as compaction, friction, and humidity.[60]

Immediately following AMI photo editor Robert Stevens's death from inhalation anthrax in October 2001, most U.S. public-health and law-enforcement officials did not even believe that the anthrax spores had been intentionally disseminated. As Leonard Cole discusses in Chapter 2 in this volume, public-health officials took samples from Stevens's house and began to trace his movements because they assumed that there was a natural explanation for the exposure. At this stage, the FBI confirmed that it was assisting, but made it clear that there was no criminal investigation. "We're out there following them just in case anything is found," a Florida FBI spokeswoman said.[61] Only after tests confirmed the presence of anthrax spores on Stevens's office keyboard and in a sample taken from an AMI mail supervisor's nose was a criminal investigation begun.

In public, law-enforcement officials cautioned against linking the case,

dubbed "Amerithrax" by the FBI, with international terrorists or those responsible for the 9/11 attacks.[62] But privately, because the mailings happened so soon
after the attacks on New York and Washington, the FBI actively pursued such a
link, searching both the Florida apartments and the cars used by the 9/11 hijackers for traces of anthrax bacteria, but none were found.[63]

Having failed to find a link between the Amerithrax case and either Al-
Qaeda or a foreign government such as Iraq, law-enforcement authorities began to consider a new hypothesis, that the letters could have been the work of
a domestic extremist group rather than overseas terrorists. White House Press
Secretary Ari Fleischer expressed a similar view in late October 2001, noting that
the anthrax spores sent to Senator Daschle's office could have been produced
"by a PhD microbiologist and a sophisticated laboratory."[64] In mid-November,
the FBI released copies of the letters that had been sent to NBC, the *New York
Post*, and Senator Daschle as well as a behavioral profile of the person believed
to be responsible for the attacks. The profile described the likely perpetrator as
an adult male, probably with a scientific background, who had access to laboratory equipment and *Bacillus anthracis* spores and the knowledge and expertise
to refine them.[65]

From outside the government, scientist Barbara Hatch Rosenberg concurred
with the FBI profile and went on to suggest that the source of the spores, or of
the information and materials to make them, had been a U.S. government or
contractor laboratory. She also argued, controversially, that U.S. government
officials had known for some time that the mailings were "an inside job," but
had been reluctant to admit it. Later, Rosenberg suggested that the FBI actually
knew who the perpetrator was but had not made a move because the individual
had information damaging to the U.S. government.[66]

But there are also other possible explanations for the absence of an arrest.
The FBI clearly did not want to find itself with another Richard Jewell–type
situation on its hands (Jewell was the janitor who was wrongly accused of the
bombing at the 1996 Olympics in Atlanta, Georgia.) Former CIA agent Vincent
Cannistraro underscored this point in August 2002, noting that some within
the FBI were convinced that they were on the right track, but did not want to
"come up with a janitor theory that's wrong again."[67]

Another possible explanation is that law-enforcement authorities needed to
be certain that they could successfully prosecute the case. In the same August

2002 statement in which he identified BW expert Steven Hatfill as a "person of interest," Attorney General John Ashcroft emphasized that, although progress was being made, "the ultimate plateau that's necessary is for us to cross the threshold which provides a basis for prosecutable facts."[68]

Over the course of the Amerithrax investigation, the FBI employed many traditional investigative techniques to try to determine the perpetrator behind the letters. Many of these were broad in scope, aimed at obtaining further information. This included releasing copies of the letters, as was done in the Unabomber case; tracking purchases of the types of centrifuges and milling machines that would have been needed to produce the anthrax spores;[69] tracing the origins of the paper, envelopes, tape, and ink used in the mailings;[70] examining thousands of photocopiers to try to identify the one used to copy the letters;[71] comparing the handwriting in the letters with Secret Service, FBI, and Capitol police databases;[72] tracking purchases of the antibiotic Cipro in pharmacies near where the letters were mailed;[73] sending out 500,000 flyers to households in those areas;[74] and e-mailing a request for help to the more than 40,000 members of the American Society for Microbiology.[75] Other steps were more focused, targeting specific individuals or facilities that could have produced the spores. This included investigating personnel at U.S. biodefense and contractor labs who had been vaccinated against anthrax and who had access to the bacteria;[76] polygraphing people at two U.S. Army labs—the U.S. Army Medical Research Institute for Infectious Diseases (USAMRIID) in Maryland and Dugway Proving Ground in Utah—who had worked with anthrax bacteria;[77] seeking samples from the labs that possessed the Ames strain;[78] and searching the homes of more than two dozen U.S.-based BW experts.[79]

The FBI also took a number of other steps that were much less familiar to its investigators, involving the relatively new field of microbial forensics. This included, for example, securing a high-containment laboratory for storing samples from the letters and other samples safely and without cross-contamination;[80] working with scientists from more than 90 outside labs to develop new tests and protocols for exploring the genetic structure of the anthrax spores;[81] and contracting with some 19 government, commercial, and university labs for assistance in analyzing the attack material.[82] This research effort reportedly has revealed at least three important pieces of information: that the anthrax bacteria in the letters was cultured no more than two years before it was mailed; that the water used in the culture media came from the northeastern United States;[83] and that the attack material most closely matches bacteria from a U.S. Army lab, specifically USAMRIID.[84] But whether the mailings were carried out by someone linked to USAMRIID is unclear, as officials there have said that their bacteria came originally from the U.S. Department of Agriculture (USDA), that other labs also likely received the Ames strain from USDA, and that USAMRIID lacked the technology to produce BW agent powder like that used in the attacks.[85] The Army lab at Dugway Proving Ground reportedly made a *Bacillus anthracis* paste using the same Ames strain identified in the mailings, as well as a powder preparation, but it is unclear which strain was used for the latter.[86]

Despite these efforts, the FBI has been unable to bring the Amerithrax case to a close, prompting criticism not only from outside the government but also from within the very agencies that have been at the forefront of the U.S. investigation. Public-health officials have pointed to a culture clash between the law-enforcement and public-health communities from the outset of the investigation. As one senior official from the Centers for Disease Control and Prevention (CDC) described it: "Public health wants the risk removed by identifying it and stopping transmission. Their [the FBI] view is that the goal is to identify the perpetrators, capture and prosecute them. Our standards are scientific. Theirs are to collect evidence."[87]

There has also been confusion about who, exactly, is in charge. In congressional testimony in the fall of 2001, Health and Human Services Secretary Tommy Thompson acknowledged that no one person was in charge of responding to a domestic chemical or biological attack. Thompson's comments prompted Senator Fred Thompson to observe that, "The good news is that there are many agencies working on all of these issues. The bad news is that there are many federal agencies working on all of these issues."[88]

Another problem area, particularly in the early weeks of the investigation, has been communication, both with the public and between government agencies. The FBI has said that all of the appropriate agencies were warned about the extremely virulent nature of the anthrax spores in the Daschle letter almost immediately after it was opened in October 2001.[89] But others say that a lack of communication between the Army, which first examined the material, and the CDC prevented public-health officials from realizing that postal workers, not just congressional staff, were also at risk.[90] FBI agents also have complained about communication problems between agencies. "The CIA and FBI are sometimes seen as rivals," an FBI linguistic forensics expert said in October 2002. "My anxiety is that the FBI agents assigned to this case are not getting full and complete cooperation from the U.S. military, the CIA and witnesses who might have information."[91]

Mistakes have been made both by public-health officials and by the law-enforcement community. Public-health officials were slow to diagnose the initial Florida AMI cases as inhalation anthrax (believing them to be pneumonia) and slow to recognize that the anthrax cases in Florida and New York were linked. This almost certainly affected the initial FBI approach to the investigation.

Many believe that the law-enforcement community waited too long before turning to outside BW experts for help. In August 2002, almost a year after the attacks, former U.S. bioweaponeer Bill Walters pointed out that he and his colleagues had yet to be consulted by the FBI. "I read where they haven't left a stone unturned," Walters complained. "There's about eight of us stones that are still unturned. It's a joke."[92] One possible explanation for the delay in contacting some experts was offered by William Patrick, another former U.S. bioweaponeer, who says that the FBI told him that they delayed consulting him for four months because he was a suspect.[93]

Perhaps most seriously, law-enforcement officials were slow to pursue certain potential leads. Samples were not sought from laboratories that possessed the Ames strain until four months after it was identified as the strain that was used in the letters.[94] In addition, little effort seems to have been made to locate a letter or other forensic evidence in the AMI building until over ten months after AMI photo editor Stevens died. In late August 2002, the FBI announced plans to return to AMI to collect additional samples using new techniques. An FBI official stated at the time that while previous sampling had focused on public health, this time the focus would be on furthering the criminal investigation. "Last year we were in the building for a different reason," FBI Special Agent Hector Pesquera said in August 2002. "It was not as comprehensive an investigation as the one we are planning. . . . It was more of a public health . . . investigation. This investigation will be scientifically driven for a criminal investigation."[95]

More than five years after the most lethal biological attack ever on U.S. soil, the perpetrator still has not been apprehended. In late 2001, several hundred

FBI agents were working the Amerithrax case, together with the U.S. Postal Inspection Service and state and local law-enforcement authorities.[96] By September 2006, only 17 FBI agents and 10 postal inspectors were still devoted to the anthrax investigation.[97] Many would agree with former FBI official Christopher Hamilton: "No matter what anybody says, if it is five years out, and we are not even seeing any smoke from the investigation, then I would say definitely that this case is cold."[98] The FBI has countered that the failure to make an arrest does not mean that it does not have a suspect in sight. "There are in my experience a lot of instances where we might know or have a good reason to believe who committed a criminal act, but we may not be able to prove it," Secretary of Homeland Security Michael Chertoff said in September 2006. "So when you say something is not solved, you should not assume from the fact that there is no criminal prosecution we don't have a good idea of what we think happened."[99] But whether the United States will ever successfully attribute the anthrax case and prosecute those responsible is still very much an open question.

Concluding Observations

In each of the cases discussed in this chapter, one or more attribution issues were left unresolved. In Korea, it was not even possible to determine conclusively which diseases were involved, as the countries concerned did not allow the ICRC or any other independent body to investigate. Whether an investigation at that time would have concluded that evidence had been fabricated intentionally by the accusers and that the outbreaks had a natural origin is unclear. In Cuba, the identification of the causative agents was never at issue, but the failure of either side to pursue a meaningful investigation of the scientific evidence has allowed Cuba to continue to characterize the outbreaks as intentionally caused by the United States. In the case of Yellow Rain, perhaps the most widely trumpeted allegation of use, mismanagement of the investigation in the early 1980s led to flawed judgments concerning the identification of the agent, the characterization of the reported illnesses, and the attribution to a source. Without further information from the countries involved, we may never know with certainty whether anything other than riot control agents really was used in Southeast Asia and Afghanistan more than a quarter century ago. Finally, notwithstanding FBI claims, the resources devoted to the Amerithrax investigation have been scaled back, and many question whether the perpetrator ever will be brought to justice.

A number of lessons can be derived from these cases for future efforts to investigate and attribute the use of biological agents. Allegations of use by their nature arise during international or internal armed conflict or when there are deep antagonisms between the parties involved. This was true in Korea, where North Korean and Chinese forces were fighting the U.S.-led UN force; during the Yellow Rain controversy, in which the United States was allied with anti-Communist forces; and in the case of the Cuban BW allegations, which took place against a backdrop of long-standing hostility between Havana and Washington. Even the anthrax bacteria mailings occurred at the outset of what would soon be described as a war on terror. This observation underscores the importance of impartial international investigations of allegations of use between countries, and of national investigations subject to independent scrutiny. Even if the particular allegations are not definitively resolved, the willingness of the parties to support a serious investigation will be viewed as evidence of the credibility of the case.

Allegations of use often have some plausibility, given the historical context in which they occur. Historian Kathryn Weathersby has suggested that during the Korean War, Chinese commanders, aware of both the U.S. BW program and of U.S. efforts to shield Japanese Unit 731 scientists and officers from prosecution, may have mistakenly linked U.S. overflights with subsequent outbreaks of disease. By the time further investigation had absolved the United States, Chinese and other officials had gone public with the charges. Evidence was fabricated, therefore, both to support their claims and to cover up their countries' public-health failures.[100] Martin Furmanski and Mark Wheelis have made a similar argument with respect to Cuba, noting that senior Cuban officials may have believed that some of the disease outbreaks there had been caused by the United States, given previous U.S. efforts to overthrow Castro and revelations of CIA interest in using BW agents or toxins in some of those efforts.[101] In the case of the Yellow Rain reports, U.S. officials were similarly inclined to believe that Moscow was responsible, given their view of the Soviet Union as an evil empire, their concerns about the Soviet BW program, and the presence of Soviet troops or advisors in all of the countries concerned. U.S. officials went public with the Yellow Rain charges over the objections of intelligence analysts and before they had been corroborated adequately. This observation under-scores the importance of not making accusations prematurely and of not doing so publicly without a strong technical case, including corroborating scientific and other evidence that will withstand outside scrutiny.

Reports of BW use generally end up having a natural explanation. Retro-spective analyses of both the Korean War and Cuban disease outbreaks sup-port the conclusion that they were both natural in origin, as U.S. officials ar-gued at the time.[102] As for Yellow Rain, Meselson and others have proven that the yellow material found in the environmental samples from Southeast Asia was pollen deposited by honeybees. They also have suggested that the myco-toxins detected in a small number of environmental and biomedical samples may have resulted from laboratory contamination, and that in some cases, refugee reports of illness following attacks may have reflected the use of riot control agents. This observation underscores the importance of considering alternative hypotheses and of pursuing rather than disregarding evidence that is at odds with established positions, even at the risk of having to acknowledge being wrong.

Finally, allegations of use that are not supported by adequate evidence are unlikely to gain broad acceptance. Neither of the two international commis-sions that examined the Korean War charges did an actual investigation or at-tempted to determine whether the illnesses were natural in origin, even though many of the diseases were endemic in the regions concerned. In the case of the Cuban allegations, no scientific or epidemiological data was ever presented by Cuba to support its claims of a U.S. role. As far as is known, the United States also never requested such evidence from Cuba in order to refute the charges. By comparison, a large body of evidence—reports from alleged attacks, environ-mental and biomedical samples said to contain mycotoxins, and information on the purported Soviet role—was released by the U.S. government in the early 1980s to support its Yellow Rain allegations. But much of that evidence has collapsed in the face of other information from U.S. and foreign government sources and from outside experts. Although the anthrax case is still open, U.S. law-enforcement authorities have made clear that their ability to prosecute the case successfully depends on sound scientific evidence. This observation un-derscores the importance of meeting established standards of scientific proof, with detailed information on the symptoms of victims and on the likelihood of natural occurrence of the disease. It requires meeting agreed standards for the collection, handling, and analysis of samples, as well as the analysis of samples by more than one lab. And it requires other confirmatory evidence, such as munitions or intercepts.

These lessons from the U.S. experience are relevant not only to U.S. policy-makers but also to officials in other countries who may need to identify, characterize, and attribute the use of biological weapons in the future.

Notes

Acknowledgements: I am grateful to Len Cole, Stephen Cunnion, Martin Furmanski, Milton Leitenberg, Matthew Meselson, Julian Perry Robinson, and Mark Wheelis for their comments on earlier drafts of this chapter. I also want to thank Milton Leitenberg for sharing his documents on the Korean War and Cuban allegations and Rebecca Katz for providing a copy of her Yellow Rain dissertation.

1. P. L. 102-182. U.S.C. 5601–6. *Legislation on Foreign Relations Through 1996*, vol. II, p. 1394.

2. The only biological weapons allegation investigated under this authority was in 1992, when Azerbaijan claimed that Armenia had used cyanide, a toxin, against Azeri villages. This is discussed in Chapter 12 by Jonathan Tucker in this volume.

3. Except where noted, this section draws on information contained in Chapter 6 by Milton Leitenberg in this volume.

4. The Communist charges are discussed in A. M. Halpern, *Bacteriological Warfare Accusations in Two Asian Communist Propaganda Campaigns*, RAND RM-796 (Santa Monica, CA: Rand Corporation, 1952). Japan's BW activities are discussed in Chapter 8 in this volume by Jeanne Guillemin.

5. Ernest A. Gross, Deputy U.S. Representative to the United Nations, "Security Council Statement of July 1, 1952," *Department of State Bulletin*, July 28, 1952, 154. The United States also may not have wanted to call further attention to its handling of General Ishii and other Japanese BW scientists.

6. See, for example, U.S. Department of State, Office of Intelligence Research, "Communist Bacteriological Warfare Propaganda," Special Paper 4, June 16, 1952.

7. Memorandum from George A. Morgan, Acting Director, Psychological Strategy Board, "Staff Study—Preliminary Analysis of the Communist BW Propaganda Campaign with Recommendations," July 25, 1952, p. 2.

8. The British may have been the source of the ICRC suggestion. See "Memorandum of Conversation, by the Deputy Assistant Secretary of State for Far Eastern Affairs (Johnson)," Washington, DC, March 3, 1952, reprinted in *Foreign Relations of the Unit-*

ed States [FRUS] 1952–1954, vol. XV: *Korea, Part I* (Washington, DC: U.S. Government Printing Office [U.S. GPO], 1984), 74.

9. The top State Department official for UN affairs predicted the Soviet veto in a memo proposing action in the Security Council. See "Memorandum by the Assistant Secretary of State for United Nations Affairs (Hickerson) to the Deputy Secretary of State (Matthews)," Washington, DC, May 20, 1952, reprinted in *FRUS 1952–1954*, vol. XV: *Korea, Part I* (Washington, DC: U.S. GPO, 1984), 210–11.

10. Some have attributed this lack of cooperation to Chinese doubts about the impartiality of the UN and the ICRC. See Martin Furmanski and Mark Wheelis, "Allegations of Biological Weapons Use," in Mark Wheelis, Lajos Rozsa and Malcolm Dando, eds., *Deadly Cultures: Biological Weapons since 1945* (Cambridge: Harvard University Press, 2006), 445, note 44.

11. U.S. Department of Defense, Office of Public Information, "Propaganda Campaign on Biological Warfare," Memorandum for Mr. William Korns, Psychological Strategy Board, March 21, 1952.

12. Psychological Strategy Board, "Staff Study," 7.

13. The White House, "Letter from C. D. Jackson to President Dwight Eisenhower," April 21, 1953.

14. Memorandum from Howard R. Penniman to Mallory Browne, Psychological Strategy Board, "Preliminary Estimate—Communist Charges of Germ Warfare," April 8, 1952.

15. U.S. Department of Defense, Office of the Secretary of Defense, Assistant for Special Security Programs, Director of Administration, "Report on Chemical and Biological Warfare Readiness," July 1, 1952, p. 1.

16. "Red Cross to Investigate 'Germ Warfare' Charges," *Department of State Bulletin,* March 24, 1952, 453.

17. The United States realized that evidence was being fabricated but could not have known the scope of the effort. See U.S. Department of State, "Communist Bacteriological Warfare Propaganda," 19–20.

18. Furmanski and Wheelis, "Allegations," 260–61.

19. See U.S. Department of State, "North Korea Persists in 54-year-old Disinformation," November 9, 2005, <http://usinfo.state.gov/media/Archive/2005/Nov/09-262154.html>, accessed May 30, 2006.

20. Except where noted, this section draws on information contained in Chapter 7 in this volume by Raymond Zilinskas.

21. U.S. Senate, Select Committee to Study Governmental Operations with Respect to Intelligence Activities, *Foreign and Military Intelligence*, Book I, 94th Cong., 2nd Sess., Report No. 94-755, April 26, 1976, pp. 360–63; and U.S. Senate, Select Committee of Study Governmental Operations with Respect to Intelligence Activities, *Alleged Assassination*

Plots Involving Foreign Leaders, 94th Cong., 1st Sess., Interim report No. 94-465, pp. 71–85.

22. Raymond A. Zilinskas, "Cuban Allegations of Biological Warfare by the United States: Assessing the Evidence," *Critical Reviews in Microbiology* 25, no. 3 (1999): 176.

23. After Cuba charged the United States with sending balloons with BW cultures over Cuba in 1964, the Department of State considered the possibility of requesting an investigation by the World Health Organization or other appropriate international body if the Cubans continued to pursue the allegations. The White House, "Cuba," Memorandum from Gordon Chase for Mr. Bundy, June 8, 1964.

24. "Epidemic in Cuba Sets Off Dispute with U.S.," *New York Times*, September 6, 1981.

25. Later analysis of samples from nearby Jamaica suggested that the Cuban epidemic may have been caused by Cuban military personnel returning from Vietnam, not from Angola. Milton Leitenberg, *The Problem of Biological Weapons* (Stockholm: Sweden, Swedish National Defense College, 2004), 82–83.

26. U.S. Department of State, "Case Study of Cuban Hypocrisy: The 1981 Dengue Epidemic in Cuba," Special Report No. 133, December 1985. Two U.S. scientific papers attached to the April note were not released publicly.

27. Requests by WHO and others for sera from Cuban dengue patients were repeatedly denied. Leitenberg, *The Problem of Biological Weapons*, 82.

28. U.S. Department of State, Office of the Spokesman, "Cuba: No Use of Biological Weapons," May 6, 1997.

29. U.S. Delegation, "Documents in Support of United States Presentation Regarding Cuban BW Allegations," August 25, 1997; and Donald A. Mahley, "U.S. Presentation on Cuban Allegations," August 25, 1997.

30. Zilinskas, "Cuban Allegations," 216–17.

31. Except where noted, this section draws on information contained in Chapter 4 by Matthew Meselson and Julian Perry Robinson and Chapter 5 by Rebecca Katz in this volume.

32. The tricothecene results were in a report marked "Preliminary Report" and contained warnings that more verification was needed. Personal communication with Stephen Cunnion, April 14, 2007. Cunnion, a retired Navy research epidemiologist and disease outbreak investigator with CBW experience, was a member of the joint State/Defense investigative team and was in Southeast Asia from 1984 to 1986.

33. Given the nature and amount of evidence, some intelligence analysts opposed going public. But according to Rebecca Katz, once Haig spoke, there was "political pressure to prove that not only were the attacks taking place but that the causative agent was a mycotoxin." Rebecca Katz, "Yellow Rain Revisited: Lessons Learned for the Investigation of Chemical and Biological Weapons Allegations," dissertation, Princeton University, 2005, pp. 56, 57, 59.

34. U.S. Senate, Subcommittee on Arms Control, International Operations, and Environment, Committee on Foreign Relations, *Yellow Rain*, Hearing, 97th Cong., 1st Sess., November 10, 1981, p. 16.

35. The White House, "United States Chemical and Biological Weapons Arms Control Policy," *National Security Decision Directive Number 18* (declassified October 29, 1999), January 4, 1982, pp. 1–2.

36. Katz, "Yellow Rain Revisited," 48, 66.

37. Katz, "Yellow Rain Revisited," 68.

38. Katz, "Yellow Rain Revisited," 63–64.

39. Peter S. Ashton et al., "Origins of Yellow Rain," Letter, *Science*, October 28, 1983, p. 366.

40. Thomas D. Seeley et al., "Yellow Rain," *Scientific American* 253, no. 3 (September 1985): 129–30.

41. Katz, "Yellow Rain Revisited," 64–66.

42. The State/Defense team ended up writing their own collection manual and had to ask colleagues elsewhere in the government for protective masks and clothing to use when collecting samples. The only equipment the team was provided officially were large (approximately 18 X 18 inch) mylar bags poorly suited for sample collection. Personal communication with Stephen Cunnion, April 14, 2007.

43. Katz, "Yellow Rain Revisited," 48.

44. Katz, "Yellow Rain Revisited," 49, 67, 74–75, 81–84.

45. One of the most active NGO medical personnel had earlier worked briefly researching protective equipment at Fort Detrick. Katz, "Yellow Rain Revisited," 49, 261, 264.

46. Labs in other countries allied to the United States could have been used for this purpose.

47. Elisa D. Harris, "Sverdlovsk and Yellow Rain: Two Cases of Soviet Noncompliance?" *International Security* 11, no. 4 (Spring 1987): 63.

48. Katz, "Yellow Rain Revisited," footnote 6, pp. 253–54.

49. In contrast to the other evidence, relatively little of the intelligence information has been released. For an early analysis of the publicly available intelligence, see Harris, "Sverdlovsk and Yellow Rain," 67–68, 85. See also Jonathan B. Tucker, "The Yellow Rain Controversy: Lessons for Arms Control Compliance," *Nonproliferation Review*, Spring 2001.

50. Lois Ember, "New Data Weakens U.S. Yellow Rain Case," *Chemical and Engineering News*, June 9, 1986, p. 23.

51. David C. Stark, James F. Hertzog, and Maria B. Filinska, "Appendix G: Assessment of Investigations of Alleged CW Use in Laos and Kampuchea," in *Chemical Weapons Convention Verification Technology Research and Development: Assessments of Inves-*

tigations of Alleged Use of CW (1970–1993) (Aberdeen Proving Ground, MD: Edgewood Research, Engineering and Development Center, May 1994), G-2.

52. U.S. Department of State, Bureau of Verification, Compliance and Implementation, "Case Study: Yellow Rain," October 2005, p. 2.

53. Except where noted, this section draws on information contained in Chapter 2 by Leonard Cole in this volume.

54. Center for Counterproliferation Research, *Anthrax in America: A Chronology and Analysis of the Fall 2001 Attacks*, Working Paper (Washington, DC: National Defense University, November 2002), 47. This report contains excerpts from statements by government officials and other experts and from press reports on the investigation.

55. *Anthrax in America*, 49.

56. *Anthrax in America*, 50; Gary Matsumoto, "Anthrax Powder—State of the Art?" *Science* 302 (November 28, 2003): 1494.

57. Peter J. Boyer, "The Ames Strain," *New Yorker*, November 12, 2001.

58. Matsumoto, "Anthrax Powder," 1493–94.

59. Matsumoto, "Anthrax Powder," 1494. The absence of additives or special coatings also was reported in the *Baltimore Sun* in April 2003. See Scott Shane, "Tests Point to Domestic Source Behind Anthrax Letter Attacks," *Baltimore Sun*, April 11, 2003.

60. Douglas J. Beecher, "Forensic Application of Microbiological Culture Analysis to Identify Mail Intentionally Contaminated with *Bacillus anthracis* Spores," *Applied and Environmental Microbiology* 72, no. 8 (August 2006): 5309.

61. *Anthrax in America*, 22.

62. *Anthrax in America*, 26, 29.

63. *Anthrax in America*, 24, 50.

64. *Anthrax in America*, 48.

65. Federal Bureau of Investigation, "Amerithrax: Linguistic/Behavioral Analysis," November 9, 2001, <http://www.fbi.gov/anthrax/amerithrax.htm>.

66. *Anthrax in America*, 70–71, 96–97.

67. *Anthrax in America*, 113.

68. *Anthrax in America*, 119.

69. Eric Lichtblau and Megan Garvey, "Loner Likely Sent Anthrax, FBI Says," *Los Angeles Times*, November 10, 2001.

70. Mark Schoofs, Gary Fields, and Maureen Tkacik, "The Anthrax Probe Ranges Far and Wide as Investigators Scour Tips, Trash for Leads," *Wall Street Journal*, December 11, 2001.

71. Marilyn W. Thompson, "The Pursuit of Steven Hatfill," *Washington Post*, September 14, 2003.

72. Schoofs et al., "The Anthrax Probe."

73. *Anthrax in America*, 40.

74. *Anthrax in America*, 93.

75. Laurie Garrett, "A Lack of Teamwork," *Newsday*, July 23, 2002.

76. *Anthrax in America*, 73, 84.

77. *Anthrax in America*, 106.

78. *Anthrax in America*, 98.

79. *Anthrax in America*, 109.

80. Mark Schoofs and Gary Fields, "Anthrax Probe Was Complicated by Muddled Information, FBI Says," *Wall Street Journal*, March 25, 2002.

81. *Anthrax in America*, 110.

82. Scott Shane, "Distinct Signature Found in '01 Anthrax," *Baltimore Sun*, July 4, 2004.

83. Lois Ember, "Anthrax Sleuthing," *Chemical and Engineering News*, December 4, 2006.

84. Debora MacKenzie, "Anthrax Attack Bug 'Identical' to Army Strain," *New Scientist*, May 9, 2002.

85. Associated Press, "Match of Anthrax Points to Multiple Possible Sources," December 16, 2001. There are multiple reports that USAMRIID distributed Ames to the other labs that possess it but no reports specifying other labs to which USDA might have sent it. Moreover, even if USAMRIID did not produce the powder itself, it would have had an aerosol preparation on hand for use in its vaccine studies.

86. Scott Shane, "Anthrax Matches Army Spores," *Baltimore Sun*, December 12, 2001; and Scott Shane, "Army Confirms Making Anthrax in Recent Years," *Baltimore Sun*, December 13, 2001.

87. Quoted in Garrett, "A Lack of Teamwork."

88. *Anthrax in America*, 37.

89. *Anthrax in America*, 45.

90. Patricia Thomas, *The Anthrax Attacks* (New York: The Century Foundation, 2003), 30.

91. *Anthrax in America*, 130.

92. *Anthrax in America*, 113.

93. *Anthrax in America*, 102.

94. FBI Director Robert Mueller has said that further sampling was not done sooner because scientific procedures had to be developed that could demonstrate a match between the samples and the attack material that would hold up in court. Josh Meyer and Megan Garvey, "Science Could Help to Crack Anthrax Case," *Los Angeles Times*, March 3, 2002.

95. *Anthrax in America*, 121.

96. Schoofs et al., "The Anthrax Probe."

97. Federal Bureau of Investigation, "Amerithrax Fact Sheet," September 2006, <http://www.fbi.gov/anthrax/amerithrax_factsheet.htm>.

98. Eric Rosenberg, "5 Years After Deadly Terror of Anthrax, Case Grows Cold," *Houston Chronicle*, September 16, 2006.

99. Allan Lengel and Joby Warrick, "FBI is Casting a Wide Net in Anthrax Letters," *Washington Post*, September 25, 2006.

100. Kathryn Weathersby, "Deceiving the Deceivers: Moscow, Beijing, Pyongyang, and the Allegation of Bacteriological Weapons Use in Korea," Cold War International History Project, Winter 1998. Furmanski and Wheelis have made a similar argument. See Furmanski and Wheelis, "Allegations," 279–81; and M. Furmanski, "Misperceptions in preparing for biological attack: an historical survey," *OIE Scientific and Technical Review* 25, no. 1 (April 2006): 58–59.

101. Furmanski and Wheelis, "Allegations," 267–68, 280; and Furmanski, "Misperceptions," 59–60.

102. Furmanski and Wheelis argue for broader efforts to resolve allegations of use retrospectively using political tools such as Article V and scientific tools such as genetic sequencing. Furmanski and Wheelis, "Allegations," 282; and Mark Wheelis, "Investigation of Suspicious Outbreaks of Disease," in Raymond Zilinskas, ed., *Biological Warfare: Modern Offense and Defense* (Boulder: Lynne Rienner Publishers, 2000), 105–17.

CHAPTER ELEVEN

A UK View on Biological Weapons Attribution Policies

The Importance of Strengthening Norms Against Biological Weapons

GRAHAM S. PEARSON

The United Kingdom (UK) has long regarded biological weapons as a class of weapons that should be totally prohibited. The UK led the way in 1969 by putting forward the first draft for what became the Biological and Toxin Weapons Convention (BWC).[1] Its Preamble states the Parties' determination "to exclude completely the possibility of bacteriological (biological) agents and toxins being used as weapons."[2]

The UK, along with the United States and the former Soviet Union (now Russia), are the co-depositaries of the BWC. The Convention opened for signature on April 10, 1972, and entered into force three years later on March 26, 1975, when 22 states, including the three depositaries, had ratified the treaty.

In this chapter the UK experience is first outlined. The chapter then sets out a UK view on biological weapons attribution policies. The manifestation of biological weapons may lie only in their eventual use—in an outbreak of disease or intoxination—but there can be earlier indicators that a biological weapons capability may be being sought. UK policy focuses on the latter, due to a clear preference for actions to deter and counter the acquisition of biological weapons over actions to respond to their use. The chapter notes what indicators there may be of possible possession of biological weapons and how these indicators may be evaluated. The aim of the chapter is to develop an overall policy strategy for deterring the possession of biological weapons, together with the elements necessary to implement such a strategy.

UK emphasis has long focused on dissuading would-be state possessors of biological weapons, rather than on evaluating or determining whether an outbreak of disease or intoxination has been intentional or natural, both because there have been few attempted uses, and because responses after use would not be as effective. Since the attacks of September 11, 2001, however, non-state possession and use—in which evaluation and determination of an outbreak is likely to be more important—have been given increased attention.

UK Efforts

The UK has been a leading player in international efforts to prohibit biological weapons totally. In July 1969, the UK put forward to the Eighteen-Nation Conference on Disarmament in Geneva the first draft for what became the BWC. The first Review Conference of the BWC in 1980 was overshadowed by the reports that an anthrax release at Sverdlovsk in April 1979 had resulted in a number of deaths. Charles Flowerree, head of the U.S. delegation, stated on the final day of the Review Conference that the U.S. government had initiated consultations with the Soviet Union under Article V of the Convention, "which raised the question whether a lethal biological agent had been present in 1979 in the Soviet Union in quantities inconsistent with the provisions of the Convention."[3] Ambassador Issraelyan, head of the Soviet Union delegation, claimed that, "The incident . . . had in fact resulted from an epidemic caused by the consumption of infected meat which had not been subjected to normal inspection before sale: it in no way reflected on the Soviet Union's compliance with the Convention."[4]

A UK statement, some five months later, expressed concern that provisions of the BWC "should not be undermined," and called the official Soviet explanations of the outbreak of anthrax at Sverdlovsk "unconvincing and self-contradictory." The Soviet authorities had, in the UK view, "fallen short of the co-operative attitude that seems necessary if the consultative provisions of Article V are to have particular meaning." Speaking approvingly of the U.S. efforts to seek clarification of the incident, the statement declared that the UK government "shares this concern and hopes that the Soviet Government will yet provide an explanation that will satisfy world opinion."[5]

These concerns were echoed in 1982 when the UK Defence White Paper emphasized the importance of adequate verification. Referring to the Sverdlovsk outbreak, it pointed out that the Soviet authorities had resisted all efforts to improve procedures for ensuring compliance with the Convention.[6] This statement reflected the UK view that there could and should be a mechanism to verify compliance with the Convention.

Further concerns in relation to the agents covered by the BWC appeared in the early 1980s in regard to the "Yellow Rain" attacks in South-East Asia (see Chapter 4 by Meselson and Robinson and Chapter 5 by Katz in this volume). The British government investigation sought to evaluate the toxicity of trichothecene mycotoxins and to develop analytical techniques for trace levels of such mycotoxins. The results, reported in a parliamentary answer published on May 19, 1986, stated that analysis at the Chemical Defence Establishment (CDE) Porton Down of a number of environmental and biomedical samples had yielded negative results.[7] The UK was confident that the analytical techniques used would have detected trichothecenes, had they been present in the alleged chemical warfare samples analyzed at CDE. The lesson from this experience was that conclusions should not be drawn about the nature of any agent until it has been rigorously and scientifically established. In regard to attribution, it is vital that any evidence provided should stand up to international scrutiny.

The next development came in the early 1990s, with concern that Iraq might have developed biological weapons. There was no doubt about Iraq's possession of chemical weapons, and it was feared that Iraq might seek toxins or biological weapons, as they could be more effective than chemicals and required smaller quantities. Following the invasion of Kuwait in August 1990, there was major concern that Iraq might use chemical or biological weapons against the coalition forces. President George H.W. Bush, in a letter to Saddam Hussein, stated plainly that, "the United States would not tolerate the use of chemical or biological weapons. . . . You and your country will pay a terrible price if you order unconscionable acts of this sort."[8] In the event, neither chemical nor biological weapons were used in the conflict, although it was subsequently found that Iraq had a massive chemical weapons program and a significant biological weapons capacity. In subsequent years, under the authority of Security Council Resolution 687 (1991), the United Nations Special Commission on Iraq (UNSCOM) worked to oversee the destruction of Iraq's weapons of mass destruction capabilities and to implement an ongoing monitoring and verification plan. The UK contributed experts both to UNSCOM and to its inspection missions.[9]

The UK chaired the Security Council when it met for the first time ever at the level of Heads of State and Government on January 31, 1992. Its statement, issued as President of the UNSC Security Council meeting on disarmament, arms control, and weapons of mass destruction, stated that "The proliferation of all weapons of mass destruction constitutes a threat to international peace and security. The members of the Council commit themselves to working to prevent the spread of technology related to the research for or production of such weapons and to take appropriate action to that end."[10]

Concerns about Soviet biological weapons capability were expressed in UK and U.S. démarches to Moscow in the early 1990s, and on April 11, 1992, President Boris Yeltsin issued a decree prohibiting work on biological weapons. Later the same year, following a visit by a joint UK/U.S. delegation to Moscow, a Joint U.S./UK/Russian Statement on Biological Weapons was issued in September 1992.[11] This statement acknowledged that the Russian government had confirmed "the termination of offensive research, the dismantlement of experimental technological lines for the production of biological agents, and the closure of the biological weapons testing facility" and had agreed to accept visits to "any non-military biological site at any time in order to remove ambiguities."[12]

In the mid-1990s, the UK and the United States made approaches to the South African government about its chemical and biological weapons programs. Although, at the time, these approaches were not very publicly visible, it has subsequently become known that South Africa was encouraged privately by both the UK and the United States to abandon these programs and to make appropriate declarations under the international regimes, which it did. In addition, South Africa took steps to contain the knowledge possessed by Wouter Basson, who had headed its chemical and biological weapons program, known as Project Coast, in the South African Ministry of Defence.[13]

More recently, on December 19, 2003, Libya announced that it was eliminating its weapons of mass destruction program. Although little has been stated officially, it is evident from media reports that the UK and the United States were together involved in encouraging Libya to make this step.[14] On January 5, 2004, the UK Foreign Secretary commented on Libya's announcement: "This agreement represents a successful outcome for the engagement by the United States and the United Kingdom with Libya over a long period. We have,

I believe, established a relationship of trust, which has enabled Libya first to renounce terrorism and now to renounce the pursuit of weapons of mass destruction."[15]

Over the years since the BWC was negotiated, the UK has put its efforts primarily into persuading states thought to be seeking or to possess biological weapons to give up such weapons. In regard to the potential for non-state or terrorist use of biological weapons, a UK government statement of October 16, 2001, said that existing extensive contingency plans for protecting the public from any possible biological or chemical attack had been reviewed in the light of the terrorist attacks just weeks earlier on September 11. A joint UK/ U.S. agreement was reached, also in 2001, to pool intelligence, expertise, and planning.[16] Later still in 2001, the UK Anti-Terrorism, Crime and Security Act adapted existing anti-terrorism legislation to deal with the threat of chemical and biological warfare, and introduced controls on possession of and access to certain biological materials.[17]

Indicators of Possible Possession of Biological Weapons

Indicators of possible possession of biological weapons are considered in four categories: statements, acquisitions, activities, and outbreaks.

Statements

Statements are fairly infrequent indicators of BW possession, as states generally give no prior notification or they lie about whether they have particular capabilities. This is increasingly so as the BWC prohibiting biological weapons has become more widely adopted. A country's declaration of non-compliance with the increasingly widespread international norm is now likely to provoke international reaction, either bilaterally, from another state, or multilaterally, through the United Nations. Conventions such as the BWC need to be strengthened and their universality promoted so that the norm that biological and toxin weapons are totally prohibited is reinforced, thereby emphasizing that any statement of non-compliance will not be internationally acceptable. For example, the entry into force of the 1925 Geneva Protocol, which prohibited the use in war of asphyxiating and toxic gases and of bacteriological warfare, was initially qualified by a number of states that entered reservations. Such reservations are incompatible with the obligations that states have undertaken under the BWC and the 1997 Chemical Weapons Convention (CWC); therefore any outstanding reservations to the 1925 Geneva Protocol should be withdrawn.[18] The withdrawal of any such remaining reservations strengthens the norm that the use of such weapons is totally prohibited—and underlines that declarations of non-compliance are unacceptable.

Statements may also be made by sub-state actors such as terrorist groups. Care must be taken in assessing such statements, as false statements may deliberately be made to cause alarm. States may counter such statements by enacting effective national legislation to implement the BWC, together with national controls on access to and transfers of biological materials. Statements of possession will be less credible when confidence is strong that the materials concerned are controlled, and that those handling them are aware of their legal responsibilities.

Acquisitions

Acquisition of materials or equipment of types and quantities that appear inconsistent with peaceful permitted uses of biological materials is another indicator that an actor may possess biological weapons. For example, in the mid-1990s, Iraq acquired biological growth material in bulk, even though its declared uses needed only much smaller packaging units. Monitoring of acquisitions can best be achieved through export controls. These typically monitor specific materials and equipment and also include a WMD (weapons of mass destruction) catch-all clause, which requires that a license be sought by the exporter for any materials and equipment which the exporter has been told, knows, or suspects could be used in activities connected with weapons of mass destruction or missiles for WMD delivery. It should also be noted that in the UK and in several other countries, legislation has introduced additional controls on the transfer, by any means, of technology or the provision of technical assistance which is or may be intended for use in connection with WMD or a related missile program.[19]

Activities

Activities which appear inconsistent with peaceful permitted uses of biological materials are another indicator of possible possession of biological weapons. This is an area in which there is much to be gained if all states parties to the BWC make comprehensive returns under the agreed Confidence-Building

Measures (CBMs), especially if these returns are made available on the Internet, as has been done by the UK and some other states parties. The CBMs, which were agreed at the Second Review Conference[20] and extended at the Third Review Conference, require the annual submission of information by states parties on biological defense programs, outbreaks of disease, legislation, past programs, vaccine production facilities, and high-containment facilities meeting the WHO criteria for laboratories designated as biosafety level 4 (bl4) or P4 or equivalent standards.[21]

This information can be compared with other information in the public domain to evaluate whether the activities are consistent with those expected for peaceful permitted purposes. Evaluation must also assess whether the alleged purposes of particular activities might have been falsely declared, in order to conceal activities that are not permitted under the BWC.

Outbreaks

There are requirements for a country to declare any outbreaks of disease, in humans, animals, or plants, to the appropriate international organization— the World Health Organization (WHO), the World Organization for Animal Health (OIE), or the UN Food and Agriculture Organization (FAO).[22] A revision of the International Health Regulations, referred to as IHR (2005), was unanimously adopted on May 23, 2005, by the World Health Assembly (the decision-making body of the WHO). These regulations are scheduled to enter into force in June 2007; they require each state to notify the WHO within 24 hours of "all events which may constitute a public-health emergency of international concern within its territory." In considering how to distinguish a natural outbreak from release, intentional or unintentional, it has to be recognized that once any outbreak is initiated, it will spread naturally, and consequently all outbreaks are to some degree "natural" whatever their initiation. The ability to discriminate between a natural outbreak and an intentional or unintentional one will depend on the characteristics, pattern, and location of the outbreak, the nature of the disease, and whether the pathogen subspecies is indigenous to the area.[23] There is no unique signature that distinguishes an intentional or unintentional outbreak from a natural one, as many natural outbreaks may have unusual characteristics.

In some alleged attacks, samples may be collected and analyzed to determine the causative agent. An illuminating example is that of the UK examination of samples collected from the "Yellow Rain" attacks in Southeast Asia.[24] A laboratory in the United States had already identified trichothecene mycotoxins. The effort in the UK focused on seeking to confirm whether or not trichothecene mycotoxins were involved. This involved, first, inquiries into the toxicology of these mycotoxins, to determine whether they would be sufficiently toxic to cause the effects observed in Southeast Asia; and second, developing and applying analytical techniques capable of detecting these mycotoxins at levels down to 1–10 nanograms per sample, well below the level at which they would have a toxic effect. The toxicological studies showed that T-2 was one of the most toxic trichothecene mycotoxins, with a systemic lethal toxicity of between 1 and 10 mg/kg of body weight. Thus a fatal dose for an average adult would be some 70 mg of toxin. The consistency of toxic effects of mycotoxins in animals as diverse as mice and cows suggested that the signs in people are likely to be similar. Mycotoxins such as T-2 do not readily penetrate skin and when they do, they are rapidly metabolized, making it highly unlikely that biomedical samples (such as blood or tissue) collected some time after an attack would still have traces of the mycotoxin. Exceptional care had to be taken in the analytical techniques, such as the use of new analytical glassware for each analysis, in order to prevent any possible cross-contamination between the samples analyzed. The UK techniques were developed at the CDE at Porton Down (now called the Defence Science and Technology Laboratory) and cross-checked by analyses at what was then the Admiralty Research Laboratory at Holton Heath (which subsequently closed). The analytical methods were checked in two interlaboratory collaborative exercises by correctly analyzing 64 samples spiked with mycotoxins at levels between 2 and 200 ng/ml, together with negative controls, all submitted blind by external laboratories. At the time, this was at the leading edge of analytical techniques, and the same standard is used today. These analyses led to the conclusion that no mycotoxins were found in the 50 or so biomedical and environmental samples collected from Southeast Asia and analyzed in the UK.

A number of lessons can be drawn from this experience. First, the collection of samples should be validated with a complete documentation of the chain of custody leading to the analytical laboratory. Second, the analytical techniques should be defined in stringent analytical protocols and proven by interlaboratory validation exercises using samples submitted blind by a third laboratory. Third, when an identification is made, whether it can cause the effects observed in the alleged attack must be validated either through pre-existing data or through experimental confirmation using appropriate models. The importance of such a validated and controlled approach to sample collection and analysis has been recognized by the Organization for the Prohibition of Chemical Weapons (OPCW) in its procedures to investigate an alleged chemical weapons attack. The UN Monitoring, Verification, and Inspection Commission (UNMOVIC) in Iraq adopted a similar approach to the collection and analysis of samples of potential chemical and biological agents.[25]

Evaluation of Indicators of Possible Possession of Biological Weapons

Several factors must be considered in evaluating the indicators of possible possession of biological weapons, including the possibility of deliberate misinformation, uncertainty, and validation or confirmation. These all affect the quality of the information and, ultimately, what action may be taken as a result of the evaluation. The goal must always be validated, accurate information.

Deliberate Misinformation

Deliberate disinformation may falsely suggest that biological weapons are possessed, in order to attract attention internationally or from the media or to create public alarm. The 2001 anthrax letter attacks in the United States (see Chapter 2 in this volume by Leonard Cole) were followed by numerous hoaxes around the world, in which innocuous packets of white powder caused disruption to a greater or lesser extent. A false claim to have biological weapons may be made by a state, if biological weapons are seen as providing an asymmetrical response or deterrent to a threat from superior conventional forces.

The second type of disinformation is where a state falsely declares that it has no biological weapons when it does indeed have a covert program. Past state programs were concealed by disinformation. A particular example was the role of Biopreparat in the former Soviet Union, which ostensibly had a public-health role, whereas in fact its central role was to support the offensive biological weapons program.[26]

Uncertain Information

A more likely situation is one in which there is uncertain or ambiguous information. In evaluating such information, the agency carrying out the evaluation must constantly keep the primary goal in sight. In many situations, evaluations are carried out by intelligence agencies, which exist to warn of possible threats to states; consequently, their assessments tend to be focused on worst-case assumptions. Any assessments must, however, be carefully labeled so that worst-case evaluations can be distinguished from balanced assessments. It is one thing for an agency to make an assessment to warn a state about a possible danger or risk, so that the state can decide what resources to devote to countering the possible threat. It is quite another matter, however, if the agency's assessment is to be the basis for action in the international arena or against the purported possessor; in such a case, it is crucial that the evaluation explicitly balance worst-case views against a full range of other possible explanations. A key tool in any such evaluation is to look for consistency, or inconsistency, in information from as wide as possible a range of sources.

Validated Information

The quest must always be for accurate, validated information. In evaluation it is vital to avoid preconceptions. After all, things are done differently for all sorts of reasons in different countries around the world: expectations that things will be necessarily done as they are in one's own country may be misplaced. All available sources of information should be used. Information is increasingly available from the Internet and through other open sources, but must also be checked for consistency with official information from both national and international sources such as WHO, FAO, and OIE.

The overall aim is for accurate and validated information. If the evaluation is to be used as a basis for national or international action, then it must be prepared in a way that will stand up to national or international scrutiny and will be persuasive nationally or internationally.

The UK Arrangements for National Evaluations of Potential BW Possession and Use

The UK national intelligence machinery is described in a publicly available 37-page booklet.[27] Top-level assessments for the UK government are made by the Joint Intelligence Committee (JIC), which is explicitly given the responsibility, "on the basis of available information, to assess events and situations relating to external affairs, defense, terrorism, major international criminal activity, scientific, technical and international economic matters." An annex to the booklet describes the "Nature, Collection, Assessment and Use" of intelligence by the UK government. Some key points relevant to the evaluation of possible possessors of biological weapons are summarized here.

Secret intelligence is information acquired against the wishes, and generally without the knowledge, of the originators or possessors. Intelligence, when collected, may be fragmentary or incomplete. The reliability of the source and the credibility of the information must be evaluated to enable a judgment about how much weight to give it. It must be analyzed to identify significant facts before it is either circulated as a single-source report or else collated and integrated with other material as part of a more comprehensive assessment. Intelligence must be situated within a sensible real-world context and elements that can inform policymaking must be made explicit. Evaluation, analysis, and assessment thus transform the raw material of intelligence so that it can be assimilated in the same way as other information provided to decision makers at all levels of government.

The annex rightly points out that intelligence has limitations which must be recognized by its ultimate recipients—policymakers and ministers in government—if it is to be used wisely. The most important limitation is incompleteness. Nations expend much ingenuity and effort on making the secret information difficult for others to acquire and hard for them to analyze. Although the intelligence process may be able to overcome such barriers, intelligence seldom acquires the full story: even after analysis it may still be, at best, inferential. Those undertaking assessments must place the intelligence in the context of wider knowledge available. Where information is particularly sparse or of questionable reliability, the risks are higher both of being misled by deception or by sources intending to influence more than to inform, and by judgments that conform to others' expectations, rather than to what the facts demonstrate. These points, although written specifically about intelligence, apply equally to evaluations about the indicators of possible possession or use of biological weapons. The example of the Yellow Rain allegations is a case where the UK analyses showed that the trichothecene mycotoxin T-2 was not a credible threat agent and consequently no effort was put into developing detection, protection, or medical countermeasures against this as a possible agent, in contrast to the U.S. effort to devote resources to defending against this as a possible agent.

Policies to Counter Possible
Possession of Biological Weapons

Policies to counter possible possession of biological weapons are considered in this section using the same terms as for the possible indicators of biological weapons, namely: statements, acquisitions, activities, and outbreaks.

Statements

There is a need for clear national and international statements that the acquisition and possession of biological and toxin weapons are totally unacceptable. Such national statements could be made by parliaments or in other public declarations, such as government statements to the UN General Assembly or to the Review Conferences of the BWC. International statements could come from the Review Conferences of the BWC, from the UN Security Council, or from other international groupings such as the G8 (group of eight major industrialized nations) or the European Union. For example, the G8 Global Partnership against the Spread of Weapons and Materials of Mass Destruction was launched in Kananaskis, Canada, in 2002, with the following declaration:

> We commit ourselves to prevent terrorists, or those that harbour them, from acquiring or developing . . . biological weapons; . . . and related materials, equipment and technology. We call on all countries to join us in adopting the set of non-proliferation principles we have announced today.[28]

More recently, the G8 meeting in St. Petersburg on July 16, 2006, issued the following statement opposing proliferation of WMD:

> The proliferation of weapons of mass destruction (WMD) and their means of delivery, together with international terrorism, remain the pre-eminent threat to international peace and security. . . . We reaffirm our determination and commitment to work together and with other states and institutions in the fight against the proliferation of WMD, including by preventing them from falling into hands of terrorists.[29]

This declaration went on to address the BWC, promising to "facilitate adoption by the [6th] Review Conference [scheduled for November 20–December 8, 2006] of decisions aimed at strengthening and enhancing the implementation of the BTWC." Statements such as these are public commitments by the G8 nations—Canada, France, Germany, Italy, Japan, Russia, UK, and the United

States—as well as the European Union, to maintain and strengthen the prohibition against biological and toxin weapons. Their visible message to the rest of the world—that these nations abhor and will not tolerate such weapons—reinforces the international norm.

Acquisitions

There is a need for effective national and international controls over access to materials, equipment, and know-how relating to biological weapons. Increasingly, export control regimes require end-user certificates and include catch-all clauses requiring that an export license be sought if the exporter has any reason to think that the material or equipment may be intended to support a biological or toxin weapons program. Additionally, some countries are introducing national controls over particular biological materials that might be misused by sub-state actors in biological weapons programs. Many such national controls complement regulations that have long been in place for health and safety reasons. The WHO is currently in the progress of finalizing its publication on laboratory biosecurity guidance, which sets out the principles to be adopted by national regulatory authorities and by laboratory directors and managers.[30] National regulations and controls on who may have access to particular biological materials that might be misused makes it clear that states are determined that such materials and capabilities shall be limited only to those that should have them.

Activities

Benefits are to be gained from national declarations of planned activities to counter outbreaks of disease and of intoxinations in humans, animals, and plants. Such declarations build international confidence that the declared national programs are intended to strengthen the ability of the country to counter such outbreaks or intoxinations, and not for prohibited purposes. There are benefits from such a transparency policy both nationally—making the public aware that the government is taking steps to protect them—and internationally, helping to prevent concerns in other countries that the national program might be for prohibited purposes. Such intended benefits underlie the Confidence-Building Measures (CBM) agreed by the Second Review Conference of the BWC in 1986 and extended by the Third Review Conference in 1991. For example, CBM "A" Part 2 requires that states parties provide, annually, detailed information on their biological defense research and development programs, including summaries of the objectives and costs of efforts performed by contractors and in other facilities. Returns pursuant to these Confidence-Building Measures are circulated to other states that are party to the Convention. There would be advantages in making them more generally available, as has been done by Australia, the United States, and the United Kingdom prior to 2006, along with Finland, Malaysia, Sweden, and Switzerland in 2006.[31] Greater visibility of and government statements on national programs build confidence that these are indeed permitted activities and are not assisting any prohibited programs.

Outbreaks

In the event of an outbreak, the requirement is to collect evidence: the precise location of the outbreak, the details of the casualties (human, animal, or plant), and any unusual characteristics. This evidence will be subjected to scientific and public scrutiny; validation of the evidence requires that the information can be checked and confirmed at a later date. Even for an outbreak not at first regarded as unusual, the collection of forensic-type evidence, with a clear chain of custody, will have huge benefits should the outbreak later be considered to be unusual and it becomes necessary to investigate the possibility that it was intentional.

This is especially true for any samples of physical evidence. The OPCW has developed a scheme for the validation and certification of designated laboratories.[32] This provides a useful model for what is required to obtain reliable and accurate results of samples collected from an unusual disease outbreak or intoxination.

Should an investigation team be sent to the site of the unusual outbreak or intoxination, it should be multinational in composition and have multidisciplinary skills. Pulling together a number of experts from a number of countries to carry out an investigation will be more effective if they have previously been trained to work together. The experience of UNMOVIC in Iraq demonstrated how a roster of trained inspectors could be created and used to carry out investigations effectively; the UNMOVIC experience could serve as a model.[33]

An investigation will take some time before it can reach a conclusion, and analytical results will require careful checking before there can be any statement about the outcome of the investigation. The host country in which the outbreak or intoxination has taken place may well have its own agenda and be seeking a particular conclusion from the investigation team; nevertheless, the team must maintain its independence, and must scrutinize all information or evidence offered, to check that such information or evidence is sound and valid.

Overall Strategy for Deterring Possession of Biological Weapons

The various policies above in relation to statements, acquisitions, activities, and outbreaks all contribute to countering the efforts of those who might seek to acquire and possess biological and toxin weapons. They suggest an overall policy strategy for deterring the possession of biological weapons. The emphasis in the UK has long been much more focused on dissuading would-be possessors from acquiring such weapons than on the analysis of evidence from an alleged attack, although the latter has certainly a role in an overall strategy.

The approach followed in the UK has been to adopt a web of deterrence that also provides a web of assurance for the public that all reasonable steps are being taken to protect them from the risk of deliberate outbreaks of disease or intoxinations. The web is made up of a number of complementary and integrated strands: comprehensive international and national prohibitions; effective international and national controls over agents and equipment; preparedness for disease outbreaks and intoxinations in humans, animals, and plants, whether caused naturally or deliberately; forceful responses, both national and international, to any statements of possession, attacks, or threats of use. Each of these element is next considered in turn.

Comprehensive International and National Prohibitions

Comprehensive international prohibition is provided by the BWC. Each state that is party to it undertakes "never in any circumstances to develop, produce, stockpile or otherwise acquire or retain: (1) Microbial or other biological agents, or toxins whatever their origin or method of production, of types and in quantities that have no justification for prophylactic, protective or other peaceful purposes; [or] (2) Weapons, equipment or means of delivery designed to use such agents or toxins for hostile purposes or in armed conflict."[34]

In October 2006, 155 states were party to the treaty and a further 16 states were signatory to the BWC (signatory states undertake to do nothing contrary to the aims and objectives of the Convention, but have yet to ratify their signature and so become full parties to the treaty).[35] There is a need for states parties to launch an initiative for universality comparable to the Chemical Weapons Convention, which has now 180 states parties and a further six signatory states; only nine states have not yet taken any action on the CWC.[36]

Article IV of the Convention requires each state party to "take any necessary measures to prohibit and prevent the development, production, stockpiling, acquisition, or retention of the agents, toxins, weapons, equipment and means of delivery specified in article I of the Convention, within the territory of such State, under its jurisdiction or under its control anywhere." In its Fourth Review Conference in 1996, the States Parties "recognized the need to ensure . . . the effective fulfillment of their obligations under the Convention in order, *inter alia*, to exclude use of biological and toxin weapons in terrorist or criminal activity."

National implementation of the BWC was achieved in the UK by the Biological Weapons Act of 1974, which introduced into British law the requirements of the Convention and provided that violators could be punished with a life sentence.[37] All states parties to the BWC should adopt national legislation, including penal legislation, to strengthen the national implementation of the Convention. The UK along with the EU has mounted initiatives to encourage other states parties to do so.

Effective International and National Controls of Agents and Equipment

Article III of the BWC requires that each state party "undertakes not to transfer to any recipient whatsoever, directly or indirectly, and not in any way to assist, encourage, or induce any State, group of States or international organizations to manufacture or otherwise acquire any of the agents, toxins, weapons, equipment or means of delivery specified in article I of this Convention." At the Fourth Review Conference in 1996, the States Parties affirmed that Article III covers any recipient whatsoever at international, national, or subnational levels.

In the UK, controls on export and transfers are detailed in the Export Control Act 2002 along with secondary legislation and regulations.[38] Internal biosecurity controls are specified in the Anti-Terrorism, Crime and Security Act 2001.[39] Comparable standards are also required in the EU.

Preparedness

The WHO has recently provided guidance on the public-health response to biological and chemical weapons; it recommends that authorities should make maximum use of existing emergency response resources and should adopt an approach that is consistent with the management of any other type of public-health emergency.[40] A parallel approach is recommended by the OIE for dealing with attacks against animals.[41] Preparedness is not limited to response; it requires action before there is any attack. An awareness that a state is well prepared for any attack serves as a deterrent because it makes a would-be perpetrator uncertain whether an attack could have effect.

Within the UK, the response to a deliberate attack using biological or toxin agents would be handled as part of the overall response to emergencies.[42] These include severe weather, flooding, drought, human health emergencies, terrorism, transport accidents, animal and plant diseases, public protest and industrial action, international events, industrial technical failure, structural failure, CBRN (chemical, biological, radiological, nuclear) events, and industrial accidents and environmental pollution. The Civil Contingencies Act 2004 establishes the legislative framework for response to such emergencies.[43]

UK preparedness for a deliberate attack using biological or toxin agents builds upon the biological defense program for the UK armed forces, as much of what is required to counter an attack by sub-state actors is also required to defend the armed forces from an attack by biological weapons.[44] Preparedness for a deliberate attack requires an ability to detect and identify the agent that has been used, to assess the hazard area associated, to provide physical protection such as respirators and clothing to personnel dealing with the incident, and undertake medical countermeasures to treat any casualties.

Forceful Responses to Any Statements of BW Possession, BW Threats, or BW Attacks

Should there be a statement of possession, threat of use, or actual attack, there must be a determined response. Nationally, action should be taken through the courts to prosecute and punish those responsible. An international response would also be required if the event takes place in another country or is caused by the actions of another country. National penal legislation should be enacted by all states parties to both the BWC and the Chemical Weapons Convention (CWC). It should be sufficiently embracing to apply to all nationals of the state and to cover their activities whether carried out within the state or abroad. Proposals have been made for an additional international treaty to prohibit biological and chemical weapons under international criminal law.[45] This proposed Convention would make it an offense for any person, regardless of official position, to order, direct, or knowingly to participate or render substantial assistance in the development, production, acquisition, stockpiling, retention, transfer, or use of biological or chemical weapons; to threaten the use of such weapons; or to create or retain facilities intended for the production of such weapons. Such a convention would provide a valuable complement to the existing BWC and CWC by closing any jurisdictional loopholes, thus eliminating any potential impunity for criminal acts involving these weapons (see Chapter 8 by Jeanne Guillemin in this volume on related issues). It could usefully be negotiated in the Sixth (Legal) Committee of the United Nations General Assembly.

In the event of any statement of possession, threat of use, or actual attack, a state party to the BWC or CWC can seek international action based on the provisions in those Conventions. The Security Council on January 31, 1992, met for the first time at the level of Heads of State and Government and, with the Prime Minister of the UK in the chair, underlined "the need for all Member States to fulfil their obligations in relation to arms control and disarmament; to prevent the proliferation in all its aspects of all weapons of mass destruction."[46] In 2004, this statement was reaffirmed and recalled in Security Council Resolution 1540 which declared that, "all States shall refrain from providing any form of support to non-State actors that attempt to develop, acquire, manufacture, possess, transport, transfer or use nuclear, chemical or biological weapons and their means of delivery." Moreover, it called for "all States, in accordance with their national procedures, to adopt and enforce appropriate effective laws which prohibit any non-State actor to manufacture, acquire, possess, develop, transport, transfer or use nuclear, chemical or biological weapons and their means of delivery, in particular for terrorist purposes, as well as attempts to engage in any of the foregoing activities, participate in them as an accomplice, assist or finance them."[47]

The Security Council has recorded its intention to take steps against all those states engaged in proliferation of biological and toxin weapons. Such action could range from diplomatic action through sanctions to military intervention.

It is important that any statement of possession, threat of use, or actual attack is met by determined action both nationally and internationally, to demonstrate that the acquisition, possession, or use of such weapons will not be countenanced. Any would-be possessor must be given to understand that the entire international community would unite in condemnation and would respond.

Conclusions

Inaccurate or incorrect attributions bring the accuser into disrepute, undermine the credibility of intelligence assessments, weaken international treaty regimes, and waste resources on unnecessary protective measures. A forceful, authoritative, consistent, and balanced approach to any suspected use, threat, or possession of biological weapons is vital, with evidence and conclusions that meet rigorous legal standards and stand up to scientific and public scrutiny.

Policies for responding to possible outbreaks or intoxinations must be part of a broader integrated strategy, both national and international, to deter the acquisition and possession of biological and toxin weapons. Such a strategy must include comprehensive prohibitions, effective controls over access to and transfers of materials and equipment, preparedness for outbreaks or intoxinations whether natural and intentional, and forceful responses to any statements of possession, attacks, or threats of use.

This overall UK strategy can be strongly commended as a model to other states, and indeed, it is increasingly evident that many states recognize the values of such an approach and are adopting its elements in their national policies.

Notes

1. Nicholas A. Sims, *The Evolution of Biological Disarmament* (Oxford: Oxford University Press for Stockholm International Peace Research Institute [SIPRI], 2001), 3–4.

2. Convention on the Prohibition of the Development, Production and Stockpiling

of Bacteriological (Biological) and Toxin Weapons and on Their Destruction, <http://www.opbw.org>, accessed September 22, 2006.

3. United Nations, Review Conference of the Parties to the Convention on the Prohibition of the Development, Production and Stockpiling of Bacteriological (Biological) and Toxin Weapons and on Their Destruction, *Summary Record of the Twelfth Meeting,* BWC/CONF.I/SR.12, March 25, 1980, p. 3, <http://www.opbw.org>, accessed September 22, 2006.

4. Ibid., 5.

5. Ambassador David Summerhayes, Record of the Conference on Disarmament, Geneva, August 5, 1970, CD/PV.97, 36–37.

6. Her Majesty's Stationery Office [HMSO], *Statement on the Defence Estimates 1982,* London, Cmnd. 8529, 1982, I, 25–26.

7. House of Commons, *Official Report, Parliamentary Debates (Hansard),* vol. 98, no. 117, Written Answers to Questions, Monday May 19, 1986.

8. George Bush Presidential Library and Museum, *Statement by Press Secretary Fitzwater on President Bush's Letter to President Saddam Hussein of Iraq,* January 12, 1991, <http://bushlibrary.tamu.edu/research/papers/1991/91011201.html>, accessed September 24, 2006.

9. Graham S. Pearson, *The UNSCOM Saga: Chemical and Biological Weapons Non-Proliferation* (Basingstoke: Macmillan Press, 1999).

10. United Nations Security Council, Note by the President of the Security Council, S/23500, 31 January 1992, <http://documents-dds-ny.un.org/doc/UNDOC/GEN/N92/043/34/pdf/N9204334.pdf?OpenElement>, accessed September 24, 2006.

11. U.S. Department of State, Office of the Assistant Secretary, *Joint US/UK/Russian Statement on Biological Weapons,* Statement by Richard Boucher, Spokesman, September 14, 1992, <http://www.dod.mil/acq/acic/treaties/joint_bio_weapons/index.htm>, accessed September 24, 2006.

12. David C. Kelly, "The Trilateral Agreement: Lessons for Biological Weapons Verification," in Trevor Findlay and Oliver Meier, eds., *Verification Yearbook 2002* (London: VERTIC, 2002), 93–109, <http://www.vertic.org/assets/VY02_Kelly.pdf>, accessed September 25, 2006.

13. Chandré Gould and Peter Folb, "Project Coast: Apartheid's Chemical and Biological Warfare Programme," UNIDIR/2002/12, United Nations Institute for Disarmament Research, 2002.

14. See, for example, Peter Beaumont, Kamal Ahmed, and Martin Bright, "The Meeting That Brought Libya In from the Cold," *The Observer,* December 21, 2003, <http://observer.guardian.co.uk/worldview/story/0,1111343,00.html>, accessed September 24, 2006; Judith Miller, "Gadhafi's Leap of Faith," *The Wall Street Journal,* May 17, 2006; <http://www.opinionjournal.com/editorial/feature.html?id=110008386>, ac-

cessed September 24, 2006; and Judith Miller, "How Gadhafi Lost His Groove," *The Wall Street Journal,* May 16, 2006, <http://www.opinionjournal.com/editorial/feature. html?id=1100083861>, accessed September 24, 2006.

15. The Secretary of State for Foreign and Commonwealth Affairs (Mr. Jack Straw), *Libya,* Hansard (Commons), January 5, 2004, 416, no. 15, cols. 21–22, <http:// www.publications.parliament.uk/pa/cm200304/cmhansrd/vo040105/debtext/40105-06.htm#40105-06_spmino>, accessed October 9, 2006.

16. The Secretary of State for Health (Mr. Alan Millburn), *Emergency Services,* Hansard (Commons), 16 October 2001, 372, no. 30, cols. 1049–50, <http://www.publications. parliament.uk/pa/cm200102/cmhansrd/vo011016/debtext/11016-05.htm#11016-05_spmino>, accessed October 9, 2006.

17. Home Office, *Anti-Terrorism, Crime and Security Act 2001,* <http://www. homeoffice.gov.uk/security/terrorism-and-the-law/anti-terrorism-crime-security-ac/>, accessed October 4, 2006.

18. Nicholas A. Sims and Graham S. Pearson, "Article VIII: Geneva Protocol Obligations," in Graham S. Pearson, Nicholas A. Sims, and Malcolm R. Dando, eds., *Key Points for the Sixth Review Conference* (Bradford: University of Bradford, Department of Peace Studies, 2006), 171–83, <http://www.brad.ac.uk/acad.sbtwc>, accessed March 28, 2007.

19. Department of Trade and Industry, *Supplementary Guidance Note on Additional Controls Relating to the Prevention of Proliferation of Weapons of Mass Destruction (WMD),* <http://www.dti.gov.uk/files/file8419.pdf>, accessed September 25, 2006.

20. United Nations, Second Review Conference of the Parties to the Convention on the Prohibition of the Development, Production and Stockpiling of Bacteriological (Biological) and Toxin Weapons and on Their Destruction, *Final Declaration,* BWC/CONF. II/13 (Part II), 1986, p. 6, <http://www.opbw.org>, accessed September 25, 2006.

21. United Nations, Third Review Conference of the Parties to the Convention on the Prohibition of the Development, Production and Stockpiling of Bacteriological (Biological) and Toxin Weapons and on Their Destruction, *Final Declaration,* BWC/CONF. III/23 (Part. II), 1991, p. 6, <http://www.opbw.org>, accessed September 25, 2006.

22. G. S. Pearson, "Public Perception and risk Communication in Regard to Bioterrorism Against Animals and Plants," *Scientific and Technical Review (World Organization of Animal Health),* 2006, 25(1), 71–82, <http://www.oie.int/eng/publicat/rt/2501/A_R2501_PEARSON.htm>, accessed March 28, 2007.

23. See Malcolm Dando, Graham Pearson, and Bohumir Kriz, eds., *Scientific and Technical Means of Distinguishing Between Natural and Other Outbreaks of Disease, NATO Science Series, 1. Disarmament Technologies,* vol. 35 (Dordrecht: Kluwer Academic Publishers, 2001).

24. R. M. Black and D. G. Upshall, "Assessing the Danger," *Chemistry in Britain* 24, no. 7 (July 1988): 659–64.

25. Graham S. Pearson, *The Search for Iraq's Weapons of Mass Destruction: Inspection, Verification and Non-Proliferation* (Basingstoke: Palgrave, 2005).

26. Ken Alibek with Stephen Handelman, *Biohazard* (London: Hutchinson 1999); Roger Roffey, Wilhelm Unge, Jenny Clevström, and Kristina S. Westerdahl, "Support to Threat Reduction of the Russian Biological Weapons Legacy—Conversion, Biodefence and the Role of Biopreparat," Swedish Defence Research Agency Report FOI-R–0841–SE, April 2003, <http://www.foi.se/upload/english/reports/foi-russian-bio-weapons-legacy.pdf>, accessed March 28, 2007.

27. Cabinet Office, *National Intelligence Machinery* (London: HMSO, September 2006), <http://www.cabinetoffice.gov.uk/publications/reports/intelligence/NationalIntelligenceMachinery.pdf>, accessed October 2, 2006.

28. Statement by G8 Leaders, *The G8 Global Partnership Against the Spread of Weapons and Materials of Mass Destruction,* Kananaskis, June 27, 2002, <http://www.g8.gc.ca/2002Kananaskis/globpart-en.asp>, accessed October 5, 2006.

29. Statement by G8 Leaders, *Statement on Non-Proliferation,* St. Petersburg, July 16, 2006, <http://en.g8russia.ru/docs/20.html>, accessed October 5, 2006.

30. World Health Organization, *Biorisk management: Laboratory biosecurity guidance,* September 2006, <http://www.who.int/csr/resources/publications/biosafety/WHO_CDS_EPR_2006_6.pdf>, accessed October 5, 2006.

31. These CBM returns are posted on The Biological and Toxin Weapons Convention website, <http://www.opbw.org>, accessed March 28, 2007.

32. Information is available from the Organization for the Prohibition of Chemical Weapons, <http://www.opcw.org>, accessed October 5, 2006.

33. Pearson, *The Search for Iraq's Weapons of Mass Destruction.*

34. The Biological and Toxin Weapons Convention website, *Convention on the Prohibition of the Development, Production and Stockpiling of Bacteriological (Biological) and Toxin Weapons and on Their Destruction,* Article I, <http://www.opbw.org>, accessed March 28, 2007.

35. The Biological and Toxin Weapons Convention website, *List of States Parties to The Convention on the Prohibition of the Development, Production and Stockpiling of Bacteriological (Biological) and Toxin Weapons and on their Destruction,* BWC/MSP/2005/MX/INF.5, <http://www.opbw.org>, accessed October 4, 2006.

36. Organization for the Prohibition of Chemical Weapons, *Status of Participation in the Chemical Weapons Convention,* <http://www.opcw.org/factsandfigures/index.html#participation>, accessed October 4, 2006.

37. Department of Trade and Industry, *Biological Weapons Act 1974,* <http://www.dti.gov.uk/europeandtrade/non-proliferation/chemical-biological/btwc/bwa-1974/page26600.html>, accessed October 4, 2006.

38. Department of Trade and Industry, *UK Legislation on Strategic Export Controls,*

<http://www.dti.gov.uk/europeandtrade/strategic-export-control/legislation/index. html>, accessed October 4, 2006.

39. Home Office, *Anti-Terrorism, Crime and Security Act 2001*, <http://www. homeoffice.gov.uk/security/terrorism-and-the-law/anti-terrorism-crime-security-ac/>, accessed October 4, 2006.

40. World Health Organization, *Public Health Response to Biological and Chemical Weapons; WHO Guidance* (Geneva: WHO, 2004), <http://www.who.int/csr/ delibepidemics/biochemguide/en/index.html>, accessed October 4, 2006.

41. World Organization for Animal Health, "Biological Disasters of Animal Origin: The Role and Preparedness of Veterinary and Public Health Services," Martin Hugh-Jones, ed., *Scientific and Technical Review* 25(1), 2006, <http://www.oie.int/eng/publicat/ RT/A_RT25_1.htm>, accessed October 4, 2006.

42. UK Resilience, "Emergencies," <http://www.ukresilience.info/emergencies/ index.shtm>, accessed October 4, 2006. UK Resilience website is a news and information service for emergency practitioners by the Civil Contingencies Secretariat at The Cabinet Office.

43. UK Resilience, Civil Contingencies Act 2004, <http://www.ukresilience.info/ ccact/cat2_info/index.shtm>, accessed October 4, 2006.

44. Graham S. Pearson, "United Kingdom: Bioterrorism Defense," in Richard F. Pilch and Raymond A. Zilinskas, eds., *Encyclopedia of Bioterrorism Defense* (Hoboken, NJ: John Wiley, 2005), 493–508.

45. The CBW Conventions Bulletin, *A Draft Convention to Prohibit Biological and Chemical Weapons Under International Criminal Law, no. 42*, December 1998, pp. 1–5, <http://www.sussex.ac.uk/Units/spru/hsp/pdfbulletin.html>, accessed October 4, 2006; see also *The HSP Draft Convention*, <http://lense.net.uk/Units/spru/hsp/Harvard-Sussex-Program-draft-convention.htm>, accessed October 4, 2006.

46. United Nations Security Council, *Note by the President of the Security Council*, S/23500, January 31, 1992, <http://documents-dds-ny.un.org/doc/UNDOC/GEN/ N92/043/34/pdf/N9204334.pdf?OpenElement>, accessed October 4, 2006; also available at <http://www.securitycouncilreport.org/atf/cf/%7B65BFCF9B-6D27-4E9C-8CD3-CF6 E4FF96FF9%7D/UNRO%20S23500.pdf>, accessed March 29, 2007.

47. United Nations Security Council, *Resolution 1540 (2004) Adopted by the Security Council at its 4956th meeting, on 28 April 2004*, S/RES/1540 (2004), April 28, 2004, <http://documents-dds-ny.un.org/doc/UNDOC/GEN/N04/328/43/pdf/N0432843. pdf?OpenElement>, accessed October 4, 2004.

CHAPTER TWELVE

Multilateral Approaches to the Investigation and Attribution of Biological Weapons Use

JONATHAN B. TUCKER

Since the end of World War II, governments, journalists, and humanitarian organizations have accused various actors of employing biological or toxin weapons in violation of international law.[1] Multilateral mechanisms for investigating such allegations can help to determine their validity and, if the incident proves to be real, assist with the process of identifying the agent, determining the detailed circumstances of the attack, and attributing it to a specific country or subnational group.

Although multilateral investigations may encounter many of the same obstacles faced by investigations carried out by individual states, the involvement of a diverse array of countries tends to generate greater international credibility and legitimacy than evidence based on national intelligence alone. For this reason, multilateral investigations provide a stronger basis for mobilizing political, economic, and even military sanctions against a perpetrator. Such investigations are also less likely to involve sensitive sources and methods of intelligence collection that cannot be shared with other countries.

To date, most multilateral investigations of alleged use have resulted in ambiguous or weakly stated findings because of a lack of timeliness, access, or cooperation by the host country. This chapter describes the various multilateral investigative mechanisms that currently exist and suggests how they might be strengthened to improve their effectiveness. Because past multilateral investigations of alleged use have often involved chemical weapons rather than biological or toxin weapons, both types of incident are covered.

The Biological Weapons Convention

The 1972 Biological and Toxin Weapons Convention (BWC) bans the development, production, stockpiling, and transfer for hostile purposes of disease-causing microorganisms and toxins (toxic chemicals of natural origin). Although the BWC does not explicitly prohibit the use of such weapons, the treaty dovetails with the 1925 Geneva Protocol banning the use in war of both biological and chemical arms. An absolute ban on use is also implied by the BWC's prohibitions on acquisition and possession. Indeed, the Fourth Review Conference of the BWC in 1996 agreed that "the use by the States Parties, in any way and under any circumstances, of microbial and other biological agents and toxins, that is not consistent with prophylactic, protective or other peaceful purposes, is effectively a violation of Article I of the Convention."[2]

The BWC was negotiated in the early 1970s, when most countries were unwilling to accept the highly intrusive on-site inspections needed to monitor compliance with a reasonable degree of confidence. As a result, the treaty entered into force in 1975 without formal verification measures. A subsequent effort from 1995 to 2001 to negotiate a compliance protocol to augment the BWC also proved unsuccessful. Although allegations of use may be addressed under two articles of the BWC, Article V (on consultations) or Article VI (on investigations), neither provision has been particularly effective, for the reasons discussed below.

Consultations Under Article V

Article V of the BWC provides that member states "undertake to consult one another and to cooperate in solving any problems which may arise in relation to the objective of, or in the application of the provisions of, the Convention." These consultations may occur either on a bilateral basis or multilaterally, "through appropriate international procedures within the framework of the United Nations and in accordance with its Charter." Although Article V does not specify how multilateral consultations are to be carried out, the Third and Fourth Review Conferences of the BWC developed detailed procedures for convening a formal consultative meeting of member states to address compliance concerns.

Such a meeting has been held only once, in response to an allegation by Cuba that a U.S. government aircraft overflying the island in October 1996 released an insect pest to damage Cuba's agricultural sector (see Chapter 7 by Raymond Zilinskas). The undisputed facts of the incident are that on October 21, 1996, a single-engine crop-dusting plane operated by the U.S. Department of State flew from an Air Force base in Florida to Grand Cayman Island, en route to Colombia for use in the coca eradication program. As the U.S. aircraft passed through the international air corridor over Matanzas Province in central Cuba, it was observed releasing a gray-white cloud. Two months later, on December 18, 1996, a serious infestation of an insect pest known as *Thrips palmi* occurred in Matanzas Province. The infestation went on to devastate 17 vegetable crops in Cuba, including potatoes, beans, peppers, cucumbers, and pumpkins, causing economic losses in the tens of millions of dollars.[3]

On April 28, 1997, the Cuban government sent a letter to the UN Secretary-General alleging that the U.S. government aircraft had released *Thrips palmi* over Matanzas Province in a deliberate effort to harm Cuba's agriculture. At Havana's request, Russia (one of the three BWC depositaries) convened a formal consultative meeting of BWC member states to address this charge. The meeting was held in Geneva, Switzerland, on August 25–27, 1997, under the chairmanship of British ambassador Ian Soutar.

The Cuban representative presented his country's case that the U.S. government aircraft had released the insect pest over the island. In rebuttal, the United States argued that as the State Department plane transited Cuba, the U.S. pilot observed an approaching Cuban airliner that did not respond to various means of notification. Fearing a possible collision, the pilot alerted the Cuban airliner by emitting several puffs of smoke from an on-board smoke generator. The U.S. government representative noted that *Thrips palmi* had been present in the Caribbean region since 1985 and had spread over the previous decade to Haiti, the Dominican Republic, Jamaica, and Venezuela. Thus, the pest could easily have been brought to Cuba by hurricane winds or the importation of goods from affected countries.[4]

When the states participating in the formal consultative meeting failed to reach consensus on the merits of the Cuban allegation, the chairman invited them to submit their observations in writing. Of the twelve countries that submitted statements, most were not persuaded of a causal link between the U.S. overflight and the *Thrips palmi* infestation and believed that the United States should be exonerated. Only North Korea found the Cuban case convincing, while China and Vietnam argued that because of the technical complexity of the issue and the lack of detailed information, they could not make a clear judgment. On December 15, 1997, Ambassador Soutar released a final report on the formal consultative meeting, noting that "due *inter alia* to the technical complexity of the subject and to the passage of time, it has not proved possible to reach a definitive conclusion with regard to the concerns raised by the Government of Cuba."[5] Although Havana accepted this inconclusive result, the outcome of the meeting suggested that politics was more important than evidence in shaping countries' assessments of the Cuban allegations. The lack of objective scientific data also underscored the need for an impartial fact-finding mechanism to investigate charges of biological and toxin weapons use.

Investigations Under Article VI

Another provision in the BWC for raising—and potentially investigating—allegations of use is Article VI, which holds that a member state that "finds that any other State Party is acting in breach of obligations deriving from the provisions of the Convention may lodge a complaint with the Security Council of the United Nations. Such a complaint should include all possible evidence confirming its validity." The UN Security Council may then decide to launch a formal investigation, but is not required to do so. Although Article VI does not specify rules of evidence or assign the burden of proof, the complainant state would presumably be expected to present clear and convincing information in support of the charge, while the accused party would be expected to cooperate in any investigation that the Security Council decides to initiate and would have the right of rebuttal.

Under Article 27 of the UN Charter, Security Council decisions on non-procedural matters must have the support of nine of the 15 members of the council and can be vetoed by any of the five permanent members (China, France, Russia, the United Kingdom, or the United States). Thus, a Security Council investigation of an alleged use of biological weapons could easily be blocked for political reasons. During the BWC negotiations, Britain proposed exempting

Article VI investigations of noncompliance from the veto, but this idea was not adopted. The resulting weakness of Article VI explains why the United States never brought its repeated allegations of Soviet noncompliance with the BWC to the attention of the Security Council.

The Failed BWC Protocol Negotiations

Between 1995 and 2001, an Ad Hoc Group of BWC member states worked to develop a compliance protocol to augment the Convention that included detailed provisions for investigating allegations of biological and toxin weapons use. In early 2001, the chairman of the Ad Hoc Group circulated a compromise draft text of the BWC Protocol, and it appeared that the negotiations were entering the final phase. But in July of that year, the new U.S. administration of President George W. Bush rejected the draft BWC Protocol and withdrew from the Ad Hoc Group talks, dooming them to failure. Although a number of other countries were unhappy with the chairman's compromise text, they were quite willing to let the United States take the heat for rejecting the draft treaty.

Investigations by the UN Secretary-General

Another mechanism for investigating the alleged use of chemical or biological weapons exists outside the framework of a formal treaty. Under Article 99 of the UN Charter, the Secretary-General has the right to bring matters that may constitute a threat to international peace and security to the attention of the Security Council and to engage in related fact-finding activities. Building on this authority, the UN General Assembly adopted a series of resolutions during the 1980s enabling any member state to report an allegation of chemical, biological, or toxin weapons use and request that the Secretary-General organize an impartial field investigation by an international group of experts. Between 1980 and 1992, the Secretary-General launched a dozen field investigations, all of them involving the alleged use of chemical or toxin weapons. The results of these missions are described briefly below.

The "Yellow Rain" Investigations

In the late 1970s, the United States alleged that the Soviet-allied Communist governments of Laos and Vietnam were employing unknown toxic agents for counterinsurgency warfare against the H'mong rebels in Laos, who had fought on the U.S. side during the Vietnam War, and Khmer Rouge forces in Cambodia (then known as Democratic Kampuchea). After the Soviet invasion of Afghanistan in December 1979, the United States also accused the Red Army of using chemical agents against the *mujahedin* resistance fighters. Eyewitnesses in all three countries described attacks with a yellow liquid that fell like rain and caused severe illness and death in humans and livestock exposed to it. The press dubbed this mysterious agent "Yellow Rain." (See Chapter 4 by Meselson and Robinson and Chapter 5 by Rebecca Katz in this volume.)

In December 1980, at the request of the United States, New Zealand tabled General Assembly Resolution 35/144C requesting the UN Secretary-General to look into the alleged "Yellow Rain" incidents in Southeast Asia and Afghanistan. The operative paragraphs of the resolution stated that the General Assembly "decides to carry out an impartial investigation to ascertain the facts pertaining to these reports regarding the alleged use of chemical weapons and to assess the extent of damage" and "requests the Secretary-General to carry out such an investigation . . . with the assistance of qualified medical and technical experts."[6] Despite strong opposition from the Soviet Union and its Communist bloc allies, the resolution was approved by a majority of UN member states. Secretary-General Kurt Waldheim then assembled a group of experts from Egypt, Kenya, Peru, and the Philippines to investigate the allegations. In September 1981, several months into the UN inquiry, U.S. Secretary of State Alexander Haig made a speech in West Berlin in which he declared that the U.S. government had analyzed spots of "Yellow Rain" material and identified a mixture of potent fungal poisons called trichothecene mycotoxins. Secretary Haig claimed the Soviet Union had developed and produced these toxins for military use and made them available to its Pathet Lao and Vietnamese allies.[7]

After the UN experts completed their investigation in Southeast Asia, they could not reach a definitive judgment on the "Yellow Rain" allegations for three reasons: the refusal by the governments of Laos and Vietnam to grant the experts access to the purported attack sites or to cooperate in any way; the long delay between the alleged toxin attacks and the start of the investigation; and the unreliable and conflicting testimony of eyewitnesses. Further, the provenance of the U.S. "Yellow Rain" samples was uncertain and the UN team was unable to obtain clear-cut forensic evidence, such as intact munitions containing the toxic agent or contaminated fragments. The final report of the

UN experts stated, "Any investigation designed to lead to definitive conclusions regarding the alleged use of chemical weapons . . . would require timely access to the areas of alleged use of chemical warfare agents in order to establish the true facts. Such an exercise has so far not been possible."[8]

Dissatisfied with this outcome, the General Assembly asked Secretary-General Javier Pérez de Cuéllar to launch a follow-on investigation in Southeast Asia and Afghanistan, which he did in early 1982. Like the first UN team, however, the second team was denied access to the alleged attack sites and was forced to rely on interviews with refugees at camps in Pakistan and Thailand. As a result, the report of the second UN investigation proved to be as inconclusive as the first: "While the Group could not state that these allegations had been proven, nevertheless it could not disregard the circumstantial evidence suggestive of the possible use of some sort of toxic chemical substance in some instances."[9]

On December 13, 1982, the UN General Assembly adopted Resolution 37/98D expanding the investigative powers of the Secretary-General beyond the specific case of "Yellow Rain" by granting him the authority to investigate any alleged use of chemical or biological weapons in violation of the 1925 Geneva Protocol, which lacks formal verification measures.[10] The Geneva Protocol is widely considered to be part of the customary international law of armed conflict as a result of general adherence and the declarations of international organizations.[11] Accordingly, the authority of the Secretary-General to investigate the alleged use of biological or chemical weapons applies to all states, whether or not they have signed and ratified the Geneva Protocol and whether or not the country with which they are engaged in hostilities is a party to the treaty. In response to Resolution 37/98D, the UN Secretary-General asked member countries to submit lists of qualified experts to conduct field investigations and of reference laboratories capable of analyzing environmental and biomedical samples. The Secretary-General also appointed a Group of Consultant Experts to draft an 80-page handbook containing criteria for when to investigate an incident of alleged use and technical guidelines for the conduct of such missions.[12]

Investigations During the Iran-Iraq War

The next investigation of alleged use took place during the Iraq-Iraq War of 1980–88. Iraq, facing a numerically superior adversary, began in 1983 to employ chemical weapons as a force-multiplier to counter Iran's "human wave" infantry tactics. Mustard gas and nerve agents were quite effective against Iranian troops and militia, who lacked gas masks and protective suits or failed to use them correctly. On November 3, 1983, Iran requested the Secretary-General to dispatch a UN team to investigate the reported chemical attacks.[13] Despite pressure from several countries not to pursue the Iranian allegations, Secretary-General Pérez de Cuéllar dispatched a group of experts to Iran on a "fact-finding visit" on the basis of "the humanitarian principles embodied in the Charter and of the moral responsibilities vested in his office."[14]

To perform this mission, the UN Secretariat selected four experts from Australia, Spain, Sweden, and Switzerland, who visited Iran on March 13–19, 1984. The Iranian government granted the UN team full access to the alleged attack sites and to injured Iranian soldiers. Based on samples collected from unexploded chemical munitions and analyzed in reference laboratories, the experts concluded that Iraq had attacked Iranian troops at various times with bombs and artillery shells loaded with mustard agent, tabun nerve agent, and an unknown pulmonary irritant.[15]

Over the course of the Iran-Iraq War, four more UN teams were dispatched to investigate Iranian allegations of Iraqi chemical warfare. In each case, the collection and analysis of environmental or biomedical samples confirmed the continued use of blister and nerve agents. Yet despite the clear evidence that Iraq was flagrantly violating the Geneva Protocol, the short-term interest of the United States and other Western countries in avoiding an Iranian victory took precedence over the enforcement of international law. Instead of imposing political and economic sanctions on Baghdad, the Security Council merely issued a declaration condemning the use of chemical weapons, without mentioning Iraq by name.

In 1987, Iraq tried to turn the political tables by accusing Iran of chemical warfare, and the Secretary-General launched an investigation into these allegations. A UN team visited Iraq from April 29 to May 3, 1987, and conducted medical examinations of injured Iraqi troops, performed autopsies on cadavers, and collected soil samples from a shell crater in the Basra area. The team's final report concluded, "Iraqi forces have been affected by mustard gas and a pulmonary irritant, possibly phosgene. In the absence of conclusive evidence of the weapons used, it could not be determined how the injuries were caused."[16] Indeed, it was possible that the Iraqi troops had been injured by accidental exposure to their own chemical agents. After the Iraqi air force dropped chemical weapons on the Kurdish city of Halabja in northern Iraq on March 16, 1988, killing thousands of civilians, several countries asked the Secretary-General to launch an investigation of the incident, but Iraqi President Saddam Hussein refused to cooperate.[17]

On November 30, 1987, in recognition of the need for the prompt investigation of allegations of chemical or biological weapons use, the UN General Assembly adopted Resolution 42/37C expanding the authority of the Secretary-General to "carry out investigations in response to reports that may be brought to his attention by any Member State concerning the possible use of chemical and bacteriological (biological) or toxin weapons that may constitute a violation of the 1925 Geneva Protocol or other relevant rules of customary international law."[18] This resolution also urged the Secretary-General to update the roster of experts and the field investigation handbook; a revised version of the latter was issued in October 1989.[19] In addition, UN Security Council Resolution 620 of August 26, 1988, encouraged the Secretary-General to investigate allegations of use and committed the council to "consider immediately, taking into account the investigations of the Secretary-General, appropriate and effective measures in accordance with the Charter of the United Nations, should there be any future use of chemical weapons in violation of international law, wherever and by whomever committed."[20]

Investigation in Mozambique

The next two investigations of alleged use under the Secretary-General's mechanism took place in 1992. On January 27, the government of Mozambique sent a letter to UN Secretary-General Boutros Boutros-Ghali alleging that the Mozambican National Resistance (RENAMO), a rebel organization supported by the apartheid regime in South Africa, had used chemical weapons against Mozambican government forces. The alleged incident occurred on January 16, 1992, when the Third Battalion of the Mozambican Army, reinforced with a company of provincial troops for a total of 382 soldiers, raided a RENAMO base near the village of Macaene in southwestern Mozambique, about ten kilometers from the South African border.

As the Mozambican army unit was returning from the operation, an artillery shell or rocket exploded overhead, releasing a cloud of black smoke that was carried by the wind over the formation and dissipated without touching the ground. Although no immediate casualties ensued, some 15 minutes later about a fifth of the Mozambican troops developed fever, thirst, dry mouth, sore throat, dilated pupils, chest pains, an inability to sweat, severe muscle weakness and lethargy, confusion, disorientation, mood-swings, and self-destructive behavior. Unit discipline broke down and some troops fired their weapons indiscriminately, killing two soldiers by accident. Over the ten-day period from January 18 to 27, twenty-eight affected troops were admitted to the Military Hospital in Maputo, the Mozambican capital.[21]

Before the UN Secretary-General became involved, the Mozambican government requested outside experts to conduct preliminary investigations of the incident. On January 27–31, 1992, John P. Thompson, a British pharmacologist with the Chemical and Biological Defence Establishment at Porton Down, interviewed hospitalized Mozambican government troops with the assistance of the British military attaché in Maputo. Thompson concluded that the reported signs and symptoms were "entirely consistent with the use of a centrally acting anti-cholinergic incapacitating agent" such as BZ (3-quinuclidinyl benzilate) or a related compound.[22] A second inquiry, conducted on February 5–11 by a group of experts from the Swedish National Defense Research Establishment (FOA), concluded that the most likely cause of the incident was the use of a toxic military smoke, such as that used to create smokescreens, rather than a chemical warfare agent.[23]

These preliminary findings persuaded Secretary-General Boutros-Ghali to launch a formal UN investigation.[24] On March 18, he appointed two experts, Sven-Ake Persson, a toxicologist at FOA, and Heiner Staub, a chemical engineer at the Swiss chemical and biological defense laboratory in Spiez, and dispatched them on short notice to Mozambique, accompanied by two UN diplomats. Persson and Staub arrived in Maputo on March 23, and Thompson joined them the next day.[25]

Over the next four days, the UN experts attended briefings by Mozambican officials, interviewed alleged victims at the military hospital in Maputo, and visited the purported attack site near the village of Macaene to collect environmental samples, which were sent for analysis at laboratories in Sweden, Switzerland, and the United Kingdom.[26] (For unknown reasons, the UN team was taken to a different site than the one Thompson had visited earlier.[27]) All of the environmental samples were negative for 20 common chemical warfare agents, including BZ and its degradation products. Nevertheless, because of confusion over the precise location of the alleged attack and the length of time that had elapsed since the incident, some uncertainties remained. It was possible that the samples had been taken at the wrong place or that the chemical warfare agent—if it existed—had degraded to the point that it was no longer detectable.

In the absence of hard analytical data, the UN investigation focused on interviews with Mozambican troops who had been involved in the incident. Staub gradually became convinced that chemical weapons probably had not been used, for several reasons. First, it is nearly impossible to place a single artillery or mortar shell precisely in the middle of a moving battalion, and a military attack involving only one round (conventional or chemical) is highly unusual. Second, a chemical artillery shell contains only about 1 to 2 kilograms of agent, far too little to affect so many troops. Third, because BZ and related compounds are solids, they require a specialized delivery mechanism for effective dispersal. During the 1960s, the United States developed small smoke generators that were released from an aerial cluster bomb and descended to earth on parachutes, disseminating BZ as they did so.[28] But eyewitness accounts of the Mozambique incident did not point to such a delivery system.[29]

After completing their investigation, the three UN experts returned home to write a final report, an arduous process that lasted three days. Whereas Persson and Staub argued that the eyewitness accounts were inconsistent with a chemical attack and that the reported symptoms could be explained just as well by severe heat stress, Thompson insisted that the symptoms were strongly indicative of BZ exposure. After the three experts had argued for hours without reaching agreement, the two UN diplomats accompanying the team helped them to craft an ambiguous statement that everyone could accept.[30] The final report concluded, "Mozambican government forces sustained casualties not entirely explicable by the kind of weapons so far in use in the conflict in Mozambique. From the material available to the qualified experts it was not possible to determine whether or not a chemical weapon was used against Mozambican government forces."[31]

In 2001, two intelligence analysts with the U.S. Department of State published an article on the Mozambique case in which they argued that the inconclusive findings of the UN investigation had been a cover-up, the result of political pressure from UN mediators who wished to avoid derailing delicate peace negotiations between the warring parties then under way in Rome.[32] But Heiner Staub, a member of the UN team that conducted the investigation, strongly denies that such political interference occurred.[33] Given the ambiguity of the physical data, the evidence for a deliberate cover-up appears weak.

Investigation in Azerbaijan

Later in 1992, the UN Secretary-General launched another investigation of alleged chemical warfare, this time in Azerbaijan. After the December 1991 breakup of the Soviet Union, Azerbaijan and Armenia had become embroiled in a war over Nagorno-Karabakh, an enclave within Azerbaijan populated by ethnic Armenians. On June 1, 1992, the Permanent Representative of Azerbaijan to the UN sent a letter to the president of the Security Council alleging that Armenian armed forces had used chemical weapons the previous month in Nakhichevan, a region of western Azerbaijan bordering Armenia, and that traces of mustard, cyanide, and phosgene had been detected in blood samples from wounded Azeris.[34] On June 8, the Permanent Representative of Armenia rejected the allegation and requested a UN inquiry to clear his country's name.

The gravity of the charges led UN Secretary-General Boutros-Ghali to launch an investigation. On June 19, 1992, he dispatched three experts on short notice to Azerbaijan: Heiner Staub of the Spiez Laboratory in Switzerland; Johan Santesson, a chemist at FOA in Sweden; and Jan Willems, a Belgian military medical doctor with experience treating chemical casualties. Accompanied by two UN officials and equipped with portable inspection equipment, the experts flew on a Swiss Air Force plane directly from Geneva to Baku, the capital of Azerbaijan.[35]

The UN team conducted its investigation on July 4–8, traveling by helicopter to two Azeri villages in Nakhichevan that had allegedly been attacked with chemical artillery shells and rockets. After meeting with villagers who claimed to have experienced strange odors and other signs of toxic warfare, the experts concluded that it was unlikely chemical weapons could have been used in such a way that no clusters of contaminated persons would have resulted.[36] Returning to Baku, the team visited the Civil Defense Laboratory, which had reportedly found trace amounts of cyanide in samples of soil and shrapnel collected from shell craters after an Armenian artillery barrage. The UN experts determined that the laboratory had used an obsolete Russian analytical technique that could give false-positive results, and that cyanide might also be present in samples for reasons not associated with the use of chemical weapons. The team's final report concluded that chemical weapons "do not appear to have been used in the ongoing conflict between Armenia and Azerbaijan."[37] Despite the weak language, the negative findings were convincing enough to end the Azerbaijani charges against Armenia.

Since 1992, no additional UN field investigations have occurred, although General Assembly Resolution 42/37C of 1987 authorizing the Secretary-General's mechanism has remained in effect and several unofficial allegations of chemical weapons use have been made (including Srebrenica, Bosnia, in 1995; Tbilisi, Georgia, in 1998; southern Sudan in 1999; the West Bank in 2001; and Myanmar in 2005).[38] Furthermore, the United States did not request a UN investigation of the letters contaminated with anthrax bacterial spores that were sent through the U.S. postal system in September–October 2001 (described by Leonard Cole in Chapter 2 of this volume). The Secretary-General's mechanism fell into disuse for several reasons. First, the CWC's opening for signature in 1993 and its entry into force in 1997 meant that the new treaty provided for investigations of the alleged use of chemical and toxin weapons. Second, during the BWC Protocol negotiations from 1995 to 2001, the Secretary-General's mechanism was put on hold to avoid preempting the development of field investigation procedures.[39] As a result, no attempt was made to update the UN roster of experts or to revise the 1989 inspection handbook.

Efforts to Revive the Secretary-General's Mechanism

After the United States withdrew from the Ad Hoc Group negotiations in 2001, it proposed reviving the UN Secretary-General's mechanism as an alternative to the now-defunct BWC Protocol. A first step in this direction was taken in 2002, when the UN Under-Secretary-General for Disarmament Affairs sent a letter to all 191 UN members requesting them to update the lists of experts and reference laboratories. Responses were received from 28 states, 24 of them positive.[40]

In July–August 2004, a Meeting of Experts in the framework of the intersessional work program established by the Fifth Review Conference of the BWC discussed the conduct of field investigations of alleged biological weapons use. The decision to include this topic in the BWC work program reflected the growing international interest in reviving the Secretary-General's mechanism. During the meeting, the British government proposed strengthening the mechanism by incorporating lessons learned from the UN weapons inspections in Iraq and advances in analytical science and technology.[41] The United States, in contrast, distanced itself from its earlier position by arguing that the Secretary-General's authority to pursue allegations of chemical and biological weapons use "stands and, in our view, should not be tinkered with. The mechanism exists outside the auspices of the BWC and it would, therefore, not be the place of BWC States Parties to revise it."[42] Despite the U.S. reservations, the Europeans continued to push for a new initiative. In an October 2005 statement to the First Committee of the UN General Assembly, British Ambassador John Freeman said on behalf of the European Union, "We believe that the [Secretary-General's] mechanism—now 15 years old—needs to be reviewed and updated so that it can take advantage of the progress of science and investigation in the intervening years and support efforts to make progress in that regard."[43]

On February 27, 2006, the European Union adopted an Action Plan on Biological and Toxin Weapons that specified measures to be taken in the event of a violation of the BWC. This plan called on EU member states to volunteer expertise to the UN Secretary-General by the end of December 2007 to help him update the lists of experts and reference laboratories for investigating allegations of biological weapons use, and to review and revise this information every two years.[44] Subsequently, on September 20, 2006, the UN General Assembly passed a resolution establishing a "United Nations Global Counter-Terrorism Strategy." Paragraph II (11) of this resolution encouraged the Secretary-General "to update the roster of experts and laboratories, as well as the technical guidelines and procedures, available to him for the timely and efficient investigation of alleged use."[45]

In a position paper distributed in December 2006 at the Sixth Review Conference of the BWC, Germany noted that all previous experience with the Secretary-General's mechanism had involved the alleged use of chemical or toxin weapons. Accordingly, it was unclear whether the existing investigation guidelines and procedures were suitable for incidents involving microbial pathogens, which presumably would require different techniques for medical examination and the collection and analysis of environmental and biomedical samples. To address this situation, the German government recommended reviewing the technical guidelines and procedures in the light of recent scientific and technological developments and adapting them to the specific characteristics of biological warfare agents; updating the lists of qualified experts and laboratories periodically; and conducting a series of exercises to test the applicability of the revised guidelines, procedures, and lists, and modifying them as necessary.[46]

The Chemical Weapons Convention

The entry into force of the Chemical Weapons Convention (CWC) on April 29, 1997, marked a critical juncture in the ability of the international community to investigate allegations of chemical weapons use. Whereas the BWC lacks any formal verification measures, the CWC contains detailed provisions for on-site inspections and field investigations, which are conducted by the treaty-implementing body, the Organization for the Prohibition of Chemical Weapons (OPCW), based in The Hague, The Netherlands.

Under Article IX (Consultations, Cooperation and Fact-Finding), each CWC member state has "the right to request an on-site challenge inspection of any facility or location in the territory or in any other place under the jurisdiction or control of any other State Party for the sole purpose of clarifying and resolving any questions concerning possible non-compliance." A challenge inspection may take the form of an investigation of alleged use (IAU), and detailed procedures for conducting an IAU are set out in Part XI of the CWC Verification Annex. The members of the investigation team would be chosen from amongst those OPCW inspectors selected for challenge inspections. In addition, the OPCW Director-General must "prepare a list of qualified experts whose particular field of expertise could be required in an investigation of alleged use of chemical weapons and constantly keep this list updated." Such experts would be incorporated into the investigation team to provide expertise not available within the organization.[47]

Immediately after receiving a request from a member state to investigate an incident of alleged use, the OPCW Director-General must contact the affected parties and arrange for the safe reception of the experts. The IAU team is entitled to visit "any and all areas which could be affected by the alleged use of chemical weapons," such as hospitals and refugee camps, and has the right "to collect samples of types, and in quantities it considers necessary," including toxic chemicals, munitions and devices, or remnants thereof, environmental samples (air, soil, vegetation, water, and snow), and biomedical samples (blood, urine, excreta, and tissue) from human or animal sources. Sample analysis may take place on-site or in an OPCW-approved laboratory. The investigation team must submit a preliminary report on its findings within 72 hours of returning to The Hague and a final report within 30 days.

The second mechanism in the CWC for initiating an investigation of alleged use is provided for in Article X (Assistance and Protection Against Chemical Weapons). This article entitles any member state that has been the victim of a chemical attack or threatened with chemical weapons—whether by a CWC party or a non-party—to request assistance from the OPCW. The request for assistance must be accompanied by substantiating information, such as the types of chemical agents alleged to have been used, the extent and time of use, and the effects on humans, animals, and vegetation.[48] Not more than 24 hours after receiving a request for assistance, the Director-General must initiate an investigation to gather "relevant facts related to the request as well as the type and scope of supplementary assistance and protection needed," providing the basis for further action.

Since the entry into force of the CWC in April 1997, no member state has asked the OPCW to investigate an alleged use of chemical or toxin weapons, despite unofficial allegations of use made by non-governmental organizations. Nevertheless, the CWC field investigation mechanism is available whenever a state party decides to invoke it. Although the treaty does not cover allegations of chemical or toxin use by non-parties to the CWC, such incidents would be covered by the Secretary-General's mechanism. In September 2001, the OPCW signed a cooperative agreement with the UN Secretariat in which it pledged to "closely cooperate with the Secretary-General in cases of the alleged use of chemical weapons involving a State not party to the Convention or in a territory not controlled by a State Party to the Convention." The OPCW has also agreed, upon request, to place its technical resources at the disposal of the Secretary-General.[49]

Role of Other Multilateral Organizations

A multilateral mechanism for the investigation of unusual outbreaks of infectious disease exists under the auspices of the World Health Organization (WHO), one of the specialized agencies of the United Nations. In 2000, WHO established the Global Outbreak Alert and Response Network (GOARN) to collect reports of infectious disease outbreaks around the world and mobilize a network of partner-agencies to contain epidemics close to the source. In 2002, in the aftermath of the September 11, 2001, terrorist attacks in the United States and the subsequent anthrax mailings, the World Health Assembly (the annual policymaking forum of WHO) passed Resolution WHA55.16 making "preparedness for deliberate epidemics" a new mission of the organization and offering assistance to member states seeking to improve their capacity for infectious disease surveillance and response.[50] Because WHO must preserve its political neutrality, which is vital to its ability to respond to natural epidemics anywhere in the world, the organization intends to investigate unusual outbreaks strictly from the standpoint of safeguarding international health. In cases where deliberate release is suspected, it would be up to individual UN member states to bring any allegations of covert biological weapons use to the attention of the Security Council.[51]

Two other UN agencies, the World Organization for Animal Health (OIE) and the Food and Agriculture Organization (FAO), have not yet received a mandate from their governing bodies to assist member states in the event of a deliberate biological attack on livestock or crops. Nevertheless, the staffs of both organizations include experts who, upon request, could help investigate an incident of "agroterrorism."[52]

Conclusions and Recommendations

Multilateral investigations of alleged use offer a number of advantages over those conducted by individual countries, including greater international credibility and the reduced risk of compromising sensitive intelligence sources and methods. Given the failure of the BWC Protocol negotiations and the constraints on WHO's field investigation capability, the UN Secretary-General's mechanism is currently the only multilateral vehicle available for investigating allegations of biological weapons use. Nevertheless, the record of UN field investigations conducted between 1980 and 1992 reveals many deficiencies. With the exception of the Iran-Iraq War, the findings were largely inconclusive because of recurrent problems with timeliness, access, cooperation by the host country, and chain of custody. All of these shortcomings must be addressed and corrected if future investigations of alleged use are to be effective.

In particular, the historical record has highlighted the need for the investigation team to arrive as soon as possible after an alleged chemical or biological attack, while the forensic evidence is still fresh; to obtain unrestricted access to the incident site; and to conduct prompt medical examinations of the dead and injured. Another useful source of evidence for chemical or biological weapons use is the physical examination of animals or livestock suffering from characteristic signs and symptoms of exposure or infection.

Prompt sample collection and analysis is essential in the case of biological agents, which tend to degrade rapidly in the environment and may not be detectable after a period of days or weeks. Samples of agent fill from an unexploded bomb or shell, or contaminated munition fragments, offer particularly compelling evidence of use. It is also vital to document a continuous chain of custody for all samples. Finally, past investigations have taught that an allegation of use can be confirmed with high confidence only if environmental and biomedical samples are analyzed by at least two independent reference laboratories. (If the initial analytical results are ambiguous, an extra set of samples should be available for analysis in a third lab.)

Experience with field investigations suggests that in the absence of tangible evidence such as positive environmental or biomedical samples, demonstrable victims, or filled munitions or contaminated fragments, claims of biological or chemical weapons use should be viewed with skepticism. Interviews with purported eyewitnesses are not always reliable and, taken alone, are rarely if ever conclusive. Attributing reported symptoms to a particular chemical or biological agent can be difficult, and accounts of toxic attacks may involve misunderstandings or deliberate distortions. A false allegation may be either an honest mistake or a deliberate attempt by one country to discredit another. Although it is impossible to disprove an allegation of use with 100 percent confidence, one can demonstrate that no plausible evidence exists to support it.

In order to correct the gaps and limitations in the existing Resolution 42/37C, the General Assembly should adopt a new resolution that strengthens the Sec-retary-General's mechanism in a number of ways. First, under the current au-thority, the Secretary-General can initiate an investigation only at the request of a UN member state and not in response to allegations made by a humanitar-ian organization, such as Human Rights Watch or the International Commit-tee of the Red Cross. Giving the Secretary-General greater flexibility to launch investigations based on credible information provided by non-governmental organizations and other unofficial sources would significantly strengthen the mechanism.

Second, it is important to clarify whether or not the Secretary-General's mandate covers the use of a chemical or biological agent by a non-state actor, such as a terrorist group or even an individual terrorist. Ensuring the broadest possible scope is important because in case of a suspicious outbreak of disease, the identity of the perpetrator—state or non-state—would probably not be known at the outset. Since the 1992 Mozambique investigation involved the alleged use of a chemical agent by a subnational organization (RENAMO), it arguably set a precedent for the coverage of non-state actors.[53] To avoid fu-ture ambiguity, however, a new resolution authorizing the Secretary-General's mechanism should explicitly cover the following alleged-use scenarios: (1) by a state against another state (armed conflict); (2) by a rebel army against a state (insurgency warfare); (3) by a state against a rebel army or against civilians who are supporting it (counterinsurgency warfare); (4) by a sub-state group against another sub-state group (civil or ethnic warfare); and (5) by a sub-state group against unarmed civilians (terrorism).

Third, a current weakness of the Secretary-General's mechanism is that the accused party is not required to cooperate with the investigators or to grant them access to the site of the alleged attacks. A strengthened resolution should include a political commitment by all UN member states to cooperate fully with field investigations, thereby establishing an important behavioral norm, albeit one that may be difficult to enforce.

Fourth, the Secretary-General's mechanism lacks a dedicated source of funding, which is needed to maintain the lists of experts and reference labora-tories and to conduct field investigations. The UN Office for Disarmament Af-fairs (UNODA), the sole branch of the UN Secretariat with the relevant exper-tise, has no discretionary funds for this purpose. In the past, all investigations of alleged use were financed on an ad-hoc basis from the Secretary-General's emergency fund and voluntary contributions by member states, but there is no guarantee that sufficient resources will always be available. One solution would be for a group of wealthy states such as the EU to commit to supporting the Secretary-General's investigation mechanism; alternatively, a special line item might be added to the regular UN budget, requiring a modest increase in annual dues.[54]

Fifth, since allegations of biological and toxin warfare are likely to be rare, it would be desirable to hold periodic training and exercises for the experts on the roster so that they are prepared to conduct a field investigation on short notice. Annual or semiannual workshops would cover the safe handling of toxic materials and personal protective equipment, procedures for the collection and chain-of-custody documentation of samples, and the conduct of interviews using standardized survey instruments. This training program should draw on the expertise of former UN biological weapons inspectors in Iraq, encourage the sharing of knowledge and experience, and foster the interpersonal relationships needed for a strong *esprit de corps* and effective intra-team communication. (The OPCW inspectorate might also provide useful assistance in this regard.) In addition to the roster of qualified experts, a list of "interpreter-experts" skilled in the speaking and reading of rare languages should be established and maintained.

Finally, future investigations of alleged use will have to cope with rapid advances in science and technology, such as the development of genetically engineered pathogens and toxins. This challenge will require more specialized training of inspectors and greater flexibility and adaptability in planning for investigations.

Making these improvements to the Secretary-General's mechanism would ensure that this vital investigative tool can be applied effectively the next time it is needed.

Notes

1. Martin Furmanski and Mark Wheelis, "Allegations of Biological Weapons Use," in Mark Wheelis, Lajoz Rózsa, and Malcolm Dando, eds., *Deadly Cultures: Biological Weapons Since 1945* (Cambridge: Harvard University Press, 2006), 252–83.

2. Fourth Review Conference of the Parties to the Convention on the Prohibition of the Development, Production and Stockpiling of Bacteriological (Biological) and Toxin Weapons and on Their Destruction, "Final Declaration," BWC/CONF.IV/9, 6 December 1996, Part II, 15, para 3.

3. Government of Cuba, "Working Paper Submitted by Cuba," Ad Hoc Group of the States Parties to the Convention on the Prohibition of the Development, Production and Stockpiling of Bacteriological (Biological) Weapons and on Their Destruction, Twentieth session, Geneva, July 10–August 4, 2000, BWC/AD HOC GROUP/WP.417, 10.

4. "Report of the Formal Consultative Meeting of States Parties to the Convention on the Prohibition of the Development, Production and Stockpiling of Bacteriological (Biological) and Toxin Weapons and on Their Destruction," Geneva, Switzerland, August 27, 1997.

5. Ambassador S. I. Soutar, Permanent Representative of the United Kingdom to the Conference on Disarmament, Geneva, "Letter Addressed to All States Parties to the Biological and Toxin Weapons Convention," December 15, 1995, paragraph 7.

6. United Nations, General Assembly, Thirty-fifth session, Ninety-fourth Plenary Meeting, Resolutions Adopted on the Reports of the First Committee, Resolution 35/144C, "Chemical and Bacteriological (Biological) Weapons," December 12, 1980.

7. Jonathan B. Tucker, "The 'Yellow Rain' Controversy: Lessons for Arms Control Compliance," *Nonproliferation Review* 8, no. 1 (Spring 2001): 25.

8. United Nations, General Assembly, Thirty-sixth session, "Report of the Group of Experts to Investigate Reports on the Alleged Use of Chemical Weapons," A/36/613, Annex, November 20, 1981, 35.

9. United Nations, General Assembly, Thirty-seventh session, "Report of the Group of Experts to Investigate Reports on the Alleged Use of Chemical Weapons," A/37/259, December 1, 1982, 50.

10. United Nations, General Assembly, Thirty-seventh session, Resolution 37/98D, "Chemical and Bacteriological (Biological) Weapons: Provisional Procedures to Uphold the Authority of the 1925 Geneva Protocol," December 13, 1982.

11. Gerhard von Glahn, *Law Among Nations: An Introduction to Public International Law*, 5th ed. (New York: Macmillan, 1986), 658.

12. United Nations, General Assembly, Thirty-ninth session, "Chemical and Bacteriological (Biological) Weapons: Report of the Secretary-General," A/39/488, October 2, 1984.

13. United Nations, Security Council, "Letter dated 3 November 1983 from the Permanent Representative of the Islamic Republic of Iran to the United Nations Addressed to the Secretary-General," S/16128, November 7, 1983.

14. United Nations, Security Council, "Report of the Specialists Appointed by the Secretary-General to Investigate Allegations by the Islamic Republic of Iran Concern-

ing the Use of Chemical Weapons: Note by the Secretary-General," S/16433, March 26, 1984, 2.

15. Ibid., 11–12.

16. United Nations, Security Council, "Report of the Mission Dispatched by the Secretary-General to Investigate Allegations of the Use of Chemical Weapons in the Conflict Between the Islamic Republic of Iran and Iraq," S/18852, May 5, 1987, 18.

17. James Bruce and Tony Banks, "Growing Concern over Iraqi Use of CW," *Jane's Defence Weekly*, September 24, 1988, 715.

18. United Nations, General Assembly, Forty-second session, Resolution 42/37C, "Chemical and Bacteriological (Biological) Weapons: Measures to Uphold the Authority of the 1925 Geneva Protocol and to Support the Conclusion of a Chemical Weapons Convention," November 30, 1987.

19. United Nations, General Assembly, Forty-fourth session, "Report of the Group of Qualified Experts Established in Pursuance of General Assembly Resolution 42/37C," A/44/561, October 4, 1989, Annex I, 11–43.

20. United Nations, Security Council, Resolution 620, August 26, 1988.

21. United Nations, "Report of the Mission Dispatched by the Secretary General to Investigate an Alleged Use of Chemical Weapons in Mozambique," S/24065, June 12, 1992.

22. John P. Thompson, "An Investigation into the Alleged Use of CW in Mozambique, January 1992," IL 2505/506/92, London, February 17, 1992, 6.

23. Robert E. McCreight and Stephen L. Weigert, "Up in Smoke: Political Realities and Chemical Weapons Use Allegations during Mozambique's Civil War," *International Politics* 38, no. 2 (June 2001): 253–72.

24. United Nations, "Report of the Mission Dispatched by the Secretary General to Investigate an Alleged Use of Chemical Weapons in Mozambique," 1 (para 2).

25. Heiner Staub, e-mail communication to the author, May 11, 2006.

26. United Nations, "Report of the Mission Dispatched by the Secretary General to Investigate an Alleged Use of Chemical Weapons in Mozambique," 1–2.

27. Graham Pearson, University of Bradford (UK), personal communication to author, London, June 13, 2006.

28. Reid Kirby, "Paradise Lost: The Psycho Agents," *CBW Conventions Bulletin* no. 71 (May 2006): 3.

29. Staub, e-mail communication to the author.

30. Ibid.

31. United Nations, "Report of the Mission Dispatched by the Secretary General to Investigate an Alleged Use of Chemical Weapons in Mozambique," 11.

32. McCreight and Weigert, "Up in Smoke."

33. Staub, e-mail communication to the author.

34. United Nations, Security Council, "Letter dated 1 June 1992 from the Permanent Representative of Azerbaijan to the United Nations Addressed to the President of the Security Council," S/24053, June 2, 1992.

35. United Nations, Security Council, "Report of the Mission Dispatched by the Secretary-General to Investigate Reports of the Use of Chemical Weapons in Azerbaijan," S/24344, July 23, 1992.

36. Ibid., 8.

37. Ibid.

38. Human Rights Watch, *Chemical Warfare in Bosnia? The Strange Experiences of the Srebrenica Survivors*, November 1998, online at <http://www.hrw.org/reports98/bosniacw/>; Physicians for Human Rights, "Chloropicrin Use in Tbilisi, Soviet Georgia," online at <http://www.phrusa.org/research/chemical_weapons/index.html#3>; afrol News, "Sudan chemical weapons allegations from Norway, Germany," September 15, 2005, online at <http://www.afrol.com/articles/13956>; James Brooks, "Israel's Chemical Weapons," AfterDawn.com, July 8, 2004, online at <http://my.afterdawn.com/hot_ice/blog_entry.cfm/1007>; Simon Jeffery, "Burma 'using chemical weapons'," *Guardian Unlimited*, April 21, 2005, online at <http://www.guardian.co.uk/burma/story/0,13373,1465052,00.html>.

39. Australia, "Alleged Use Investigation—Authority to Trigger," Ad Hoc Group of the States Parties to the Convention on the Prohibition of the Development, Production and Stockpiling of Bacteriological (Biological) and Toxin Weapons and on Their Destruction, Third session, 27 November–8 December 1995, Geneva, Switzerland, BWC/AD HOC GROUP/WP.13, 29 November 1995.

40. As of July 2006, the updated roster had the names of 92 biological experts, 41 chemical experts, and 35 laboratories, including one field laboratory. Gabriele Kraatz-Wadsack, Chief, WMD Branch, Office for Disarmament Affairs, United Nations, personal communication to author, July 6, 2006.

41. United Kingdom, "Enhancing the International Capabilities for Responding to, Investigating and Mitigating the Effects of Cases of Alleged Use of Biological or Toxin Weapons and Suspicious Outbreaks of Disease," Second BWC Meeting of Experts, Geneva, Switzerland, BWC/MSP/2004/MX/WP.56, July 23, 2004.

42. United States of America, "U.S. Views on Enhancing International Capabilities to Investigate, Respond to, and Mitigate the Effects of Alleged Use of Biological Weapons or Suspicious Outbreaks of Disease," Second BWC Meeting of Experts, Geneva, Switzerland, August 4, 2004, 2.

43. United Nations, General Assembly, Sixtieth session, First Committee, 10th meeting, "Agenda items 85 to 105 (continued): Thematic discussion on item subjects and introduction and consideration of all draft resolutions submitted under all disarmament and international security agenda items," A/C.1/60/PV.10, October 12, 2005, 3.

44. European Union, "General Report 2006: European security strategy and European security and defence policy," online at <http://europa.eu/generalreport/en/2006/rg98.htm>.

45. United Nations, General Assembly, Sixtieth session, Resolution 60/288 ("United Nations Global Counter-Terrorism Strategy"), A/RES/60/288, September 20, 2006, 6.

46. Germany, "Article VI and the UN Secretary-General's Mechanism for Investigating Alleged Use of Chemical and Biological Weapons," Sixth Review Conference of the BWC, Geneva, Switzerland, BWC/CONF.IV./WP.36, December 6, 2006, 2–3.

47. Organization for the Prohibition of Chemical Weapons, "Fact Sheet 5: Three Types of Inspection" (revised July 25, 2000).

48. Organization for the Prohibition of Chemical Weapons, "Fact Sheet 8: OPCW Assistance and Protection Against Attack with Chemical Weapons" (revised July 25, 2000).

49. United Nations, General Assembly, Fifty-fifth session, Resolution 55/283, "Cooperation between the United Nations and the Organization for the Prohibition of Chemical Weapons," September 24, 2001, Article II.2(c), 3.

50. World Health Organization, 55th World Health Assembly, Agenda Item 13.15, "Global Public Health Response to Natural Occurrence, Accidental Release or Deliberate Use of Biological and Chemical Agents or Radionuclear Material That Affect Health," WHA55.16, Geneva, Switzerland, May 18, 2002.

51. World Health Organization, webpage on "Preparedness for Deliberate Epidemics," <http://www.who.int/csr/delibepidemics/en/>.

52. J. Lubroth, "International Cooperation and Preparedness in Responding to Accidental or Deliberate Biological Disasters: Lessons and Future Directions," *Scientific and Technical Review of the OIE* 25, no. 1 (2006): 361–74.

53. There may also be some precedent in the fact that the International Criminal Tribunal (ICT) for the Former Yugoslavia, the ICT for Rwanda, and the International Criminal Court (ICC) have all characterized the use of "poison," "poisoned weapons," or "poisonous gases" as war crimes that apply explicitly to individuals.

54. Jonathan B. Tucker and Raymond A. Zilinskas, "Assessing U.S. Proposals to Strengthen the Biological Weapons Convention," *Arms Control Today* 32, no. 3 (April 2002), online at <http://www.armscontrol.org/act/2002_04/tuczilapril02.asp>.

CHAPTER THIRTEEN

Building Information Networks for Biosecurity

ANNE L. CLUNAN

In the event of the release of harmful biological agents, which could spread across borders before being detected in the country originally affected, the benefits of information sharing are obvious. Governments currently seek to develop organizational and institutional innovations in response to perceptions that nontraditional transnational threats are on the increase and that intelligence failures have been widespread. A pressing threat is that biological weapons may be used against states by other states or by non-state or state-sponsored terrorists.[1]

Accurate and timely information to help manage such threats is therefore of central concern to policymakers. This is illustrated by the November 2002 outbreak of Severe Acute Respiratory Syndrome (SARS). SARS spread within 24 hours from China to six countries, and within five months to 28; it is estimated to have caused global economic losses of $40 billion in 2003.[2] China was widely criticized in the international community for withholding information about the outbreak of the disease; it was blamed for delaying identification and response, and thus facilitating the spread of the disease. The SARS outbreak highlights the problematic nature of biological agents and the vital importance of establishing transnational early warning and information networks before a crisis—intentional or otherwise—occurs.

Sharing information about the possessors and users of biological warfare

(BW) agents is essential for deterrence, because a credible threat of retaliation requires the capacity to attribute a biological attack accurately. The threat of retaliation is only credible if would-be perpetrators and sponsors of biological attacks expect to be caught. Information is also critical to deterrence by denial; for example, identification of the particular biological pathogen used may significantly improve medical management of the consequences of an attack. Correctly characterizing the outbreak as an attack also allows other protective measures to be brought into play in order to hinder or even prevent further attacks, perhaps denying the attackers the impact they seek. The rapidly evolving state of biotechnology places an ever-higher premium on the acquisition of information.

In this chapter, I argue that managing BW attribution and other problems arising from nontraditional threats requires shifts in how governments acquire and use information. The first shift requires changing the understanding of information, from *intelligence,* as something to be kept secret in order to gain relative advantage over an adversary, to *information*, as a resource to improve government management of and response to threats. In other words, governments must move from "need-to-know" limitations on intelligence sharing to a "need-to-share" paradigm of information sharing.[3]

The move beyond hierarchical responses and the traditional intelligence culture toward a "need to share" paradigm involves the second shift: development of networks for information sharing. This shift requires greater understanding of the nature of information networks, and addressing the challenges of establishing trust among members of such networks and between networks and the public.

This chapter draws on the rest of this book and other literature, especially studies of organizations, to suggest ways to develop and strengthen national, subnational, and transnational information networks to build capacity for quickly and accurately establishing whether BW has been used and by whom. It assesses the policy issues involved in moving from a "need-to-know" paradigm to a "need-to-share" information environment. It surveys the perspectives of critical stakeholders in the attribution process: policymakers, the intelligence community, business sectors, non-governmental organizations, and public-health agents, as well as intergovernmental organizations such as the World Health Organization (WHO), the UN Food and Agriculture Organization (FAO), and the World Organization for Animal Health (OIE).

New information-sharing relationships linking the intelligence community, international public-health agencies, and non-state actors could aid the timely sharing of information that meets standards of public and scientific scrutiny to facilitate attribution. Developing a network for BW attribution that would and could be trusted raises a central issue at the heart of attribution: the need to share often sensitive information among a wide range of players across local, regional, and national boundaries raising concerns over privacy, liability, democratic accountability, and reciprocity. The chapter concludes by considering how to address the trust problem: both trust within a network, and the public's trust of that network. I suggest that development of "information brokers" and meta-networks could facilitate BW attribution while lessening concerns over the misuse of information.

Disparate Actors and Their Information

Governments have made recent efforts to improve technical and technological capacity to aid in BW detection, including early detection and warning systems. For example, in 2003 the United States adopted a nationwide system of sensors to detect pathogens in 31 U.S. cities, called the BioWatch program.[4] The U.S. Centers for Disease Control and Prevention (CDC) actively promote the wider adoption of U.S. technical standards to increase international interoperability of information systems that address BW information needs.[5] The CDC's "Epi-X" program was developed to help public-health professionals nationwide share preliminary health surveillance information. Internationally, the WHO has created the Global Outbreak Alert and Response Network (GOARN) to support specialized investigations and to offer direct assistance in the event of a disease outbreak, including investigation and verification teams, transport, and sample testing. Together with Health Canada, the WHO has created an open-source Global Public Intelligence Network, an early-alert system that disseminates unofficial, informal, and open sources.[6] In 2006, the OIE, the FAO, and the WHO jointly created the Global Early Warning and Response System (GLEWS) for diseases transmissible from animals to humans.[7] Should the Verification Protocol to the Biological and Toxin Weapons Conventions (BWC) ever come into effect (see Jonathan Tucker's chapter in this volume), it would also offer a framework for early detection of BW events. Domestic and international alert systems face interoperability problems: they may rely on different types and sources of data and coding, and are often incommensurable and of questionable reliability for accurate identification.[8]

Concerns with biological terrorism have also prompted many countries to adopt "syndromic surveillance" for early detection of both biological terrorism incidents and newly emerging diseases, such as SARS and avian influenza. Syndromic surveillance relies on databases of indicators such as over-the-counter sales of medicines, absenteeism, and calls to medical information hotlines, which can indicate a disease outbreak long before patients turn up at emergency rooms or doctors' offices for diagnosis. BioSense is one such system introduced by the U.S. CDC.[9] The BioSense program is designed to look for early indicators of a biological attack. The U.S. National Biosurveillance Integration System (NBIS) is also designed to improve early detection and characterization of a biological event through the integration of information about a biological event and historical data about the human, plant, and animal disease profiles of the locale. Great Britain has adopted a system similar to BioSense, the NHS Direct Syndromic Surveillance Project.[10] These systems use advanced statistical methods to collect, analyze, and search public-health data for anomalies. These anomalies could then be followed up with an epidemiological investigation, but in practice, such systems are hampered by the need for tradeoffs between sensitivity, specificity, and timeliness. A highly sensitive system will lead to many false alarms, as diseases detected may be endemic to a region rather than an intentional attack, while less sensitive systems may not be able to pick up a specific disease and may not allow for rapid verification of the data needed for public-health response. In 2003, BioWatch sensors detected tularemia on three consecutive days in Houston's air. Lacking confidence in the results of the system and knowledge on whether the disease was endemic to the area, public officials did not issue a public-health response but increased surveillance.[11]

The effectiveness of such surveillance systems varies with the type and nature of pathogen involved. Such systems can only detect non-contagious agents (anthrax, for example) after everyone is already infected. For contagious agents such as smallpox, early detection could prevent the spread of infection. Speed of detection also varies with whether a pathogen spreads quickly or slowly.[12] Questions have been raised about the public-health value of surveillance systems: studies suggest that syndromic surveillance systems cannot detect an attack within hours of symptoms developing unless the number of infected victims is exceptionally large.[13] Such a large number would be recognizable even without a surveillance system; an example was the 1984 salmonella outbreak in Oregon in which 750 people took ill. In the absence of such large numbers, several days must pass before enough cases would mount for a surveillance system to trigger an alarm.[14]

Actors with Crucial Information May Have Competing Values and Interests

At the core of creating a need-to-share information system is the issue of establishing trusted networks among the producers, analyzers, and users of relevant information. The range of actors involved in such networks can be breathtakingly large, and the data to be processed can be massive, collected for a variety of purposes, and difficult to interpret.[15]

To attribute the deliberate use of a biological agent to an international terrorist organization or a state, the actors in the network might include first responders, such as medical and veterinary staff, police officers, emergency teams, and nongovernmental humanitarian assistance organizations; provincial public-health and law-enforcement officials and medical epidemiologists; national law-enforcement, public-health, and intelligence services; military medical and operational personnel; policymakers, and the counterparts in other countries of any or all of these roles. These actors are involved in different parts of the attribution process: identifying what biological agent, if any, was released; characterizing the release as an intentional attack or unintentional; and attributing the release to the perpetrator.

Linking such disparate actors into trusted networks is a challenge. In the United States, for example, the problem of creating trusted networks seized the attention of policymakers when nontraditional security threats were pushed to the fore by the September 11, 2001, terrorist attacks on the United States, and by recognition of the intelligence failures that preceded and followed them.[16] Senior Pentagon officials in the Bush Administration echoed Clinton Administration calls for the "need to share" information and intelligence.[17] Although there was much talk of information sharing and "fighting networks with networks," the dominant U.S. government response to the changing threat environment was to create more large and hierarchical administrative structures, such as the Department of Homeland Security.[18]

However, without information sharing, medical professionals, public-health, and law-enforcement officials cannot adequately respond to the use of biological weapons. Governments that cannot demonstrate their capacity to identify and mitigate a biological outbreak may be unable to persuade would-be terrorists that a BW attack would be ineffective. Law-enforcement and intelligence officials depend on receiving information from actors in the epidemiological and intelligence communities—public and private, domestic and foreign—to gather the evidence necessary to make the case against a perpetrator, whether an individual, organization, or state. Humanitarian aid organizations rely on access to scientists capable of testing samples and to policymakers able to take action to bring to light and end the use of BW agents.

Yet the various actors involved in the problem of BW attribution may have different and even conflicting purposes and constituencies, which significantly complicates sharing information. Political and military decision makers have a need for actionable information in order to plan an appropriate response, and may be reluctant to reveal the sources and methods by which they acquired such information. Law-enforcement officials seek to build a case that can stand up in court, and must comply with relevant laws in collecting, sharing, and using information. They are likely to resist the use or disclosure of methods and sources that would compromise their case. Healthcare professionals and humanitarian organizations are generally interested in protecting individual privacy while promoting transparency in healthcare, and are wary of the competing motives of the policy, military, and intelligence communities. Biotech companies will seek to protect proprietary information. Other businesses and healthcare providers may worry about liability in the event that shared information is misused or leaked. Citizens want assurances that information about them will be kept secure and will not be misused, and that its collection is actually necessary for their protection. They worry about loss of privacy to an "intelligence state" that engages in widespread collection of data, data-mining, and profiling technologies. Such data-mining is often conducted by private contractors, who may not be subject to the same accountability rules as the government itself, and this deepens concern over the potential for misuse.[19]

These problems grow when correct attribution of biological agents requires transnational cooperation. International organizations and international non-governmental organizations have different constituencies and missions that may make them reluctant to work with intelligence, military, or governmental personnel for fear of compromising their neutrality or alienating their constituency. Foreign governments may have differing legal restrictions on the sharing and use of personal and health information. Civil libertarians and citizens in democracies are worried about lack of accountability of such transnational networks.[20] As the outbreaks of SARS and avian influenza demonstrated, states have abundant economic incentives to withhold information about the presence or absence of biological agents that are naturally occurring, let alone covert biological warfare programs. Unilateralism and lack of reciprocity may make other countries unwilling to share information about their own biological technology; of particular concern are the U.S. unwillingness to sign the verification protocol to the Biological Weapons Convention and suspicions regarding U.S. bioweapons programs.[21] Biotech industries have little desire to allow outsiders access to proprietary information. Motivated biases may lead policymakers and others to politically driven misattributions rather than attributions based on credible science.[22]

Information Networks for Biological Warfare Attribution

It is widely recognized that the need for information sharing is the key problem to be solved when dealing with transnational terrorism and the use of unconventional weapons.[23] In this section, first, I offer a brief overview of the nature of networks, which I argue are essential to information sharing.

Recent attention to the need for networks and information sharing highlights core features of world politics that scholars have long studied. Much of the study of international relations is about networks: explaining why and how networks—formal, institutionalized ones, such as international regimes, or informal ones, such as epistemic communities and advocacy networks—are built and maintained, and how they affect world politics.[24] Sociologists and organization theorists, too, study network forms of organization.[25] The issue of information sharing has also occupied social scientists: given that information is an important resource, much scholarship has focused on why actors seek to spread, share, hide, or ignore it.

Beginning in the 1970s, academics described networks as an increasingly prevalent organizational form in both economic and public domains.[26] Although definitions of networks vary widely, Podolny and Page offer a useful one: "a network form of organization [is] any collection of [two or more] actors . . . that pursue repeated, enduring exchange relationships with one another [in the absence of] a legitimate organizational authority to arbitrate and resolve disputes that may arise during the exchange."[27] Some might suggest that network forms of organization cannot be found in government bureaucracies, which are often seen as classic hierarchies. Yet the internal behavior even of military organizations—among the most deliberately hierarchical of organizations—is shaped by formal and informal networks.[28] Students of international politics are familiar with network forms of organization: international politics essentially comprises networks of various sorts, and much literature on global governance is premised on the existence and proliferation of transnational and transgovernmental networks.[29]

One of the great strengths of network forms of organization is their ability to build on the "strength of weak ties," the connections with persons and organizations beyond one's usual cohort of interlocutors.[30] This suggests that successful networks are not necessarily constructed among players at the same levels of their respective organizations or within a set group of organizations. Rather, networks that incorporate actors that only peripherally interact with each other can prove most fruitful in providing timely access to desired resources, especially information. With respect to BW attribution, this is particularly likely to be the case for intelligence and law-enforcement officials, biotechnologists in industry and academia, and epidemiologists, pathologists, or medical staff, such as doctors in local hospitals or humanitarian aid workers in a field camp. For example, decision makers may need to tap into medical professionals' local knowledge of the disease profile of the afflicted community, particularly in cases of conflict, where medical staff in camps may have local knowledge on disease (like the Yellow Rain case). They may look to demographers and migration experts, as in the Indian plague outbreak, in order to verify or disprove a claim of BW use. Despite their competition, rivals in biotechnology frequently share information through both formal and informal networks. They are often aware of what their competitors are working on and of security breaches in their community; such information can be very useful in identifying unknown or novel pathogens.[31] Similarly, intelligence, military, and law-enforcement officials may have information that can help epidemiologists and public-health officials determine whether an event was deliberate or not.

Key benefits of networks are timely and flexible access to information, referrals to new sources or verifiers of information and (most importantly for attribution), accuracy, and credibility, as external verification of information helps keep "groupthink" or motivated biases from dominating the attribution process.[32]

Anne-Marie Slaughter provides a useful way of thinking about networks that can contribute to an information network for BW attribution; she characterizes them as harmonization, enforcement, and information networks.[33] Harmonization networks promote common standards at the domestic and international levels. Helpful for BW attribution would be those promoting adoption of common standards governing public-health infrastructure, syndromic surveillance, systems interoperability, forensic and microbial epidemiology, and criminal legislation and evidentiary standards. The BWC and the Chemical Weapons Convention (CWC), for example, seek to standardize national laws criminalizing the development and possession of such weapons. Key legal, scientific, and policy standards used in identification, characterization, and attribution need to be harmonized. Enforcement networks include national regulations governing compliance with the BWC and CWC, and WHO monitoring of disease outbreaks. Information networks can range from information exchange to more purposive ends such as agreeing "best practices," which can then become the focus of harmonization efforts.

Meta-networks and Information Brokers

When considering what players are essential to building a trusted information meta-network, decision makers must account for a variety of scenarios in which attribution would be necessary, such as a biological event among a domestic civilian population (like the U.S. anthrax and Indian plague cases); a BW incident among a foreign civilian or military population (like most of the historical studies included here); or a BW event among military forces stationed abroad (such as that feared by Iranian military personnel during the Iran-Iraq War, by U.S. service personnel during the first Gulf War, or the Korean War allegations against the United States discussed in Leitenberg's chapter). Each scenario would require different combinations of networks of information;

conditions would also differ depending on whether the environment for investigating the incident is permissive or non-permissive, the target population consisted of non-combatants or combatants, and the perpetrator was a state or a non-state actor.

The network players in the BW attribution process will include health and medical professionals and other first responders, epidemiologists, entomologists, toxicologists, animal and public-health experts, agencies such as the CDC, WHO, and OIE, biotechnologists in industry and academia, law-enforcement officials, military personnel, and policymakers. Network players operate at multiple levels across local, provincial, national, and transnational jurisdictions. All have their own formal or informal networks.

For policymakers concerned with BW attribution, the central challenge is to link up key nodes in those preexisting networks into a meta-network devoted to BW attribution, connecting the separate social worlds of academics, healthcare professionals, biotechnologists, law-enforcement officials, intelligence agencies, and others.[34]

Studies of business networks suggest that "information brokers"—especially venture capitalists and law firms—have played a vital role in the biotechnology industry, connecting academic experts with financial backers.[35] Brokers "bring together different social worlds, bridging networks and making possible new combinations of resources."[36] An agency seeking to develop a meta-network might establish or designate a broker whose explicit role is to create a meta-network among the many groups. Such brokers might take the form of government contractors who are paid to set up linkages among the relevant networks for the purpose of enhancing BW identification, characterization, and attribution.

The creation of two types of information meta-networks might allay concerns regarding information sharing while facilitating the BW attribution process, provided that they take into account the problems associated with trust discussed below. One meta-network would link various actors who can assess the background noise (such as existing or endemic diseases), both domestically and internationally. It would rely on existing networks among actors in public-health, private, nongovernmental, and intergovernmental sectors and academia as well as published or open-source information. The other meta-network would focus on signals, or the presence of anomalies. It would connect law-enforcement, policy, military, and intelligence communities. Brokers would connect together all of the networks within the two meta-networks, and would also link the two meta-networks together.

Addressing Issues of Trust

The essential problem at the root of developing networks is helping disparate actors to trust one another enough to share information. Without trust, networks and indeed cooperation more broadly breaks down. Trust has increasingly interested scholars in a variety of disciplines, but the problem of trust is as old as societal organization: it arises whenever there is uncertainty.[37] Trust implies confidence in the face of risk.[38] There are two aspects to building trusted networks for information sharing: trust among the network members, and public trust in the network.[39] Trust is both a cause and a consequence of cooperation, through the development of norms of competency, fairness, and reciprocity.[40]

Much of the recent work on the need for information networks to counter terrorism has focused on technical aspects such as interoperability; this neglects the harder problem of norms and ideologies.[41] If we are to witness a move to a "need-to-share paradigm," it implies changes in the values that underpin the norms and ideologies affecting networks and the societies that surround them. Network forms of organization are notable for being "cooperative, and to a significant degree self-reinforcing."[42] Networks are not bound together through directives backed by fear of punishment, as in classic hierarchies, nor are they purely based on contracts coordinated by the price mechanism, as in a classic market.[43] Instead, "networks are based on some common informing logic that is persuasive to its members in providing guides that order their relations with each other."[44] These cohering logics are the central influence shaping the network's structure and its rules of engagement. Some of these logics are technical, as in requirements for interoperability of technology, particularly in an information network. Others involve professional norms and ideologies, such as standards of scientific validity or acceptable legal evidence.[45] In others, a common purpose joins a community together; for example, in the biotech industry, competitors have developed information networks concerning research and development that advance the entire industry.[46]

The sociological literature emphasizes that networks are embedded in the social structures and in the norms surrounding and constituting them.[47] These norms are a vital source of trust among network members. Another key feature of networks is that they depend, to a large degree, on interpersonal trust. This trust is in part derived from adherence to network norms, but it is also based on personal ties. Seekers of information will turn to a friend for information, who will then refer the seeker to a third friend, unknown to the seeker, who might have the necessary information. This is the central logic of networks and the "strength of weak ties." Government designers face the difficulty of attempting to create meta-networks for the purpose of BW attribution, an aim that may be at odds with the purpose, norms, and interpersonal trust of existing sub-networks.

The challenge for policymakers who seek to build information networks for BW attribution and other problems is that the trust that is at the heart of networks is difficult to create deliberately. If the aim is to create such a network, designers must take network social structures, norms, and trust into account. The demands of information-sharing networks may be at odds with the purposes, norms, and social structures of the existing public-health, intelligence, and law-enforcement communities, particularly with regard to the compartmentalization of information, sharing only on a "need-to-know" basis, and the legal and societal norms that govern the collection and sharing of information collected domestically and abroad.

Legal-scientific Standards Versus Political Standards

Two sets of standards for information are important to the BW attribution process: legal-scientific standards and political standards. The former turn on different but overlapping sets of objective assessments. Legal evidentiary standards require that procedural rules are followed in terms of search and seizure, wiretapping, and other forms of information collection. Scientific standards require the replication of tests by independent researchers and other means of confirming accuracy. Sharing information among a variety of actors who can verify and confirm its accuracy is a major benefit of networks, and doing so on the basis of accepted standards may facilitate the creation of trust.

There is substantial evidence that norms of scientific validity can create consensual knowledge that eases distrust and facilitates cooperation. Studies of international and interagency cooperation suggest that institutional innovation and collective learning are easiest when science and scientific knowledge are at the core of a set of problems involving substantial interdependence.[48] BW attribution is clearly such a problem set. Standards of scientific validity could provide the basis for consensual knowledge on how to conduct BW attribution. The centrality of scientific norms to the attribution process makes it more likely that trust can be developed within a meta-network and that the meta-network would survive. The development of "information brokers" who can conform to network norms and scientific and legal standards may be an important step in developing information sharing networks for BW attribution.

Political decisions about which standards to apply to information are more problematic for the question of trust than scientific standards; even if the latter are contentious, they are inherently amenable to resolution. However, attribution of a biological weapons attack to a state or non-state actor can be highly political, with significant political and military consequences, as the case studies in this volume highlight. Political and military standards may differ from legal-scientific standards, but the costs, if political/military information standards are set too low, can be significant, as the controversy over the 1998 U.S. bombing of the al-Shifa chemical factory in Sudan and U.S. claims of ongoing Iraqi biological and chemical weapons programs in the run up to its 2003 invasion of Iraq highlighted. Policymakers would therefore be well-advised to rely on the more demanding legal and scientific standards of evidence before making an attribution. As the chapters by Jeanne Guillemin, Elisa Harris, Milton Leitenberg, Graham Pearson, and Ray Zilinskas highlight, where policymakers subordinated accurate attribution of the use of BW agents to other political and strategic goals, such as reputation tarnishing or harassing an adversary, or their own development of BW, the results were to reduce confidence in the veracity of the allegations, decrease willingness to use multilateral organizations for attribution, and prevent the development of international laws banning BW use and legal standards for attribution.

As the most difficult challenge is figuring out how to generate trust, by both domestic and international publics, in a meta-network, policymakers would be well-advised to give network norms and scientific and legal standards priority over immediate political gains. The ability of governments to quickly access a meta-network of sources and verifiers of key information about biological agents and events would substantially enhance BW attribution and mitigation capacity. It would increase the probability of deterring would-be users of biological weapons by credibly threatening punishment and improving public resistance to biological attacks. Such networks would also enhance the ability of multilateral organizations and independent investigators to accurately conduct attribution investigations and strengthen international norms against the manufacture and use of BW. Such benefits outweigh the political gains of shaming or harassing geopolitical adversaries through unverified attributions of BW use.

Notes

The views expressed in this chapter do not represent the official position of the Department of Defense or the U.S. government, but are the sole responsibility of the author.

1. President of the United States, *National Strategy for Combating Terrorism*, September 2006, 14–15, <http://www.whitehouse.gov/nsc/nsct/2006/nsct2006.pdf>, accessed September 7, 2006.

2. Jong Wha-Lee and Warwick J. McKibbin, "Estimating the Global Economic Costs of SARS," in Stacey Knobler, Adel Mahmoud, Stanley Lemon, Alison Mack, Laura Sivitz, and Katherine Oberholtzer, eds., *Learning from SARS: Preparing for the Next Disease Outbreak* (Washington, DC: The National Academies Press, 2004), 103. Available at <http://books.nap.edu/openbook.php?isbn=0309091543>, accessed April 3, 2007.

3. The essential problem for managing twenty-first-century security threats such as biological weapons attribution, according to a former senior U.S. official, requires moving from a "need to know" method of collecting and managing information to one guided by the "need to share." Anne Clunan, interview with James B. Steinberg, deputy national security advisor to the Clinton Administration, Washington, DC, October 14, 2004.

4. Dana A. Shea and Sarah A. Lister, "The BioWatch Program: Detection of Bioterrorism," *CRS Report for Congress* RL32152, November 19, 2003, 2.

5. Claire V. Broome, "Federal Role in Early Detection Preparedness Systems," *Morbidity and Mortality Weekly Report, Syndromic Surveillance: Reports of a National Conference, 2004*, 54, Supplement (August 26, 2005), 7–10; and Alexander Doroshenko, D. Cooper, G. Smith et al., "Evaluation of Syndromic Surveillance Based on National Health Service Direct Derived Data—England and Wales," in *Morbidity and Mortality Weekly Report, Syndromic Surveillance: Reports of a National Conference, 2004*, 54, Supplement (August 26, 2005): 117–22.

6. World Health Organization, "Epidemic Intelligence—Systematic Event Detec-

tion," <http://www.who.int/csr/alertresponse/epidemicintelligence/en>, accessed June 21, 2006; and World Health Organization, "A New Threat . . .Global Alert and Response: Responding to Potential Intentional Use of Biological Agents," <http://www.who.int/csr/outbreaknetwork/newthreat/en>, accessed June 21, 2006.

7. World Organization for Animal Health, "Launch of Global Early Warning System for Animal Diseases Transmissible to Humans," Press Release, July 24, 2006, <http://www.oie.int/eng/press/en_060724.htm>, accessed August 21, 2006.

8. Anne Clunan, personal communication with State Department official responsible for biological weapons verification and attribution, September 6, 2006.

9. Broome, "Federal Role in Early Detection Preparedness Systems," 7–10; and Colleen A. Bradley, H. Rolka, D. Walker, and J. Loonsk, "BioSense: Implementation of a National Early Event Detection and Situational Awareness System," *Morbidity and Mortality Weekly Report, Syndromic Surveillance: Reports of a National Conference, 2004*, 54, Supplement (August 26, 2005): 11–20.

10. Lord Jopling, "Chemical, Biological, Radiological, or Nuclear (CBRN) Detection: A Technological Overview," Special Report to the NATO Parliamentary Assembly, 167 CDS 05 E rev 2, November 2005, <www.nato-pa.int/Default.asp?CAT2=0&CAT1=0&CAT0=576&SHORTCUT=669>, accessed June 21, 2006.

11. Shea and Lister, "The BioWatch Program: Detection of Bioterrorism."

12. Michael A. Stoto, "Syndromic Surveillance," *Issues in Science and Technology*, Spring 2005, <http://www.issues.org/21.3/stoto.html>, accessed June 21, 2006.

13. Stoto, "Syndromic Surveillance."

14. Ibid.

15. Anne Clunan, personal communication with U.S. Department of State official responsible for biological weapons verification and attribution, September 6, 2006; Barry Kellman, "The International Matrix for Biosecurity," paper presented at the Los Angeles Terrorism Early Warning Group Conference on Terrorism, Global Security, and the Law, Santa Monica, CA, June 1–2, 2005.

16. See National Commission on Terrorist Attacks, *The 9/11 Commission Report: Final Report of the National Commission on Terrorist Attacks Upon the United States* (Washington, DC: U.S. Government Printing Office [U.S. GPO], August 2004), for a thorough critique of the bureaucratic obstacles that prevented information sharing between and within the FBI and other agencies prior to 9/11. The WMD Commission found numerous problems within the intelligence community, especially with regard to biological weapons intelligence. *The Commission on the Intelligence Capabilities of the United States Regarding Weapons of Mass Destruction: Report to the President of the United States* (Washington, DC: U.S. GPO, March 31, 2005), 5–6, 28–34, and chs. 9–10 and 13.

17. Senior Pentagon official, speaking on a non-attribution basis at the Naval Postgraduate School, January 31, 2006.

18. Comfort, "Risk," 343.

19. Phillip B. Heymann, *Terrorism, Freedom, and Security: Winning Without War* (Cambridge: MIT Press, 2003), 135–39.

20. Slaughter, *New World Order*, 10–11; Kenneth Anderson, "Squaring the Circle? Reconciling Sovereignty and Global Governance Through Global Governance Networks," *Harvard Law Review* 118, no. 4 (February 2005): 1299–1300.

21. Milton Leitenberg, "Biological Weapons and 'Bioterrorism' in the First Years of the 21st Century," paper prepared for Conference on the Possible Use of Biological Weapons by Terrorist Groups: Scientific, Legal, and International Implications, ICGEB, Landau Network, Ministry of Foreign Affairs, Italy, Rome Italy, April 16, 2002, 2–20.

22. Robert Jervis, *Perception and Misperception in International Politics* (Princeton, NJ: Princeton University Press, 1976).

23. See the 9/11 Commission Report; WMD Commission Report; U.S. Government Accountability Office, "Bioterrorism: Information Technology Strategy Could Strengthen Federal Agencies' Abilities to Respond to Public Health Emergencies," *Report to Congressional Requesters* GAO-03-139, May 2003; Markle Foundation Task Force on National Security in the Information Age, "Creating a Trusted Network for Homeland Security, Second Report of the Markle Foundation Task Force," December 2, 2003; Markle Foundation Task Force on National Security in the Information Age, "Protecting America's Freedom in the Information Age, First Report of the Markle Foundation Task Force," October 7, 2002; Markle Foundation Task Force on National Security in the Information Age, "Mobilizing Information to Prevent Terrorism, Third Report of the Markle Foundation Task Force, July 13, 2006 (all three Markle Foundation Task Force reports are available at <http://www.markletaskforce.org/>; and U.S. Government Accountability Office, "Information Sharing: The Federal Government Needs to Establish Policies for Sharing Terrorism-Related and Sensitive but Unclassified Information," *Report to Congressional Requesters* GAO-06-385.

24. See, for example, Ernst B. Haas, *When Knowledge Is Power* (Berkeley, CA: University of California Press, 1990); Robert O. Keohane and Joseph S. Nye, Jr., eds., *Transnational Relations in World Politics* (Cambridge, MA: Harvard University Press, 1972); Robert O. Keohane and Joseph S. Nye, Jr., *Power and Interdependence in World Politics* (Boston: Little and Brown, 1977); Margaret E. Keck and Kathryn Sikkink, *Activists Beyond Borders: Advocacy Networks in International Politics* (Ithaca, NY: Cornell University Press, 1998); Thomas Risse-Kappen, *Bringing Transnational Relations Back In: Non-State Actors, Domestic Structures and International Institutions* (Cambridge: Cambridge University Press, 1995); and Anne-Marie Slaughter, *A New World Order* (Princeton, NJ: Princeton University Press, 2004).

25. Harrison C. White, Scott A. Boorman, and Robald Briefer, "Social Structures from Multiple Networks, I: Blockmodels of Roles and Positions," *American Journal of Sociology* 81, no. 4 (January 1976): 730–80; Nitin Nohria and Robert G. Eccles, *Networks*

and Organizations (Boston: Harvard Business School Press, 1992); Mark S. Granovetter, "Economic Action, Social Structure, and Embeddedness," *American Journal of Sociology* 91, no. 3 (November 1985): 481–510.

26. Todd R. La Porte, "Shifting Vantage and Conceptual Puzzles in Understanding Public Organization Networks," *Journal of Public Administration Research and Theory: J-PART* 6, no. 1 (1996): 49. Earlier work by industrial sociologists highlighted the role of informal networks in formal organizations; see Donald Roy, "Efficiency and 'the Fix': Informal Intergroup Relations in a Piecework Machine Shop," *American Journal of Sociology* 60: 255–67; and Melville Dalton, *Men Who Manage* (New York: Wiley & Sons, 1959).

27. Joel M. Podolny and Karen L. Page, "Network Forms of Organization," *Annual Review of Sociology* 24 (1998): 57–76.

28. La Porte, "Shifting Vantage," 49–50.

29. For example, see Robert O. Keohane and Joseph S. Nye, Jr., eds., *Transnational Relations*; Slaughter, *New World Order*; Keck and Sikkink, *Activists Beyond Borders*.

30. Mark S. Granovetter, "The Strength of Weak Ties," *American Journal of Sociology* 78, no. 6 (May 1973): 1360–80; and Mark S. Granovetter, *Getting a Job: A Study of Contacts and Careers* (Cambridge, MA: Harvard University Press, 1974).

31. Walter W. Powell and Laurel Smith-Doerr, "Networks and Economic Life," in N. L. Smelser and R. Swedberg, eds., *The Handbook of Economic Sociology* (Princeton, NJ: Russell Sage Foundation and Princeton University Press, 1994), 373–75; Walter W. Powell, Kenneth W. Koput, and Laurel Smith-Doerr, "Interorganizational Collaboration and the Locus of Innovation: Networks of Learning in Biotechnology," *Administrative Science Quarterly* 41, no. 1 (March 1996): 116–45.

32. Powell and Smith-Doerr, "Networks and Economic Life," 371.

33. Slaughter, *New World Order*, 52–61.

34. Jeremy Boissevan, *Friends of Friends* (New York: St. Martin's Press, 1974).

35. Everett M. Rogers and Katherine Larsen, *Silicon Valley Fever* (New York: Basic, 1984); and AnnaLee Saxenian, *Regional Networks: Industrial Adaptation in Silicon Valley and Route 128* (Cambridge, MA: Harvard University Press, 1994).

36. Powell and Smith-Doerr, "Networks and Economic Life," 375.

37. Guido Möllering, Reinhard Bachmann, and Soo Hee Lee, "Understanding Organizational Trust—Foundations, Constellations, and Issues of Operationalization," *Journal of Managerial Psychology* 19, no. 6 (2004): 557.

38. J. David Lewis and Andrew Weigert, "Trust as Social Reality," *Social Forces* 63, no. 4 (June 1985): 967–85.

39. La Porte, "Shifting Vantage," 67–69; Todd R. La Porte and Daniel S. Metlay, "Facing a Deficit of Trust: Hazards and Institutional Trustworthiness," *Public Administration Review* 56, no. 4 (July 1996): 341–47; Comfort, "Risk," 352.

40. Möllering, Bachmann, and Lee, "Understanding Organizational Trust," 556–70.

41. This is true of the CDC's BioSense project, which is designed for interoperability across all jurisdictional and professional levels. It is also reflected in the advocacy of interoperability in the reports on information sharing issued by the Markle Foundation Task Force on National Security.

42. La Porte, "Shifting Vantage," 58.

43. Oliver Williamson, *Markets and Hierarchies: Analysis and Antitrust Implications* (New York: Free Press, 1975).

44. LaPorte, "Shifting Vantage," 58.

45. Ibid.

46. Powell and Smith-Doerr, "Networks and Economic Life," 373–75.

47. Granovetter, "Economic Action and Social Structure," 481–510.

48. Peter M. Haas, "Introduction: Epistemic Communities and International Policy Coordination," *International Organization* 46, 1 (Special Issue: Knowledge, Power, and International Policy Coordination) (Winter 1992): 225–64; Haas, *When Knowledge Is Power*; and Craig W. Thomas, "Public Management as Interagency Cooperation: Testing Epistemic Community Theory at the Domestic Level," *Journal of Public Administration Research and Theory: J-PART* 7, no. 2 (April 1997): 221–46.

CHAPTER FOURTEEN

Conclusion

The Role of Attribution in Biosecurity Policy

SUSAN B. MARTIN AND ANNE L. CLUNAN

How can governments improve their ability to determine whether an unusual biological event is an act of terrorism or of war, or is instead merely a disease outbreak? In this chapter, we draw conclusions based on the previous chapters in an effort to better the investigation of such events. We find that politically credible attributions of BW use must be based on investigations that are procedurally sound and that rely on a high degree of confidence—based on accepted scientific standards—that a particular culprit perpetrated a biological weapons attack. The development of scientific capabilities for identification, characterization, and attribution of BW use enhance both a state's ability to deter such use by the threat of punishment (by increasing the likelihood that a perpetrator will be identified), and to deter by denial (by reducing the consequences of a BW attack, through the strengthening of the public-health system).

The chapter begins with a summary of the requirements for successful identification, characterization, and attribution, and briefly analyzes some of the issues that arise with each of these tasks. It then discusses the policy issues raised by the case studies, including the issues surrounding political decisions about how to use the results of investigations into unusual biological events. It concludes with a brief examination of the role of attribution in overall policy to counter the threat from biological weapons.

Investigating Unusual Biological Events

When considering the problem of BW attribution, the starting point is understanding what first prompted questions about whether a specific biological event might have been intentional. The perception of an event as unusual may be based simply on an event's comparative characteristics, for example, the number of people reporting similar symptoms, the rarity of those symptoms, or the presence of armed conflict in the region. Here three points are key: the importance of knowledge about the background of disease and toxins against which unusual events stand out; the importance of first responders and diagnosticians, since in most cases it is symptoms of illness that first prompt concern about an unusual event; and finally, the importance of a willingness to entertain alternative and even seemingly far-fetched hypotheses about the cause of the disease.

The case studies also demonstrate that the perception of an event as unusual can be influenced by the presence of political and ideological conflict and instability. Such conflict and instability can generate fear and suspicion of the use of biological weapons, which may predispose actors to interpret biological events as unusual. Conflict and instability can also provide the opportunity to make, for political ends, false accusations that biological weapons have been used.

Clunan's analysis in Chapter 13 suggests that information networks may have a particularly important role to play in the recognition of unusual events. The information required to spot unusual events is both diverse (including, for example, knowledge of the normal disease and toxin profiles of an area as well as of its human, plant, animal, and insect populations) and large (the concern is with biological events around the globe, not just in particular areas). Networks may be the only way to efficiently exchange and process so much information. Such networks can also serve to double-check interpretations of events, helping to insure both that anomalies are recognized as such and that background conditions are not mistaken for anomalies.

Once questions have been raised about a biological event, the process of identification, characterization, and attribution goes forward. Table 14.1 on pages 314–15 compiles the requirements for identification, characterization and attribution, categorizing the requirements into four types: background information, scientific procedures and capabilities, data on the event under investigation, and political. This list represents the ideal—what we would like to have in any investigation of an unusual biological event. In the case of identification, fulfilling the checklist should give a correct identification of the biological agent. However, even a complete fulfillment of the list may not be enough to provide characterization and attribution; the list accounts for this by including the establishment of a "standard of proof" as a political requirement for each of the tasks.[1]

Although we separate identification, characterization, and attribution here for the sake of analytic clarity, in practice the relationship among the three tasks is complex. While the successful completion of each step in the process requires the success of the one before, the relation among the tasks is not linear and it is possible to engage in all three tasks simultaneously.

Identification

Once a suspicion is raised that an unusual biological event has occurred, the first task is to identify the agent or agents involved. Usually identification begins with diagnosis by medical personnel, veterinarians, or plant pathologists, often aided by public-health officials.

Correct identification requires background knowledge of endemic diseases, local toxin profiles, and biological warfare agent profiles. Knowledge of local human, plant, and animal ecology will also aid the correct identification of the source of symptoms. As Chapter 13 notes, states have taken steps to improve their technical capacity by setting up syndromic surveillance systems to collect relevant data on human disease events; although these systems are primarily intended for other purposes, they can form the basis for background data on local disease profiles going forward. However, such surveillance systems today would be insufficient to provide the necessary baseline data for detecting an intentional attack without additional information. Also helpful would be massive data-mining programs that could gather global public-health data, data on ongoing research and development in the biotech industry and academia, and data on biodiversity changes. Developing such a system would require use of existing international organizations and databases in the area of public health, the environment, and microorganisms and bio-science to create a complete

TABLE 14.1

Requisites for Identification, Characterization, and Attribution

	Identification	Characterization	Attribution
Background knowledge	Knowledge of disease and toxin profiles Knowledge of human ecology	Knowledge of endemic diseases and toxin profiles Socioeconomic histories of human communities as part of larger system of species interaction (including behavioral and environmental factors) Information on prevalence and susceptibility to disease and toxins in area Catalogue of known strains of pathogens and toxins Knowledge of general political conditions	Catalogue of known strains of pathogens and toxins and their locations Information on terrorist groups and other actors with capabilities and/or motives for such an attack
Scientific capabilities and procedures	Strict procedures for sampling and lab analysis Suitable laboratory capability Procedures and equipment for proper storage of samples Labs in local area Proper procedures for interviews Proper training of first responders and investigators Consideration of alternative hypotheses Pre-existing public health infrastructures	Consideration of alternative hypotheses Pre-existing public health infrastructures	Pre-existing public health infrastructures
Data on event under investigation	Biomedical samples and controls Environmental samples and controls Medical records Interviews with and medical records of victims	Pattern and timing of disease outbreak(s) and/or intoxication Pattern and timing of any military or terrorist activity in area Weapons or weapons fragments	Method of attack Motives of attack Contact histories of known cases Access to/ability to produce and weaponize agent used in attack Connection between attacker and victim Confessions

	Identification	Characterization	Attribution
Political	Timely access to purported attack site(s) and victims	Timely access to purported attack site(s), victims	Multilateral and/or independent investigations
	Multilateral and/or independent investigations	Multilateral and/or independent investigations	Need for cooperation among governments, academia, NGOs
	Need for cooperation among governments, academia, NGOs	Need for cooperation among governments, academia, NGOs	Standard of proof
	Standard of proof	Standard of proof	Knowledge of politics surrounding allegation
		Access to event data	

picture of the background data of biological agents in order to pick out anomalous events.[2] Yet, as Clunan highlights in Chapter 13, many of the organizations collecting such information may be reluctant to share data with law-enforcement, military, intelligence, or other government agencies.

Data on the particular event is also critical. Obtaining biomedical samples and controls, environmental samples, medical records of those affected and unaffected, and interviews with victims and others present at the outbreak sites are essential for understanding the source of symptoms.

Background information and event data could allow diagnosticians and public-health officials to develop and consider alternate hypotheses regarding the cause of the outbreak, potentially averting misidentification and misdiagnosis. Information networks may be the only means of bringing such a wide array of background information and diagnostic expertise to bear quickly in the identification of the cause of a biological event. Such knowledge might, for example, have improved the chances of the American media and postal workers infected with anthrax in 2001 being more speedily and accurately diagnosed, and might thus have prevented deaths.

Two additional factors are key at the identification stage: appropriate scientific procedures and capabilities, and political cooperation to facilitate timely access to the victims and sites in question. The case studies show that, under ideal circumstances, laboratories would be available near the outbreak site and scientifically valid procedures would be used for sampling and lab analysis. These entail the development and strict adherence to sample and control collection protocols and interviewing procedures; training of first responders, public-health officials, and lab technicians in these procedures; uncontaminat-ed lab facilities and equipment; repeat testing of the same samples by two or more independent labs and procedures; and equipment for proper storage of samples.

The ideal political requirements for successful identification include politi-cal willingness to grant access to the affected populations and sites; to develop the requisite capacity for the collection and dissemination of background in-formation and data to first responders, diagnosticians, and public-health au-thorities; and to mandate the establishment and use of appropriate scientific standards and procedures.

Given the difficulties in meeting these requirements, it is not surprising that the average length of time between the biological event and its identification is almost two and a half years (see Chapter 9). In the above case studies, none of the unusual events appears to have involved multiple biological agents. The use of multiple agents in an attack would significantly complicate the process of identification, although it might simplify the process of characterization.

Characterization

With characterization, the central task is to generate and evaluate hypothe-ses to account for presence of the disease or toxic agent that has been identified, and to determine whether the identified agent is a result of intentional attack or rather an unintended disease outbreak. Background information and data on the event occurrence are again of central importance. The case studies empha-size the wide range of background knowledge that may be required, including knowledge of disease and toxins, the prevalence of and susceptibility to disease in the area, catalogues of known strains of the pathogens, socioeconomic his-tories of the human communities suffering the unusual symptoms, and the habits of honeybees and other insects. This raises the importance of communi-cation across disciplines, and among governments, academia, NGOs, medical professionals, and the general public. Collection of data on the pattern and timing of the suspect disease outbreaks and of any military or terrorist activity in the affected area may also be necessary to evaluate hypotheses regarding un-intentional causes of the outbreak. As Chapter 13 notes, states have established syndromic surveillance systems to detect unusual disease outbreaks quickly, but there are questions about their usefulness to detect an attack very quickly unless the number of infected victims is exceptionally large.[3] Here, again, information networks could play a useful role in bringing together the required knowledge, generating alternative hypotheses, and validating analyses.

Cole's chapter suggests that finding a BW agent in improbable locations may be indicative of intentional attack. Meselson and Robinson caution, however, that the simple presence of such an agent is not enough to sustain such a characterization. What is needed in addition is an analysis of alternative hypotheses that might also account for the presence of the agent. For example, what if the anthrax letters had never been found, but anthrax spores were found in post office facilities? While that would be suggestive of intent, since anthrax is not normally found in post offices, it would still be necessary to investigate how legitimate samples of anthrax are shipped and whether such shipments could have been responsible for the contamination, or whether a shipment of anthrax-contaminated wool could somehow have polluted the facilities. If these and other possible explanations of how the post office facilities could have been contaminated unintentionally are found to be unlikely, then the hypothesis that the contamination was intentional would be strengthened. Evaluating alternative hypotheses may require the development of new scientific and investigate capabilities. As Harris notes, the FBI created new microbial forensic capabilities and procedures for the anthrax case, which substantially aided in characterization of the anthrax strain.

The recovery of munitions or weapons fragments containing the disease agent or toxin would strengthen a characterization as intentional; however, it is unclear whether this would be either necessary or sufficient for such a characterization. In the Yellow Rain case, the lack of discovered weapons lent support to the characterization as unintentional. The case of the anthrax letters suggests that recovery of weapons or weapons fragments containing the disease agent or toxin may sometimes be sufficient for a characterization as intentional. However, there could also be alternative explanations for the presence of such weapons; for example, they might have been left over from previous conflicts.[4]

A characterization of a biological event as intentional will also be strengthened by a correlation between the suspected attack and the known motives, capabilities, and activities of a suspect group, but this is unlikely to suffice on its own as evidence of intentionality.

Mark Wheelis has suggested in his book on biological warfare that the likelihood of mischaracterization depends on the type of attack in question. Military and terrorist attacks, in his view, are unlikely to be mischaracterized as a natural event. He argues that military attacks that involve large quantities of an aerosolized, non-communicable disease agent are unlikely to be misinterpreted as a natural disease outbreak, while terrorists, who seek to generate fear, are likely to advertise their attack.[5]

Wheelis also argues that only attacks designed to imitate naturally occurring epidemics are likely to be mischaracterized. In his view, there are two primary ways of distinguishing a deliberate epidemic from an unintentional one: "The outbreak might have unusual epidemiological characteristics at its very beginning as a result of unnatural means of introduction. Or, it might be caused by an agent that is genetically distinct from its contemporaries, showing closer relationship to agents identified as having caused past outbreaks than to its contemporary cousins."[6] Like the case studies in this book, his argument emphasizes the importance of having catalogues of all known strains of pathogens, epidemiological knowledge, and good data on the event under investigation.

Our case studies indicate, however, that characterization is more complicated, more important, and more difficult than Wheelis suggests. Wheelis has not addressed an important set of cases where mischaracterization can occur: those where unintentional outbreaks of disease or exposure to toxins could be mischaracterized as intentional, as suggested by the controversy over the Yellow Rain case as well as by the Korean War and by the Cuban allegations and the Indian plague case. Moreover, terrorists may not, in fact, always announce their attacks. The anthrax letter attacks did conform to the expectation that terrorists will announce their attacks to gain publicity or to generate fear, but in contrast, the contamination of the salad bars by the Rajneeshees, as well as the attacks launched by Aum Shinrikyo, suggest that terrorists may sometimes seek to employ biological or chemical agents in pursuit of ends that would be undermined by announcing the attacks.[7] This emphasizes the importance of a knowledge of political conditions and the consideration of alternative hypotheses in the process of characterization.

Attribution

Ideally, background information for attribution would include an up-to-date catalogue of pathogens, toxins, and their locations, and information on terrorist groups and other actors with capabilities or motives for such an attack.

Desirable data on the event itself would include the method of attack, the motives for attack, and information on who has access to or the ability to produce and deliver the agent used in the attack. Among the scientific procedures and capabilities required for attribution are well-developed public-health infrastructures, trained first responders, and microbial forensics capacity. Politically, the most important requirement is a determination of what standard of proof will be used in the investigation.

In some sense, the investigation of an unusual biological event parallels that of a standard criminal investigation. The process of characterization determines whether or not a crime has taken place; the process of identification points to the weapon (the agent involved), and the aim of attribution is to find out who is responsible for the crime. In the latter, as suggested clearly by the discussion of the anthrax letters case by Harris and Cole, there are three primary lines of investigation: motive, means—that is, connections with the BW agent used and with the delivery system, and opportunity—that is, access to the target.

There are difficulties, however, in each of these lines of investigation into attribution. Because biological agents were not strictly controlled in the past and because many are available in nature, identification of the means does not necessarily narrow the range of suspects significantly. In the case of the anthrax letter attacks, some distinguishing characteristics of the agent were evidently identified, but it has not been made public what these are or how helpful they have been in determining who had access to this material.[8] In the Yellow Rain case, the finding of trichothecene mycotoxins was at first thought to be anomalous. Even when it was found that these can occur naturally in Southeast Asia, the presence of PEG, a chemical stabilizer, and "strong intelligence linking a mycotoxin research lab in the Soviet Union with the application of yellow mist from helicopters in Afghanistan, a laboratory in Cambodia, and a yellow substance loaded into Pathet Lao planes in Laos" was thought by some to indicate the use of toxin weapons and Soviet involvement.[9] However, as Meselson and Robinson, Harris, and Pearson make clear, this has not been enough to sustain the attribution. Opportunity is also very difficult to investigate, since biological agents can be dispersed in indirect ways, even without direct contact with the target. In the anthrax letters case, all that was needed was access to a mailbox, which obviously does not limit the suspect pool greatly, even if the mailbox or zip code is identified.[10]

In addition, attribution of a biological attack generally involves politics to a much greater degree than most standard criminal investigations. First, the motives for an attack with biological weapons are not generally money or passion, but rather military advantage, political protest, or the desire for political change.[11] Second, an allegation of BW use can have political consequences, some of which stem from the general disapprobation of BW use and the opportunities it creates for politicization. The chapters by Guillemin, Meselson and Robinson, Leitenberg, Zilinskas, and Harris all make clear that the political context in which BW attribution takes place may determine whether political considerations will predominate over scientific standards. Harris finds that in the Yellow Rain case the political pressure to attribute use to the Soviet Union outweighed concerns within the U.S. intelligence community about the validity of the evidence. Leitenberg and Zilinskas both show how politics drove the fabrication of allegations against the United States. Political consequences can also stem from possible public reactions to allegations of BW use. For example, public officials may be reluctant to publicly attribute or acknowledge BW use, fearing that violence might be sparked by rumors of BW attacks by one ethnic community against another, as might have happened in the Indian plague outbreak, or if the U.S. public had suspected Arab-Americans of causing the anthrax attack. All of this emphasizes that attribution is inherently a political process.

Adherence to scientific standards can lessen the negative impact of politics on the process of attribution, but it cannot guarantee a high rate of definitive BW attribution. The difficulties in attribution are reflected in the relatively low rate of successful attributions to a specific perpetrator in past cases. Out of 31 alleged biological weapons episodes, Ackerman and Asal find only 6 (just over 20 percent) in which attribution was confirmed to any extent. What is striking in successful attributions is the role played by confession and captured or found primary documents. This suggests that, without confession by the perpetrators or actual documents that create a record of BW use, it may be very difficult to make a definitive attribution.

Policy Implications

These findings raise some key questions for policymakers: what must and can be done to improve our ability to investigate unusual biological events, and what considerations should guide decisions about how to use the results of those investigations?

Political, technical, and fiscal realities will constrain improvements in policies that have to do with investigation capabilities. While the prior chapters all stress the importance of political cooperation in investigations of unusual biological events, the cases, along with the recent failure of the proposed BWC protocol, also make it clear that such cooperation is difficult. Reasons for this include state actors' reluctance to be found culpable either of using BW agents or of making deliberately false allegations, and their fear that investigations might be unable to establish innocence and could, even if inadvertently, lend credibility to malicious BW allegations. Additionally, they may fear that such investigations could cause domestic problems by revealing that a country's public-health infrastructure and disease control capabilities are in poor condition.

Leitenberg suggests that a refusal to cooperate with such investigations may, in and of itself, be suggestive of deliberate falsification of alleged use or culpability: an accuser may refuse to cooperate with an investigation of the charges it has brought, or an accused may refuse to cooperate with an investigation.

But refusal to cooperate with an outside investigation may not be enough to disprove the allegations, in the former case, or to confirm the allegation, in the latter. Reasons other than guilt or innocence, including a lack of faith in the integrity and efficacy of the proposed investigation, may influence a state's decision not to cooperate with an investigation. While the United States pushed for an investigation into the Korean War allegations, Harris suggests that this may have been a dangerous strategy because, given that evidence was fabricated, an investigation might not have detected the false nature of the allegations against the United States.

Recognizing these limitations and the lack of a perfect solution to the problem of politics, Harris, Pearson, Tucker, and Zilinskas all recommend multinational and independent investigations as the best way to establish the veracity and political credibility of BW allegations. Pearson and Zilinskas suggest that only investigations carried out by a standing team of trained experts and operating under the authority of the UN Secretary-General are likely to be an effective instrument for attribution and for deterring politically motivated allegations. Tucker suggests that a UN General Assembly resolution could mandate compliance with the Secretary-General's investigatory team and its timely and free access to alleged attack sites. Other mechanisms for carrying out multinational investigations are not subject to enough scientific rigor and they leave too much room for politically motivated accusations; for these reasons they are unlikely to engender state confidence in their findings. Investigations under the UN Secretary-General's authority have succeeded in negating claims of BW use in the case of Azerbaijan and Armenia, and confirming chemical weapons use in the Iran-Iraq war, although in the latter, the investigation was unable definitively to attribute use to one party or the other.

Independent investigations that adhere to internationally recognized scientific standards could also limit the success of politically motivated false accusations of BW use. As Harris and Leitenberg emphasize, independent investigations may be the only way to assess claims of BW use in cases where politics prevent the deployment of a UN investigation. In the Korean War, for example, the willingness of the United States to submit its claims to independent verification by the International Committee of the Red Cross bolstered the credibility of its claim that it had not used BW. In the Yellow Rain case, the investigations conducted by independent scientists, including Matthew Meselson and British government scientists, undermined the credibility of U.S. allegations of Soviet trichothecene mycotoxin use. In the case of Cuban allegations of BW use by the United States, independent investigations might have been able to determine whether the disease outbreaks were indeed anomalous, or were instead the result of natural causes. Independent scholarly investigation of a biological event may be necessary in order to attribute blame accurately to unintentional sources such as, in the Indian plague case recounted by Barrett, labor migration patterns, earthquakes and unsanitary urban conditions, rather than to intentional causes, such as interethnic terrorism.

Adherence to strict scientific standards could also help minimize politicization, foster states' willingness to participate in investigations, and increase the credibility of the findings. There are two elements here: one is the scientific method and process by which an investigation proceeds. The other is the scientific consensus on what degree of uncertainty is acceptable before a disease can be definitively identified, an event can be declared deliberate, or an actor can be declared the perpetrator. A scientific attribution process does not guarantee that a perpetrator will be definitively blamed or exonerated, but, it would reduce uncertainty about the identification and characterization of the agent. This prospect could dissuade claims that might be revealed as incorrect because their procedures were biased or because scientific assessments were not met. Together, a scientific process and a scientific consensus on the required degree of certainty can help reduce political uncertainty about the nature of a biological event.

If sound scientific procedures are followed but the results are still unclear, policymakers should focus on efforts to continue multiple investigations and to consider alternative hypotheses and new information to ensure an accurate characterization and attribution. To facilitate this, policymakers should develop information-sharing networks among government agencies, academics, and first responders, and should also encourage development of such networks involving health agencies and intelligence agencies of other countries. The sharing of information may prove the most robust means of eliminating inaccurate hypotheses and analyzing information. Given the long delay in identifying biological agents, let alone attributing their use, information sharing may be the only realistic means to improve speed without sacrificing the accuracy of scientific standards of proof.

Fiscal realities mean that policymakers must weigh resources to be devoted to identification, characterization, and attribution of unusual biological events against other priorities, including public health, other security threats, and other BW policies. This suggests that priority should be given to increasing funding and improving resources that serve dual purposes: both identifying and characterizing an outbreak, and mitigating the harm an outbreak could cause. For example, public-health capabilities and training should be funded before air sensors that could detect deliberate biological attacks, but would not aid in managing their consequences.

Despite the political, technical, and fiscal realities, there is a great deal that can be done to improve our ability to identify, characterize, and attribute unusual biological events, ranging from the collection and sharing of the necessary background data as laid out in Table 14.1 and Chapter 13, to the establishment of the scientific capabilities needed to investigate unusual events when they occur, as highlighted in Chapters 7 and in Chapters 10, 11, and 12. The Yellow Rain and anthrax investigations emphasize the importance of improvements. As Tucker outlines in Chapter 12, this need has been addressed, at least in part, by the UN Secretary-General's handbook on protocols for investigations, the Secretary-General's roster of acceptable experts and laboratories, and also in the arrangements for inspections under the Chemical Weapons Convention. It has also been reflected in the anthrax letter investigation, for example in the care devoted to the samples and the development of new methods of microbial forensics, as explained by Harris in Chapter 10.

Conclusion: Attribution and Deterrence

The discussions throughout this volume suggest many steps that could improve our ability to attribute unusual biological events. However, our ability to do so will always be imperfect. Attribution is difficult, successful attribution is rare, and even when the evidence for accurate attribution of a BW event exists, states may choose not to act on it. However, even though attribution is difficult, biological attacks can still be deterred through both denial and punishment.

Deterrence by punishment depends to a large extent on attribution, especially if the victim of a BW attack wants its retaliatory strike to be seen as legitimate. Retaliation will have widespread legitimacy only if the victim can persuade the international community that the target of the retaliatory strike is really the party responsible for the biological attack. The political risks of an uncertain attribution can be quite high. If the policymaker acts on a preliminary suspicion that another state has attacked it with biological weapons, and decides to retaliate, the results could range from political embarrassment to unnecessary war. To avoid this, states should rely on rigorous scientific standards of proof that are capable of withstanding legal scrutiny. If every good faith effort is made to attain that standard, policymakers can act with much greater certainty that they have the best possible information and that international or domestic legal scrutiny of their case will validate their claims. A sound basis of scientific evidence thus increases the credibility of threats to punish users of biological weapons, and thus enhances deterrence.

In evaluating the possibility of deterrence, it is important not to over-state the requirements for success. Successful deterrence does not require convincing the would-be attacker that he will be caught and punished. All that deterrence requires is a negative expected utility: a BW attacker may be deterred if the expected cost of using biological weapons is greater than the expected gain. Thus deterrence may depend not just on considerations of attribution, but also on other factors that affect the likelihood that punishment will be carried out, the scale of the punishment that could be imposed, and the expected benefits of using biological weapons. Indeed, even this might overstate the requirements for deterrence, because would-be attackers do not have to choose between using biological weapons and not attacking at all; they can use other weapons. So deterrence of biological attack may require only that the expected utility of using biological weapons is less than that of using other kinds of weapons.

Here it is important not to exaggerate the benefits to attackers of using biological weapons. It is often hypothesized that biological weapons are an attractive weapon, capable of carrying out anonymous and deadly attacks that can impose great economic costs and create fear and instability. But the relative scarcity of known attacks using biological weapons suggests that the actual benefits of using such weapons may be less. It may not be very hard to deter the use of biological weapons by an attacker who seeks mass casualties, because there is not actually much incentive to use them: relatively few deaths have been caused by known attacks. This does not mean that biological weapons will not be used; biological weapons may appear attractive to an attacker who seeks to terrorize a population or cause economic disruption. But there are other factors that could discourage the use of BW for these purposes, including the scarcity of the specialized skills, materials, and training required for their use.[12]

Nonproliferation policies and consequence mitigation can also increase the disincentives to use BW. Pearson notes that the United Kingdom has chosen to emphasize the prevention of BW capability over an ability to investigate and retaliate against biological attacks when they occur. Such prevention helps to deter BW use by increasing the costs and difficulties of acquiring biological over other types of weapons. In and of themselves, biological weapons place new demands on their users: as compared to conventional weapons, new technologies and materials are needed to produce them, and new knowledge and strategies are needed to use them. These demands are themselves a disincentive. States and international organizations can also take steps to make it more difficult to acquire these weapons, such as establishing export controls, creating a standing UN team of trained specialists to investigate allegations, bolstering international norms against their development and use, and reducing the effectiveness of potential attacks through improved public-health defenses.

The general moral disapprobation of biological warfare is also important.

As Guillemin notes, the United States missed an early and critical opportunity to establish the norm that individuals who use BW will be held accountable for war crimes and crimes against humanity. As Pearson highlights, the creation and sustainment of a moral taboo against BW use is a central part of a strategy of deterring BW use. There are suggestions that at least some terrorists worry that using such abhorrent methods would alienate their supporters.[13]

Deterrence by denial is an essential means of decreasing the incentives to use BW; efforts to address the effects of biological weapons (and other kinds of disease outbreaks) help to deter the use of biological weapons, by undercutting the effectiveness of such use. As suggested by the plague outbreak in India, biodefense can benefit greatly from improvements to sanitation, drainage, and public-health infrastructure, with the added benefit of increasing capacity to manage unintentional disease outbreaks as well. The Korean case highlights the benefits of widespread vaccination programs in reducing public susceptibility to biological agents. Drug stockpiles, epidemiological surveillance programs, and training for first responders in BW agent recognition and treatment all reduce the risk that a biological agent—whether avian influenza or weaponized anthrax—could cause mass death or disruption.

Given that the burden involved in acquiring and using biological weapons is greater than for other weapons, attackers are only likely to seek BW capabilities if they see a potential gain from using them. Measures that limit the risks that biological attack can cause disease and death undermine incentives to acquire these weapons. The fear and terror associated with biological attack may also be decreased if the public has confidence in a government's ability to limit the damage caused by such attacks. Information sharing among government agencies, public-health authorities, and first responders is essential for the development of robust public biodefenses.

The ability to attribute unusual biological events is an important component in a state's security policy. Even a possibility of attribution can help to deter biological attacks through the threat of punishment. A robust attribution process also complements efforts to defend against such attacks and thus to contribute to deterrence by denial, because more efficient and successful identification and characterization allows for better treatment of the victims of a biological attack and may allow for measures to stop the spread of disease or intoxination. In addition, many of the capabilities and resources needed for identification and characterization can also contribute to general disease control. Efforts to prevent biological weapons attacks are most likely to succeed when they seek to deter use through reducing the incentives to use biological weapons, as well as increasing the probability that the terrorist or state that uses biological weapons will be identified and punished.

Notes

1. Standards of classification are also important in identification, particularly in the definition of what counts as a case of a disease, as discussed by both Cole and Barrett.

2. Barry Kellman, "The International Matrix for Biosecurity," paper presented at the Los Angeles Terrorism Early Warning Group Conference on Terrorism, Global Security, and the Law, Santa Monica, CA, June 1–2, 2005.

3. Michael A. Stoto, "Syndromic Surveillance," *Issues in Science and Technology* Spring 2005, <http://www.issues.org/21.3/stoto.html>, accessed June 21, 2006.

4. While the finding of a weapon or records of use may suffice as evidence that an attack took place, it does not suffice to prove that the weapon was the cause of the reported symptoms. In the history of biological warfare there are numerous instances where, although it is generally accepted that attacks took place, the effectiveness of those attacks in causing disease is still debated. These include the British "gift" of smallpox-infected blankets to Native Americans in 1763 and the German attempt to infect animals with glanders in World War I. See Erhard Geissler and John Ellis van Courtland Moon, eds., *Biological and Toxin Weapons: Research, Development and Use from the Middle Ages to 1945*, SIPRI Chemical and Biological Warfare Studies, 18 (Oxford: Oxford University Press, 1999).

5. Mark L. Wheelis, "Investigation of Suspicious Outbreaks of Disease," in Raymond A. Zilinskas, ed., *Biological Warfare: Modern Offense and Defense* (Boulder, CO: Lynne Rienner, 2000), 107. See also David R. Frantz, Peter B. Jahrling, Arthur M. Friedlander, David J. McClain, David L. Hoover, W. Russell Byrne, Julie A. Pavlin, George W. Christopher, and Edward M. Eitzen, Jr., "Clinical Recognition and Management of Patients Exposed to Biological Warfare Agents," in Joshua Lederberg, ed., *Biological Weapons: Limiting the Threat* (Cambridge, MA: MIT Press), 77–79.

6. Wheelis, "Investigation," 109–10.

7. The Rajneeshees sought to influence the outcome of a local election, while Aum Shinrikyo sought to use unconventional attacks to interfere with investigations into the group. See John V. Parachini, "Comparing Motives and Outcomes of Mass Casualty Terrorism Involving Conventional and Unconventional Weapons," *Studies in Conflict and Terrorism* 24, no. 5 (September–October 2001), 389–406.

8. See Chapters 2 and 10 by Cole and Harris in this volume.

9. Chapter 5 by Katz in this volume.

10. See both Cole and Harris chapters for details on the investigation into the anthrax letter attacks.

11. This depends on how one understands the motives behind war and terrorism and on whether, and if so how, one distinguishes terrorism from crime, a debate that is beyond the scope of this volume.

12. For an analysis of the utility of biological weapons, see Susan B. Martin, "The Role of Biological Weapons in International Politics: The Real Military Revolution," *Journal of Strategic Studies* 25, no. 1 (March 2002), 63–98. It is also important to note that a biological attack can impose large economic costs on the victim, although there is no evidence that attacks have been carried out with this specific goal.

13. Edward Wong, "Al Qaeda Video Hails Iraq Insurgent Leader," *International Herald Tribune*, April 21, 2006, http://www.iht.com/articles/2006/04/13/news/iraq.php, May 13, 2007.

Glossary and Index

Glossary of Technical Words and Terms

Anthrax—*Bacillus anthracis*

Bacteria—these are one-celled organisms lacking a nucleus and having a plasma membrane cell wall. Bacteria can be aerobes or anaerobes; only a small percentage of bacteria are pathogenic. They store most of their DNA in one long looping molecule (chromosome), but can also contain plasmids, which are small, circular, double-stranded DNA molecules that replicate independently from their host (see Plasmid, below).

Bacteriophage (phage)—a virus that attacks or colonizes a bacterium. Bacteriophages are specific; one type of phage will attack only one species of bacteria.

Biosafety—in activities involving life forms or their parts, the observance of precautions and preventive procedures that reduce the risk of adverse effects.

Biosecurity—activities designed to secure for humans, animals, and plants freedom from possible hazards attending biological activities, such as research, development, testing, and applications; measures taken by governments to guard against damage that may be brought about by accidental or intentional exposure to biological agents or toxins.

Biotechnology—a collection of processes and techniques that involve the use of living organisms, or substances from those organisms, to make or modify products from raw materials for agricultural, industrial, or medical purposes.

Botulism—botulinum toxin

Brucellosis—caused by any of a number of species of the genus *Brucella*; the species that most often cause disease in humans are *Brucella suis* and *Brucella abortus*.

Catalyst—a substance that affects the rate of a chemical reaction but remains itself unaltered in form or amount.

Cholera—*Vibrio cholerae*

Contagion—the transmission of a disease by direct or indirect contact.

Contamination—contact with an admixture of an unnatural agent.

Cytotoxin—a toxin that kills the cells of a host.

DNA—deoxyribonucleic acid; the carrier of genetic information found in all living organisms (except for a small group of RNA viruses). Every inherited characteristic is coded somewhere in an organism's complement of DNA.

Dysentery (shigellosis)—*Shigella dysenteriae*

Enzyme—a special protein produced by cells that catalyze chemical processes of life.

Enzyme-linked immunosorbent assay (ELISA)—a rapid and sensitive means for identifying and quantifying small amounts of virus antigens or antiviral antibodies.

Epidemiology—the study of the distribution and dynamics of diseases and injuries in human populations. Specifically, the investigation of the possible causes of a disease and its transmission.

Escherichia coli (*E. coli*)—a species of bacteria that commonly inhabits the human lower intestine and the intestinal tract of most other vertebrates as well. Some strains are pathogenic, causing urinary tract infections and diarrheal diseases. Non-pathogenic strains are often used in laboratory experiments.

Fomite—an object or material, including medicine, which can act as a carrier of infectious agents.

Fraction—a chemical agent or compound that may be separated out by chemical or physical methods from a solvent containing a mix of substances.

Fungus—this is a general term for a group of eukaryotic protists, which are distinguished from plants by a lack of chlorophyll and the presence of a rigid cell wall. The majority of fungi are made up by yeasts and mold, but also include mushrooms, rusts, and smuts. Mold represents a large group of fungi, such as *Penicillium*. Yeasts are fungi that usually remain unicellular for most of their life cycle and belong to the fungal families, ascomycetes, basidiomycetes, and imperfect fungi. Pathogenic yeasts included the genus *Candida*.

Gene—the fundamental unit of heredity. Chemically a gene consists of ordered nucleotides that code for a specific product or control a specific function.

Gene splicing—the use of site-specific enzymes that cleave and reform chemical bonds in DNA to create modified DNA sequences.

Genetic engineering—a collection of techniques used to alter the hereditary apparatus of a living cell enabling it to produce more or different chemicals. These techniques include chemical synthesis of genes, the creation of recombinant DNA or recombinant RNA, cell fusion, plasmid transfer, transformation, transfection, and transduction.

Genome—an organism's complete set of genes and chromosomes.

Genomics—the scientific discipline of mapping, sequencing, and analyzing genomes. Structural genomics is the construction of high-resolution genetic, physical, and transcript maps of organisms. Functional genomics is the use of information generated by structural genomics to develop experimental approaches for assessing gene function.

Glanders—*Burkholderia mallei* (previously *Pseudomonas mallei*)

Hemorrhagic fever—a general term that could be any of a number of fevers, such as Ebola fever, Marburg fever, Lassa fever, etc., which are caused by two types of viruses, arenaviruses and filoviruses. For our purposes it is sufficient to identify the causative organism by using terms such as Ebola virus, Marburg virus, Lassa virus, etc.

Host—a cell whose metabolism is used for growth and reproduction of a virus, plasmid, or other form of foreign DNA.

Host-vector system—compatible host/vector combinations that may be used for the stable introduction of foreign DNA into host cells.

ID_{50}—the number of microorganisms that would probably infect 50 percent of exposed individuals.

Incidence—the number of new cases of a disease in a population over a period of time.

Infection—the invasion and settling of a pathogen within a host.

Infectious—capable of causing infection; spreading or capable of spreading to others.

In vitro—literally "in glass"; pertaining to biological processes or reactions taking place in an artificial environment, usually the laboratory.

In vivo—literally "in the living"; pertaining to biological processes or reactions taking place in a living system such as a cell or tissue.

LD_{50}—the dose, or amount, of a chemical that would probably cause death to 50 percent of exposed individuals.

Melioidosis—*Burkholderia pseudomallei* (previously *Pseudomonas pseudomallei*)

Metabolism—the sum of the chemical and physiological processes in a living organism in which foodstuffs are synthesized into complex biochemicals (anabolism); complex biochemicals transformed into simple chemicals (catabolism), and energy is made available for the organism to function and procreate.

Metabolite—a substance vital to the metabolism of a certain organism, or a product of metabolism.

Microorganism—a microscopic living entity, including bacteria, fungi, protozoa, and viruses.

Molecular epidemiology—a field of scientific study that uses the techniques of molecular biology (such as PCR) to identify microorganisms responsible for causing diseases, determine their physical sources, and clarify their routes of transmission.

Morbidity—the relative incidence of disease.

Mortality—death; the death rate; ratio of number of deaths to a given population.

Mortality rate—the number of deaths that occur in a given population during a given time interval; usually deaths per 10^3 or 10^5 people per year. Can be presented as age, sex, race, or cause-specific.

Nucleotide—the fundamental molecule that makes up DNA and RNA. Each nucleotide constituting DNA consists of one of four nucleic acids (adenine, guanine, cytosine, or thymine) linked to the phosphate-sugar group deoxyribose; each nucleotide constituting RNA consists of one of four nucleic acids (adenine, guanine, cytosine, or uracil) linked to the phosphate-sugar group ribose.

Objective—the ultimate outcome that a terrorist group seeks to accomplish by successfully conducting an attack.

Pathogen—an organism that causes disease.

Pathogenic—causing or capable of causing disease.

Plasmid—small, circular, self-replicating forms of DNA existing within bacteria. They are often used in recombinant DNA experiments as acceptors of foreign DNA.

Plasmid transfer—the use of genetic or physical manipulation to introduce a foreign plasmid into a host cell.

Plague—*Yersinia pestis*

Polymer—a linear or branched molecule of repeating subunits.

Polymerase chain reaction (PCR)—a technique used in laboratories to quickly create thousands or millions of copies for purposes of analysis.

Poxes—There are many poxes, which usually are caused by members of the genus *Orthopoxvirus*. For our purposes, it is sufficient to use terms such as monkeypox virus, camelpox virus, etc. Note that smallpox, monkeypox, camelpox, etc., are one word.

Prevalence—the number of existing cases in a population who have the disease at a given point (or during a given period) of time.

Probability—a probability assignment is a numerical encoding of the relative state of knowledge.

Q fever—*Coxiella burnetii*

Respirable particle—particle of the size (<5.0 μm) most likely to be deposited in the pulmonary portion of the respiratory tract.

Risk—the probability of injury, disease or death for persons or groups of persons undertaking certain activities or exposed to hazardous substances. Risk is sometimes expressed in numeric terms (in fractions) or qualitative terms (low, moderate or high).

RNA—ribonucleic acid; found in three forms—messenger, transfer, and ribosomal RNA. RNA assists in translating the genetic code of a DNA sequence into its complementary protein.

Smallpox—variola virus (or smallpox virus)

Toxicity—the quality of being poisonous or the degree to which a substance is poisonous.

Toxicology—the scientific discipline concerned with the study of toxic chemicals and their effects on living systems.

Toxin—toxic organic chemical produced by living organisms, including bacteria, fungi, plants, insects, and mammals. The most toxic toxins are proteins of bacterial origin. As a result of advances in biotechnology, some protein toxins can be produced by engineered industrial strains of bacteria in culture. In the future, it should be possible to use peptide synthesis to synthesize non-proteinaceous toxins and their analogs. Toxins are sometimes called "mid-spectrum" agents, which suggests that they are classified as something between living organisms and chemical agents.

Toxinology—the study of toxic substances produced by or accumulated in living organisms, their properties and their biological significance for the organisms involved. Toxinology therefore covers venoms and poisons produced by animals, plants, fungi, and bacteria.

Tularemia—*Francisella tularensis*

Typhoid fever—*Salmonella typhi*

Typhus—*Rickettsia prowazekii* or *Rickettsia typhi*

Vector—a transmission agent, usually a plasmid or virus, used to introduce foreign DNA into a host cell.

Virus—a virus particle after it has entered a host cell and has subverted or is in the process of subverting that cell's genetic mechanism to ensure the virus's replication.

Weaponize—the process of developing a pathogen or toxin to the point where it becomes usable for a weapons system.

Warhead—the part of a bomb, missile, or shell that houses the explosive charge, or in the case of biological or chemical weapons, the pathogenic or toxic agent.

Zoonosis—a disease communicable from animals to humans under natural conditions.

Index